Mike Bouchet
Selected Works 1989-2009

Sternberg Press

Table of Contents

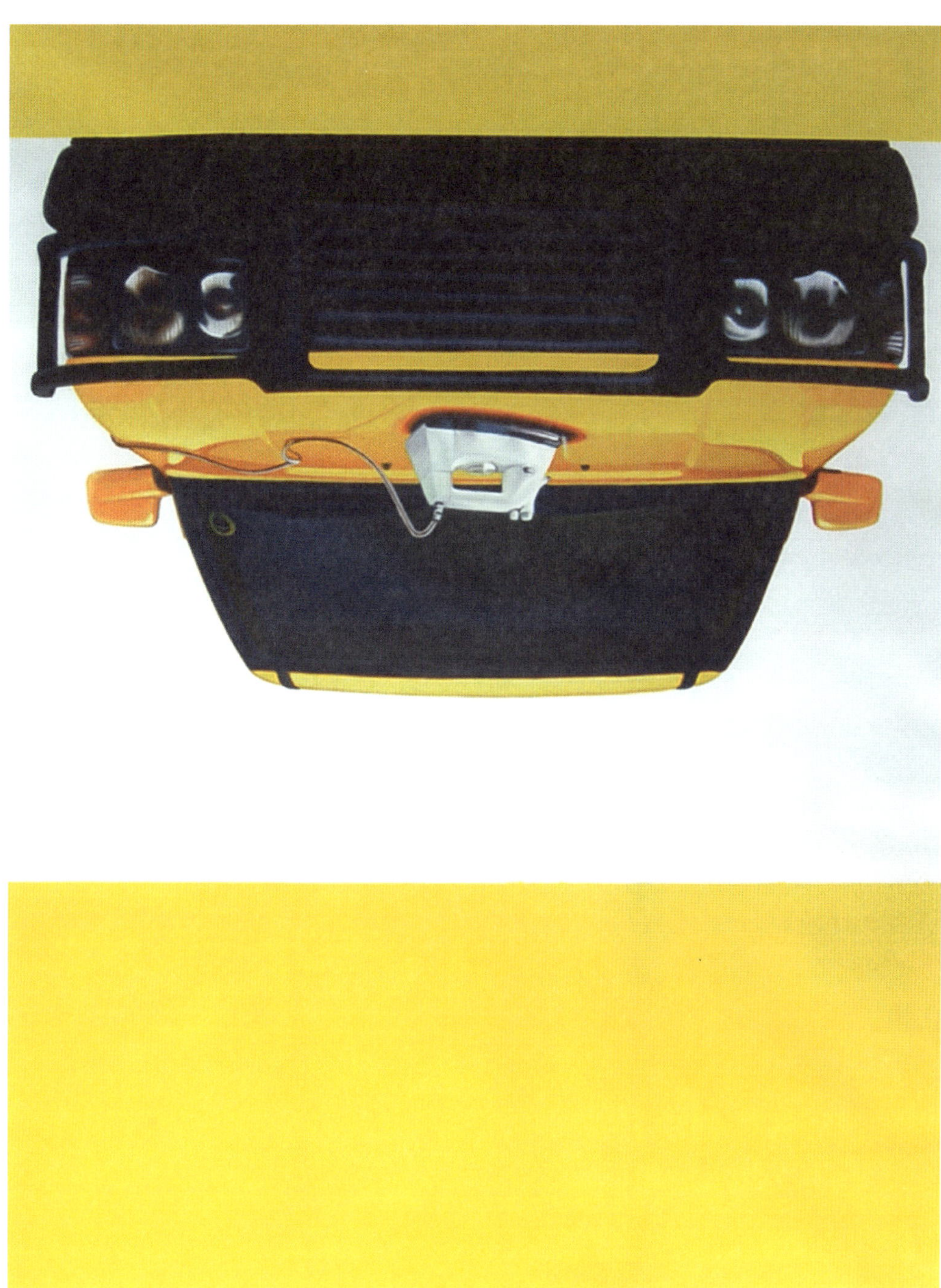

Upsidedown Layer Cake 2007

Conversation between Daniel Birnbaum and Mike Bouchet
Visible Strangeness
October 2008

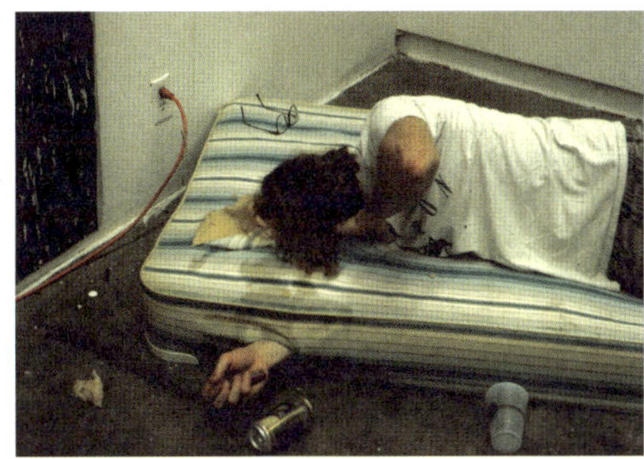

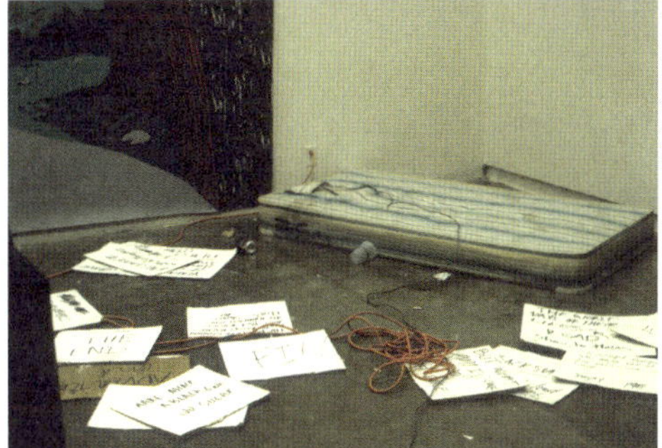

Behavior Direction 1993

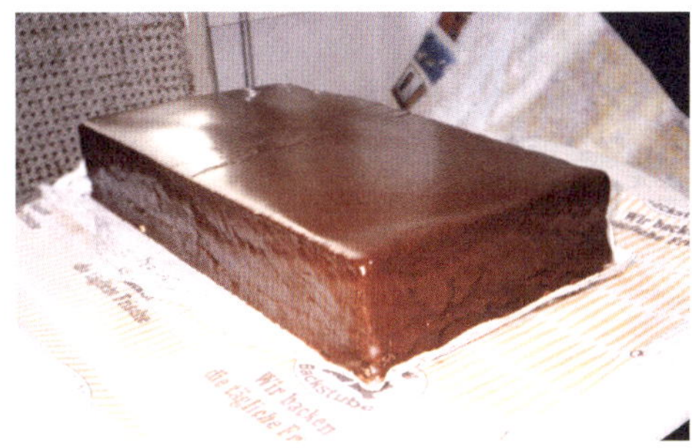

Prison Cake 1996

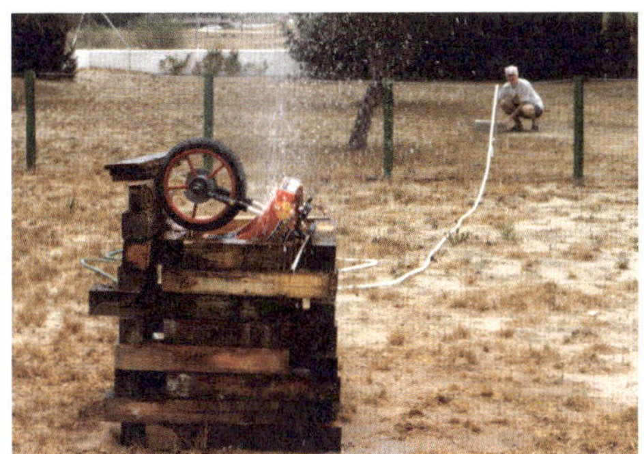

Carl Laundry 1993

Daniel Birnbaum (DB): Where were you born?

Mike Bouchet (MB): I was born in California.

DB: When were you in art school?

MB: From 1990-93, at UCLA. Luckily at that time art schools were easy to get into.

DB: It's interesting that so much of the discourse on the West coast about art seems to center on schools, at least if you compare it to Europe or the East coast where it is more about galleries and museums.

MB: I think the West coast is probably the same way now, as far as galleries and museums go. I get the impression that art schools are more like career schools. When I went to school, it felt different; there wasn't as much interest in art outside of the art community. It was a different kind of atmosphere. It was serious, but probably more like a literature or a philosophy department. They were teaching different views or approaches to making and looking at things. There was a kind of ethos there about what makes something valid as art.

DB: And which professors were the most important for you?

MB: At that time not one person in particular per se. I was getting feedback from several professors – Paul McCarthy, Richard Jackson, Charles Ray, Lari Pittman, Robert Heinecken were really supportive.

DB: Much of the work you were making then seems social and sculptural. Did you see yourself as a sculptor from early on?

MB: At that point, I tried not to categorize too much. I was interested in a lot of things. Some things came more intuitively than others – such as thinking in terms of sculpture. But when I started working on my own after school, I considered myself more as a kind of performance artist, whose works often manifested themselves through objects. Objects were either the result of actions, or came about in association with actions, or with the thought of an action.

DB: Were the objects documents, or, not to sound negative, souvenirs of the performances? Maybe residue is the right word - the performance itself being the important thing and these being its traces.

MB: At times, but also the performances inspired me to make sculptures. I think this is an important point. What an artwork "does" so to speak. Where it goes, and how it "acts". This criteria for me stems from a notion of performance, or as I prefer to use the word "action". How does something "act"? Other types of questions around this are dealt with differently – what aspects of the action or investigation are left, or revealed or even discarded. It's a big part of my art thinking.

DB: Were the performances ever visible or were they only a part of the process behind the object making?

MB: The early performances were visible, but not many people saw them. Oftentimes the performances were carried out in non-art settings, you know, out in public, and they weren't always documented. For me, the action and the object, everything sort of becomes tied together. I tried and still try not to restrict the definitions of these things too much. It takes the life out of ideas.

DB: When was this?

MB: I graduated from Art school in 1993, so around then and afterwards.

DB: In 1993 I lived in the US also, but just for a year, and I was in New York, I was a student of art and philosophy, but the most visible people I met by coincidence were people coming out of Yale, such as Matthew Barney and Michael Joo. Both of them had this double performative aspect to their work … where one doesn't maybe show the performance live, it's all on videotape or it's a photograph. It was this dialectic between object and performer … and what they were doing had these blurry lines in a sense.

MB: I was aware of their work at that point. Some of it had a theatrical element to it that I did not respond to though. I was more interested in how latent content is manifested in everyday or common things. But this dialectic between the object and the performer was an active discussion at the time I remember being interest-

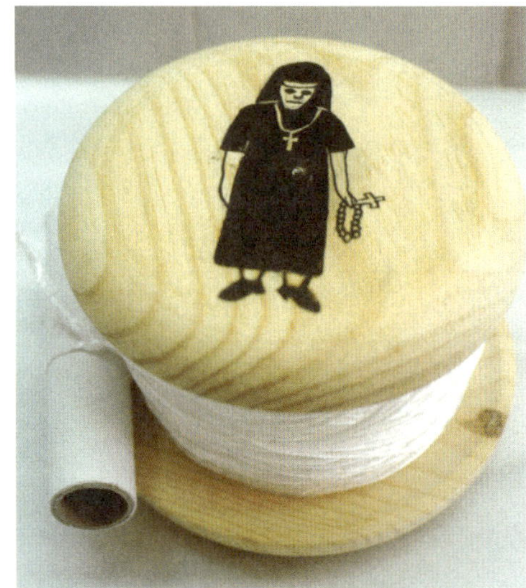

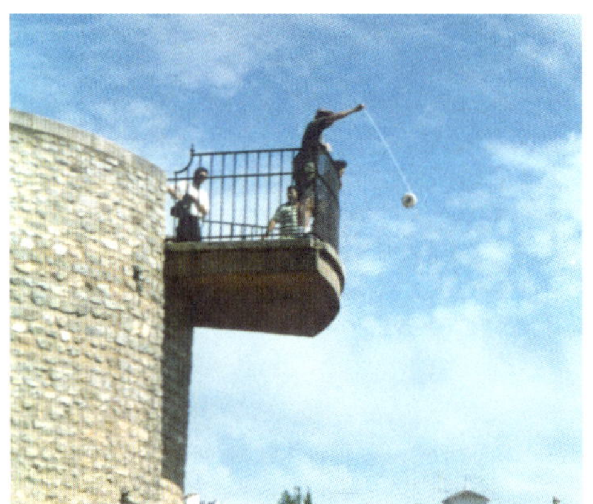

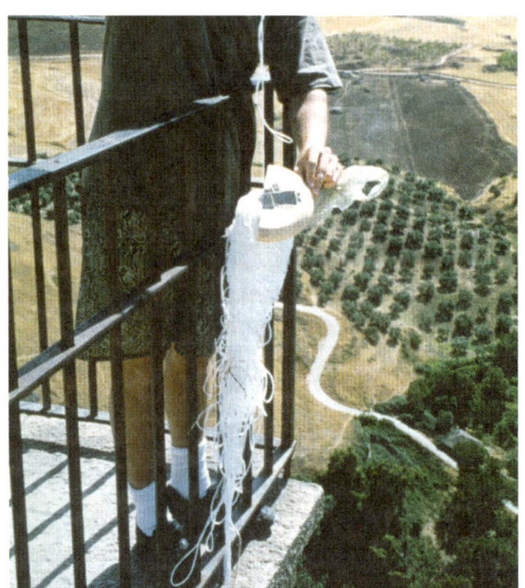

RongLevolutions 1993

ed in the aesthetic of information. I still see a big difference between making an action for a camera in a studio and making an action in the public realm. I trace this dialectic back to artists like Tristan Tzara, Kurt Schwitters, and of course Otto Muehl. He was making deliberate performances with audiences, both private and public. Afterwards the films and photographs, were treated as separate autonomous objects. I think he was mostly interested in the meaning behind the action. There are a lot of artists in the last 50 years who have made art within this messier system of categorization. I also had an interest in messing and dirtying up the art process. I felt that art criticism was repressive, somehow old fashioned and opinionated. Working from this perspective was a way to create a situation where one couldn't say: "Lets analyze the object on its own merits, in a vacuum". The action, and the resulting works couldn't be divorced from each other- it also kept them real, because something real had happened. It gets very confusing when you try to divorce the one from the other. Maybe the confusion is the most interesting part of it all. It's probably closer to the original impetus, which isn't so easy to define. Aside from a kind of methodology, from making something new, there was also a social element. I am interested in how actions, objects or documents become springboards for ideas, or for other actions and objects.

I also think that the question of remnants or of representations within this dialectic come down to just having something physical, i.e. having something to show or save or whatever… it's still about creating an art object. I like that- I've done a lot of things just to leave a trace. It depends on the work, sometimes it's the object first, other times it's the action, and things grow from there. At some point, I realized that objects could carry a real cultural power or have their own interesting complicated information, and that they could communicate those things over a longer period of time. Quite simply, there are issues that objects carry that are unique, and that people relate to uniquely. There's a kind of vanity to creating something that lasts a longer time as well. It allows you to communicate differently, to think about communication differently. You can warp a language, create a weird vocabulary, and communicate in a way that is direct and indirect at the same time.

It also has to do with the mind frame of my generation. No one was running away from any fear of object making. I felt divorced from discussions of traditional art making. What mattered to my peers, and me, was whether something was real, concrete, in terms of an attempt or an undertaking. Shopping became an important, almost political part of art making. And I mean this in a different sense from "appropriation art". This wasn't about the gesture of putting a ready-made into an art space- but about the cultural meaning and formal properties of materials that have a particular vernacular. For me, I am interested in putting things together- conflating things for an uncomfortable effect. Every store is an art supply store. So somehow that gesture - the direct response – is an action that translates directly into object making.

DB: When you say art criticism, do you mean criticism in a kind of standard sense of reviews or do you mean specific theoretic, strong theories, academic people who are writing essays and books?

MB: I wouldn't trace my negative sentiment back to specific writers per se. It probably had to do more with a popular sentiment towards art, and also reviews. I don't think that Los Angeles as an art scene, or most of America for that matter, is very influenced by art theory the way New York or Europe are, or were. For me there was also the issue of exhibition opportunities. When I was younger, living in a place like LA, there just wasn't that much opportunity for doing shows. You made your work for colleagues and for your own entertainment. It's probably changed by now, but in general if I had ideas for things to do, I just wanted to do them. I also became interested in the idea of an artist being an uninvited guest.

DB: But when you said that one aspect of the kind of art that your generation was

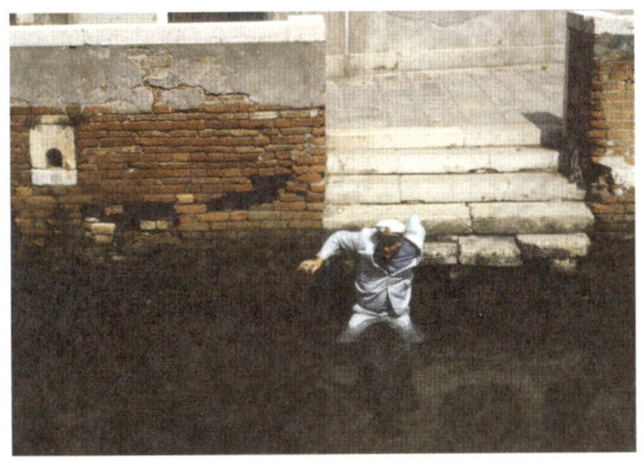

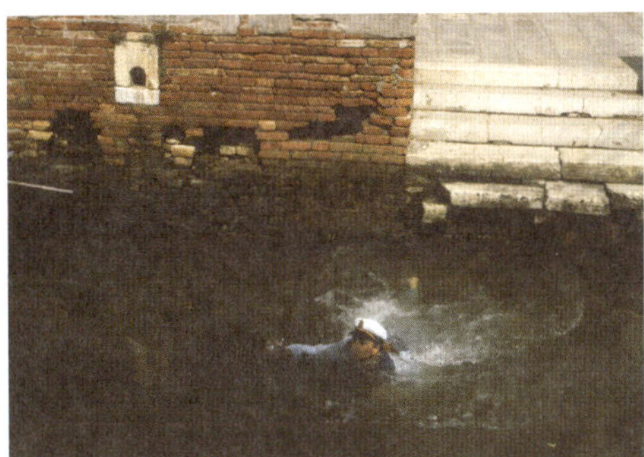

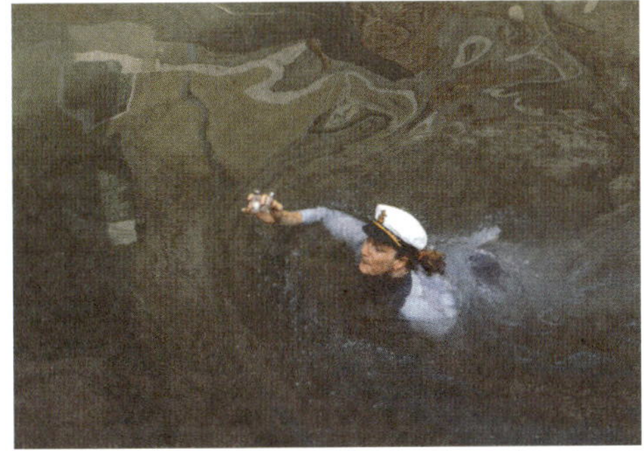

Venetian Salt Smuggle 1993

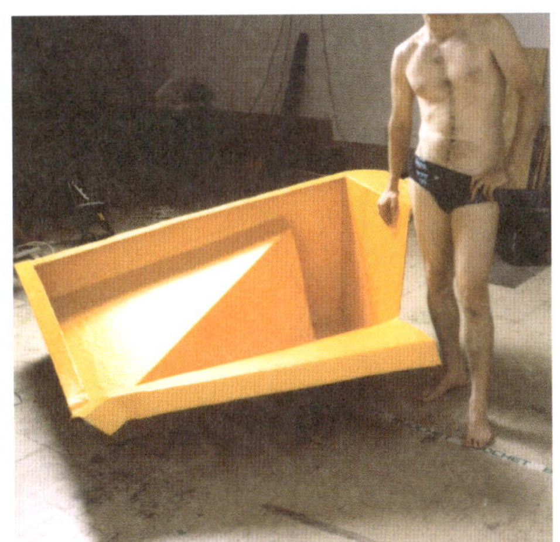

Steffi Graf Jacuzzi 1999

involved in had a political implication, then it was political more in a limited sense of art institutions. Was it trying to dodge the predictable mechanisms of the art market in some sense?

MB: Yes and no. There was a definite fear of de-contextualizing an artwork's meaning or original scope. Gallerists like small things that they can sell, generally speaking. I think the only politics that are overt in the art world are those regarding the politics of the art apparatus so to speak. Collections, museums, galleries, curators, …

DB: Of institutions.

MB: Institutions. The "political" content of the work is totally indirect. But on the other hand, when you start dealing with topics like consumerism or materialism and things like that directly from a gut feeling, I think that they are perhaps quite political. ... There are a lot of agreed upon unwritten rules in the artworld– I'm personally often very suspicious of the people that work with or supposedly work for artists in the commercial sector. What's really behind the decisions that are made? Where does the artist end up? What is the artist's real role? What does someone's word mean? Who's being catered to?

Having such opinions hasn't made things easy for me. But there is a huge gap in America. Most people don't have any interest in art whatsoever - outside a few big cities. And that also changes how people view themselves as an artist or of what kind of work they're making. I thought that what I was doing was not necessarily political. I didn't have – I've always been interested in politics on a personal level but I don't feel like what I am doing is entering in any kind of political sphere or discussion directly. I view Art as more of a construct- it should be interpreted in this way too. I think it's far more generous as well if it seems to exist in a rarified world. I also think there is an insincere element to a construction that is interesting, and really open.

But I have the feeling that it is political in an indirect sense. There is some connection. One can look at American modernism as a big anti-social movement. Perhaps much modernist artwork is really about „Fuck you, Mom and Dad". Culminating with Ad Reinhardt. In fact, I prefer this view of it. But I think because of my dislike of pretentiousness and having grown up with very little exposure to art, I am much more interested in making work that people recognize immediately. I'm interested in affect. Afterwards the dynamic of meaning or an art experience unfolds.

DB: What would be an example? A piece of yours that you could explain in such terms like this...this immediacy and then you get it, but then you...

MB: The Jacuzzis for instance.

DB: Yes, they're sculptural pieces, they have a certain formal structure, even beauty to them, I would say, and then...

MB: There is of course a familiarity to them. The Jacuzzis, in general, have recognizable features, and the materials have a strong immediacy. There's a contrast between how they're made and what they're supposed to be, i.e. Jacuzzis. Then when you factor in the fact that they're all made for someone, something happens. But as with other works of mine, it's pretty direct. I don't want people to feel like they are stupid or didn't do their homework, or that I'm better than them. I don't like that kind of attitude in art. There is a mystery or an ambiguity to certain aspects of my work, but I try not to stage them in a pretentious way.

DB: Where did you get the idea of the Jacuzzis from?

MB: The Jacuzzis came about through a process. The culmination of the Jacuzzis came from actually a number of ideas. At that time I was thinking about art patronage systems. Historically artists have had patrons, and were either producing works for them- painting their family, their dogs… But there must have been untold amounts of people making work without patrons. I thought about all the paintings, the crucifixions and church paintings, the portraits of kings that were

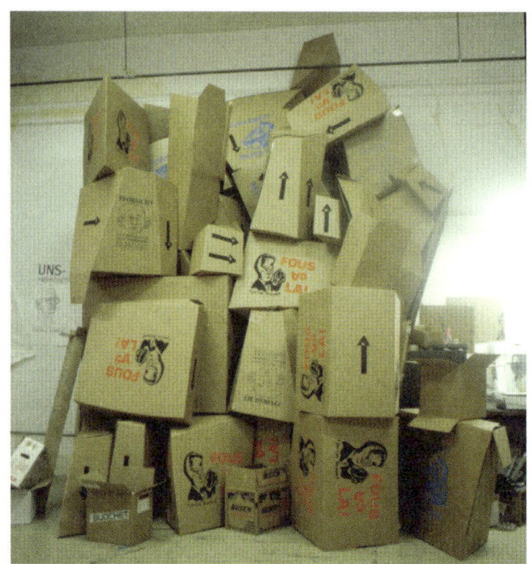

Endless Irregular Boxes 1995

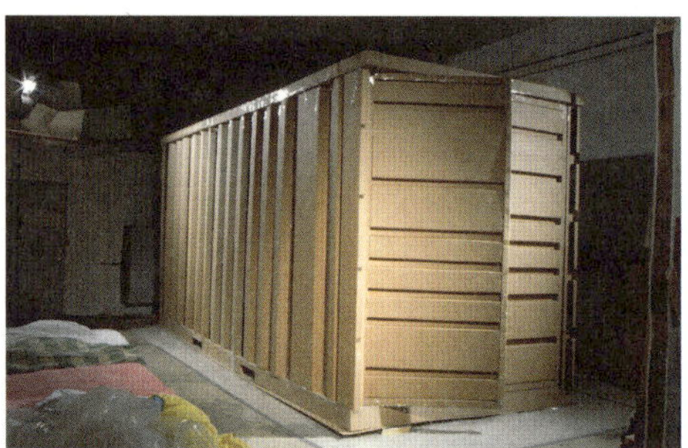

Next Onassis 1998

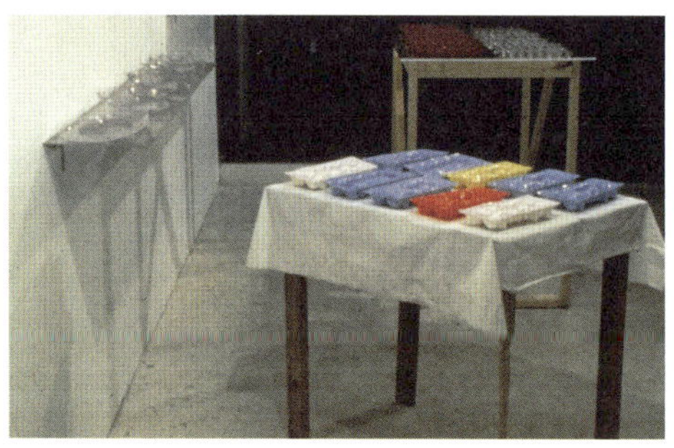

Testicle Trays 1994

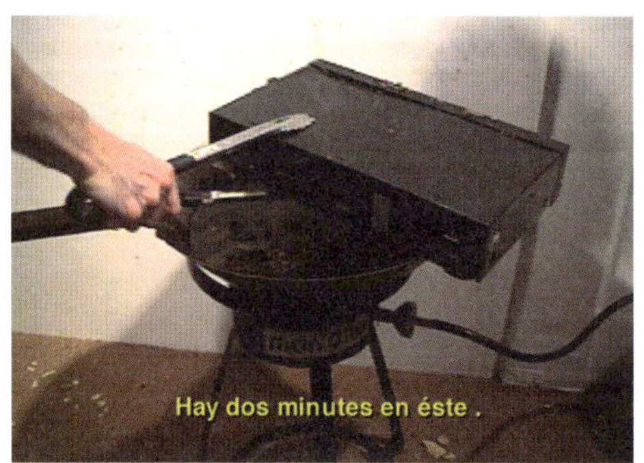

Travel Agency Cooking 2001

never commissioned! There must have been a lot of that being made over the centuries!

DB: They (patrons) probably said: "No, thank you."

MB I think that many people now want to have custom architecture commissions. Generally speaking, when you want to flaunt it, you ask Frank Gehry to make something for you. You don't ask artists to make things for you in that sense anymore.

DB: Right.

MB: My feeling was that in Los Angeles being a Jacuzzi designer, making un-commissioned Jacuzzis, was appropriate. Of course I was influenced by a certain approach to architecture, using trash and just making these forms. They certainly require purely formal decisions- I like that, a sort of abstract art making. When you look at them, you think about a number of things; your body position, how they could be plumbed, the materials, how well they are made, the celebrity they are named for, how the title functions like a color.

I was also influenced by El Greco in respect to these works. He's a really interesting historical figure- both in terms of his unique paintings, and how he worked within this patronage system we're discussing. I was also thinking of Frank Gehry's studio process. But the original impetus of work was the combination of this idea of patronage and un-commissioned artworks, making something valuable for specific people, but actually producing these strange forms out of cheap primary materials. I still am very enthusiastic about making Jacuzzis. I am often thinking about new forms, persons to make them for, and making sketches of them.

DB: The first time I got an introduction to work of yours was in relationship to this project with Hans Ulrich Obrist, We made this show about young American artists – The Uncertain States of America exhibition. We were thinking in terms of who and what belonged together, what they come out of, the backgrounds of the different groups. I would say we saw a kind of post-post-appropriation artist in New York. Some even did a few collaborative things together. We had sculptors from California, and we had a few we couldn't really fit into any pattern. I can remember that we were very convinced, but we couldn't group your work. We couldn't really grasp it all.

MB: That's a common situation with my work. I think that in general it's because I am often making very different things simultaneously. Some people are familiar with certain works but don't know anything about my practice in general at all- they think I am strictly a Jacuzzi designer, and others think I'm the artist who works with Cola.. I can tell you that changing your work all the time doesn't make it easy! That said, though I like the absurdity of the term post-post appropriation, I prefer the idea of misappropriation- this term strangely enough has remained strictly tied to the financial world at this point… I also like the term inappropriate... Post-post-post-inappropriate artist…

DB: Talking about this whole social-cultural connection … you are now living in a German context, things look different. Could that have affected your work somehow?

MB: I'm not sure. It probably has. A few things have become clearer for me, and in the work. People often say that my work is very American. Even though I have an approach that can seem very American at times, I am more interested in taking from a larger common source, from things that people everywhere in the world have access to, whether they're American or not. I do feel that living here in Germany has given me some clarity about what pierces through the cultural fog or filters so to speak.

DB: Tom Cruise is kind of American.

MB: Sure, but it's filtered, it becomes more monolithic when it's placed within an international spectrum. Tom Cruise is perhaps the definition of international.

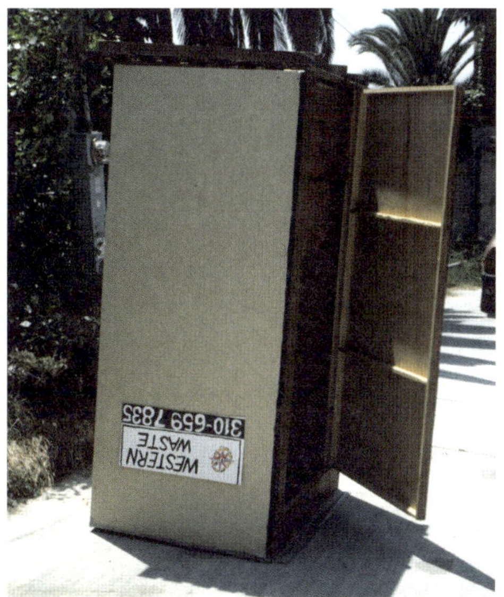

Translation Booth 1994

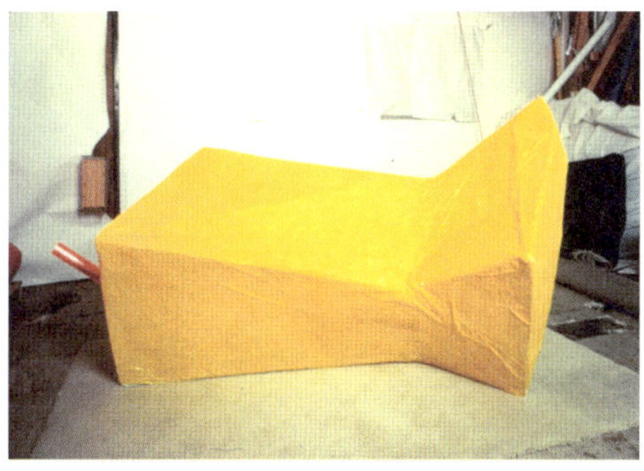

Bong 1995

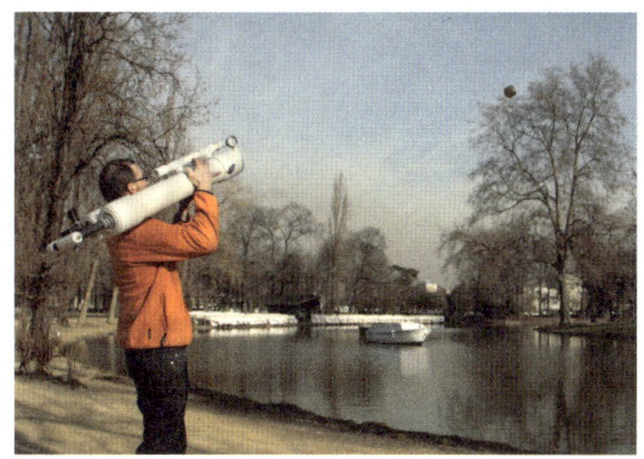

Canburger cannon shooting 2008

He´s everywhere, and everyone knows him- and I mean everyone. He just happens to have been born in America, and the forces that propagate his image are generally based in America. Schwarzenegger isn't American legally, but he might reflect America even more than Tom Cruise. My view of these things, of these elements of American pop culture, is more akin to an alien's view of America. I'm interested in how they circulate and manifest themselves around the world. I'm interested in how they function in people's headspace. How Tom Cruise lives in our heads. I like how these things tap into a rich vein of impulses and desires, and how they maintain this rather unbelievable historical presence. I worked in advertising for a long time editing television commercials. The imagery that I was looking through and these discussions with writers and art directors were amazing, looking back at the meetings, there were always these discussions about "top of mind" and "market share". People would ask things like: is this "too much about death"? "too overtly sexual"? "too last year"? etc… Very broad strokes. Far more consequential than the Psychology classes I studied at University. But what they were discussing was an informed layman's notion of an average human being's headspace. Amateur Psychology on a massive scale. These are common notions in advertising, peer and focus testing, branding strategies, mass appeal, integrated marketing, so on and so on... They are talking about how to get into people's heads and fantasies in as many places in the world at once- the more the better. It must get harder by the day, as populations and societies sort of subdivide in terms of interests, but it remains interesting. It's like discussing how wide of a spray a particular shotgun shell can make, but with products and images.

DB: Would you say this position of being a little bit outside growing up, that you felt, made things visible, clearer somehow.

MB: This experience often informs my interests and criteria with respect to the materials and ideas that I am drawn toward. Some of it is also just personal. I feel like those interests are just as well represented here in Germany. Some of them have become clearer for me here.

DB: To put an American suburban home outside an Italian city floating on a river - how does this in fact relate to the predicament you were just describing now?

MB: That's an interesting question for me actually.

DB: Even if it doesn't happen it still has happened in your head already.

MB: I've had this idea for a long time. There is actually something very very strange about a really new contemporary American house. The overall design and the details are also a byproduct of this weird system of commodification- we're talking about shelter fantasy. It touches deep nerves that go beyond a political or social discussion. I´m not interested in discussions of re-contextualization. I'm interested in the effect of putting this house into this unique context. I think it creates a giant backdrop for a really strange object, historically speaking.

DB: It doesn't make it happen on its own, it's not the displacement itself, it's making the strangeness of that "so-called normality" even more visible.

MB: Yes, and for me, that's something that I like about the neutrality of art spaces, that it has helped me reinforce that strangeness in a lot of the objects that I'm interested in. Some of the things I work with, like jeans, coca-cola, Jacuzzis, suburban houses, are simply strange, and they're strangely loaded. My feeling is that America happens to be the weirdest place in the world.

Painting as Illuminated Advertising
By Lucas Ajemian

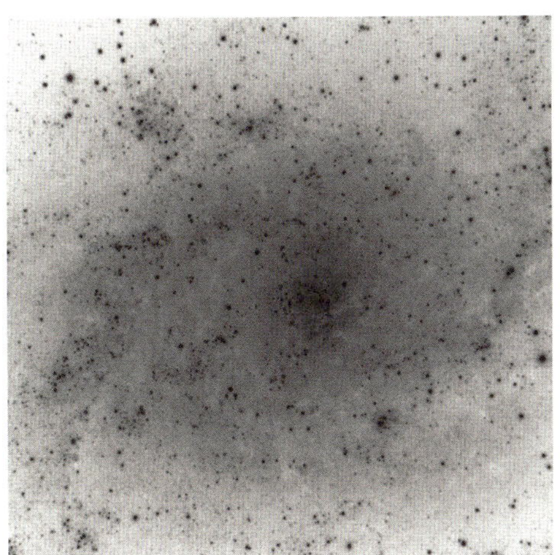

Negative Space 2002

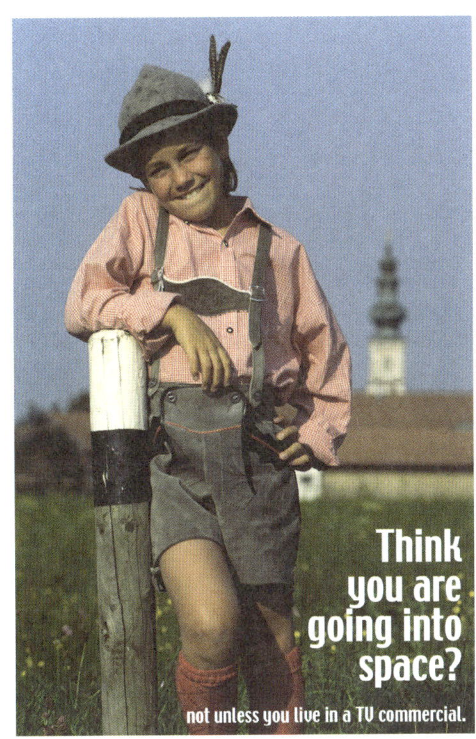

Where you going kid? 2003

Positive Thinking I:

A web of images and transactions, essential elements, bare necessities, fashionable commodities - lifestyle images in movement, images made culturally or geographically specific, things high and low… we've watched them act as relays across vast distances, we've seen them become more interconnected, less denominational. These images are the byproducts of the systems that they reflect and uphold, they are shorthand representations by means of which we align and realign our own movements through these systems. From blunt mimicry to Pop Psychology, we are well stocked with ways of representing ourselves in the world. That is to say the spectacle has won out – it is everlasting. Banging your head against that paradigm will not wrench you free from the consumed consumer alien that you have become.

The work (the output, the product) produced by Mike Bouchet in recent years seems to present a compulsion to alter one's place in the world by reproducing and re-contextualizing "desirable" things in and of the world. His projects and exploits are one-to-one models – real transactions with their own autonomy and agency. You cannot alter your place in the world without first altering your image of the world. Bouchet's endeavor goes beyond representation or a kind of DIY prudence, into what can best be described as a real-life parody. This artist uses everything at his disposal to grow, package, and pitch his own products. In systems such as these, even real transactions are not completely convincing, the reification of one's product through extensive image production is needed to make it completely viable.

Campaigning I: Think you're going to Saturn kid?
Not unless you live in a commercial.

Moving from the premise that space would soon become the emerging status destination, Bouchet embarked on a negative publicity campaign, titled Overhead Baggage Treatment in 2002. For this project the artist accumulated a brand of commercial imagery so antiseptically inflected as to craft itself into near in-distinction. Stock Photography, in Bouchet's hands is damned and damning. Each image was loaded with discontinuities in graphic overlay and text suggesting that these innocuous farm-raised shots were not as benign as they wanted to seem. At the very least, they reveal themselves to be guided by a simple presupposition – that of the ascendancy of the corporate eye.

The exhibition became a bureau of information and propaganda – phrasing and rephrasing an argument, through different aesthetic means. The inundating effect of the installation seemed to maroon the viewer in some parallel dimension - "put me in a wheel chair, put me on a plane" . Hoards of paintings, all executed with an inkjet printer, lined the walls of the gallery, stacked 3 to 4 deep. Though they stood passively, as if waiting to be examined at the viewer's leisure, they also seemed poised for broader dissemination.

As adamant as the artist was about where the viewer should not go, the only indication of a preferable destination was perhaps revealed on the sides of the panels, which were surreptitiously wrapped with custom-made tape bearing the phrase "Travel Warsaw". Travel Warsaw was the name of Bouchet's first studio in New York, which he converted into a functioning travel agency. Up until the time of his Anti-Space travel campaign Bouchet had outfitted this studio with brochures, travel magazines, and a SABRE connection (the connection used by travel agents to access and book flight reservations). His only stipulation to his clients was that all flights booked by Travel Warsaw be routed with a stopover in Warsaw, Poland. The tape around the sides and the haphazard stacking of the panels pulled these paintings away from the exalted position of being "a painting." They also allowed

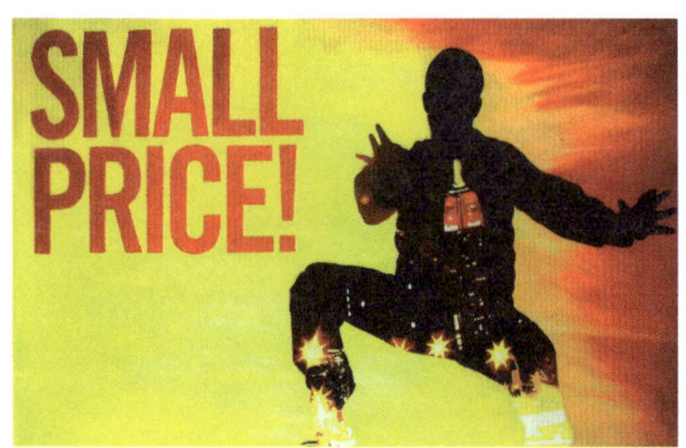

Small Price 2008

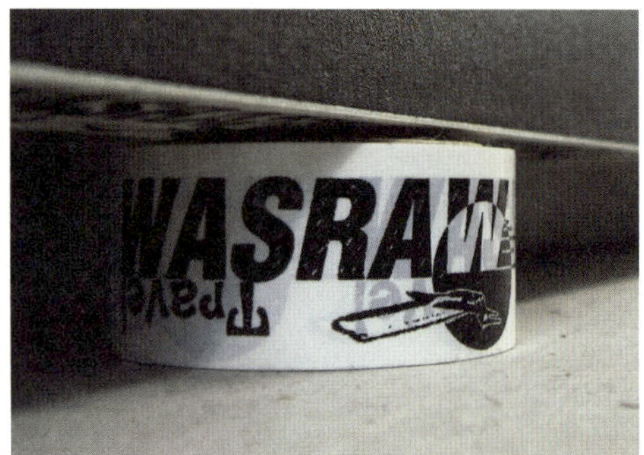

Warsaw Travel/Travel Warsaw Tape 2003

the artist to articulate a simple position, i.e. these are objects of display, propaganda, and circulation. I feel that this project was the beginning of a programmatic use of painting by Bouchet, as well as his first direct foray into what I will call Ad Grammar.

Positive Thinking II:

Mike Bouchet's visual syntax draws heavily from a media grammar - specifically that of advertisement. Ad Grammar draws on the innateness of language and on the equally innate awareness in our culture of the ways in which images can project complicated reactions and liminal directives that elude description. Deconstruction of this grammar would be one area of focus, but with this artist it seems more important to model and redeploy it as a more expressive language of endeavor – to demonstrate a fluency and command over its myriad affectations. This innateness can be best measured in the wrong-sided thing, which has the power to form the fastest and most enduring bind to the subconscious. Utilizing a broken grammar, the skewed message remains instantly decipherable while priming the subconscious to suggestion, and exemplifying the virtues of an obtuse approach to a subject. The awkwardness of much of Bouchet's image construction and as well as its inextricable ties to the rest of his enterprise disallows that contemplative state traditionally associated with the reception of painting by disrupting these innate constructions in new, often ineffable ways.

I find it productive, when thinking of Bouchet's work, to consider a field of study like Neuro-Linguistic Programming, a heady cocktail of ideas drawn from Noam Chomsky's Transformational-Generative Grammar with a bit of Gestalt Therapy and Eriksonian hypno-therapy thrown in to the mix. NLP is practiced by therapists and motivational speakers like Tony Robbins. It focuses on manipulating the dynamics of personal interaction to provoke a change. Inherent in that change is the reconfiguring of one's image of the world. Modeling oneself and one's image of the world through an attitudinal lens of power. Model the message. Prime the mind. Frame the change. When I speak of modeling, my intention is to use the term in line with the way it is put forth by NLP.

Campaigning II:

Lance Bass is Jumping Off a Bridge.
~~Lance Bass is Jumping Off a Bridge.~~
Lance Bass is Jumping Off a Bridge.
~~Lance Bass is Jumping Off a Bridge.~~
Cindy Crawford is Jumping Off a Bridge.
~~Join Him.~~
Join Her

The urgency of Overhead Baggage Treatment's poise immediately comes off as critique. It is meant as social commentary without a doubt, but what becomes clear is that mimicry or deconstruction cannot account for Bouchet's affection for the Ad campaign and his thrust toward the entrepreneurial. He recognizes this visual language as a contemporary vernacular, the right kind of voice to move his program along. He can be the most aggressive of pitchmen, presumptuous, even patronizingly so, in the way he propagates a dizzying intellectual position while holding the lowest common denominator close to his heart as his most precious subject. These motivations and sentiments represent a more problematic stance on the conflation of art and mainstream culture, advertising and economics, one that becomes even more complex and embedded in his later painting projects.

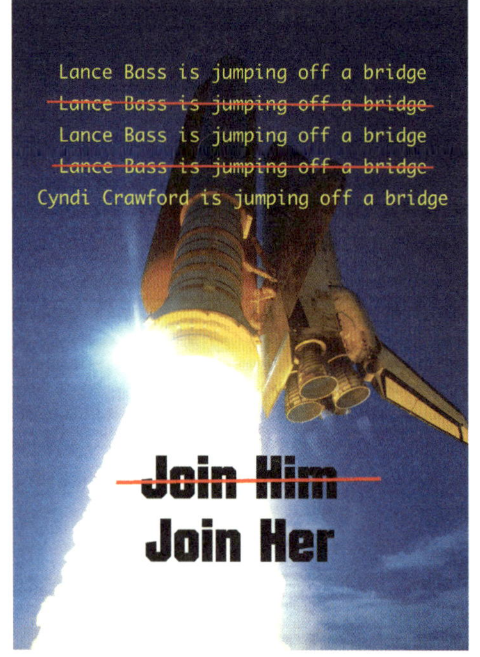

Join Her 2002

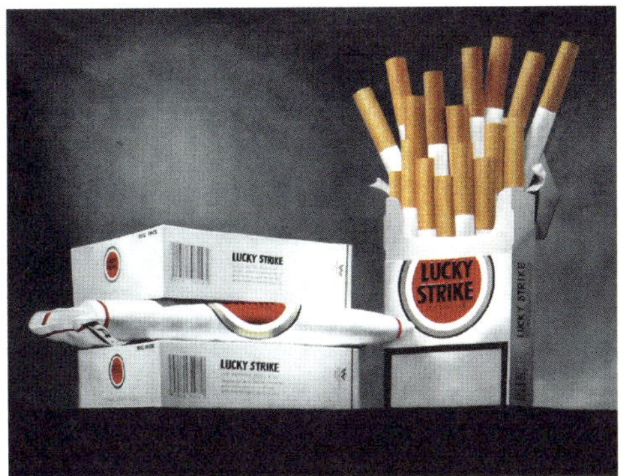

Lucky Meal 2008

Zero Painting 2007

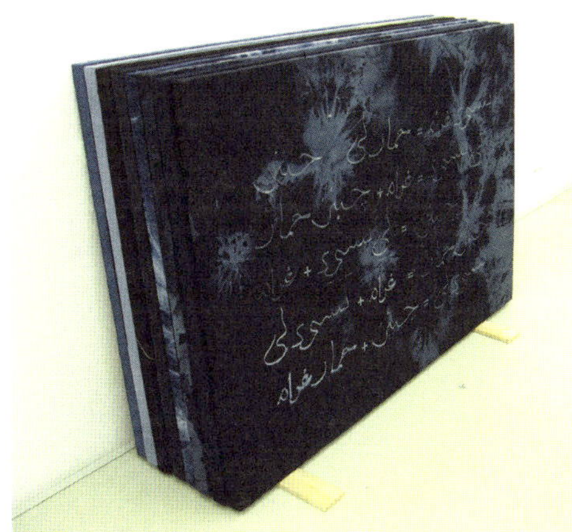

Denim Panel Stack 2004

Staging I: Spokesperson/Integration (One other thing about Spectacle).

What might the future hold? Shifts. Why not celebrate the growing innateness of the Ad Form, the Ad Grammar; commercial jingles are soon to be folk-forms. As CD and record sales slow to a halt, the record industry wanes in parallel to that of the commercial jingles. Pop Musicians are more open to licensing songs to corporations. The two forms, the jingle and the pop song, switch places. What was the purpose of a pop song in the first place? Representation. Of course. A jingle. Is that too reductive? Ringtones are to follow. Visual Artists are also making their way into the world of commerce and advertising. It's a good thing… Oh, one could say, the shape of things to come is the contour of a single all-encompassing industry where toilets designed by Rem Koolhas, manufactured by Waterworks and exclusively licenced to Target are featured in a new commercial directed by Francesco Vezzoli scored by Radiohead starring Meryl Streep. Complicity and Consolidation and Consumption… Paranoid? Ridiculous!

Product Placing: draped over stretchers in the Carpe Denim Series:
Stretched Tight around the Panels
Seeped in linen like dirty sheets in the My Cola Light Series:
Sweet Shirt Stain/Dirty Sheet. Bubble Shit

In the two series that accompanied the Carpe Denim and My Cola Light projects, Bouchet executed paintings with the surplus and leftover parts from the central works. Not only does this present an interesting reanimation of discarded materials while illustrating the frenetic note-taking and reflexive propositioning involved in Bouchet's practice, it doubles down on the propagating power of image-making and the way he floods his objects with near-ritualistic powers through reification. Letting „no idea go incognito" as it were. Forcing focus so that all thoughts are swathed in denim or drenched in cola. Viewers are directed to the necessity to visualize. To multiply the central theme across a vast field of activity, in an inundating manner. Pressing our image of the world through the thing in order to test and expand the scope of these new tenets. Here the Ad-logic is turned around on itself– lifestyle isn't the reason for the thing, the thing is a pocket of knowledge unto itself. The thing is a spokes-thing for the mind.
It's liberating. Streams of associations, litanies of connections, corrections, boasts and confessions. Detail after detail, banality after banality passing through the prism, these groups set out to describe the world in its entirety while making insights and predictions for the world to come.
What comfort it is, with feet planted firmly at the fixed location of this narrow lens of power - tapered to the dimensions of a pair of pants or the cubic volume of 2 liters - through which to look at the world and know where you stand.
As for the paintings themselves, they do not always present themselves as windows or screens hung on the wall. They are often crowded together, stacked, or leaned in tiers. Beyond the images dyed into, burned out of, or printed onto the supports, viewers are directed to the cumbersome, man-sized Rolodex of their display - gallery stockroom shopping or surplus-type handling. Inventory: Moving Product/ Product Moving.

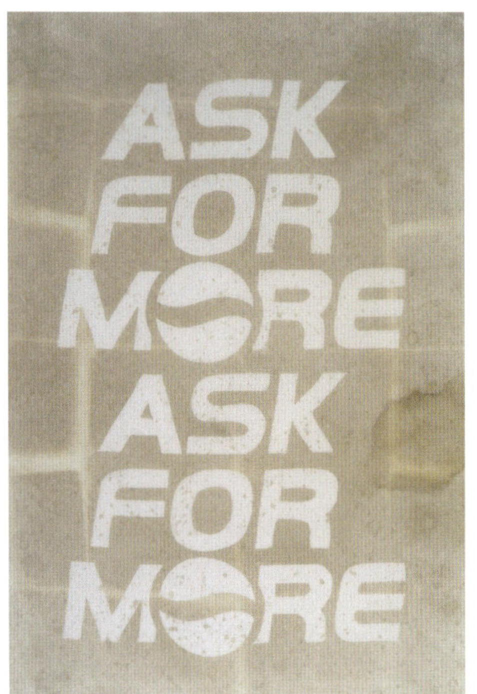

Ask For More Twice 2007

Ass Rub 2004

Real Life Parody: The material reuse of the central piece (usually a product as sculpture) takes the form of an image, or of an image in the form of a painting that comments on the central piece. Then said paintings are stacked, strewn, piled, and propped in a display similar to that of the central piece (usually a product as sculpture) with some variation.

In his sculptures, in particular, Bouchet skews material slightly to answer to his demands. These shifts and interventions follow a fairly conventional purpose, but they do retain a strange and displaced air about them. Is it just contextual? It could be – after all he does air-drop his jeans down from airplanes or building, or stipulate that his Cola only be consumed in certain regions of China - but it isn't until the material makes its way to the paintings (a fantastic convention!) that things really click into place.

Since Duchamp, any material is subject to be transformed into an artwork, transformation meaning that some extreme effect or misappropriation disguises the material make-up of a work, thus allowing for the expansion of that work's meaning and reception by the viewer. Denim and canvas are both made from cotton (there is a distinction in the weave of the fabrics and denim is usually dyed, but otherwise the material is very similar). The Carpe Denim images are rendered through washing and bleaching the fabric in ways similar to those used by the fashion industries or fashion-conscious consumers. The cola paintings are stained cotton. They work against preservation in as passive a way as you could not bother to imagine; the pictures, spills, spatters, will simply disappear unless carefully acted upon.

These paintings are extensions of a performative practice. The overarching performative aspect consists in utilizing the scope of commercial production for commercial products that are also artworks. That means deploying images in decisively manipulative roles, i.e. that of slogan-slinging visual peddlers or flashy billboards. No matter how protracted or elliptically contingent, the painted images make the actions and everything else seem more real. The staining of the My Cola Light Paintings with his own concoction of soft drink or the bleaching of the denim material, which would otherwise go into the production of Carpe Denim brand jeans, are actions indicative of a volatile rather than transformative construction. Volatile, not only because they are images made of stains that may not last or erasures produced by a chemical deterioration of the support, but also because the lines they draw to the world as it exists at the very moment of their creation are equally contingent. The work happens by way of the spilling of this or that. The work reflects the accidental nature of the things around us, and the inadvertent way we consign ourselves to those things. Though each work, each excursion, can be seen as autonomous, the adherence to the program suggests that the transformation occurs within this ecological approach to the things we consume as epistemological vessels, and how, through them, we can convey our moral, amoral, or immoral character, plot our lifestyles, and stage our self-image.

Staging II: Americaning

In the land where obsessive meets compulsive, it's no surprise that we rely on our entrenched media literacy for our internal representations. We quote to explain. We quote to express our inner thoughts. Sometimes a pop song, a jingle, or a line from a movie is the closest proxy to our true feelings. We frame the lives we want, selected from within the large swaths of lives and lifestyles we witness in the image world, via a kind of modeling.

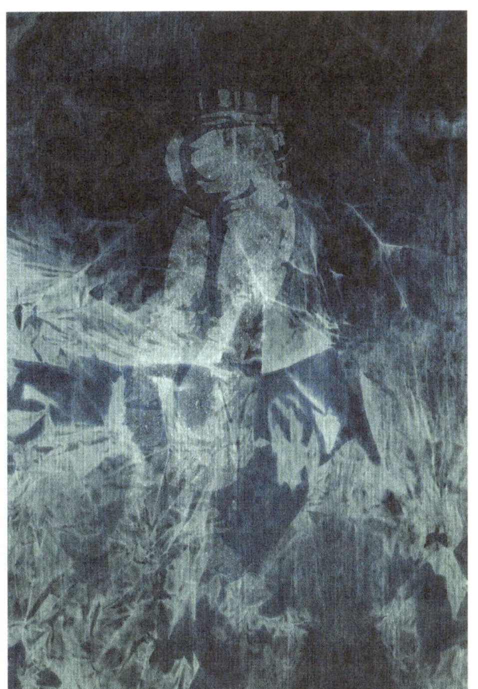

Tom of Frankfurt 2004

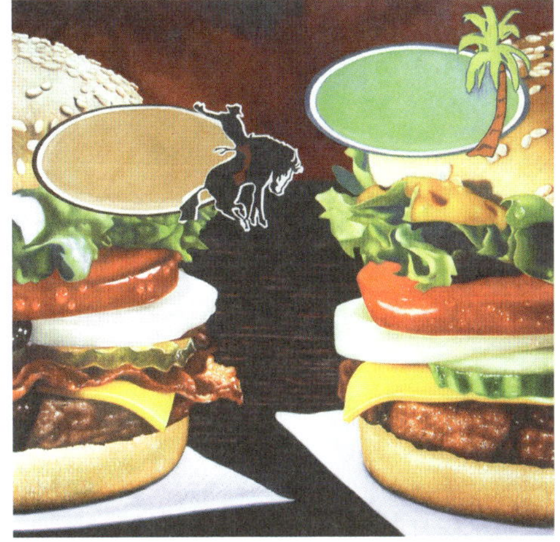

Tourists 2008

Logo Lines 1 2005

With works like Tom of Frankfurt and Long and Skinny (among others), Bouchet delves into this cultural matrix. His intent, once again, is to broaden the scope of what is looked at through the lens of power provided by the product. His are not obscure sources as much as they are smoke signals tailored to particular consumers or particular groups. The apposite use of Tom of Finland in a jeans campaign or the rockabilly quality of some of his bottle cap paintings goes to show that the power of advertising and the prowess of some of his art lies in its ability to allow the viewer to have little knowledge or understanding of the source and still come away with an abiding understanding of each image and its intent. These images of beautiful people, family dynamics, leisure, sex, or patriotism are subject to affect. They are customizations. You want a Jacuzzi? Of course you do. Do you want the Jacuzzi in the beer commercial or the Jacuzzi in Architectural Digest? Or do you want the one you saw in Lil' Wayne's House on that episode of CRIBS ? Wait, you wanna be Lil Wayne? You need the Lil'Wayne Jacuzzi from Bouchet.

The art and science of Public Relations is more pervasive in times of economic prosperity, like those of the last several years in which Bouchet's practice has matured. Visibility is important when you're trying to push for change. So are branding and spin. Public Relations makes style more corporate in its idealism and more ideal in its derivation. That's peddling good influence. A brand's rapport with its user, its client, its audience is based in large part on certain visual traits, styles and associations, cultivated by the brand as a means of address – artists do the same. Branding strives for familiarity, trust, and ultimately loyalty – don't all images? Painted ones especially, right? Isn't that why the inclination to treat painting as some estranged, deadbeat parent crops up every couple of years in art criticism?

"I am rather like a traveling salesman. I deal in ideas." Martin Kippenberger

Build on the tried and true; advocate a hyper-awareness of surface style. Work within a genre. Style for Bouchet is codified less in terms of visual constructs than it is expressed in terms of use, distribution, and effective behavior. Nevertheless, in the quality of their rendering and the blunt compositing, the Canburger and Tapestry Cartoon paintings clearly owe something to James Rosenquist and Francis Picabia. But the Logo Lines of the My Cola Light series look like Brice Marden paintings. They articulate the double talk of Bouchet's paintings.
The artful sell. The sign. The signature element. The signature.
Reducing the logo down to some bare element unmistakably identifiable with the brand as its most iconic signature. The brand should exhibit some propriety over seemingly inconsequential details like wavy lines, I suppose.
A capital A. A hierarchical format in the field of high production. Painting is a construct. It exists in Bouchet's practice as a construct. The vessel and showcase for a hybridization of the image and a syntax of epistemologies.
The artist is the spokesperson for the idea. And the idea, in our shared context of global capitalism, is a product.

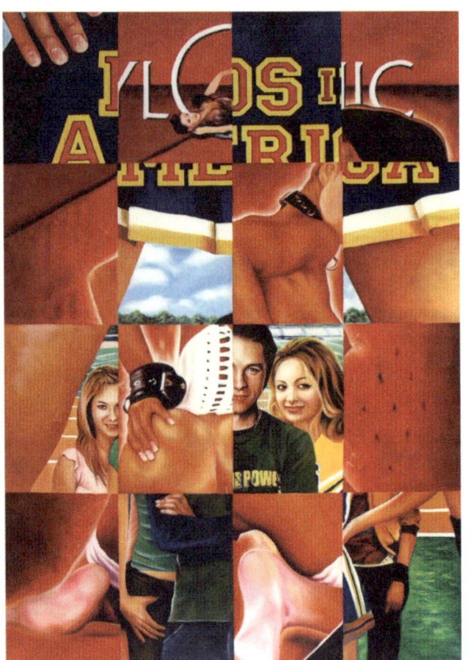

Vinyl High 2007

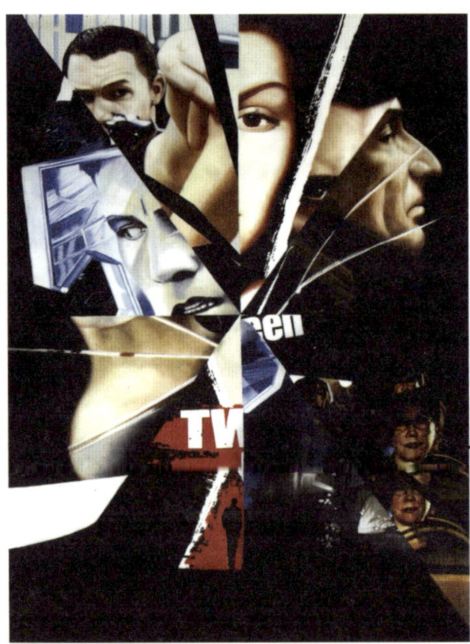

Shattered 1 2007

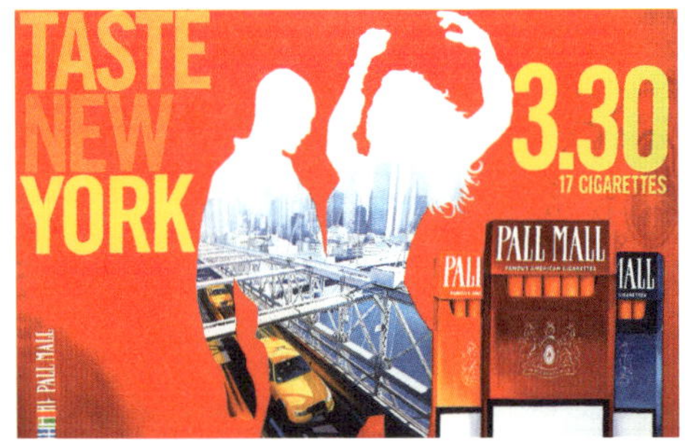

Taste New York 2007

Spinning Off:

A shift takes place with the commercial film poster based paintings of the Tapestry Cartoons. In spite of his own fluency, rather than generate his own advertising idiom, Bouchet builds narratives of potentiality by compositing existing promotional images, penetrating and exploiting the existing codes in a manner that goes beyond a typological interest. In doing so, Bouchet moves away from creating his own product from scratch to the creation of hybridized forms and a more reactionary interaction with the media world. This is a more participatory mode of interaction as made evident by his use or misuse of that most reviled of contemporary business practices: outsourcing. Unlike many artists working today, Bouchet's factory does not work on the Warholian model, one of exclusivity and bohemian ardor. Bouchet steps out of the process by taking on a more overtly executive position, outsourcing the painting of his collaged images to artisans in Mexico, Italy and China. His endeavor is more remote, more alienated, and brings up issues of labor and exploitation over apprenticeship, mastery, or scene as may be the case with the administration of Takashi Murakami's Kaikai Kikki, LLC., for example. Just as the workforce is remote, so is the CEO's proximity to the product.

Just as films themselves are pirated from DVD's and crushed together, the paintings are composed by compositing actual film posters, which are sent to professional labor contacts in other countries. These standard dimension pieces are like architectural models, the artisans work backwards from Bouchet's collages to execute these paintings. This marks an evolution in Bouchet's entrepreneurial praxis. Rather than overseeing each mark, the artist produces paintings at a distance that advertise his idea, his "brand."

Formatting:

Uniform folds, cuts, and overlays determine most of the Tapestry compositions. Seldom is a section moved by the artist to accommodate itself or the image below. Each image retains its original format and is merged with another. Elementary compositional techniques come across as proxies to pictorial craft in these images that could easily be read as typological sketches. There is a breadth of minor strategies that play out throughout this series. While most of the pieces are amalgams of images, some works focus on cataloguing elements (as in Blue Run, Blue Arms, Guns, or Shattered 1). Others, like the audacious Mister Sister or European Gigolo, are copied with most or all of the typography removed in a kind of slack-jawed amazement.

These geometries deployed by Bouchet throughout the Tapestry paintings (and later on in the advertisement based paintings) seem animated by a kind of lenticular bluff. Relying heavily on the choice of images in order to establish some semblance of continuity, the best of these works simultaneously tease and explore the gaps in that continuity . Intersecting lines, latches and hooks, look-a-likes that draw out a prosodic uniformity.... Take the following works for example: Bad Bad Boys, 2006, Extended Bad Hours, 2006, and Into the Bad Yakuza 2007, Jersey Dark, 2007, Detention, 2007. The original films and poster images live on within these genetic amalgams, making the flux and fissures that traverse them seem like the stuff of heredity.

Book-By-Its-Covering: People like to know what they're paying to see.
How shall we let them know what they're paying to see?
Green is Supernatural or Science Fiction.
Amber-Red is Action/Thriller
Red & Black is Horror/Thriller
White is Comedy
Kodacolor is Sentimental Drama and/or Romance.

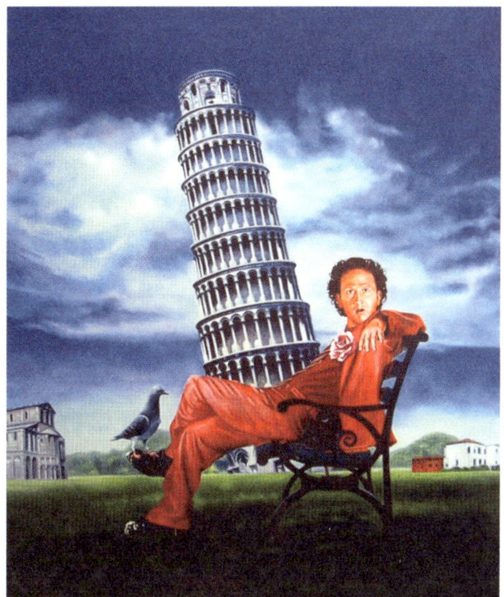

European Gigolo 2007

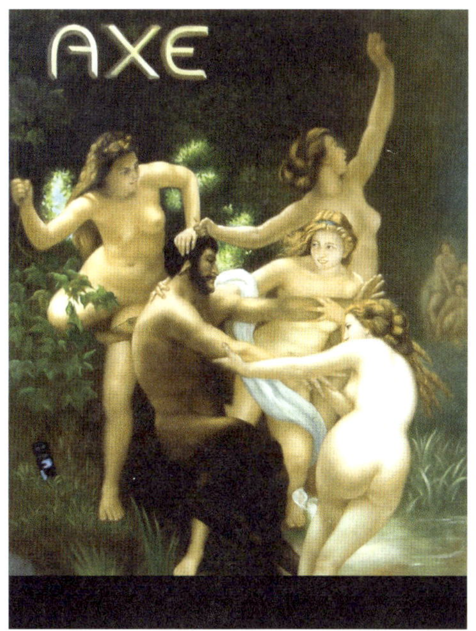

Voodoo 2008

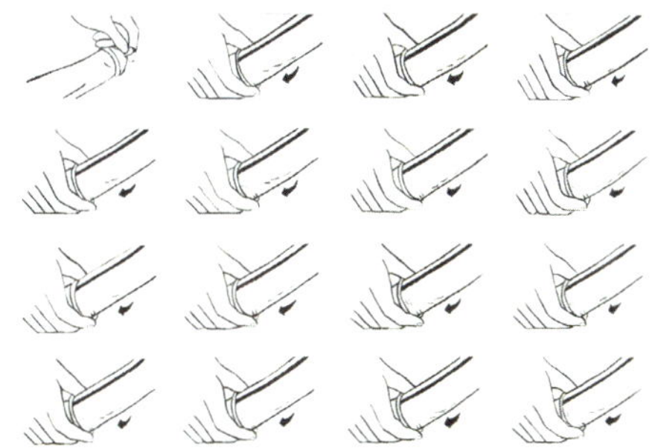

XXXXXXXXXXXXXXXL 2008

One can't help but look upon this as evidence of a kind creativity by committee. Messages squeezed out of brainstorming sessions around the conference table, mapped out through the listing of initiatives for the painstaking development of the promotional image. This is a system of color-coding that no doubt has been arrived at through a flood of loose pop-psychology and filtered through focus group after focus group, then retroactively put through market and profit analysis, before being screened for a test audience. Along with Bouchet's physical remoteness from the process, the formatting geometry of the works acts as an effective means of detachment for the artist and by extension, his committee.

Orgone Machinery: Whether you're talking about Gustave Courbet or Axe Body Spray, the cyclical loosening of mores and taboos follows similar sequences, depending on their spheres of influence.

Typologically, this uniformity in the way we as viewers determine what images we pay attention to, is dubiously effective – which is to say that our focus is easily focused. Whether his ultimate goal is to seize some autonomy within these systems or to mold a future generation of viewers, Bouchet seems to revel in the persistence of conventions in their present form. These are splendid models often approached as behaviors and predispositions to usurp or run from. The artist is a practitioner, not a critic here. It is apparent that the contour of this investigation is one he sees as having an expansive aesthetic use. (Did Cubism have such a mechanism in place?)

"There is a river of sex, you dip your toes in. It is an endless stream of fetish and affection with changing social and political repercussions - nothing ages faster than sex." Mike Bouchet

Recently, Bouchet has been collecting and working with Ads that exhibit an extremely blatant sexuality and sending them off to artisans for reproduction. The artist cites an interest in Wilhelm Reich's theory of Orgone energy and Advertising as a superlative Orgone Machine and Orgone generator.
Rather than an ironic stance, these paintings almost seem to belie a backhanded prudishness on Bouchet's part. Just as he adopts the agency of the ironist he puts forth his work and his positions in an earnest manner. Irony is a conservative position, a distance from the fulcrum of change. Both art and advertising venture to cultivate a subjective adherence. Grandiose and megalomaniacal at times, or simply fraught with ultra-creative propositioning, Mike Bouchet's work functions in more or less the same way. Ad Grammar is a language of endeavor. It is the inflection inherent in the broadcasted message, and is as such much obliged to its audience. Within this web of images and transactions, Bouchet's is a subjectivity that must adopt the collective temperament even while exploring its potential by the redeployment and redistribution of things and constructs in the image world through very industrious and systematic means. The product (the output, the work), its physical manifestation, its appraisal and propagation, these things are there to stabilize or anchor or in the very least demarcate the epistemological persuasion he wishes to impose on his audience. All this to say that the scandal of advertising is that there is no scandal and that, perhaps, the propriety of art is that it is all scandal.

Cube 1994

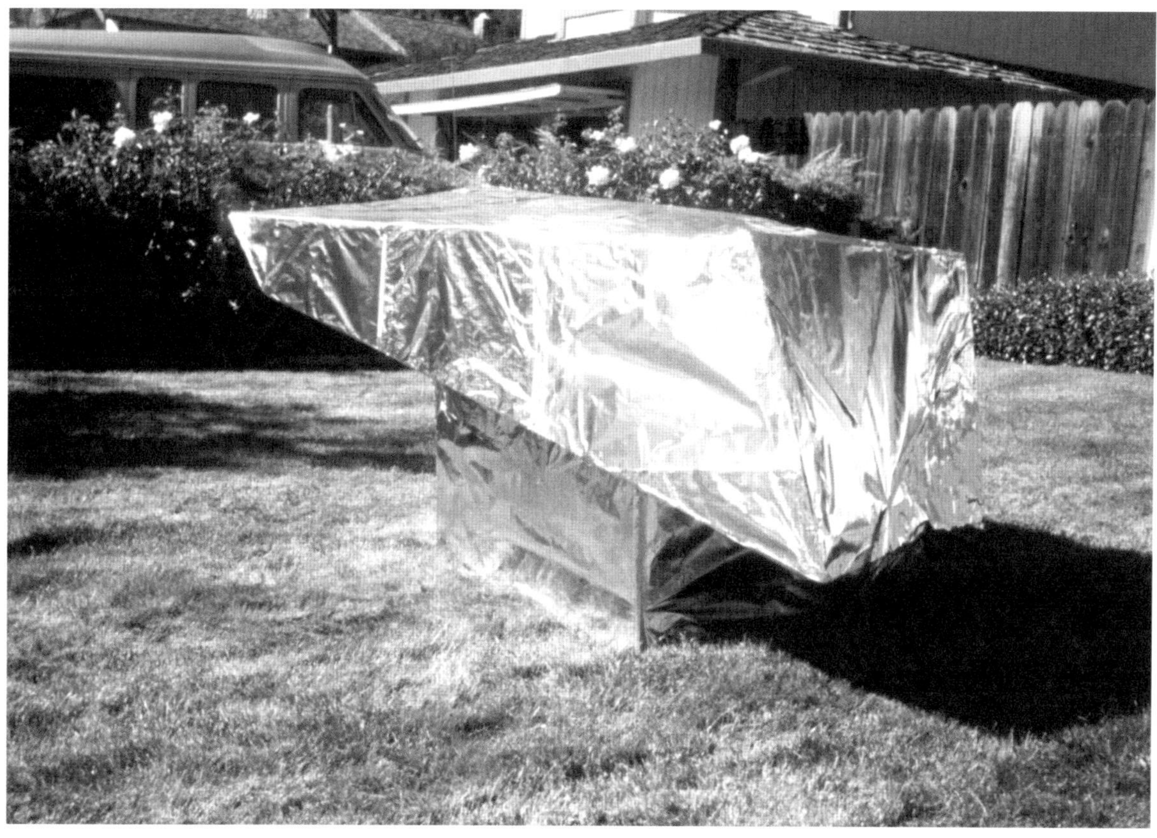

A large motor driven sculpture that rotates at approximately 10 RPM. Constructed out of wood and cardboard, and covered in aluminum foil. It is designed to fit tightly in a specific room, creating a strong wind, and leaving a narrow space between the walls of the room and the sculpture itself.

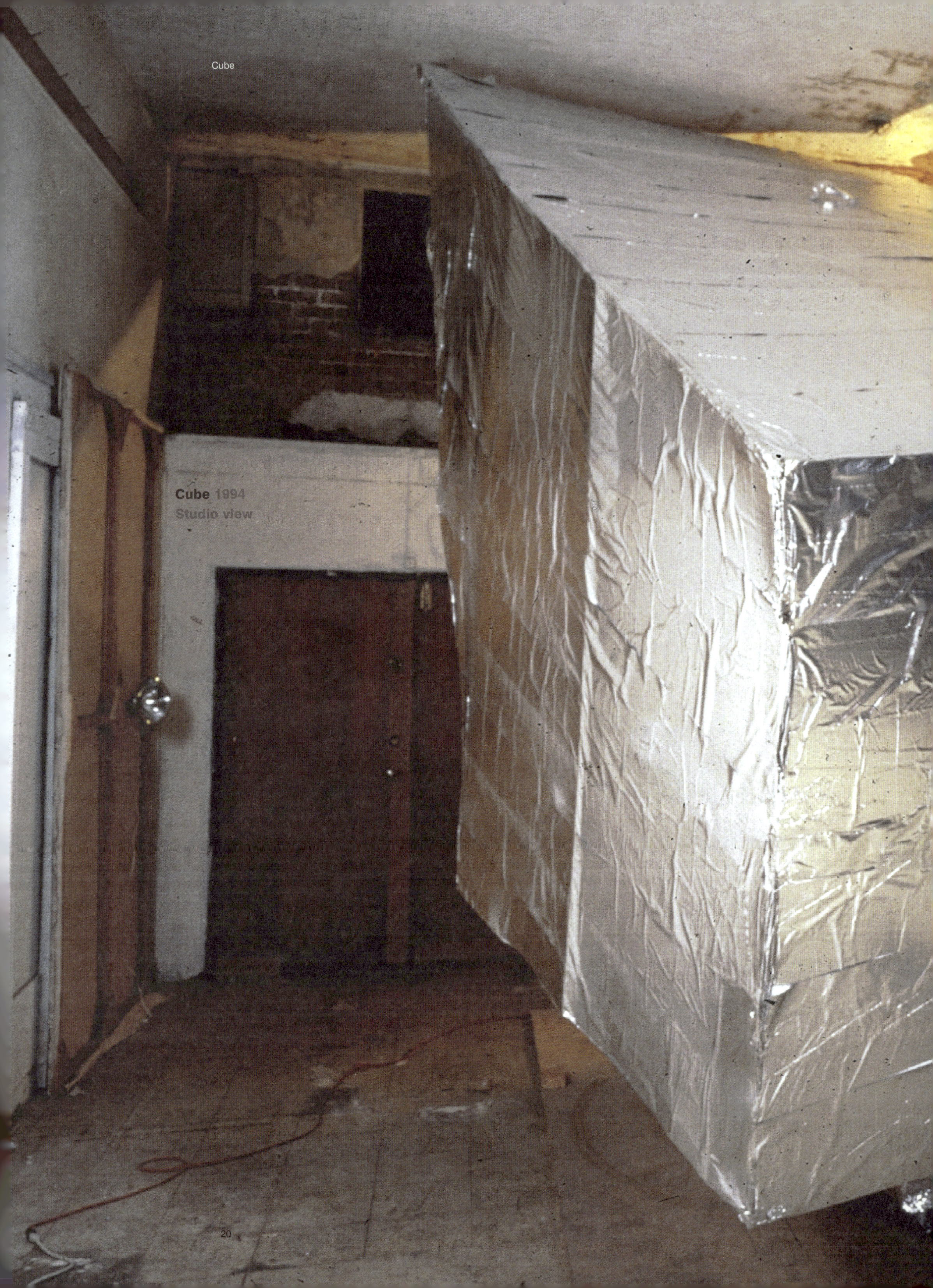
Cube
Cube 1994
Studio view
20

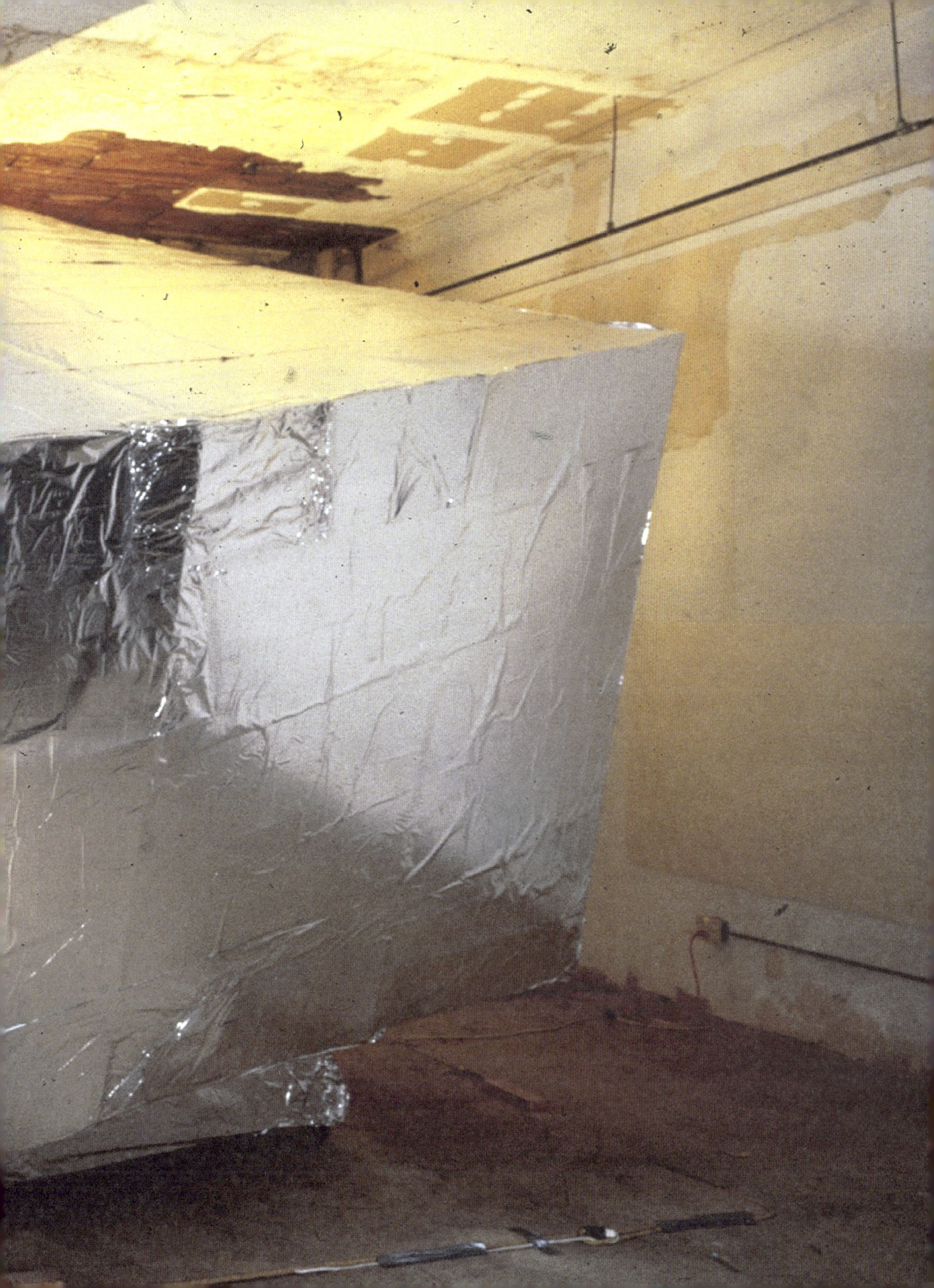

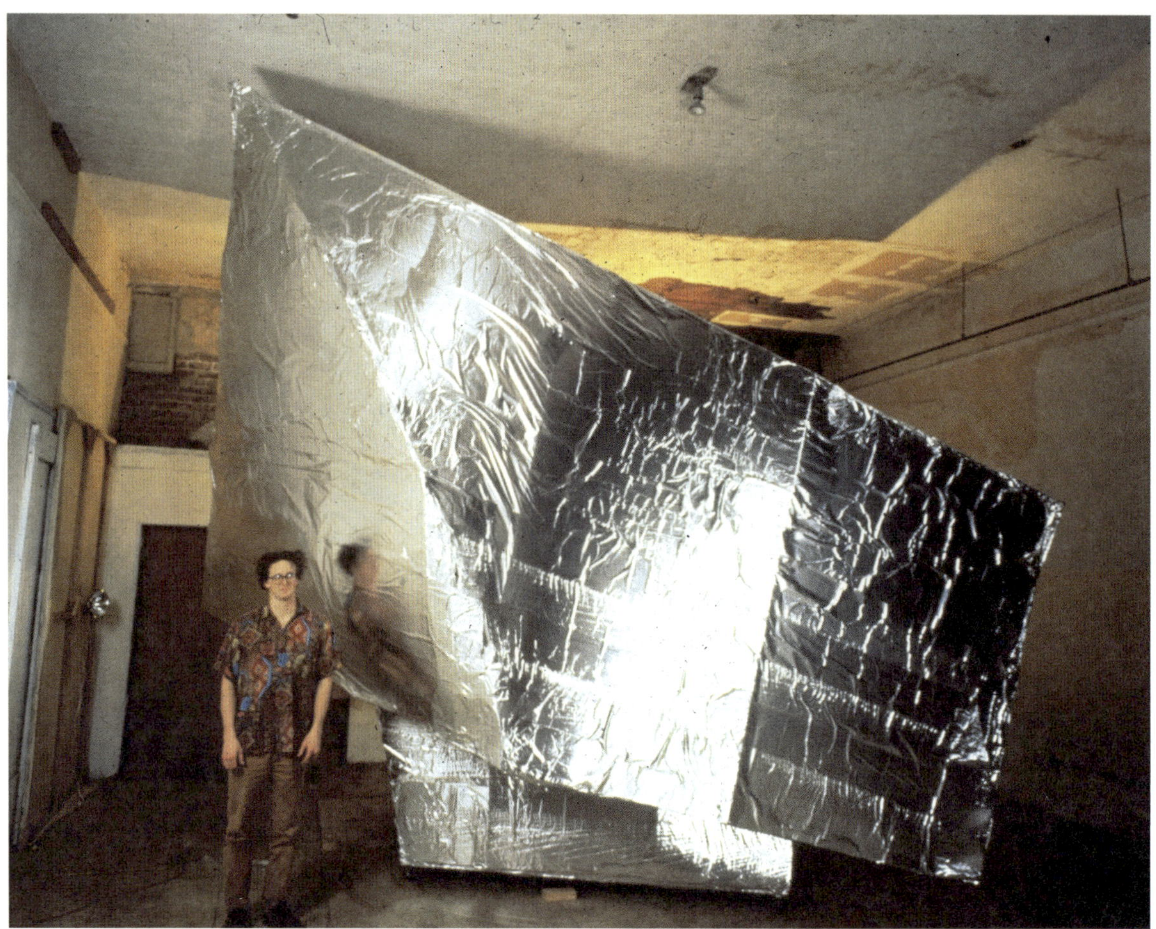

Cube, Studio view (with artist) 1994

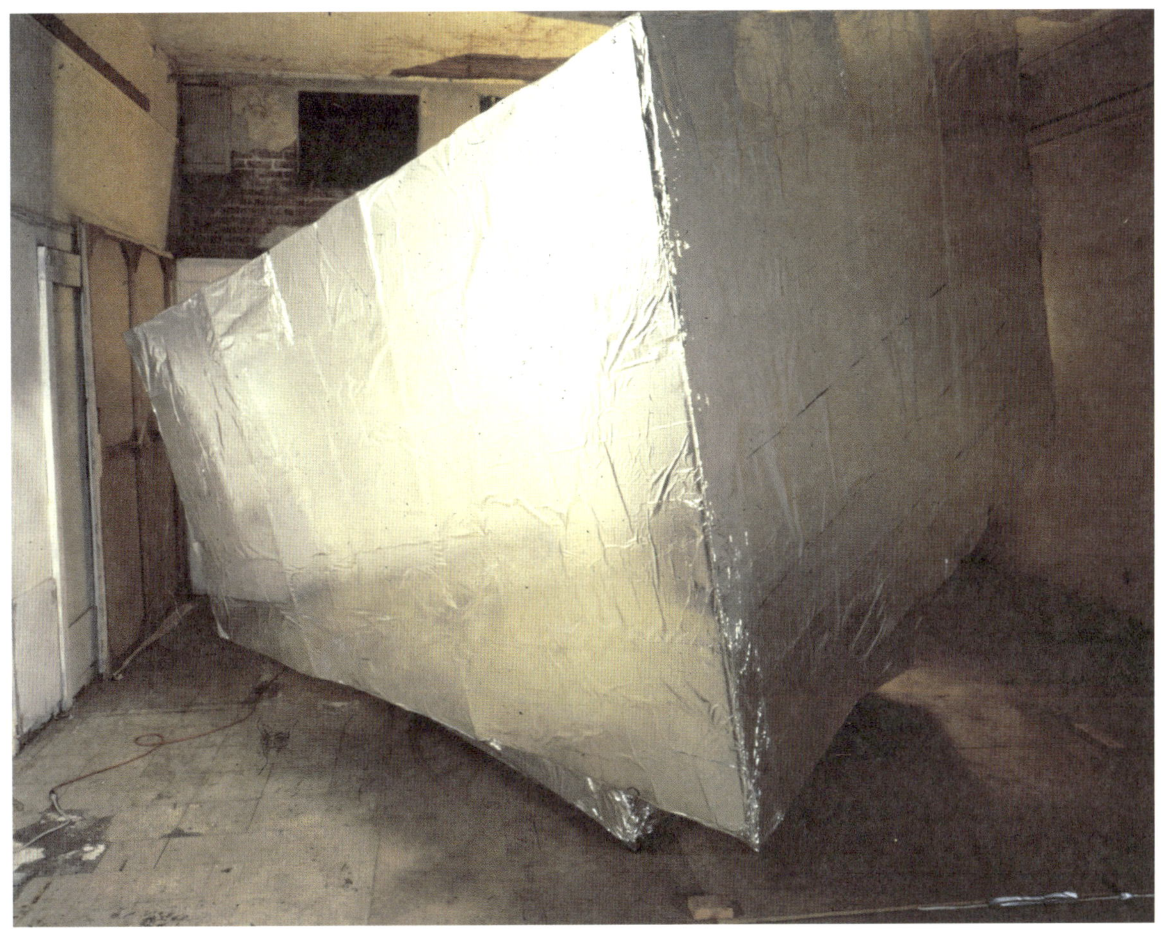

Cube, Studio view 1994

My Toothbrush is your Toothbrush 1995

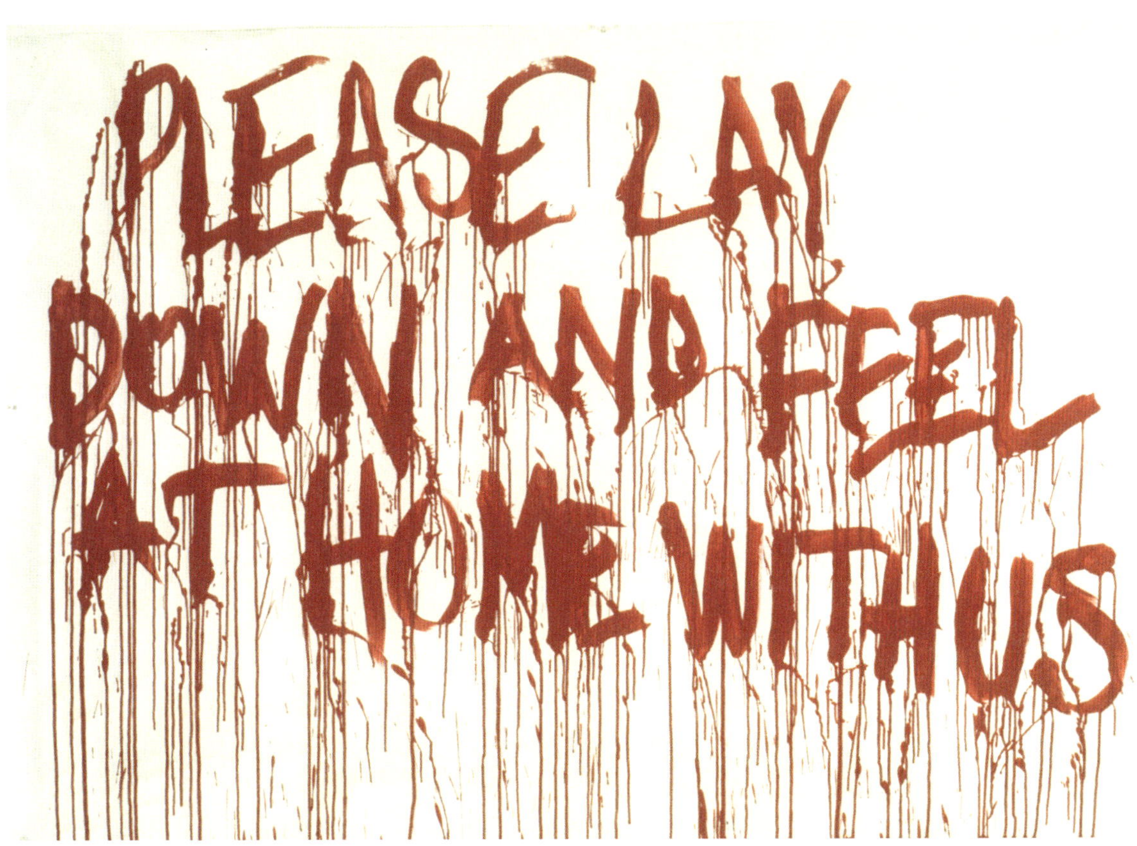

For this body of work, the artist invited various friends and acquaintances to come and live in his studio for three days: January 19-21, 1996. During the event, the participants were then asked to stay as long as they wanted. The artist provided food, marijuana, and bathrobes for approximately 40 people in an attempt to convince them to move into the studio and live in and around a 17 meter long, fully-functioning futon sofa, titled "Commune Futon".

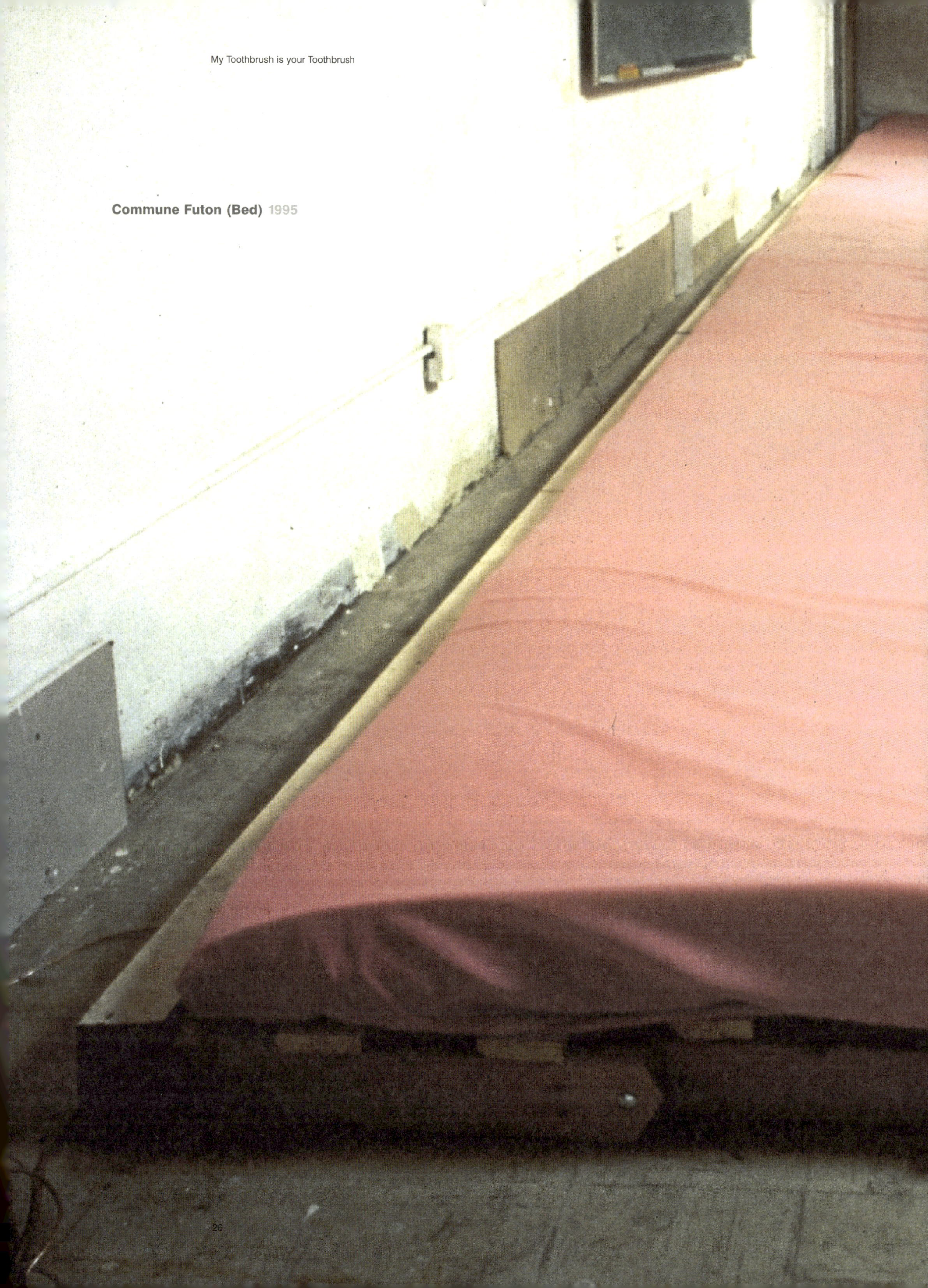

Commune Futon (Bed) 1995

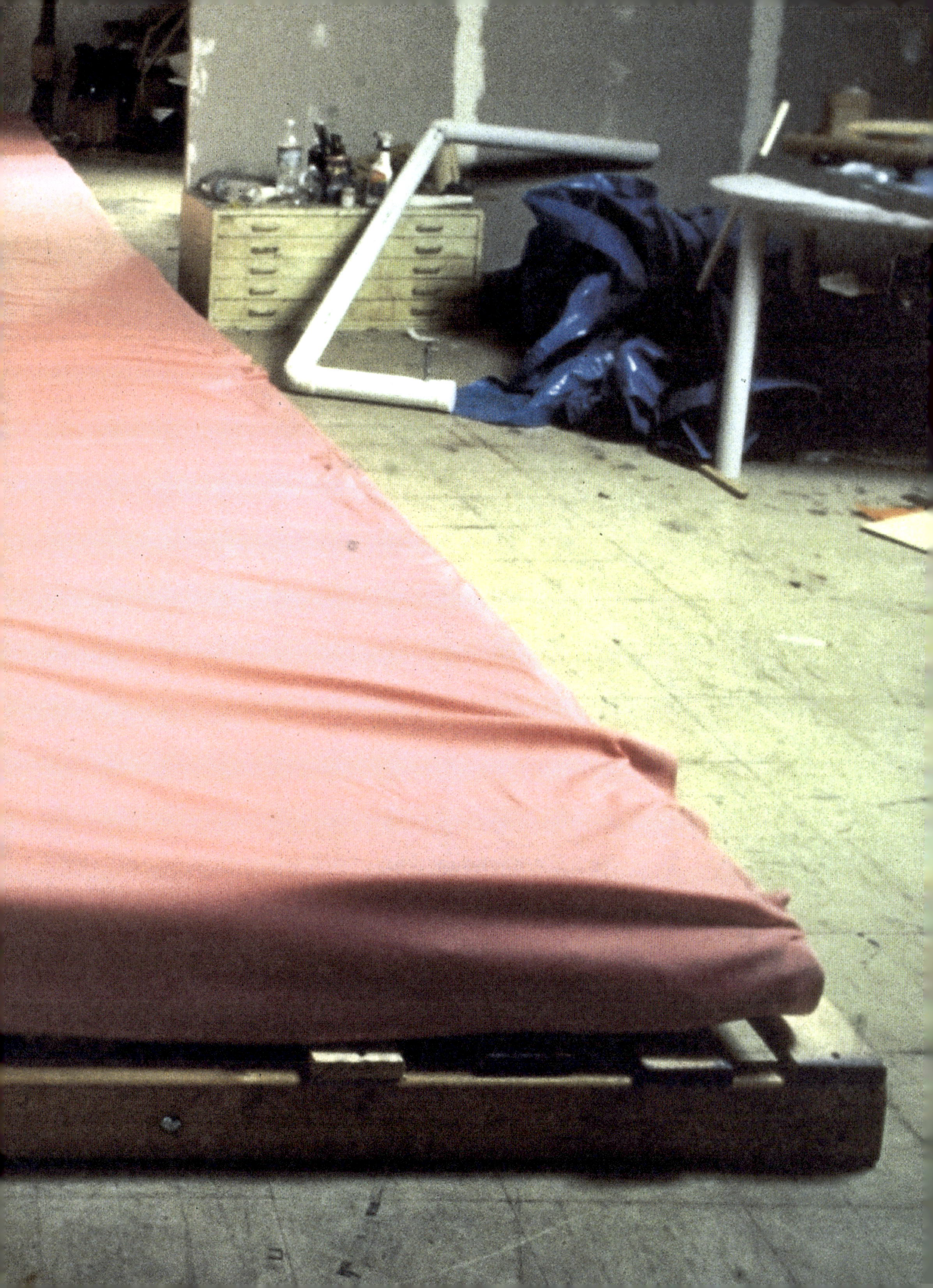

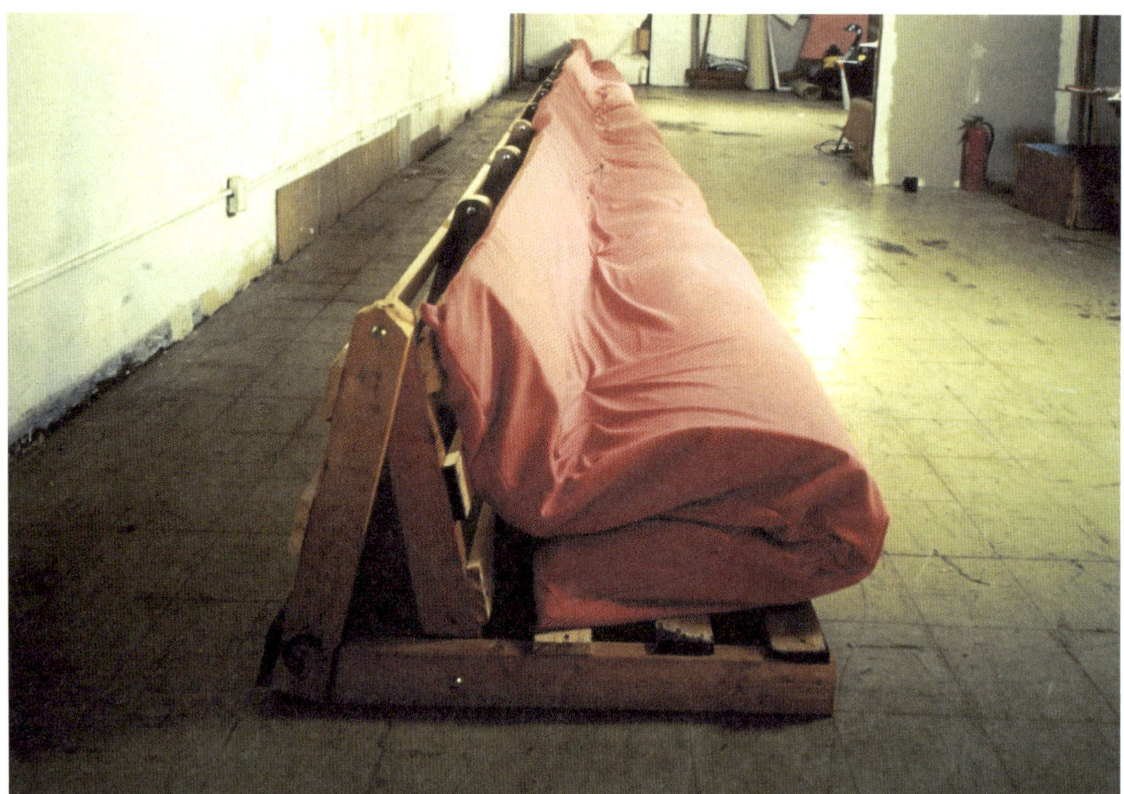

Commune Futon (Couch) 1995

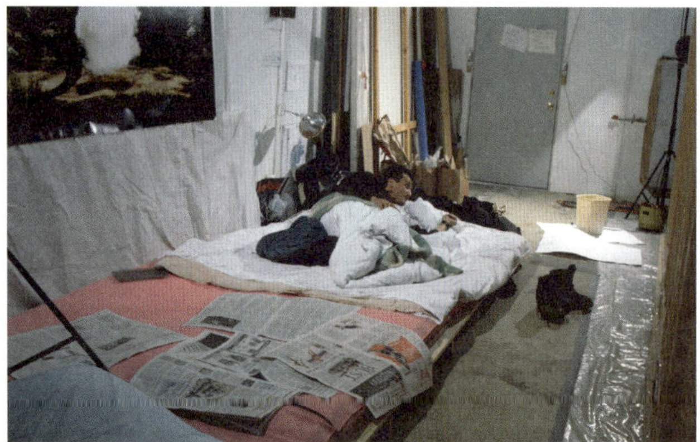

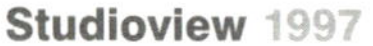

Studioview 1997

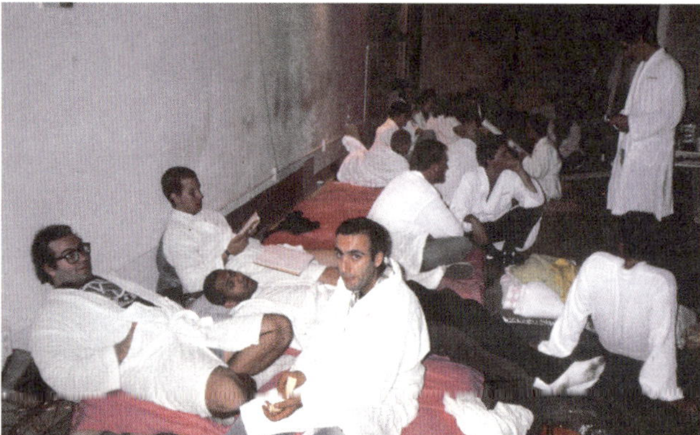

Studioview 1995

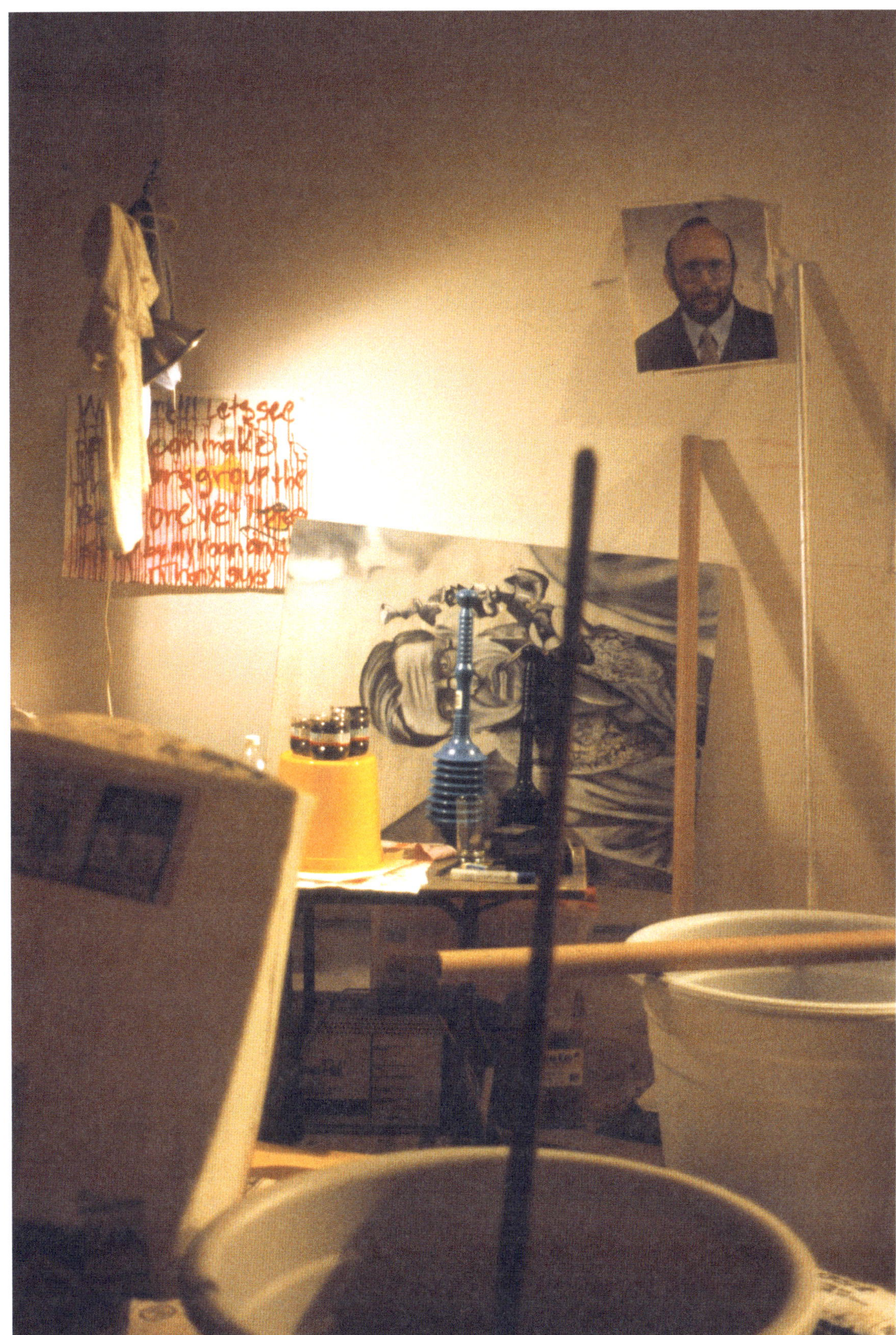

Studioview 1995

Eagle Rock ShitRock 1997–2000

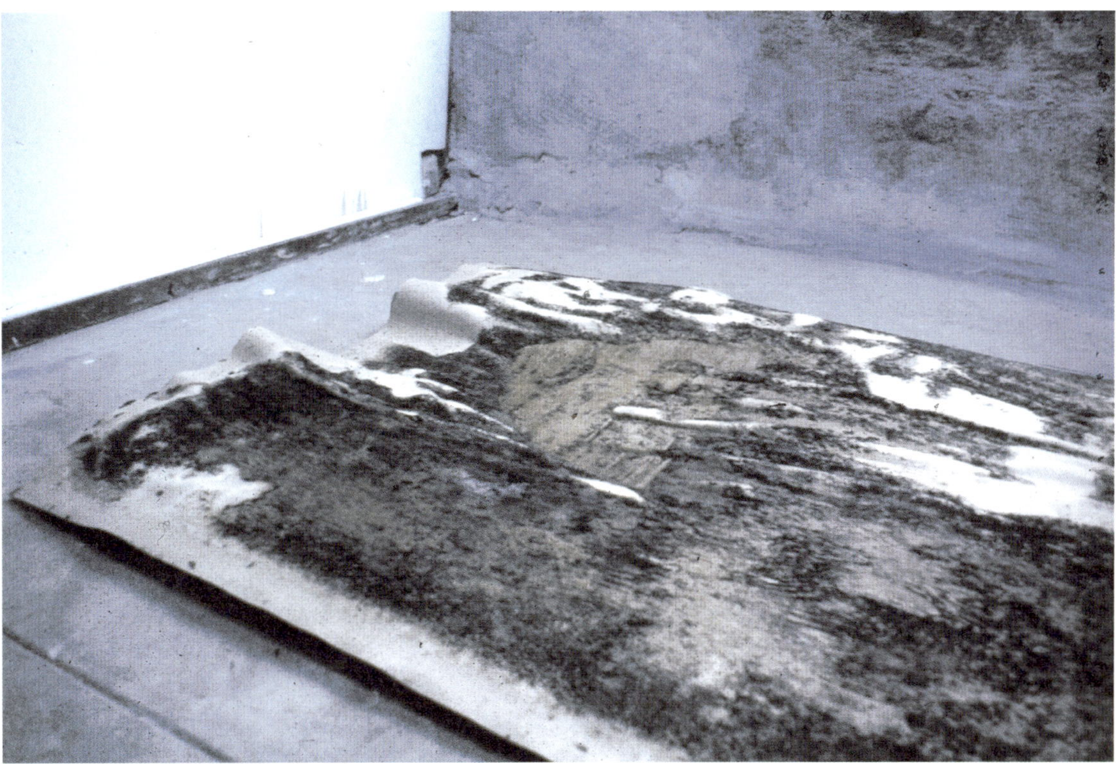

The interior scenes of the ERSR (Eagle Rock Sheet Rock) wallpapers are of a "studio" which the artist had in Los Angeles, for a project that he worked on for nearly three years. Bouchet used the space primarily to manufacture sheetrock and bricks out of steer manure. He also named the studio space "Giverny", after Monet's studio, and subsequently began producing copies of Monet's water lily paintings on commercial sheetrock, using such disparate materials as toothpaste, manure, transmission fluid, paint, and plaster. These large paintings were cut down into smaller pieces once they were finished. The "Giverny" studio was a work into and unto itself, equal parts work environment and art installation.

The site was photographed by a fashion photographer before being destroyed. The resulting 22 interior scenes provided a visual tour of the space. The subsequent photographs were then blown up into mural-sized canvas prints ("ERSR Wallpaper"), which were then installed in a variety of locations, from private apartments, to art galleries and museums.

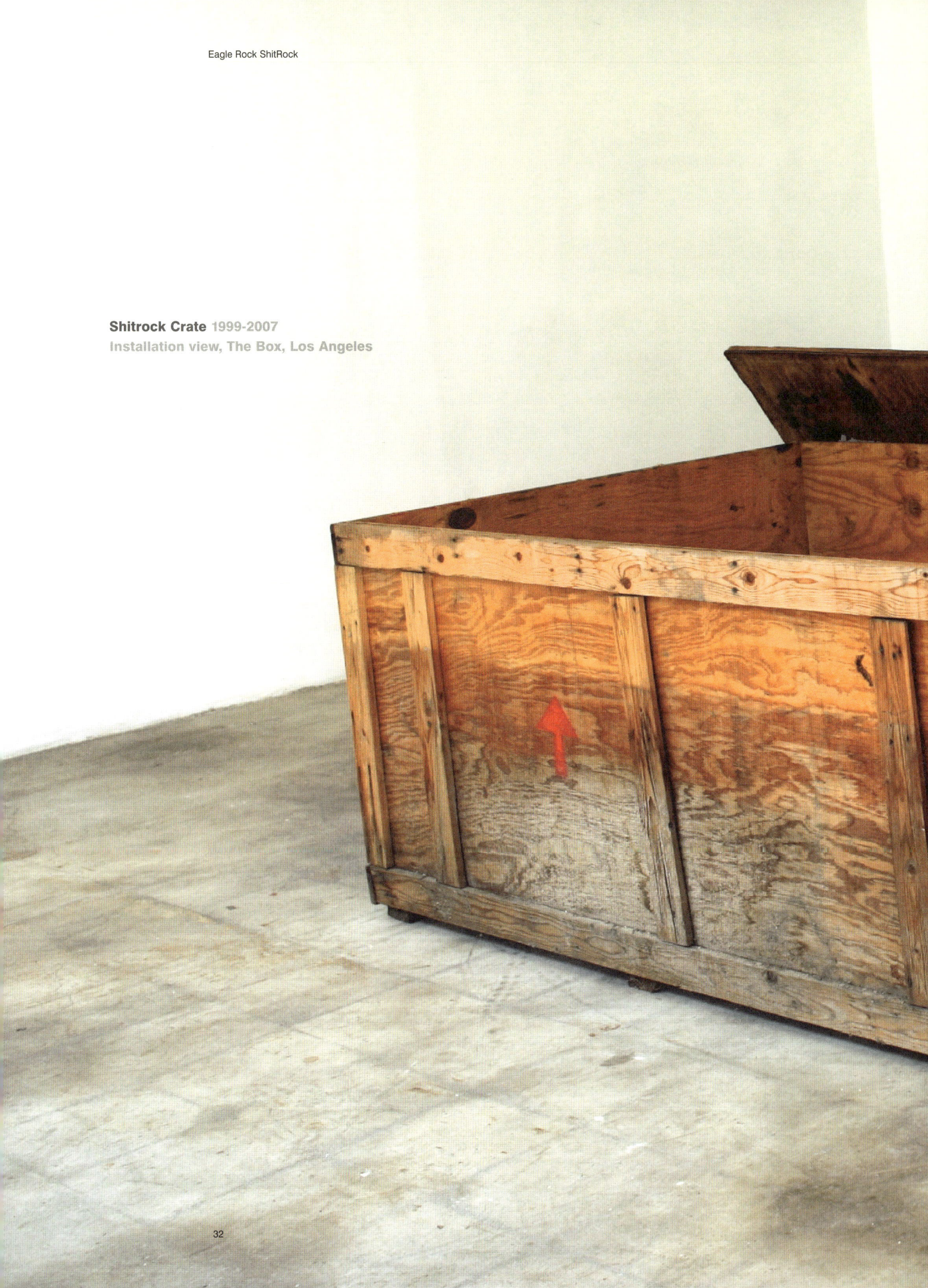

Shitrock Crate 1999-2007
Installation view, The Box, Los Angeles

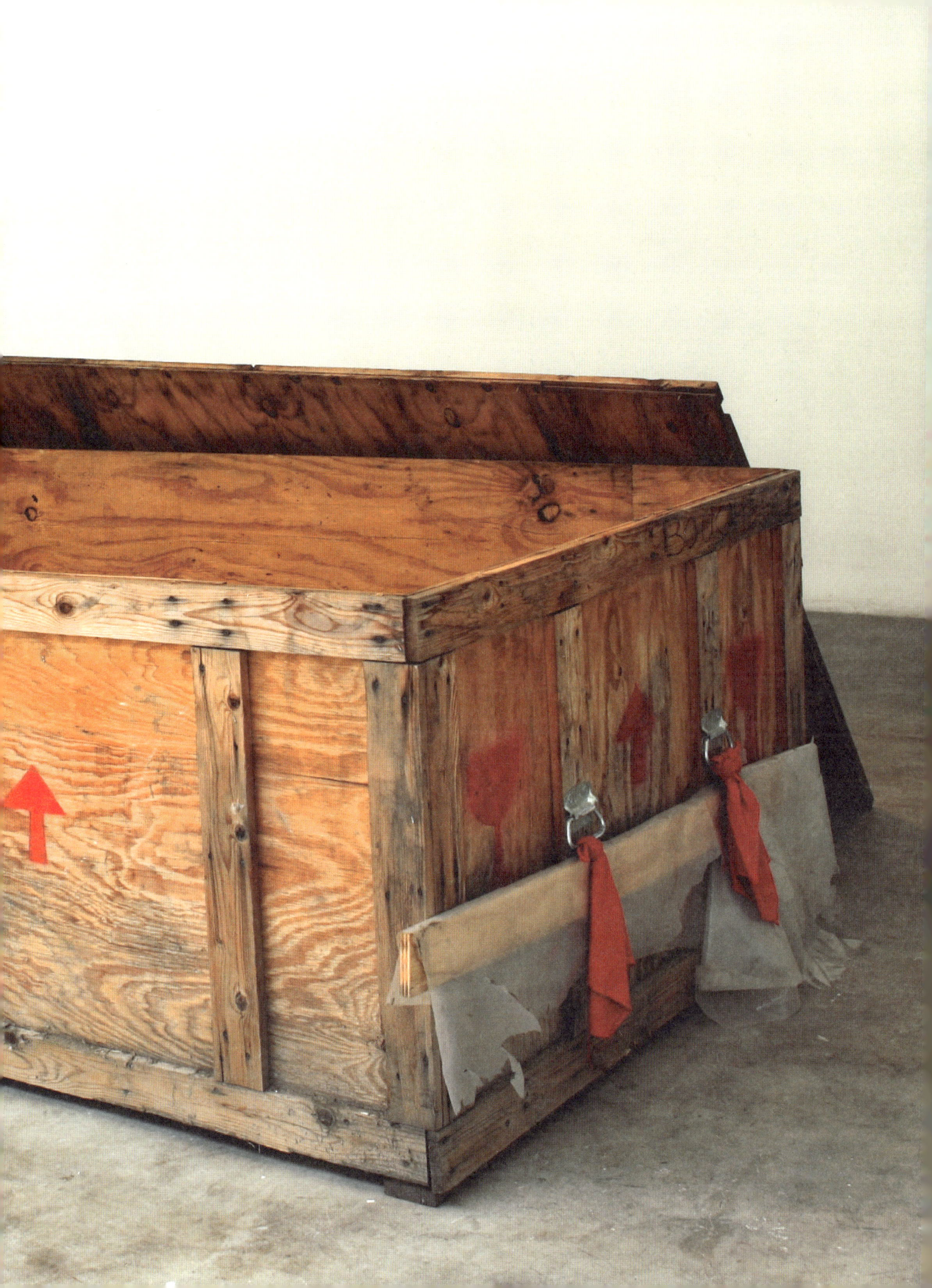

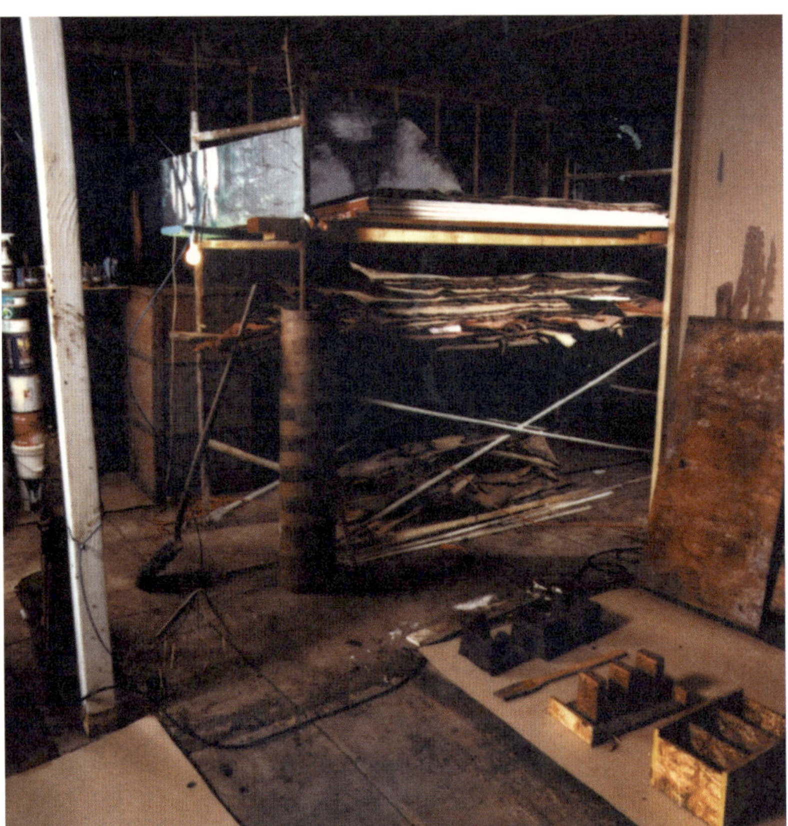

Eagle Rock ShitRock 1999
Installation view, artist's studio
Los Angeles, California

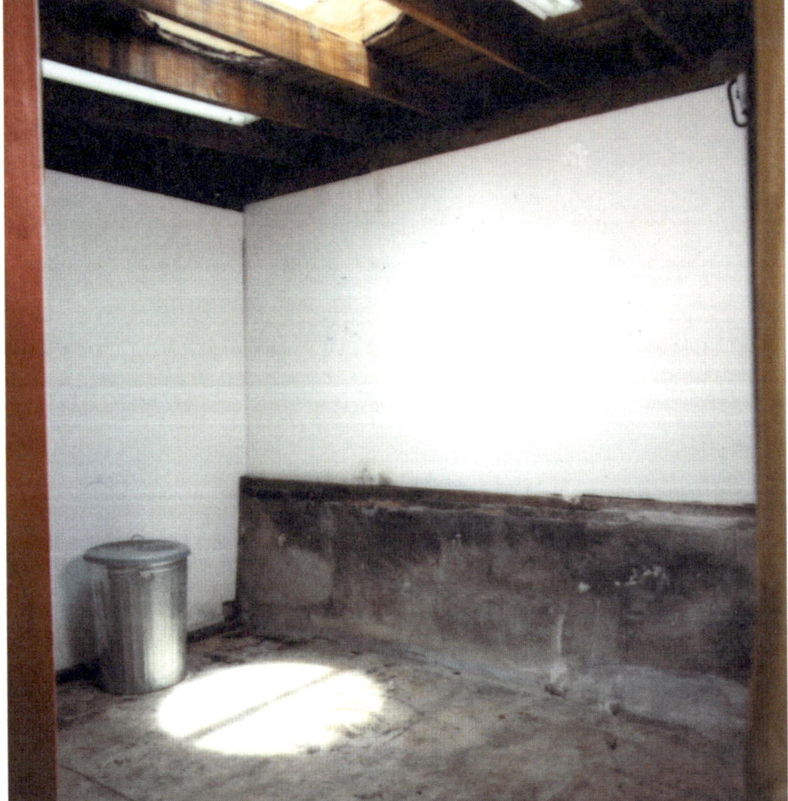

Eagle Rock ShitRock 1999
Residency studio,
Los Angeles, California

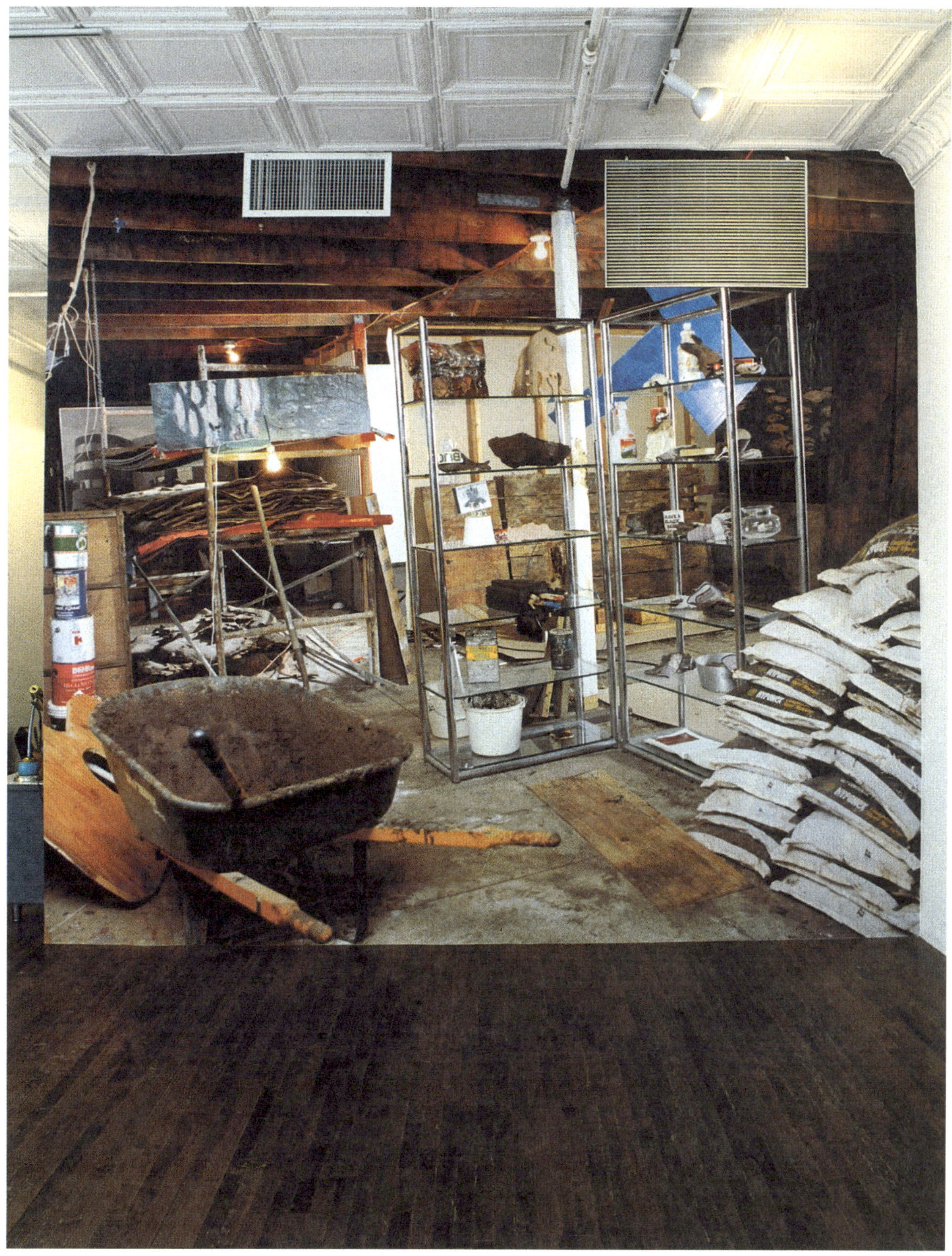

Eagle Rock Shitrock Sheet 2000
Installation view, Anton Kern Gallery, New York City

WarsawTravel/TravelWarsaw 2001

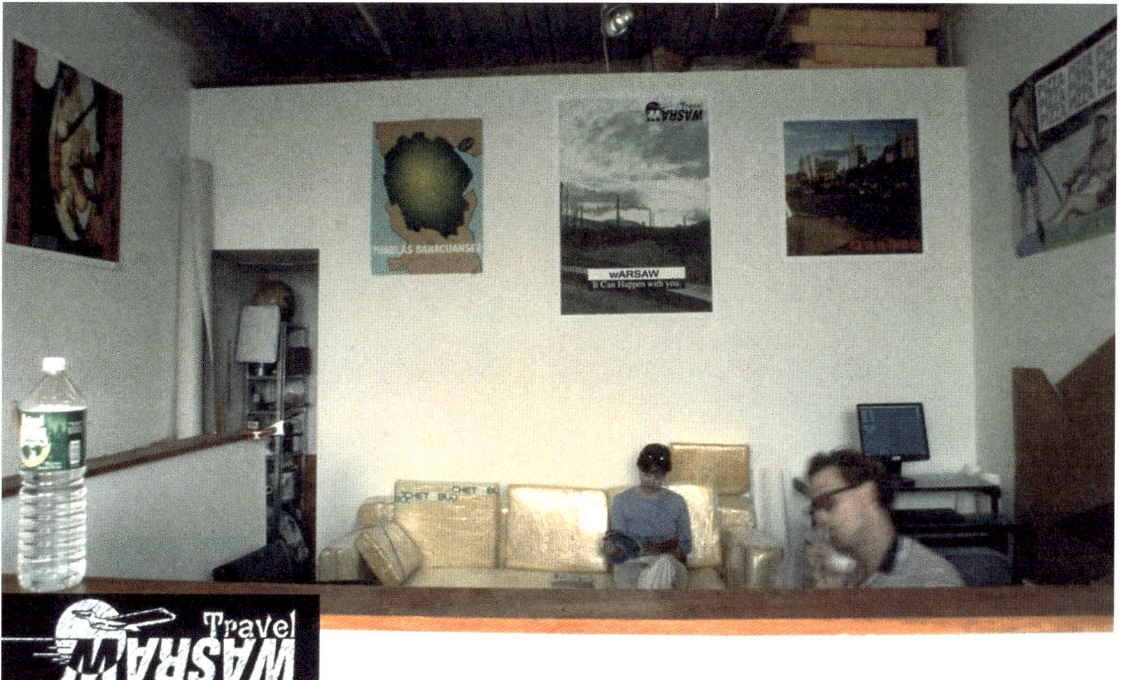

In 2001 the artist converted his art studio into a functional travel agency. The object of this agency was to book international flights, routing any and all itineraries through Warsaw, Poland. This agency was open to the general public. Bouchet offered to make reservations and generate tickets for international travel to any destination, on the condition that there be a stopover in Warsaw. Travelers who purchased their tickets through Warsaw Travel/ Travel Warsaw would have their photograph taken upon arrival in Warsaw. The piece was designed to cater to the needs of an art clientele, as well as to those of other clients looking for flight tickets and/or photo portraits.

The Warsaw Travel Agency was marked off from the rest of the studio by a 48" high oak capped wall, often used in offices to define work areas. The travel agency had a SABRE computer terminal for directly booking flights, a custom couch, several travel magazine subscriptions and various travel posters that Bouchet had designed. By building the travel office in his art studio, a contrast was created, as if the office had been 'collaged' onto a raw industrial work space.

Over Head Baggage Treatment 2003

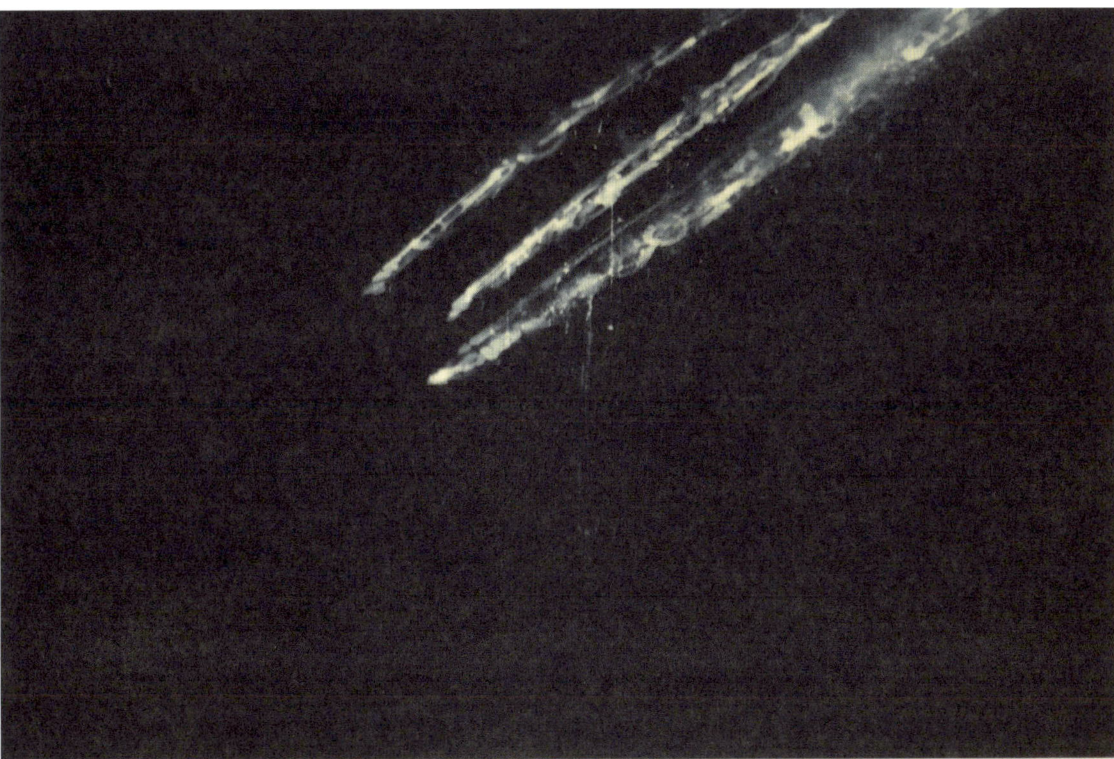

In this exhibition, Bouchet developed a layered body of work around the idea or ideal of space travel. This complex installation included stacks of paintings, video works, a refrigerated closet, and various other components. To quote Bouchet, "I wanted to tackle space travel in this exhibition, specifically the idea that we could somehow move off of this planet sometime in the near future. This mass psychosis- the world's second largest in my opinion (religion being the first)- is more insidious and widespread than we tend to think...I wanted to bring a different perspective to this question, to poke fun at the enduring appeal of this simplistic fantasy." This installation marks Bouchet's first extended foray into a more "industrial" mode of image production, in this case the series of layered text and image ink jet prints on canvas that he produced for the show.

The Other Europa Coffee Table 2003
Installation view, Maccarone, Inc., New York City

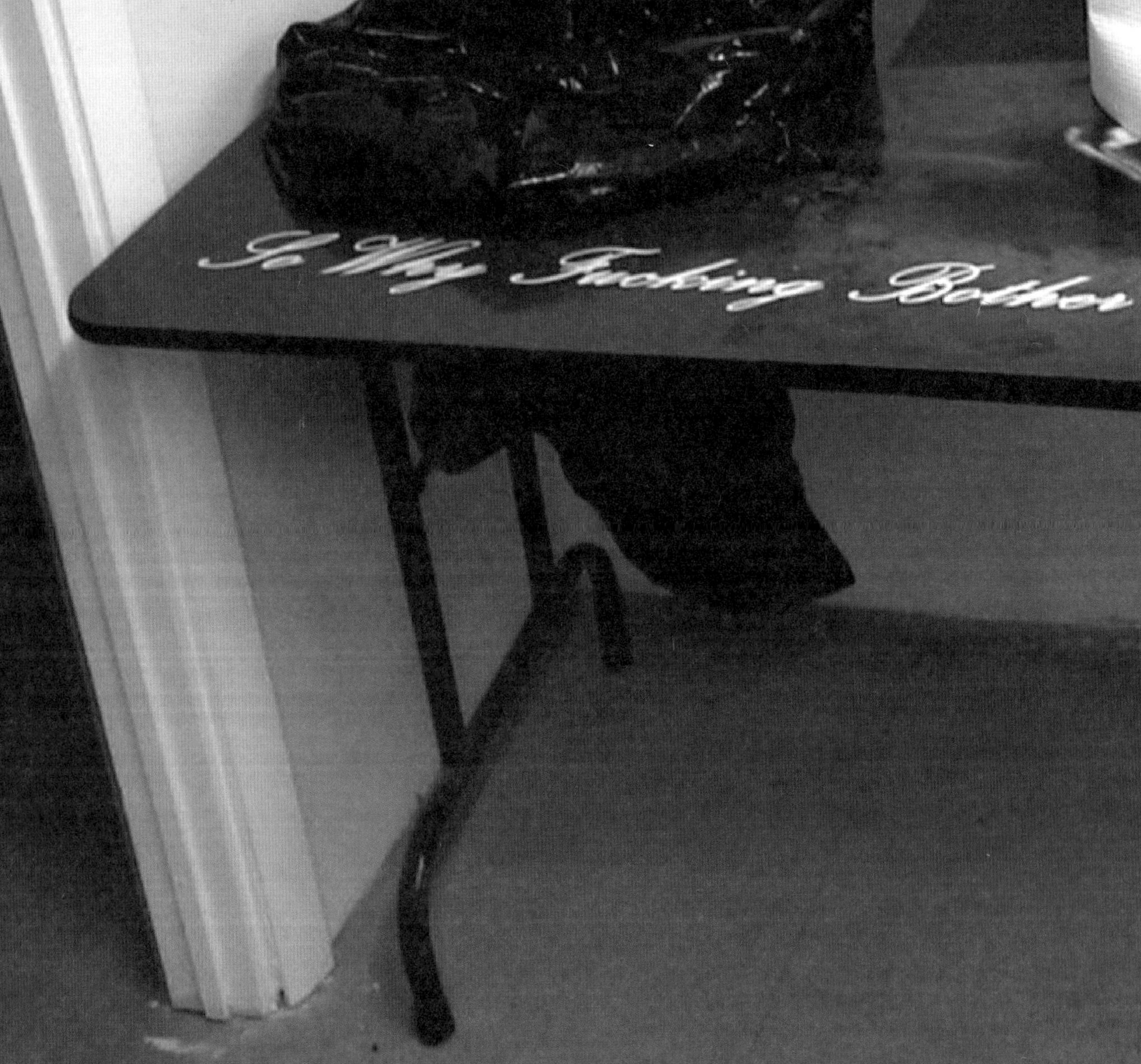

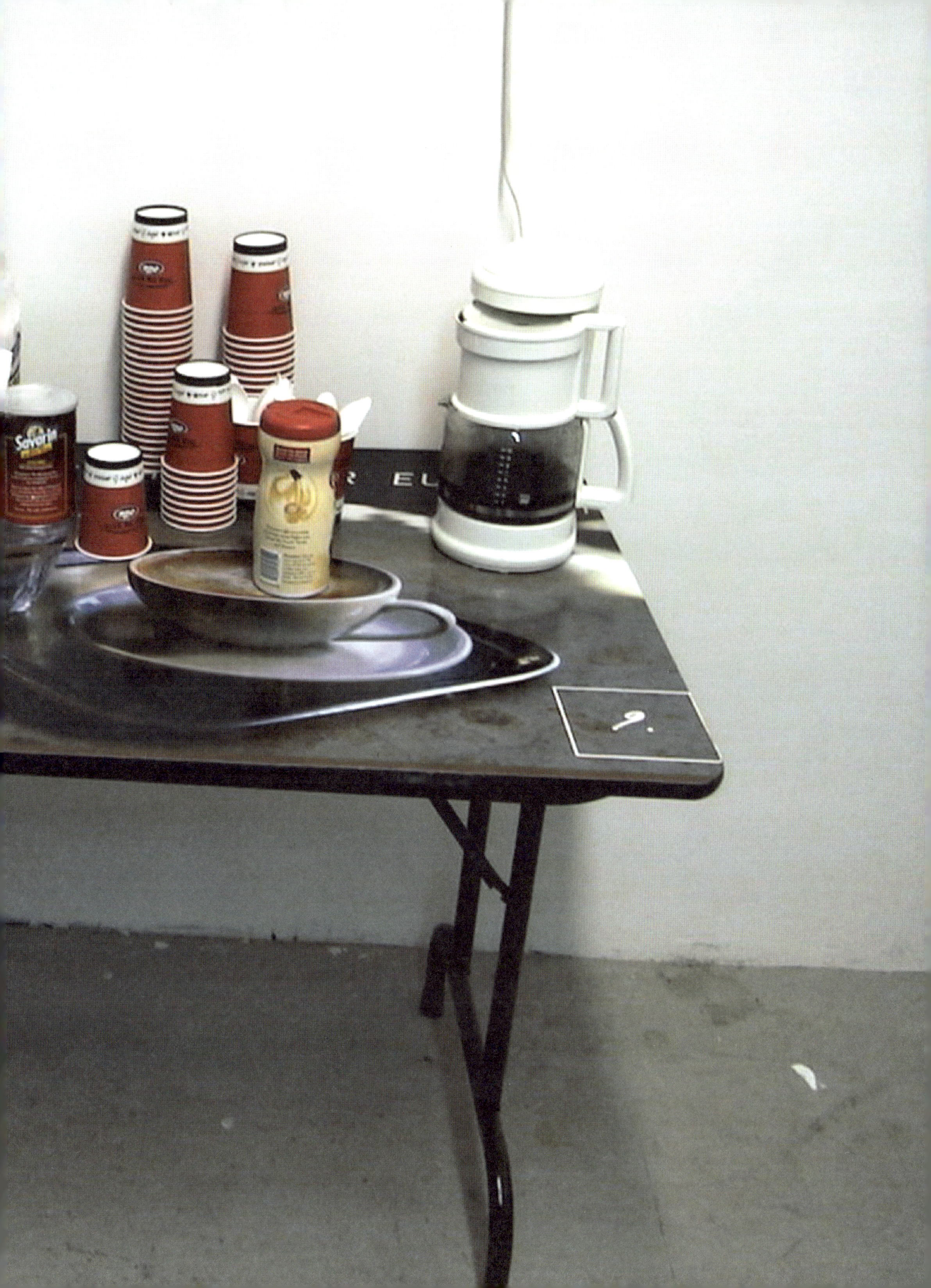

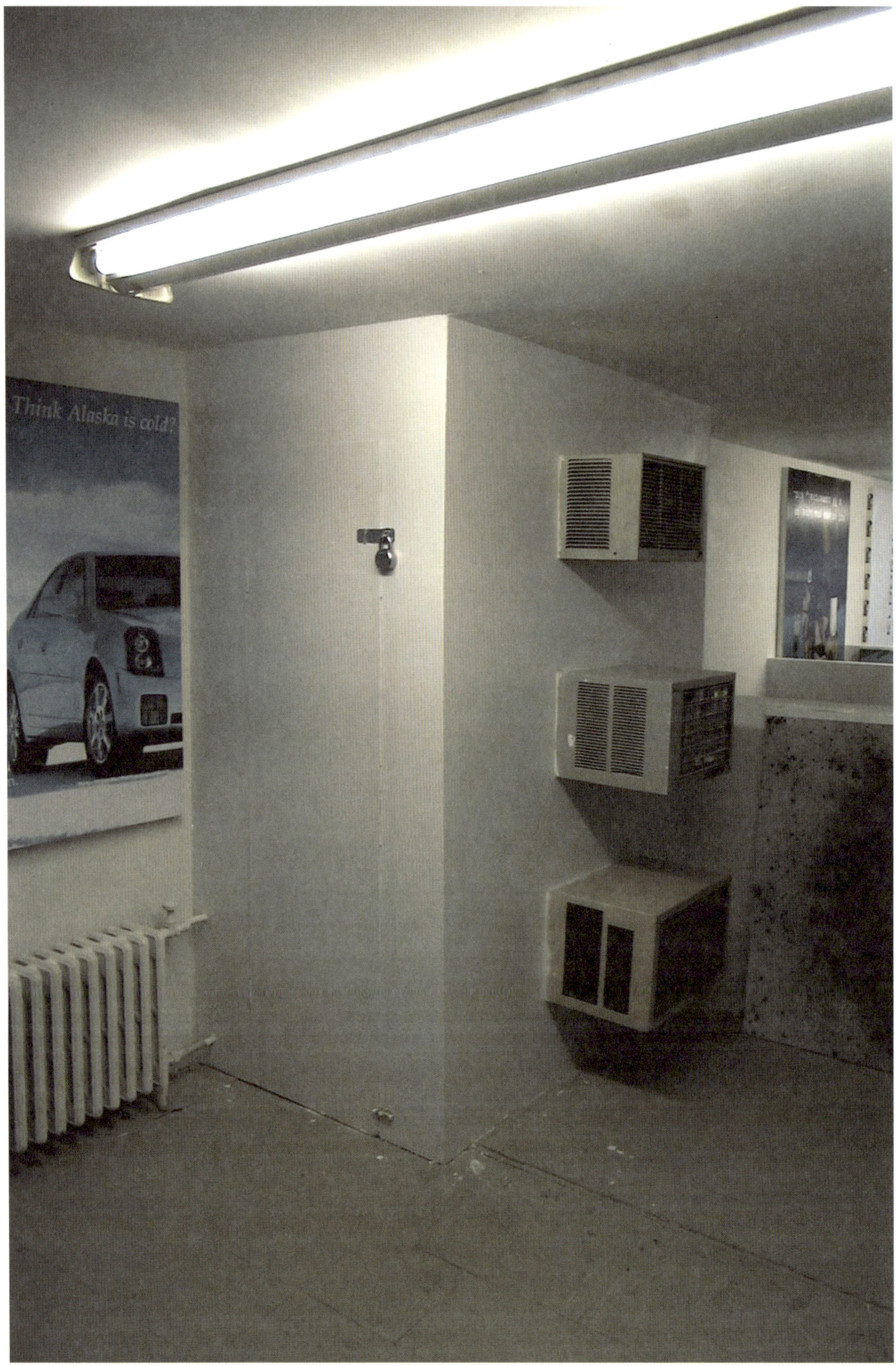

Overhead Baggage Treatment (Space Simulator) 2003
Installation view, Maccarone, Inc., New York City

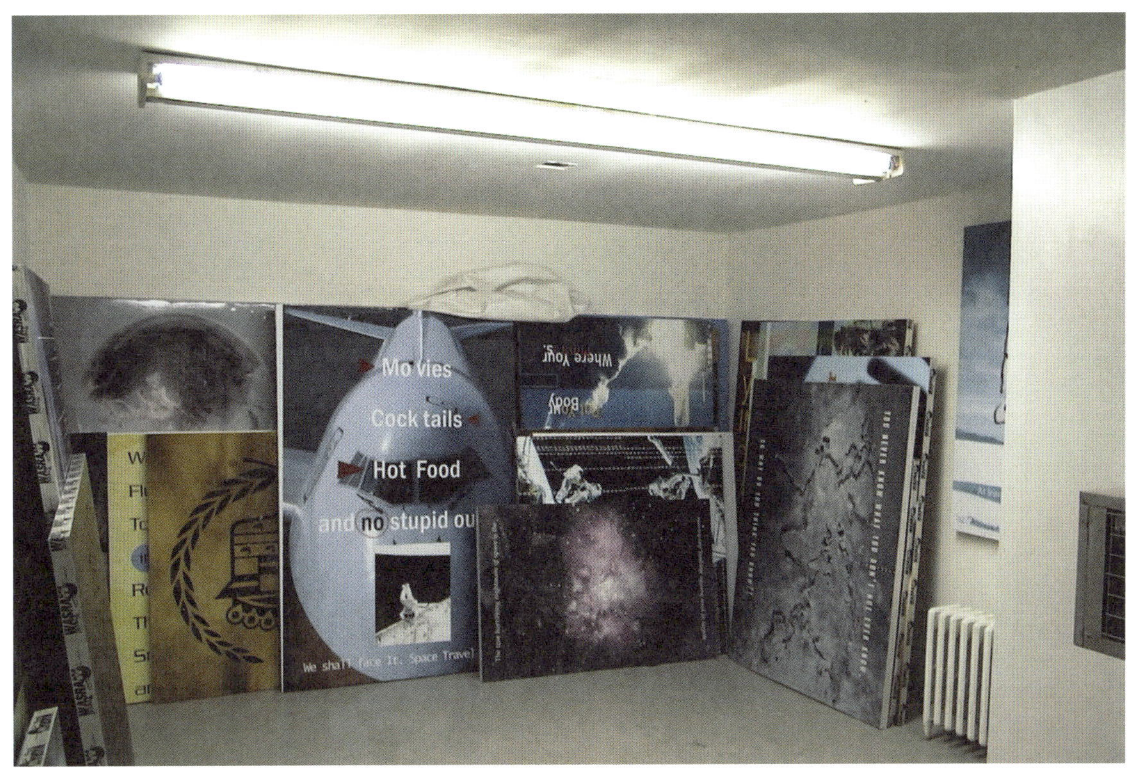

Overhead Baggage Treatment Panels 2003
Installation view, Maccarone, Inc., New York City

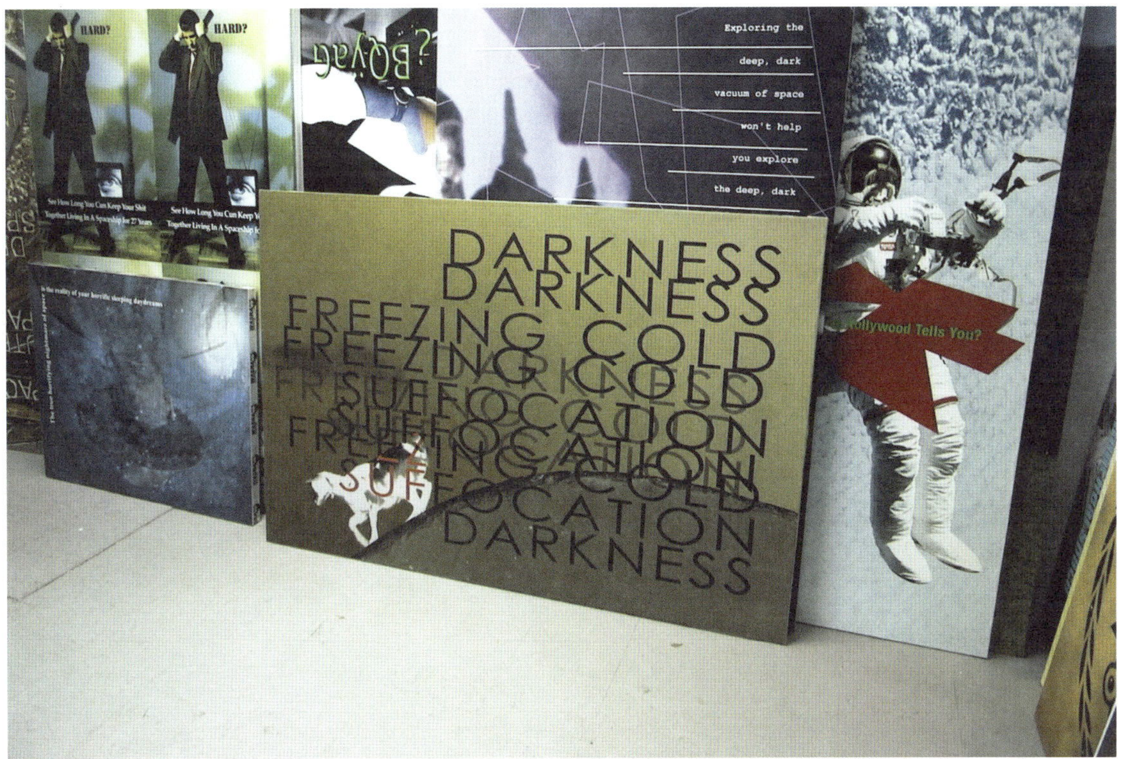

Overhead Baggage Treatment Panels 2003
Installation view, Maccarone, Inc., New York City

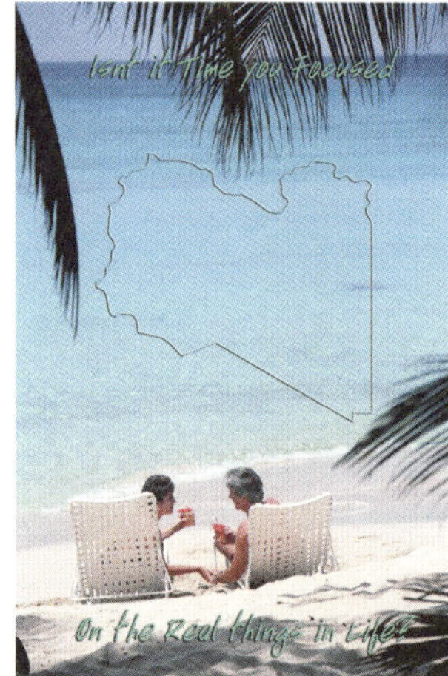

Going on Vacation 2003

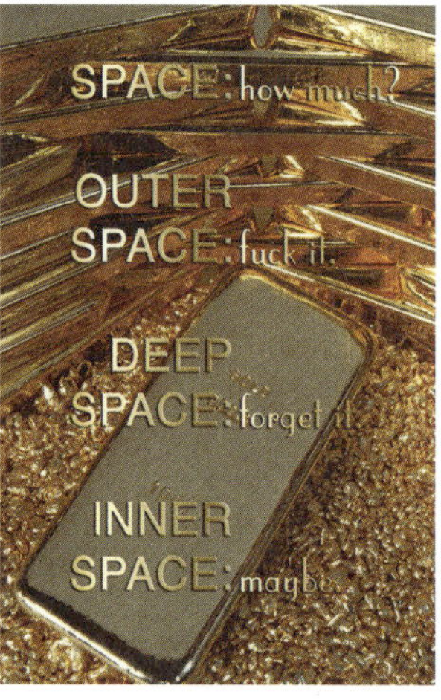

Darkness Freezing Cold Suffocation (Gold) 2003

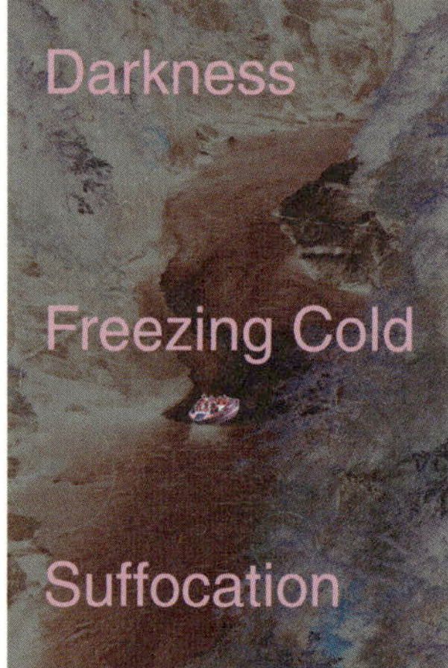

Darkness Freezing Cold Suffocation (River) 2003

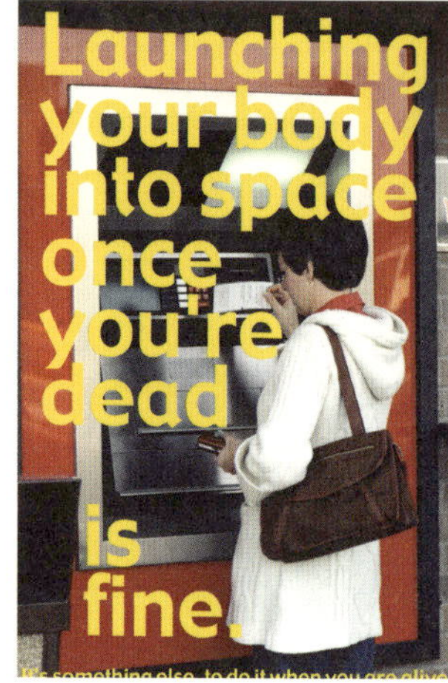

Launch Your Body 2003

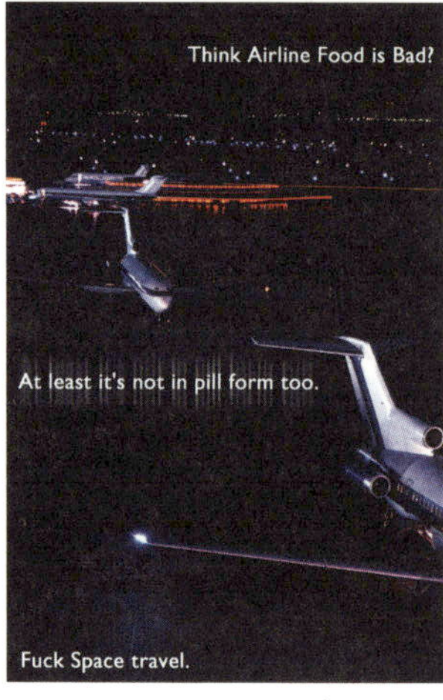

Think Airline Food is Bad? 2003

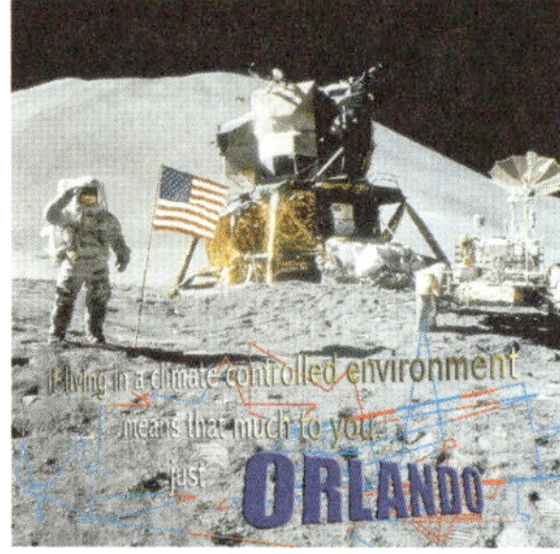

Orlando 2003

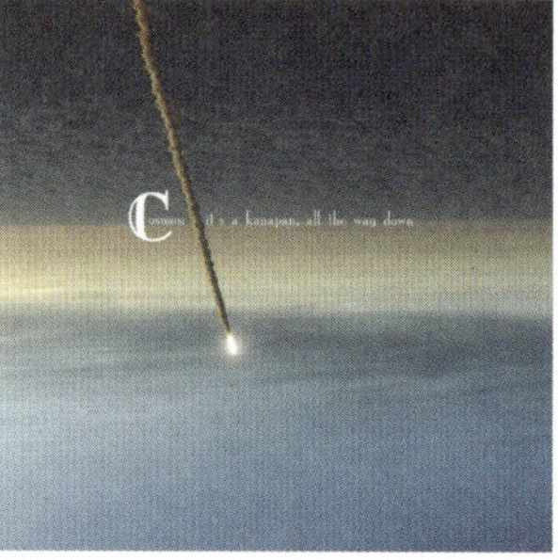

All The Way Down 2003

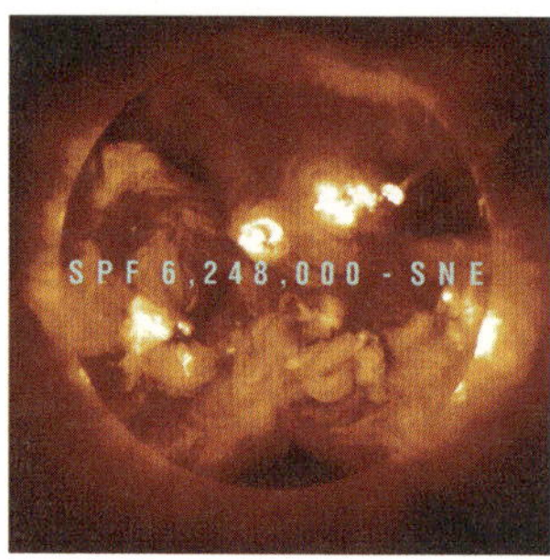

Still Not Enough 2003

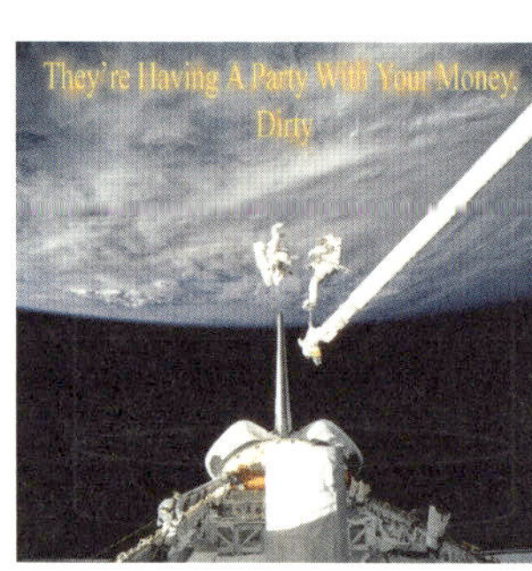

Dirty's Money 2003

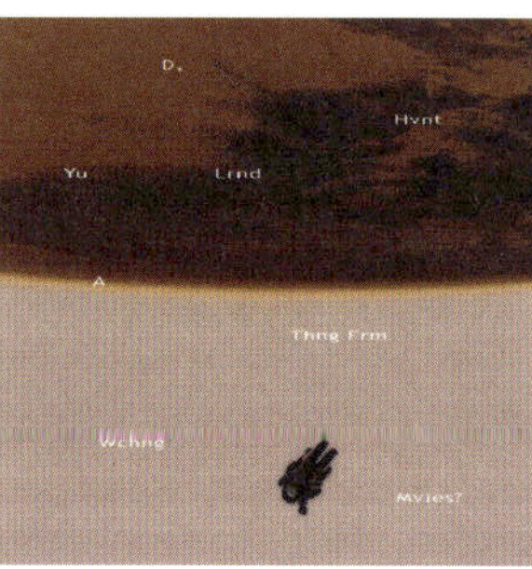

Hvnt U Lrnd A Thng? 2003

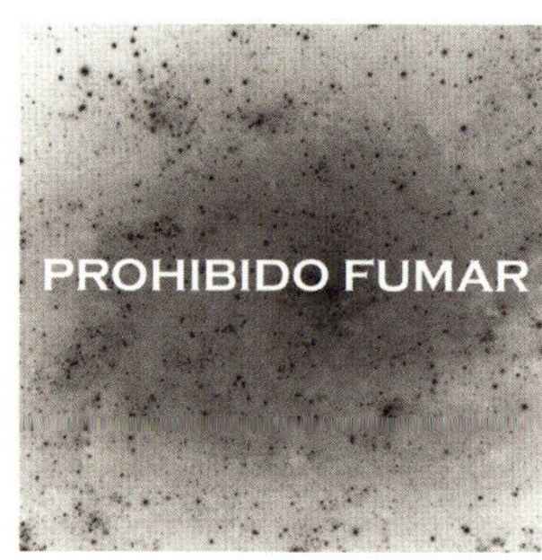

Prohibido Fumar 2003

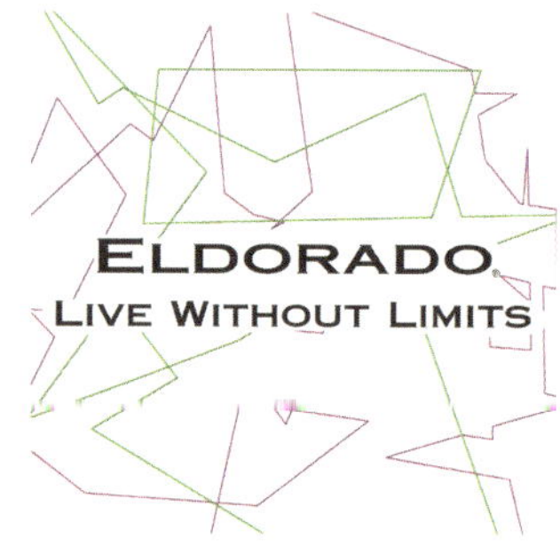

El Dorado Life 2003

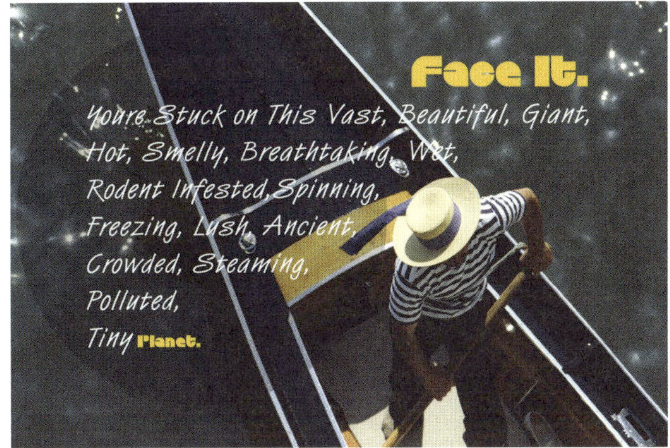

Face It 2003

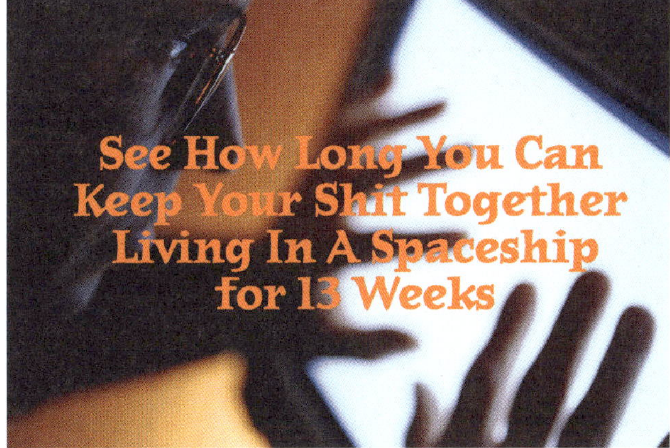

See How Long 2003

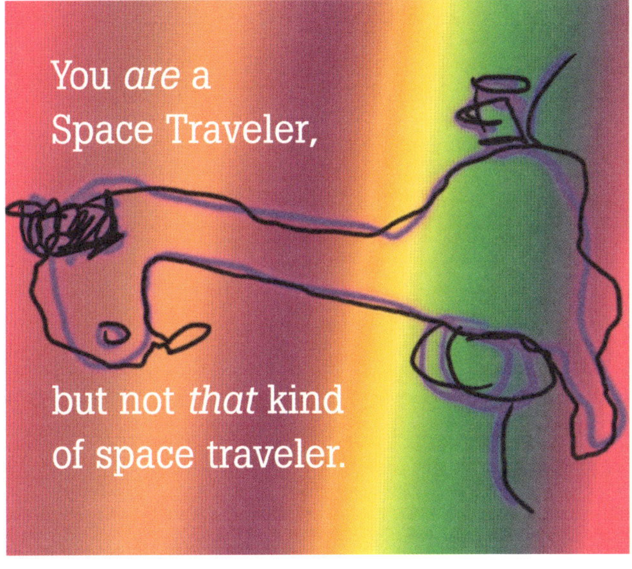

You Are A Space Traveler 2003

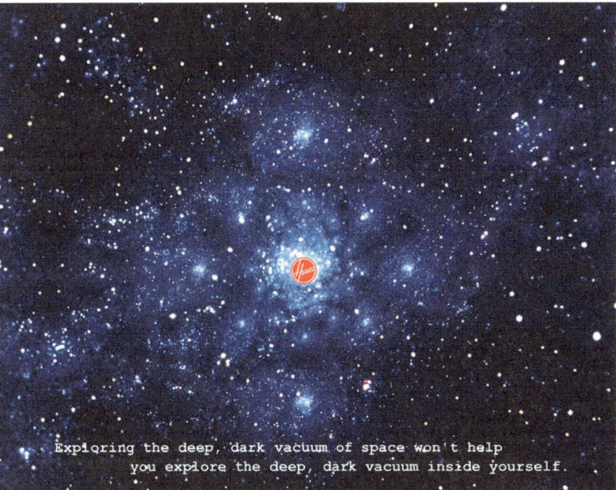

Exploring The Deep Dark Vacuum (Hoover) 2003

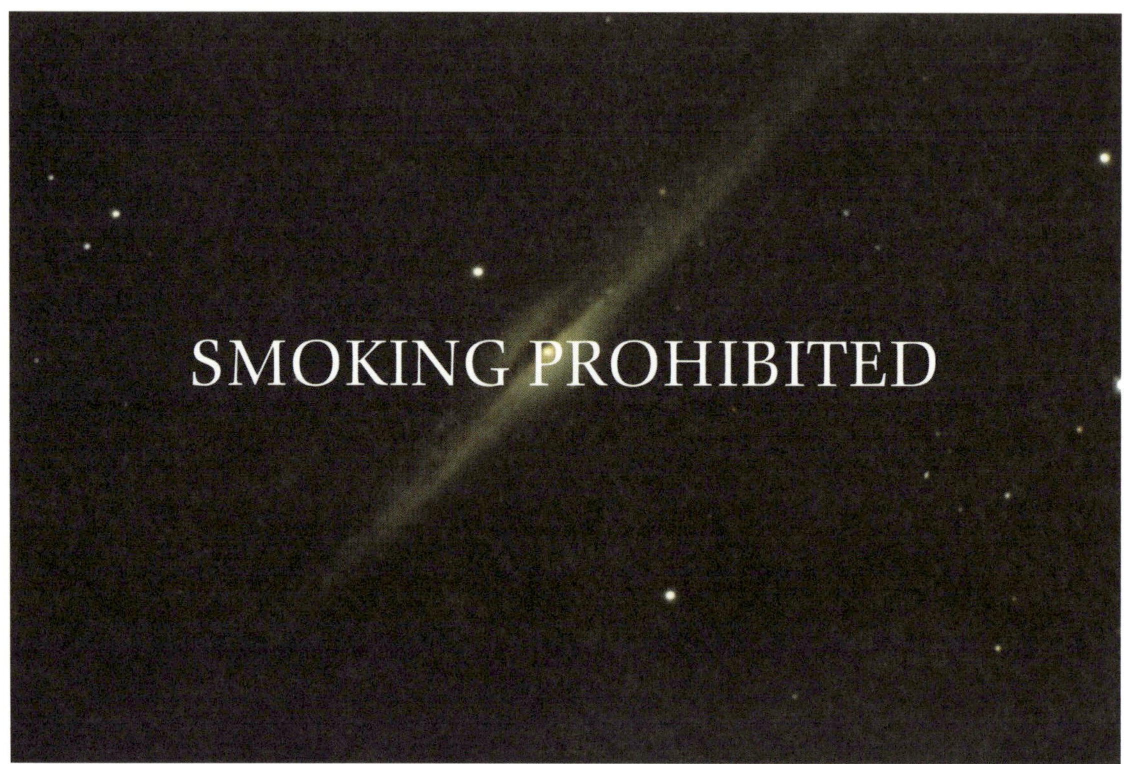

Smoking Prohibited 2003

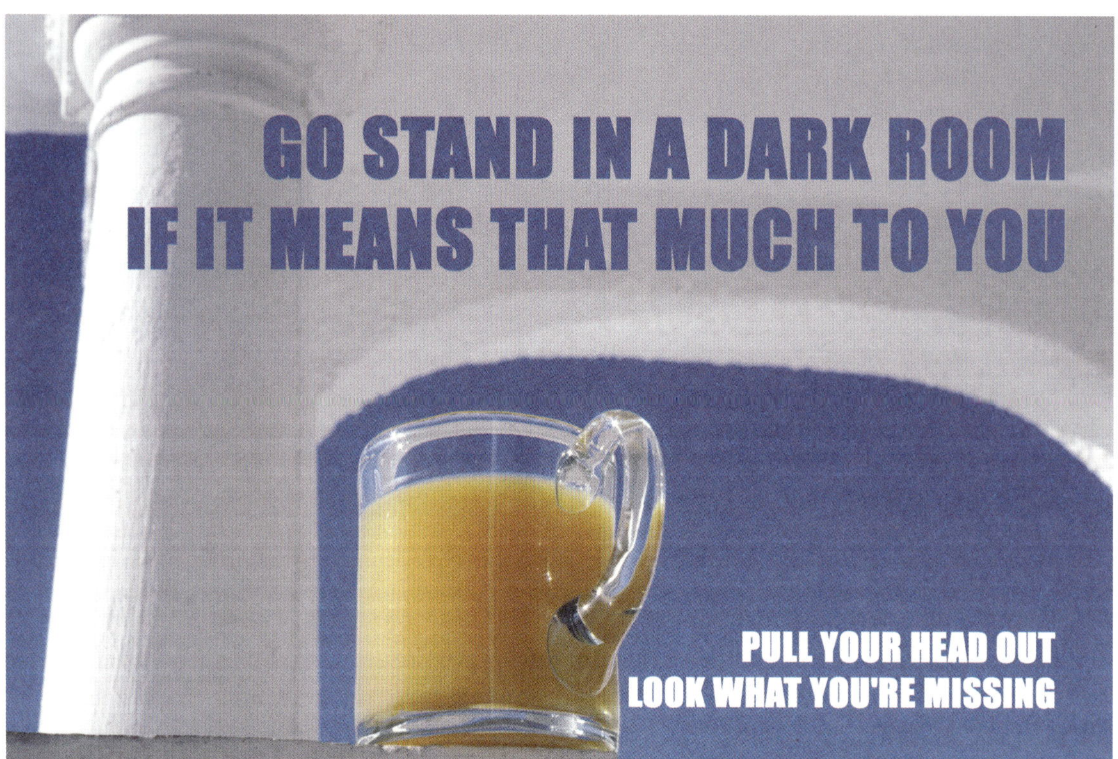

Pull your head out 2003

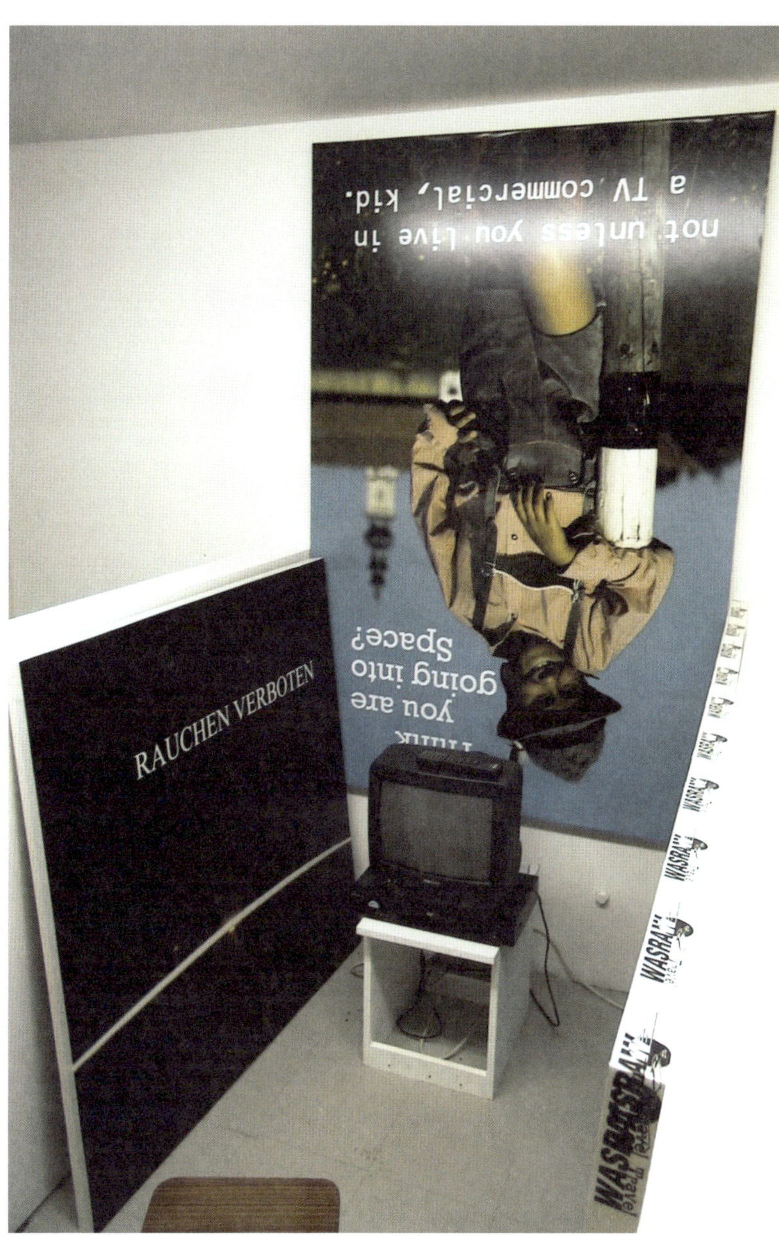

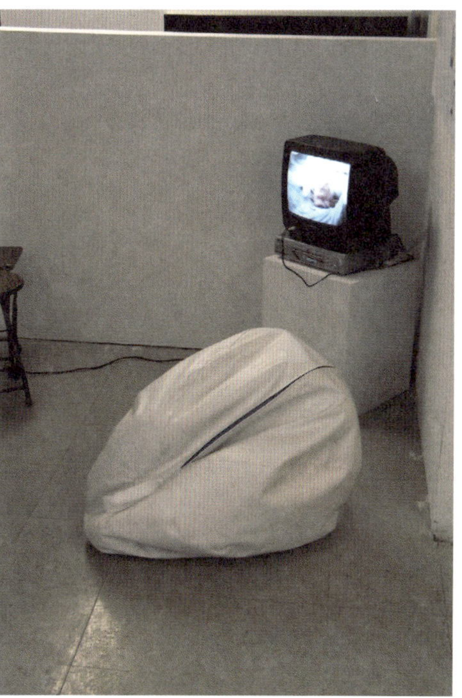

Overhead Baggage Treatment 2003

Overhead Baggage Treatment 2003
Installation view, Maccarone, Inc., New York City

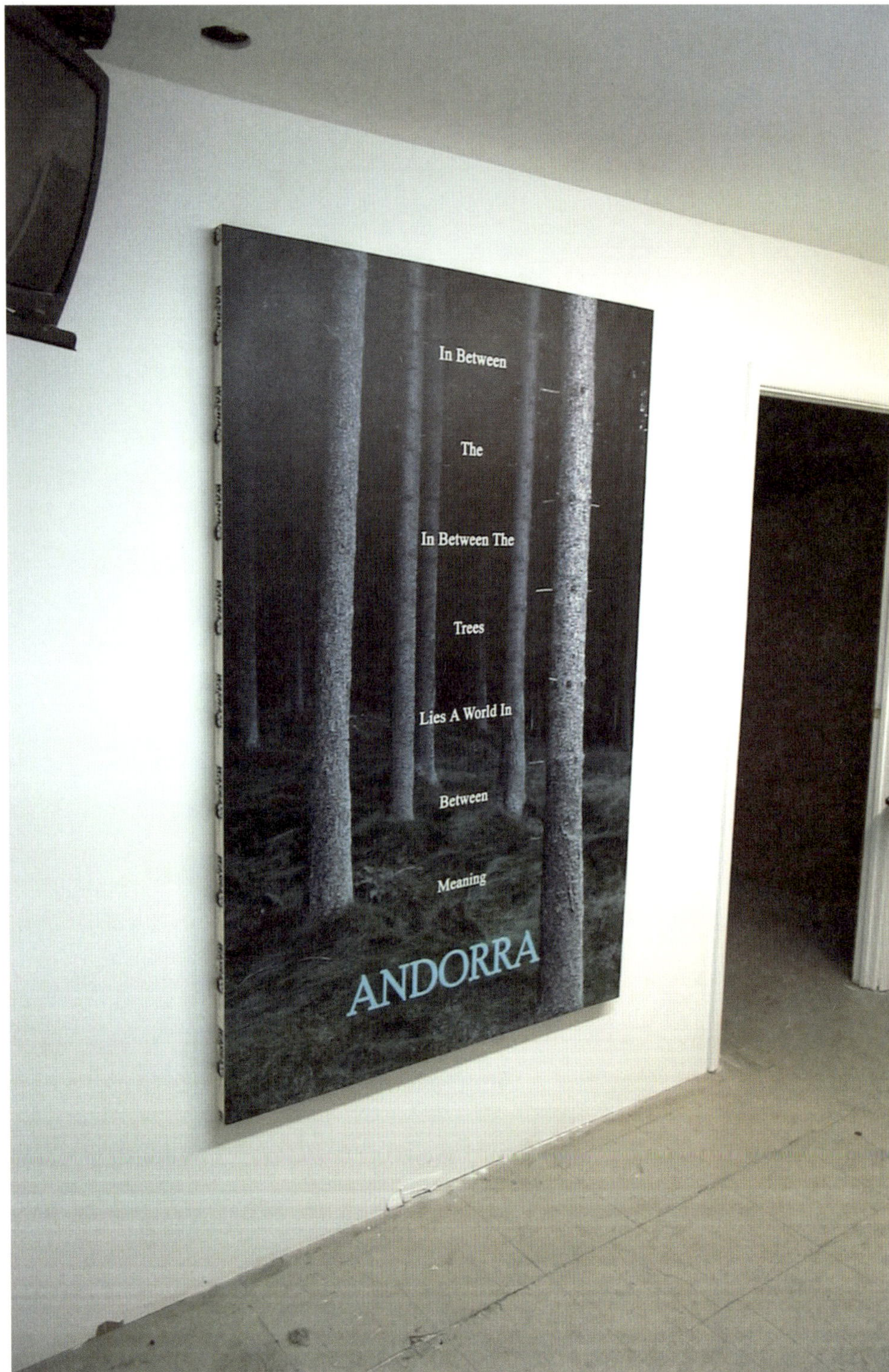

Andorra 2003
Installation view, Maccarone, Inc., New York City

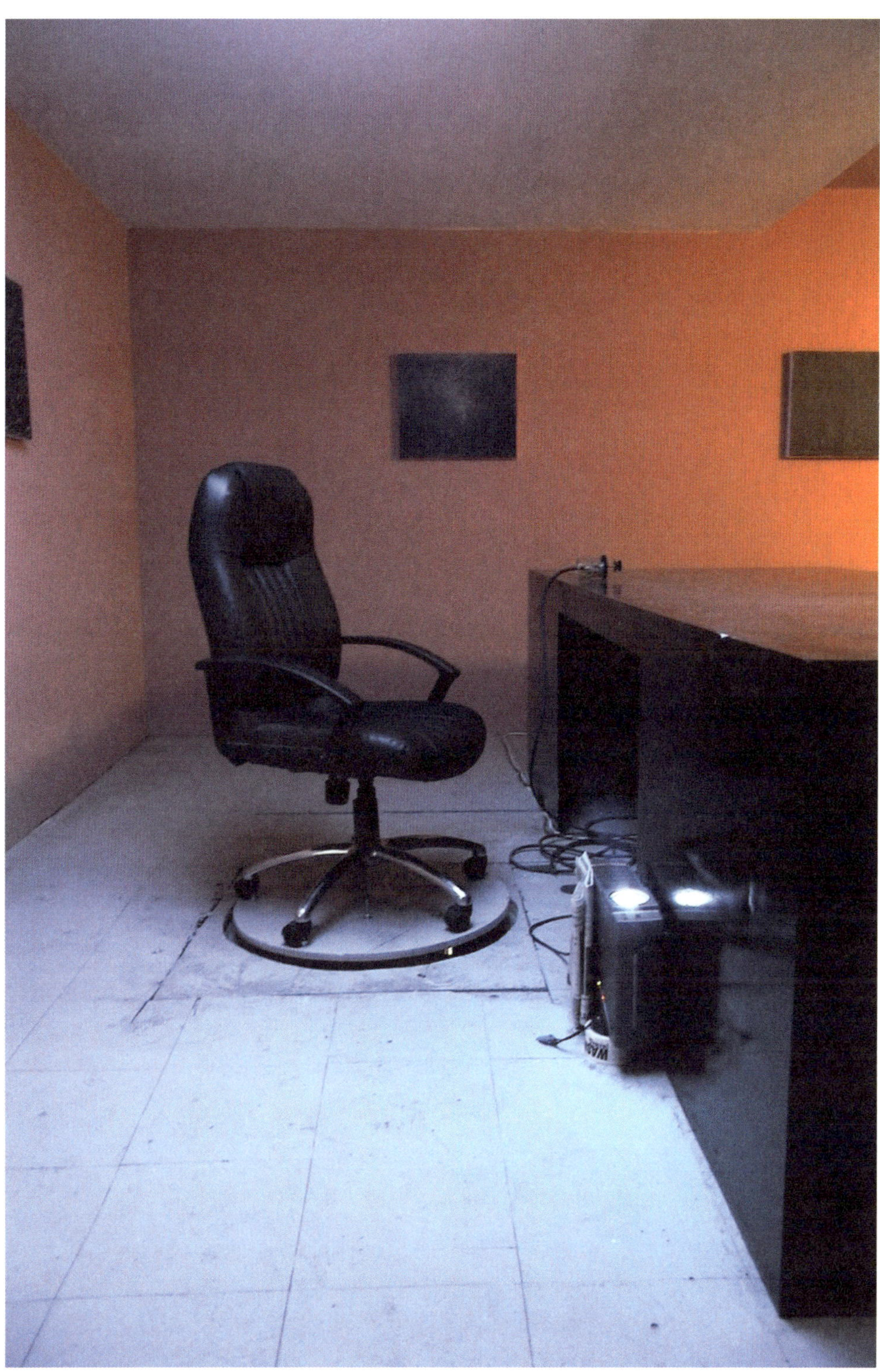

Master and Commander 2003
Installation view, Maccarone, Inc., New York City

Carpe Denim 2004

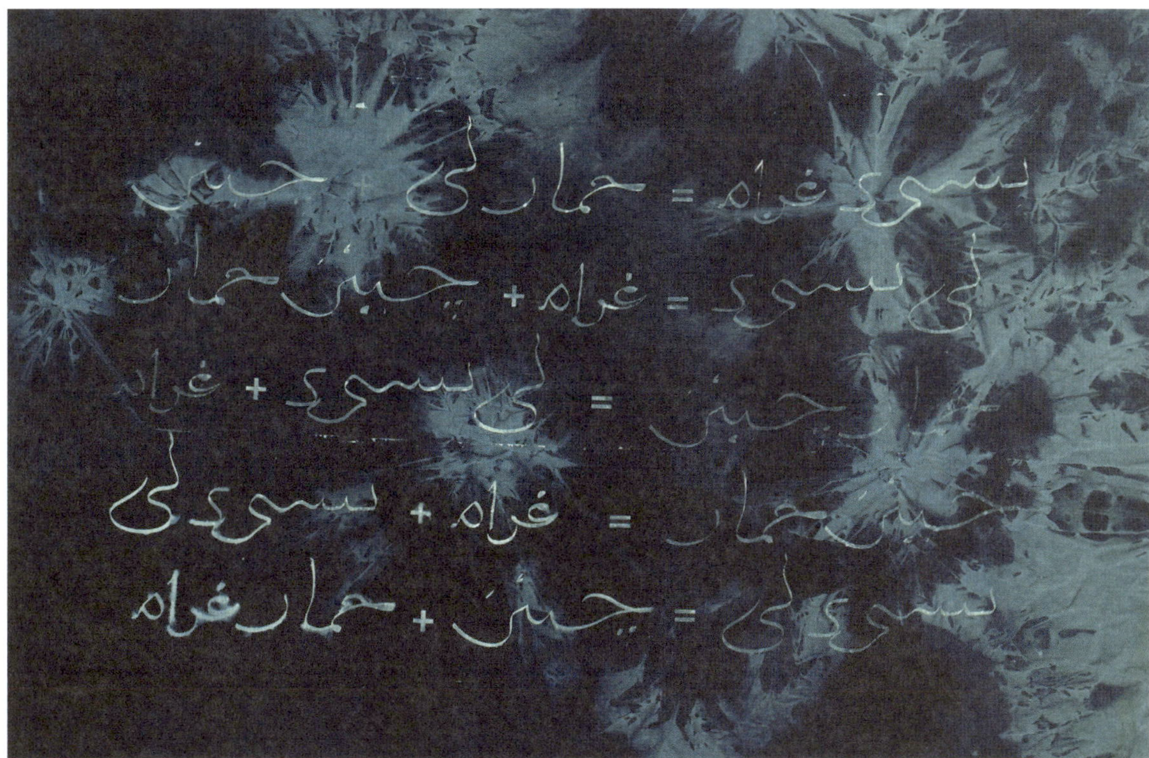

In March of 2004, Bouchet produced several thousand pairs of jeans in a small garment factory in Colombia. The jeans are of his own design: "one-size fits all" elastic waist-band leisure pants with two large back pockets, a marsupial-style pocket on the front, as well as a long side pocket with his emroidered signature that runs down most of the length of the right leg of the pants.

Once the jeans were completed, Bouchet threw half of them out of an airplane over the town in which they were produced. The remaining pairs were subsequently exhibited, and at times even similarily "distributed" to the public. Bouchet's jeans were thus thrown out of the window of a building in New York, as well as from a convertible car in Antwerp, Belgium, and from the roof of a shopping mall in Frankfurt, Germany.

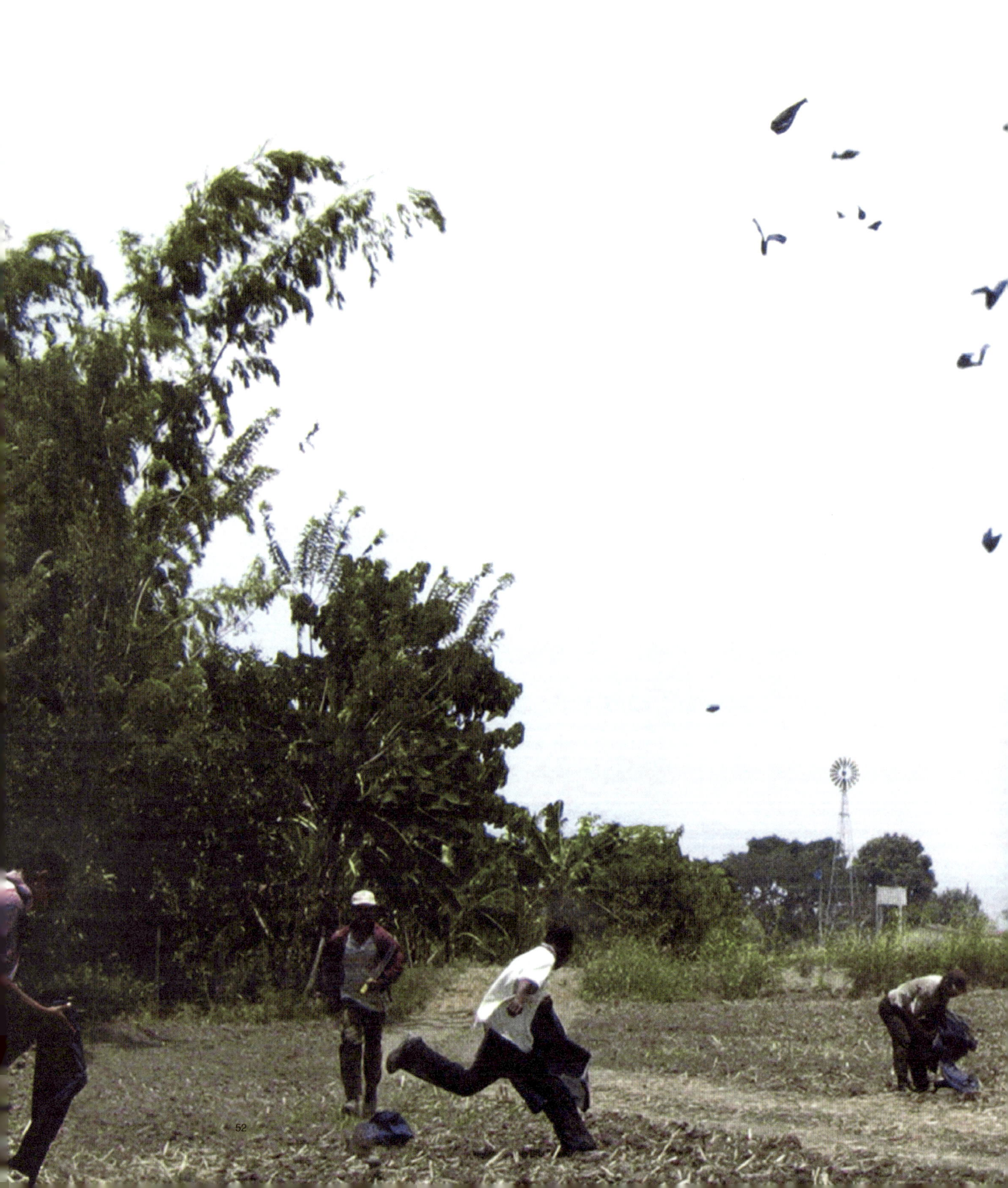

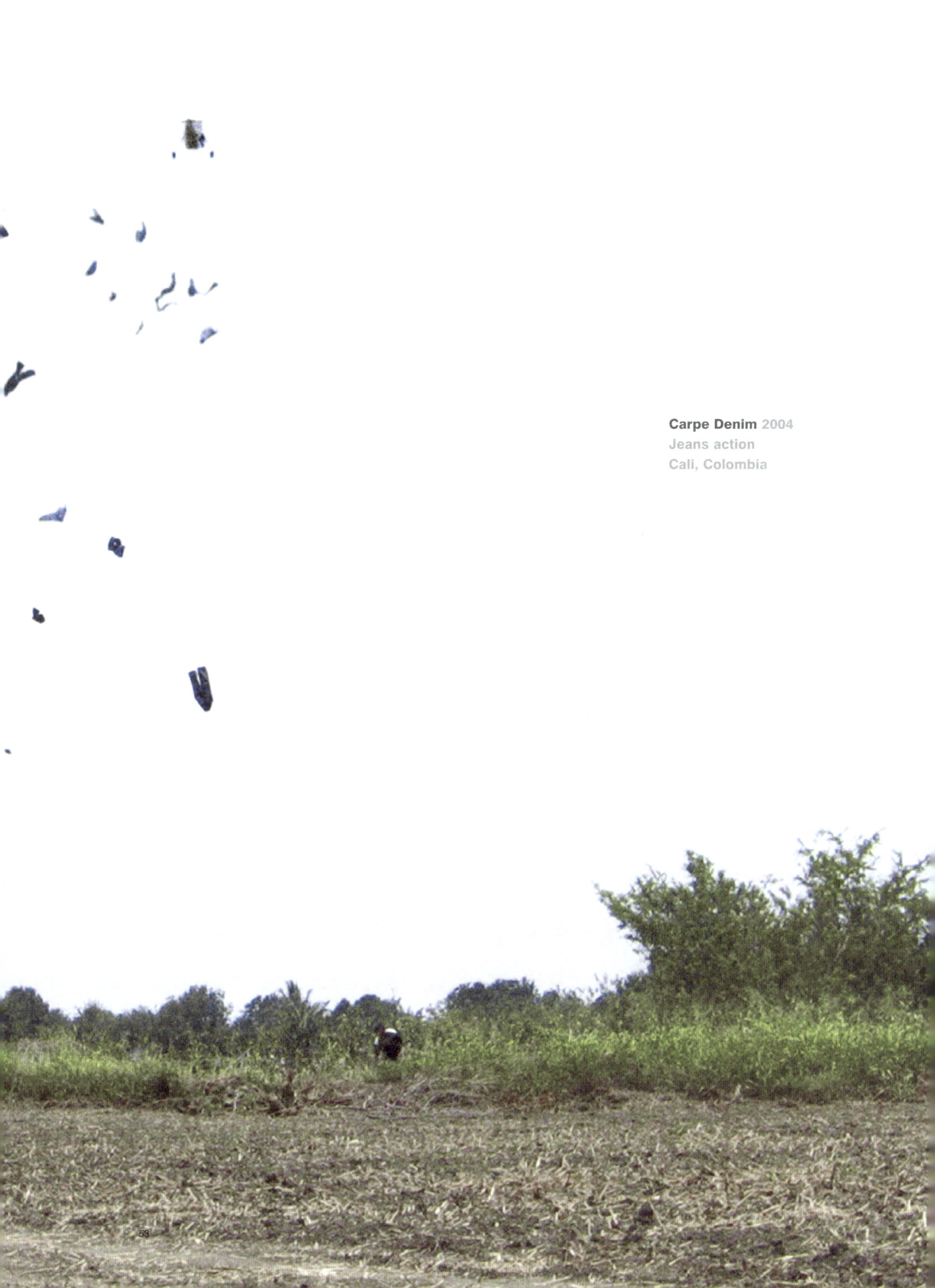

Carpe Denim 2004
Jeans action
Cali, Colombia

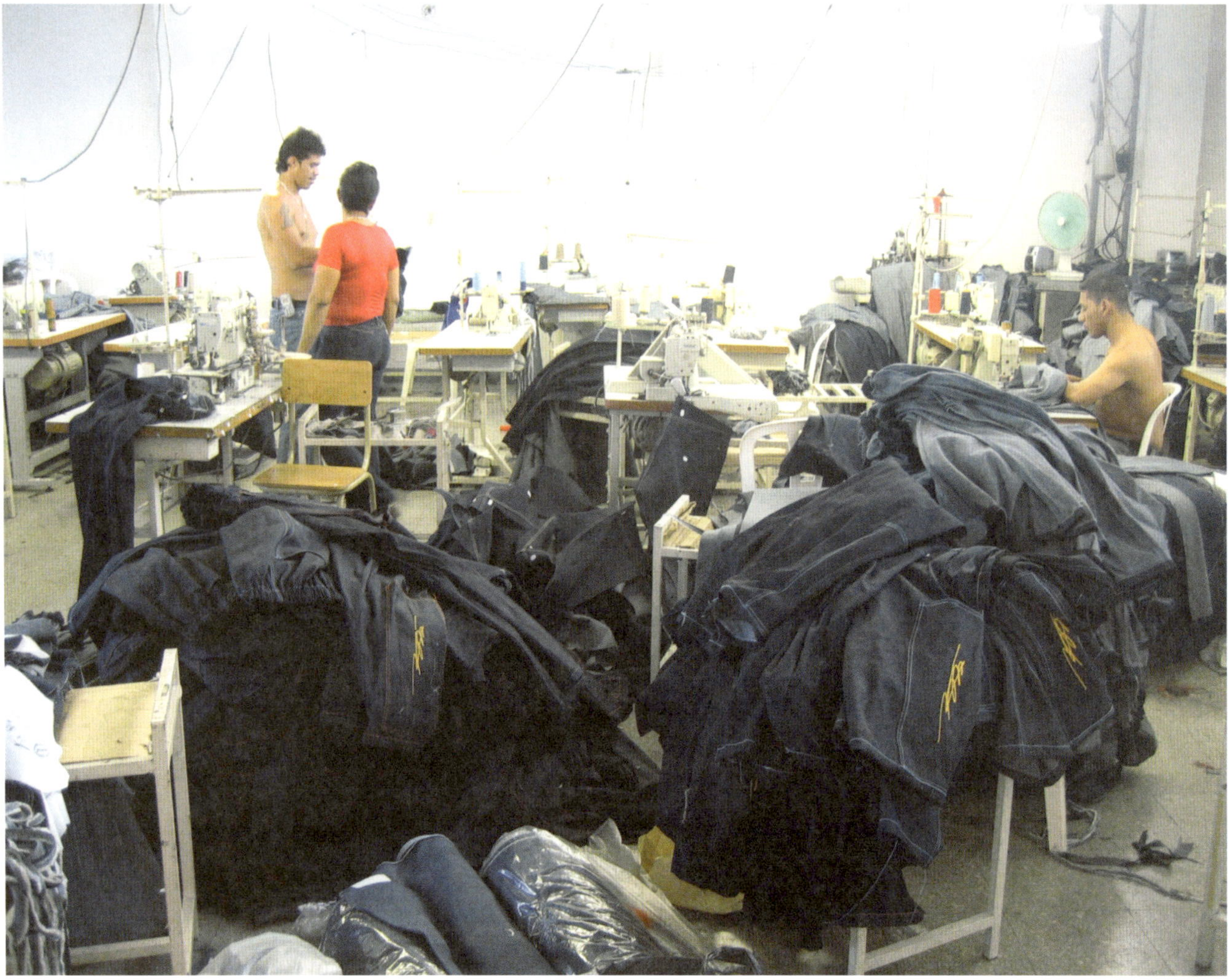

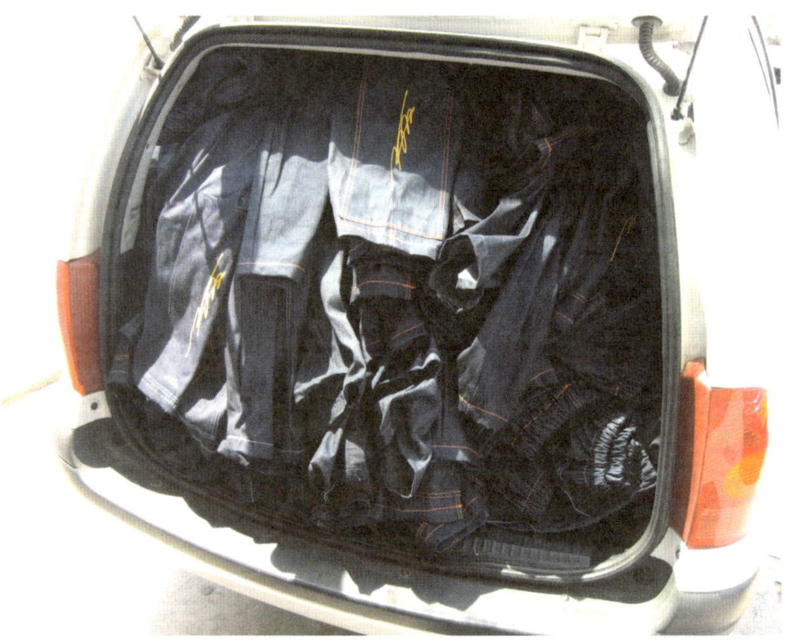

Carpe Denim, Colombia 2004
Production facility, Cali, Colombia

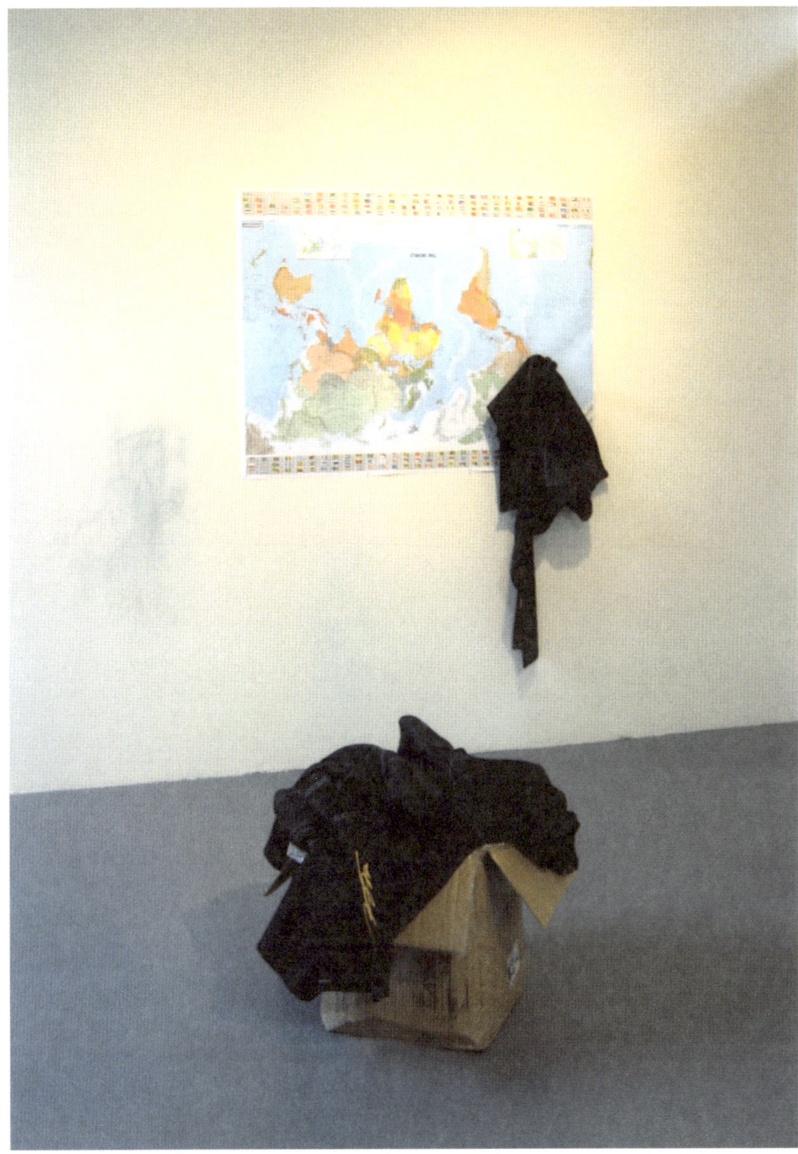

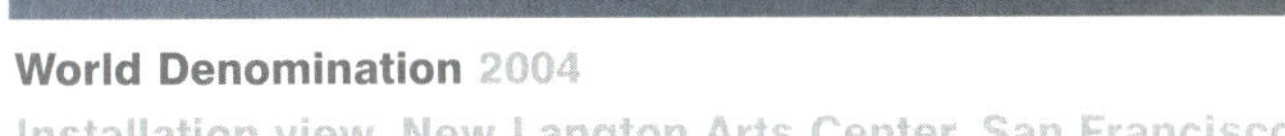

World Denomination 2004
Installation view, New Langton Arts Center, San Francisco

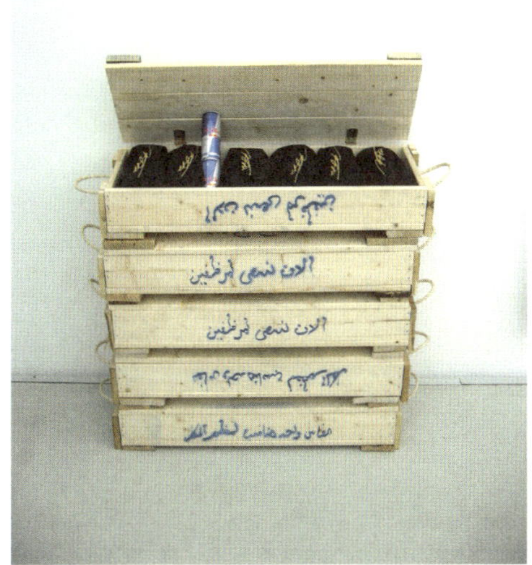

Mortar Ammunition Crate 2004

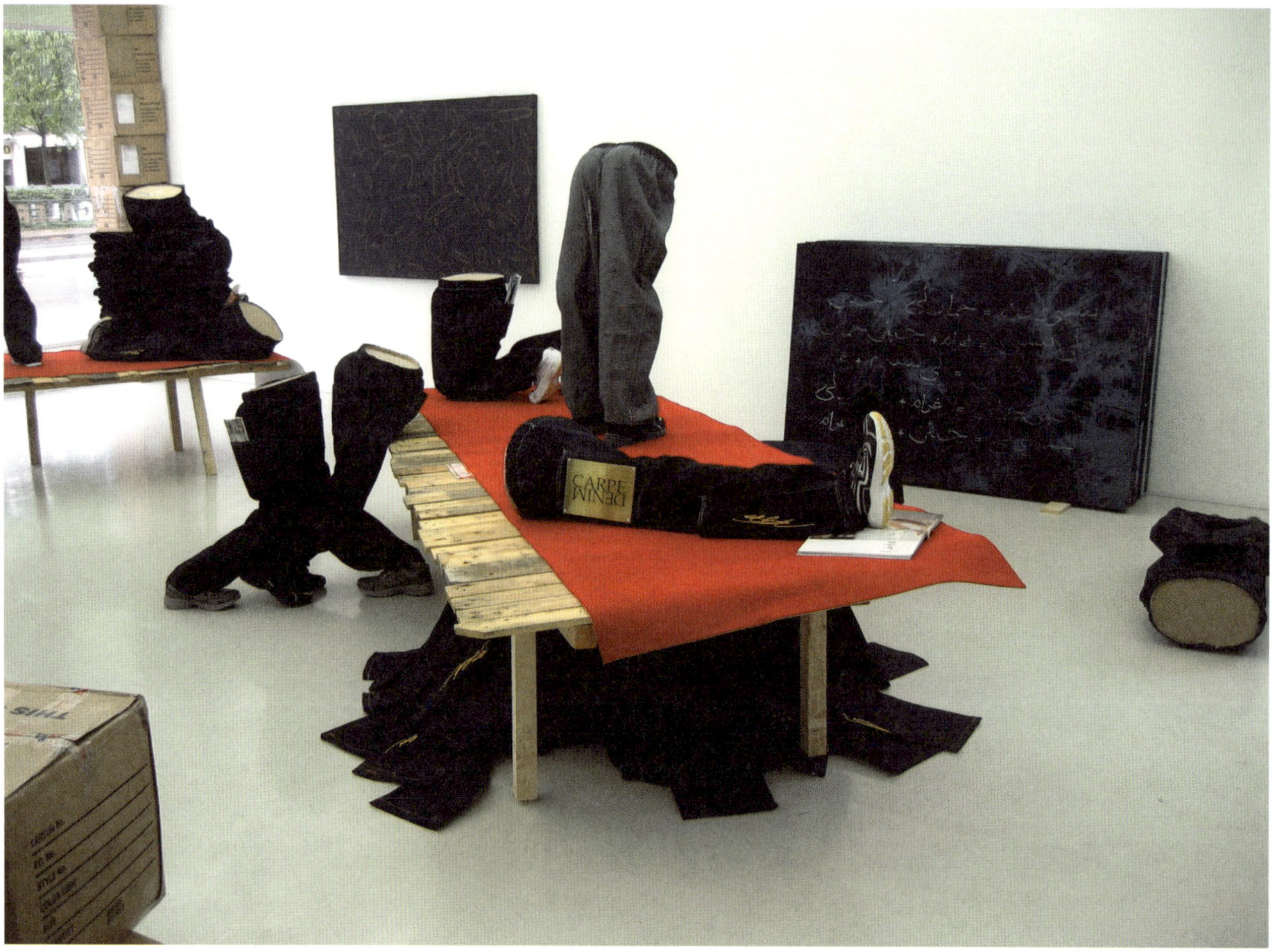

Carpe Denim 2004
Installation view, Galerie Michael Neff, Frankfurt, Germany

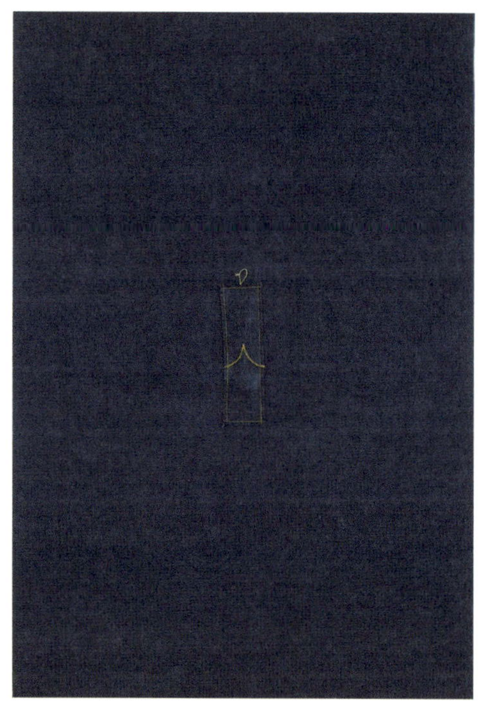

Hot Pocket 2004

 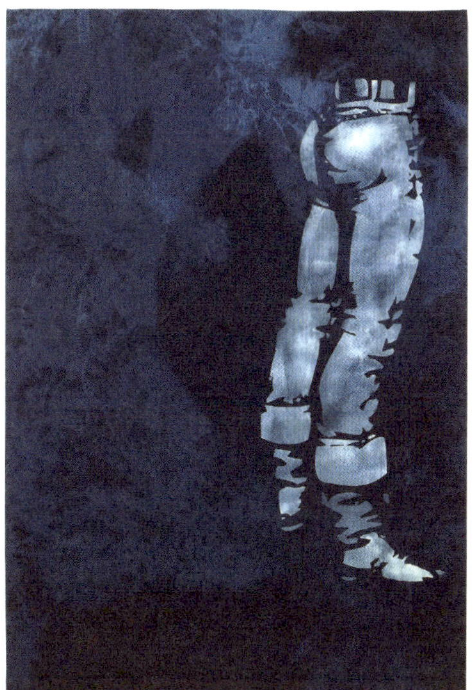

Ass Rub 2004

Tom of Frankfurt II 2004

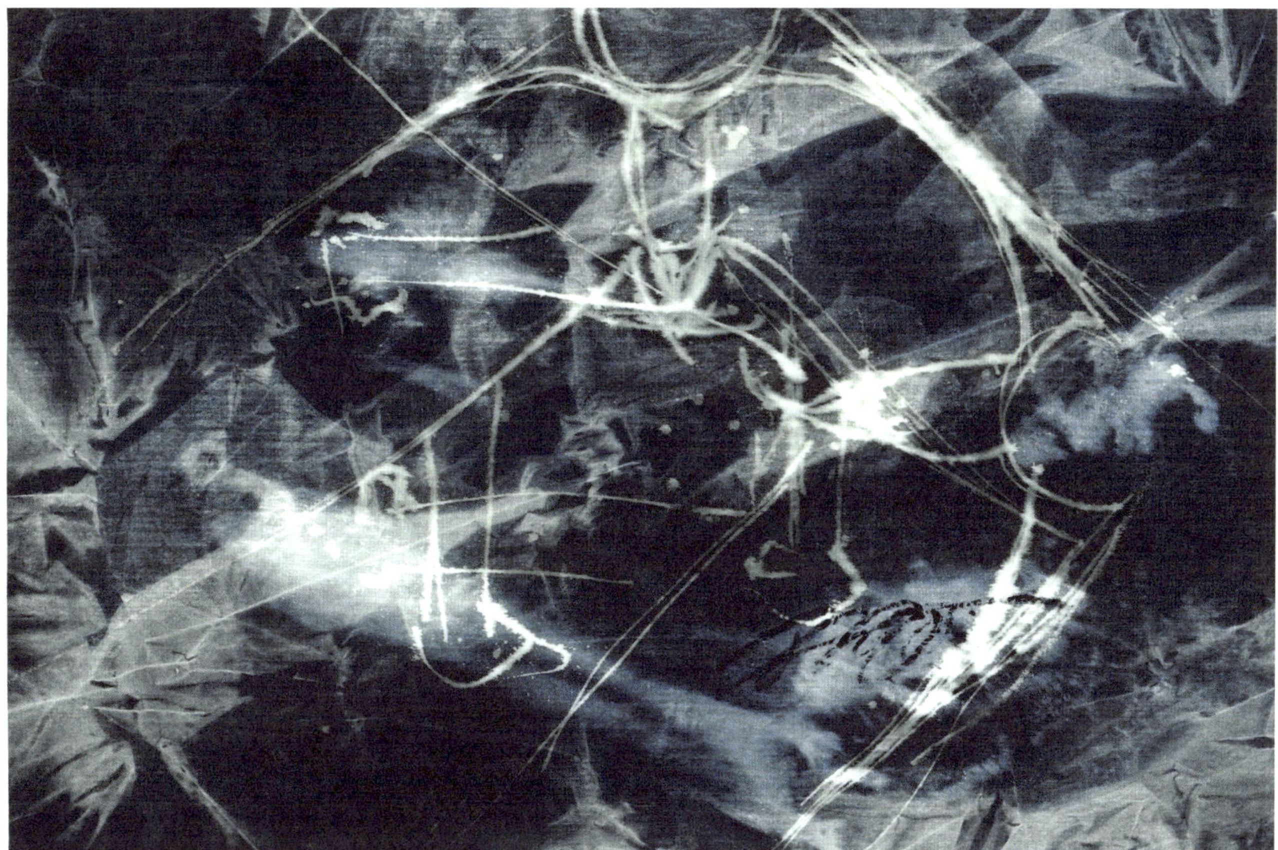

Vertical Horizontal 2004

57

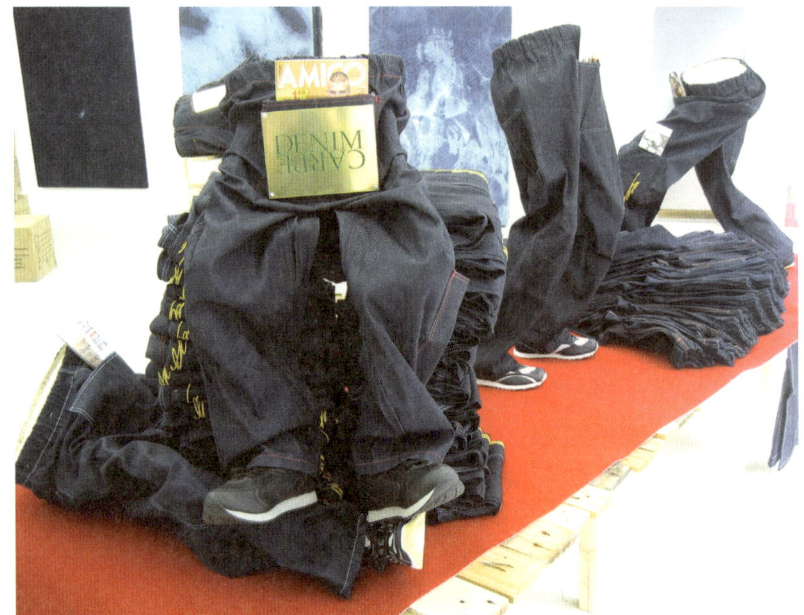

FallWinterSpringSummer 2004
Installation view, Galerie Michael Neff,
Frankfurt, Germany

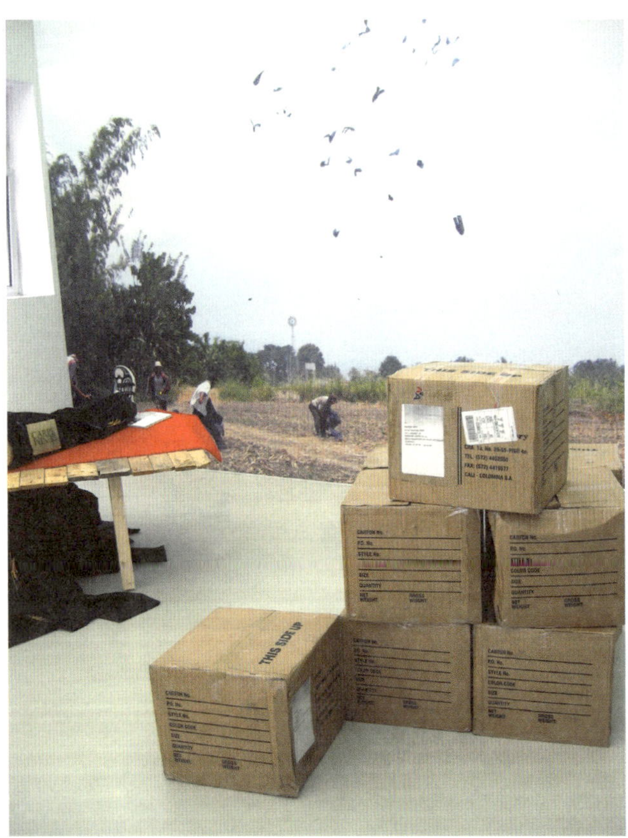

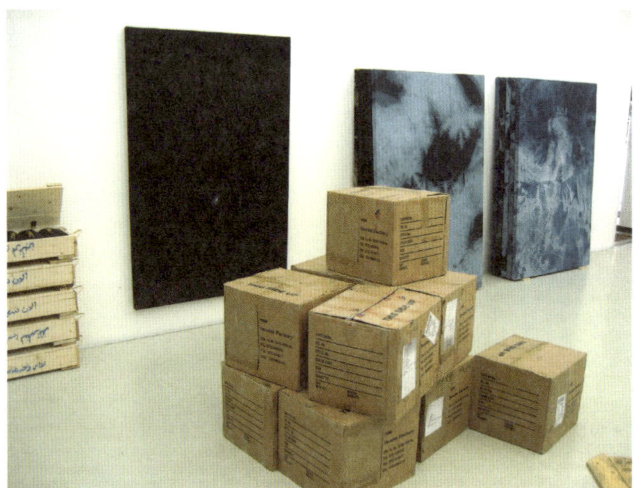

Sierra Leone Boxes 2004

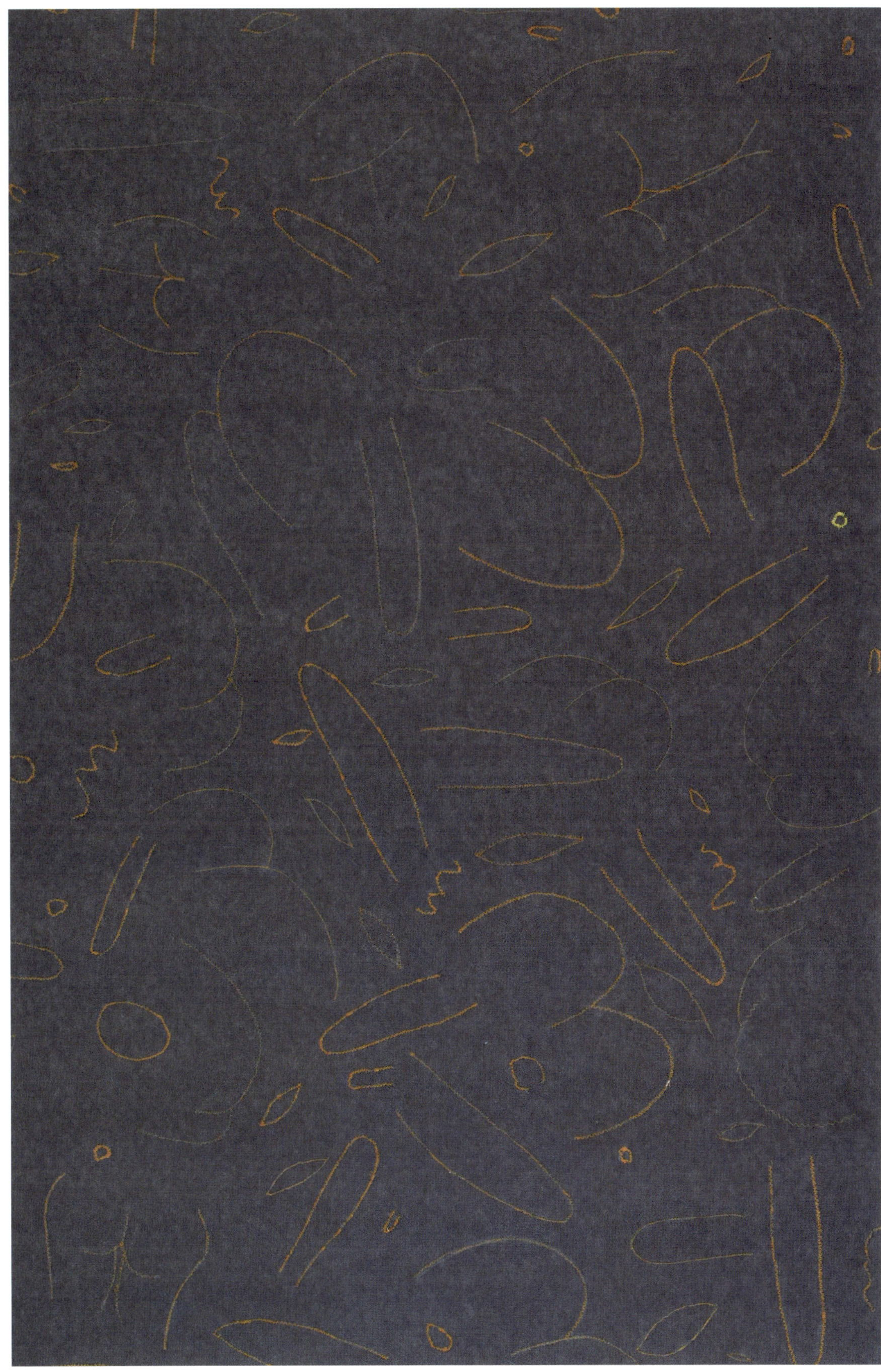

Dicks n Butts 2004

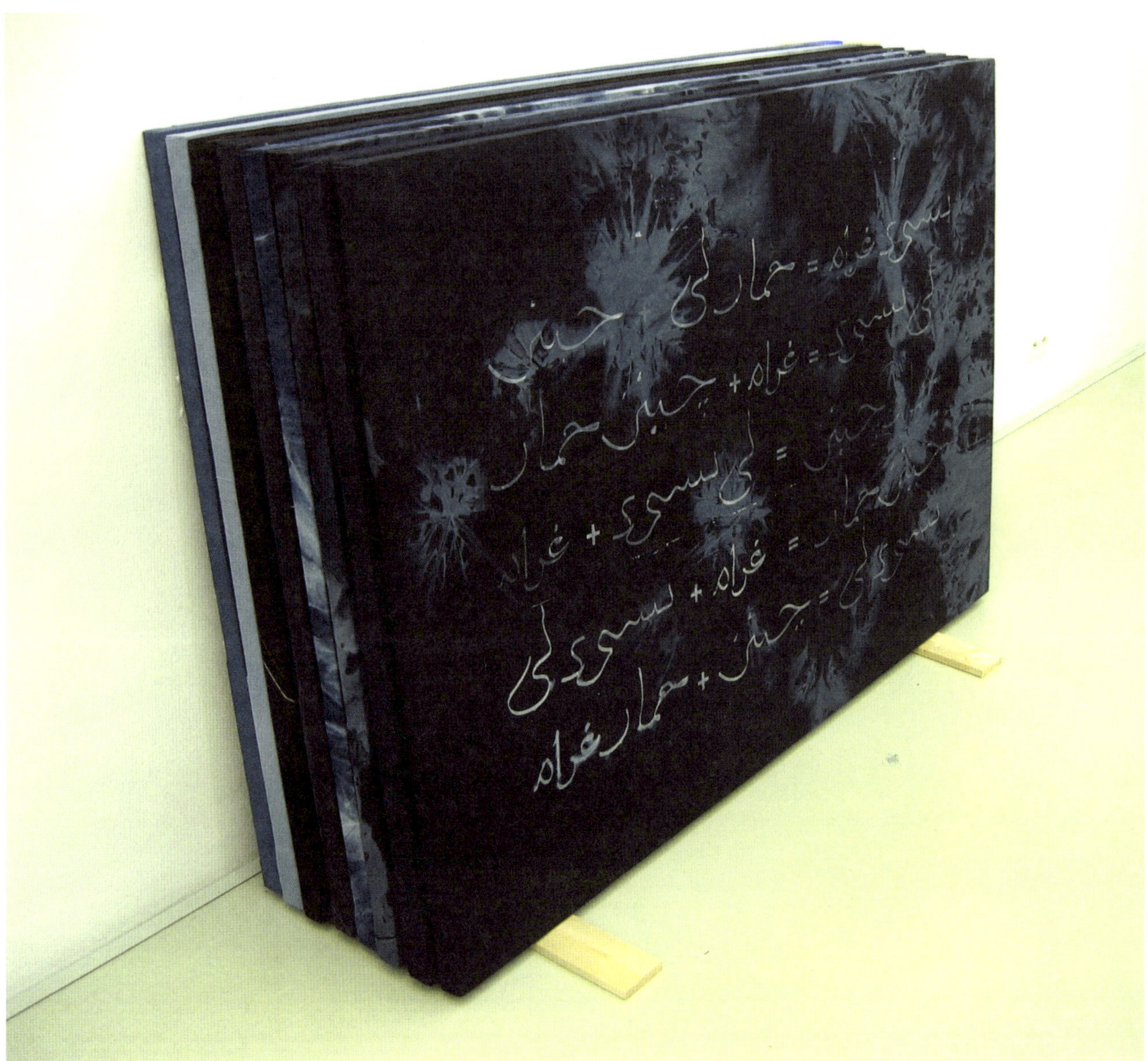

Denim Stack 2004

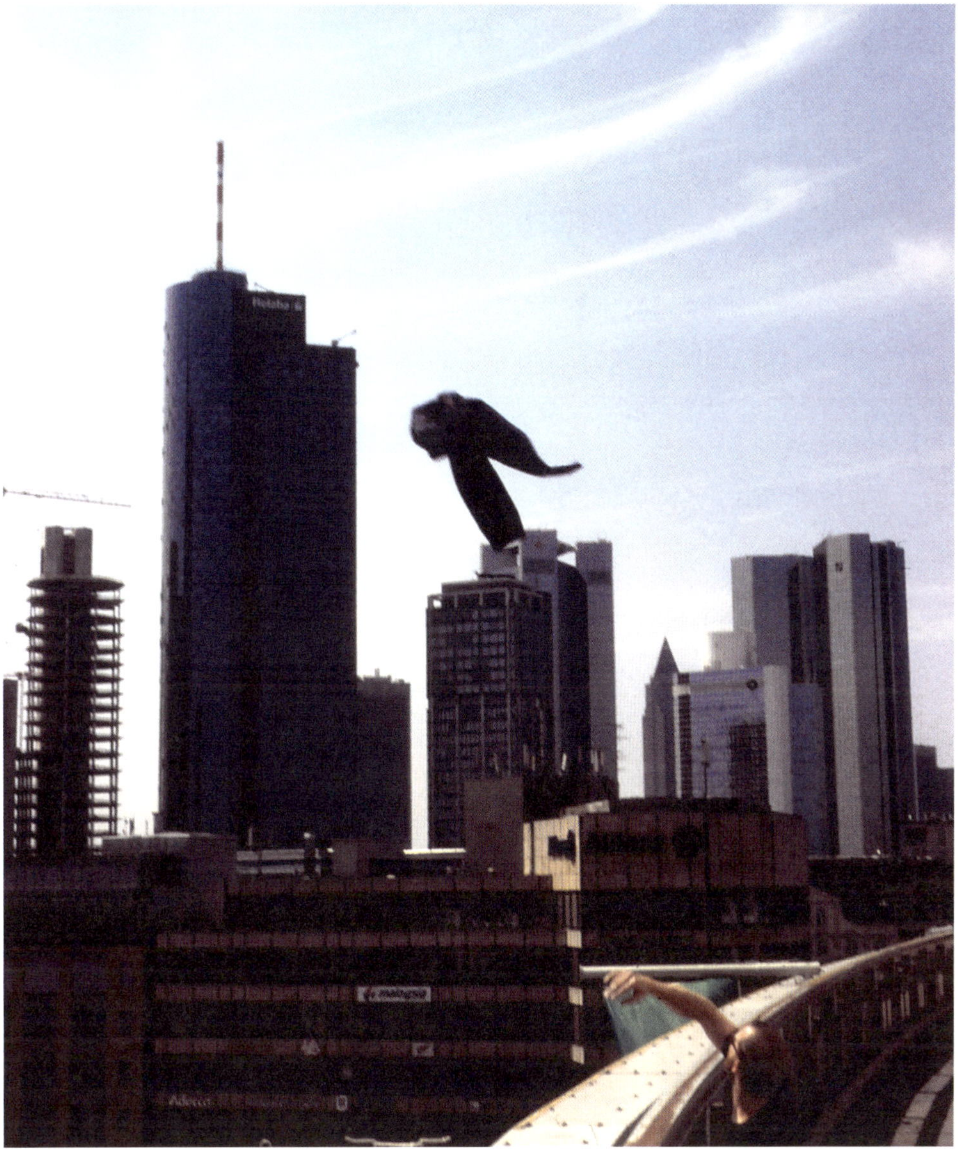

Carpe Denim 2004
jeans action, Frankfurt, Germany

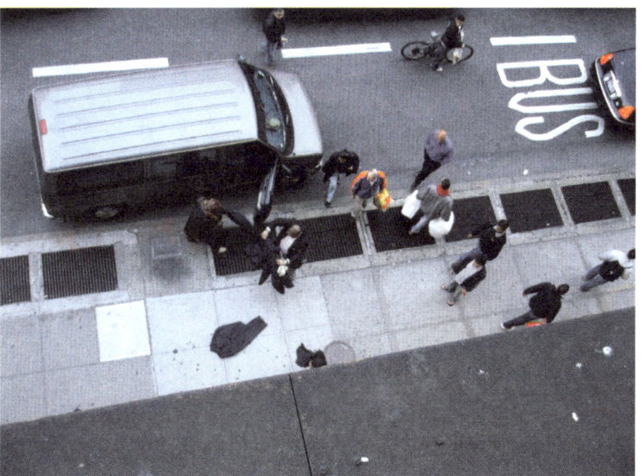

Carpe Denim 2004
jeans action, Swiss Institute, New York City

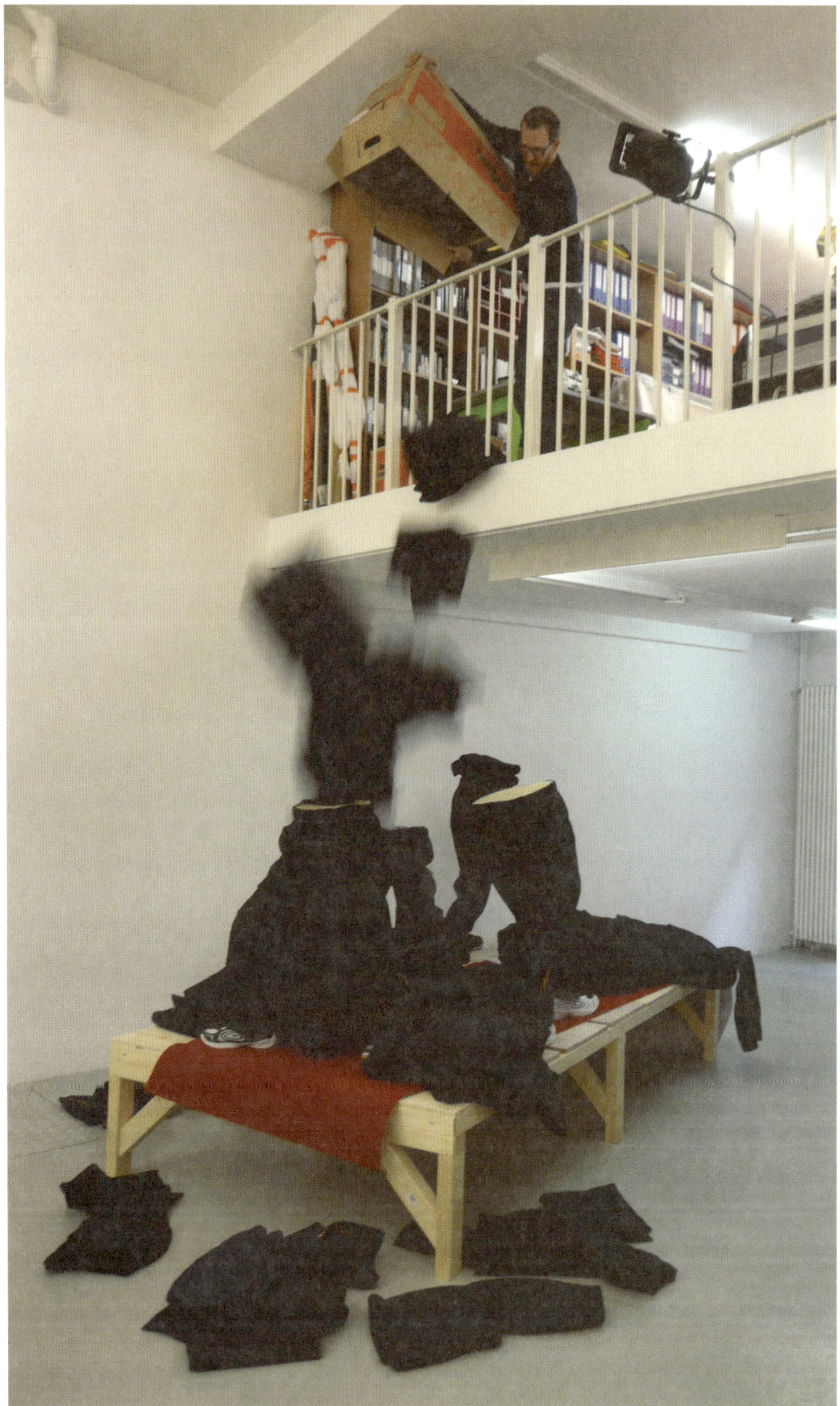

Carpe Denim 2008
installing artwork, Galerie Analix Forever, Geneva

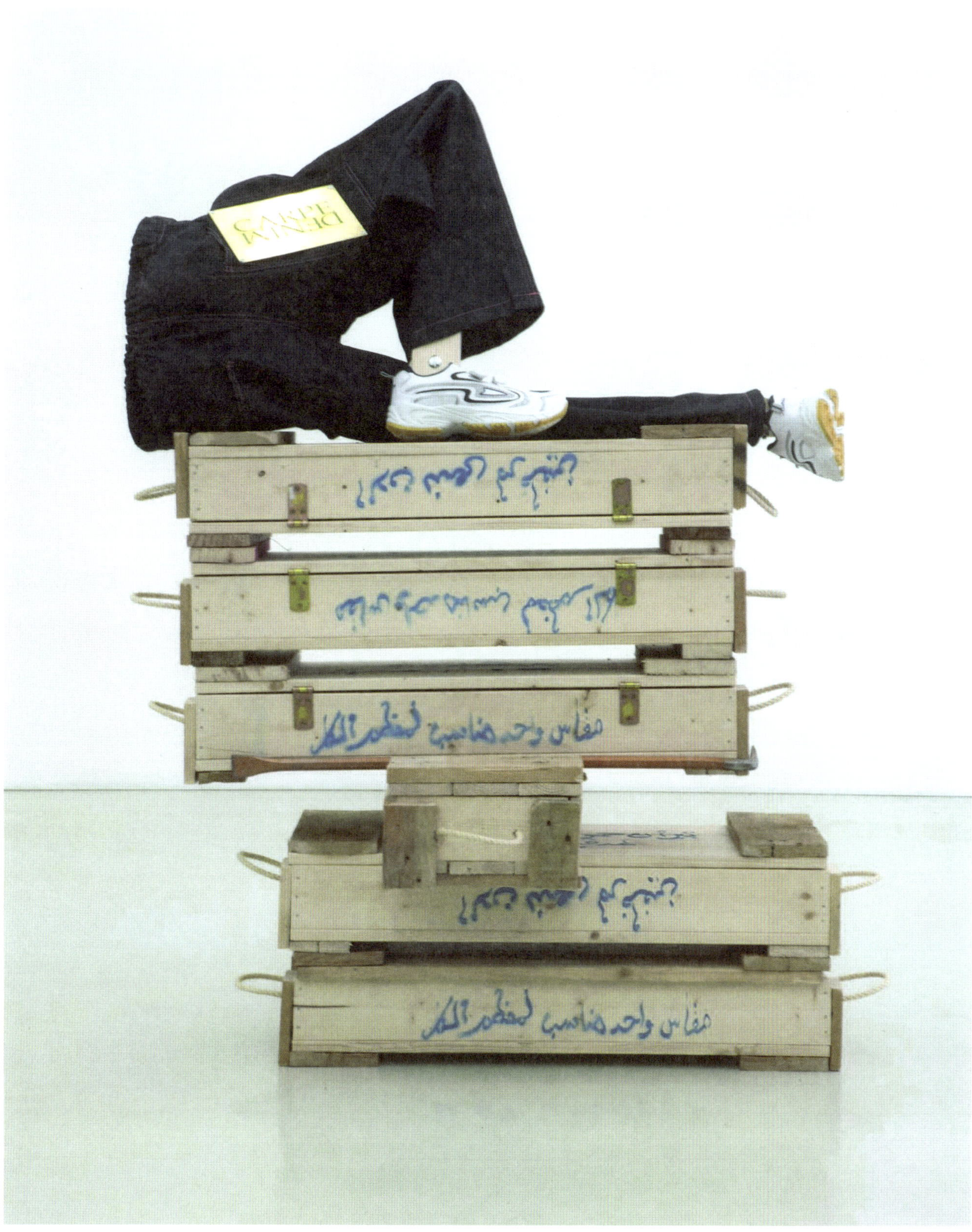

III Queda 2004

My Cola Lite 2004

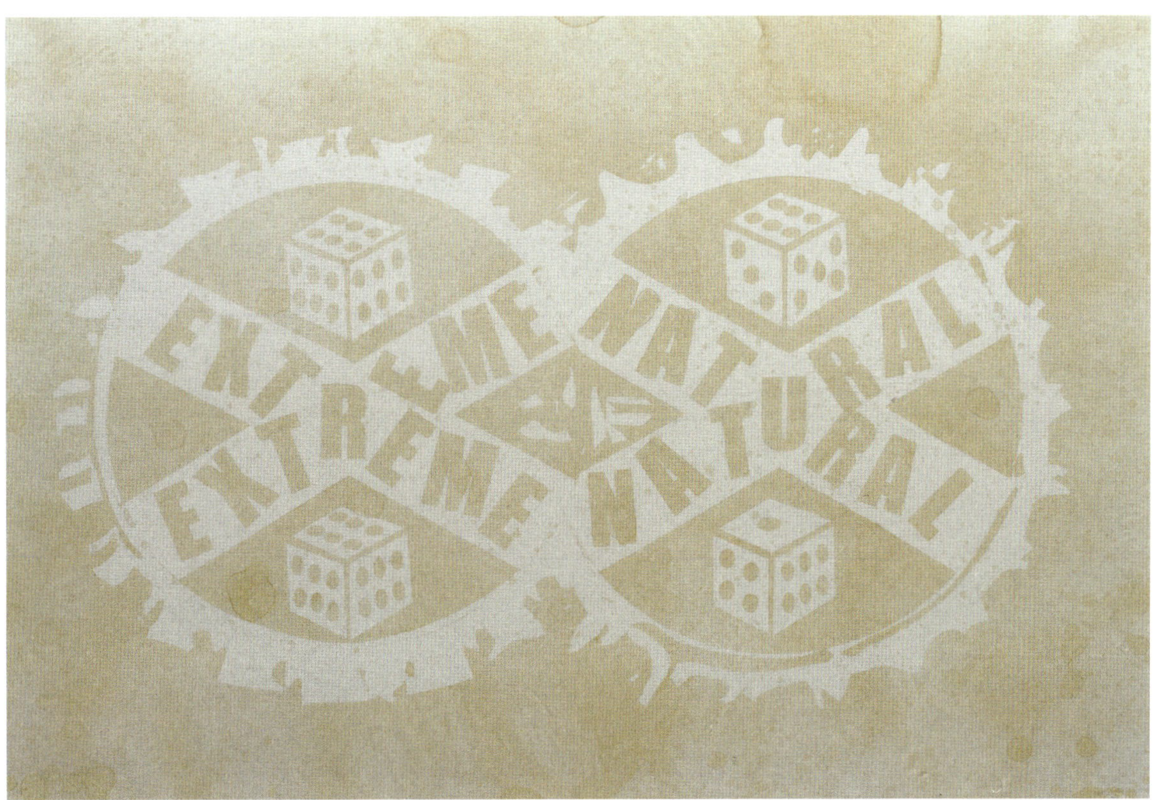

"I want to produce my own diet cola. I will make my own diet cola formula, and then I would like to produce and bottle enough cola to fill a sea shipping container. I would like to bottle the cola in large bottles. They will be printed with labeling that I will design. The sea container will also be painted like the cola logo. I will leave the sea container in the exhibition space for half the time of the show, and then ship the sea container to a destination in China. Once My Cola Light reaches China, it will be available for people there to drink for free."

The final artwork resulted in a sculpture composed of 2000 one liter bottles of diet cola and a 5 meter long painted shipping container. The artist produced the cola with no sweetener or sugar, hence the "Lite" or diet moniker. The artist wanted the cola to be black, like oil, and had the cola produced with the maximum amount of caramel coloring possible.

The resulting "Black American Water" is also used as a pigment for paintings. The paintings, more properly referred to as stainings, are created by staining white cotton with this cola.

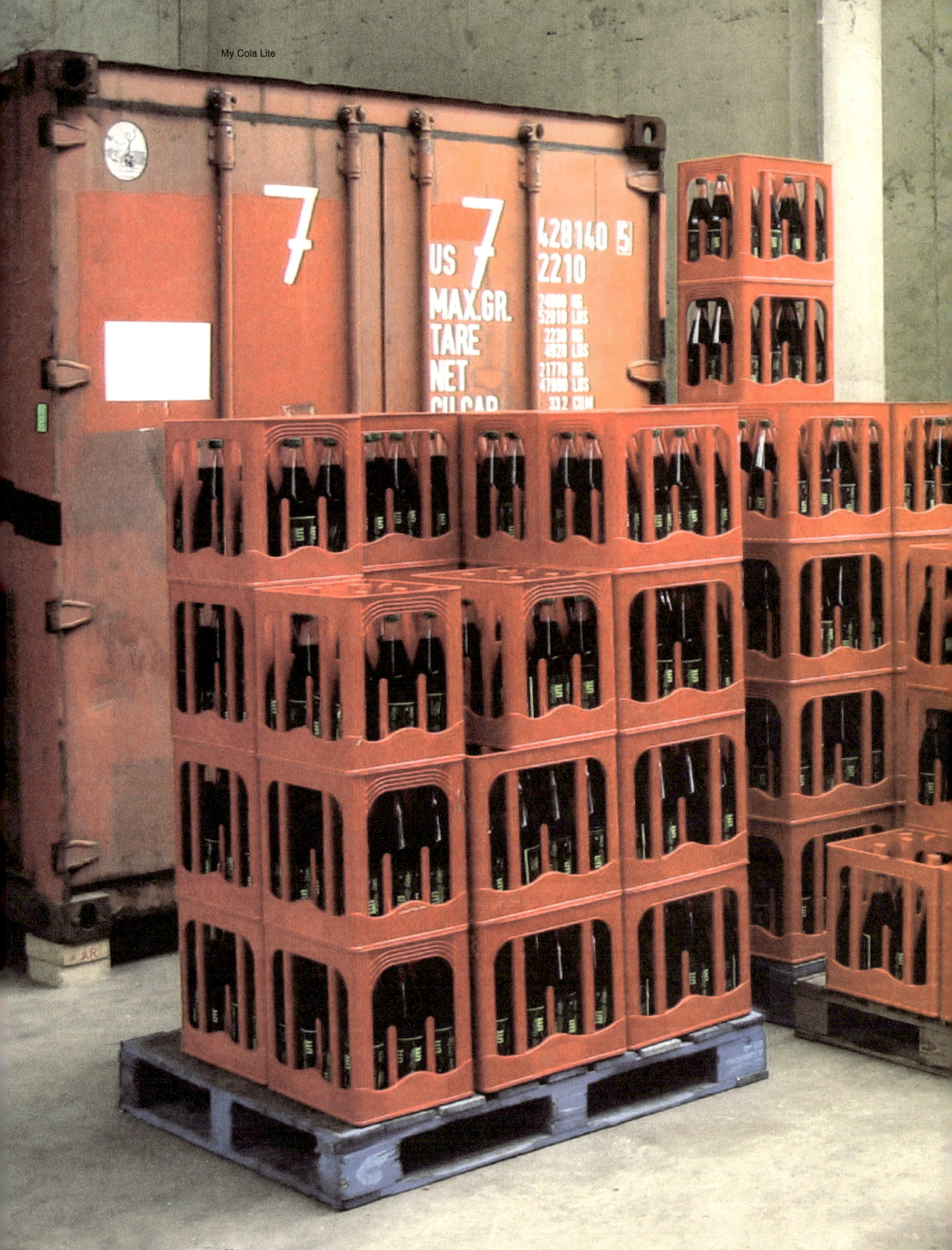
My Cola Lite
7
US 7
428140 5
2210
MAX.GR.
TARE
NET
CU.CAP.

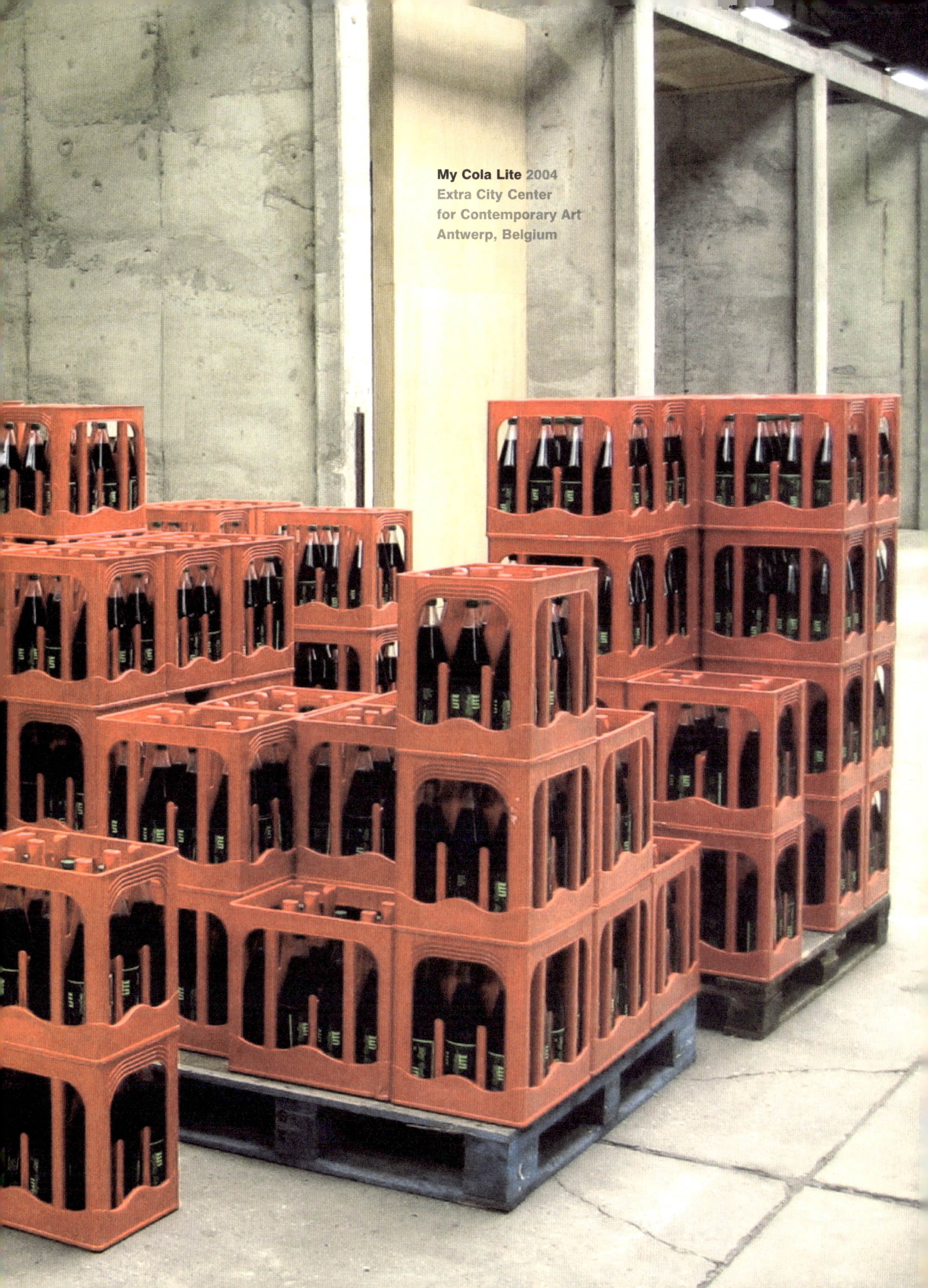
My Cola Lite 2004
Extra City Center
for Contemporary Art
Antwerp, Belgium

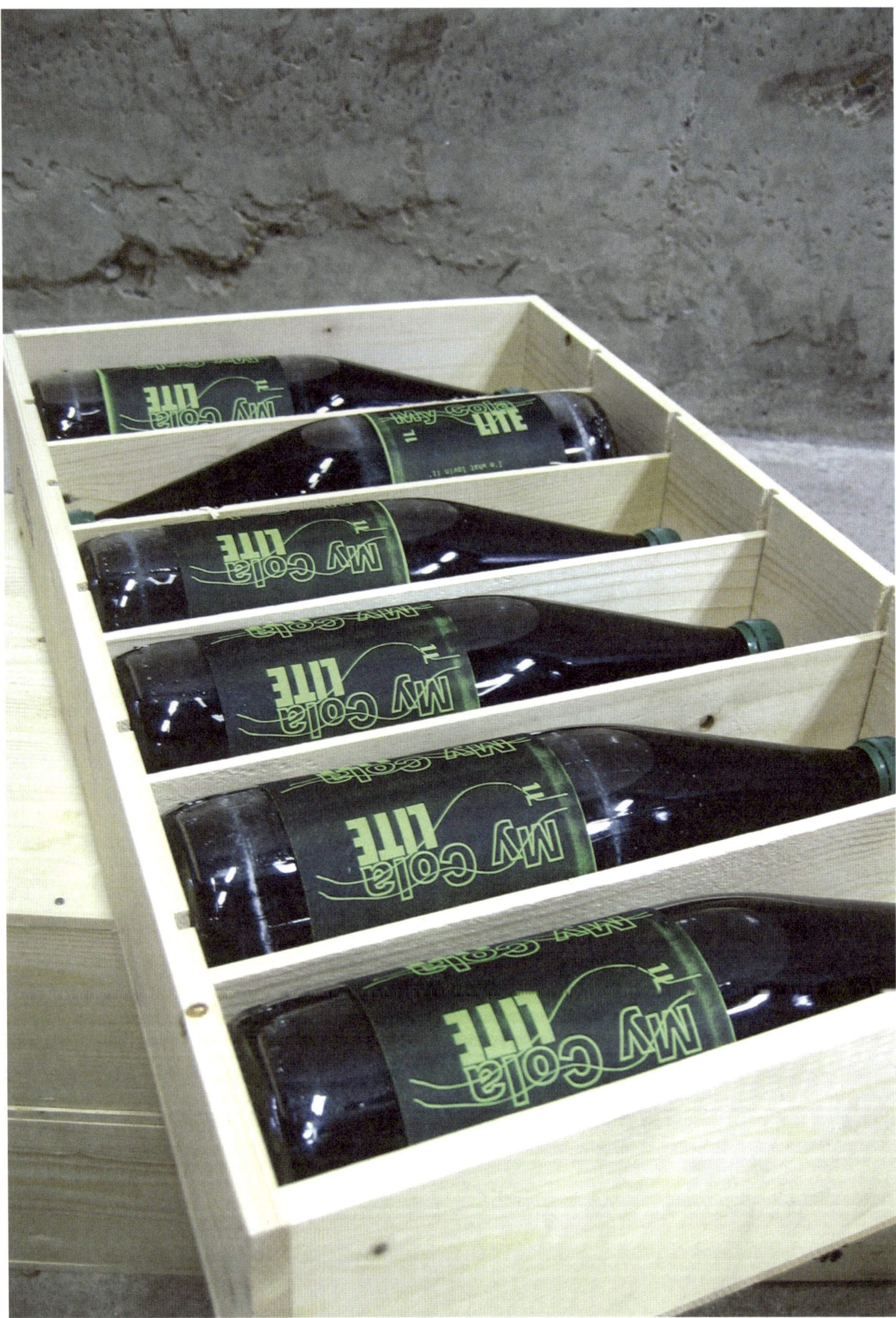

My Cola Lite (Six pack) 2004

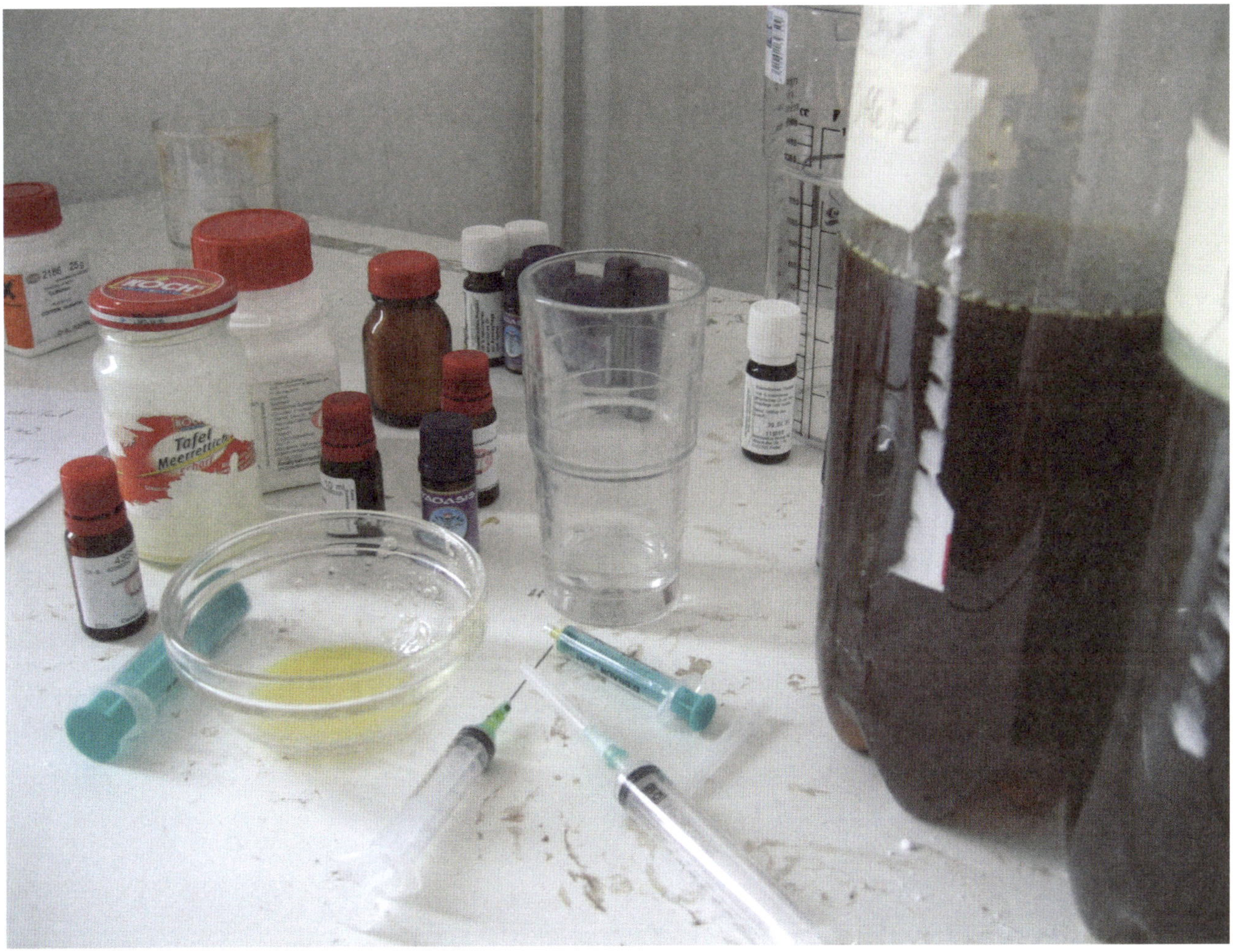

Studio Table 2004

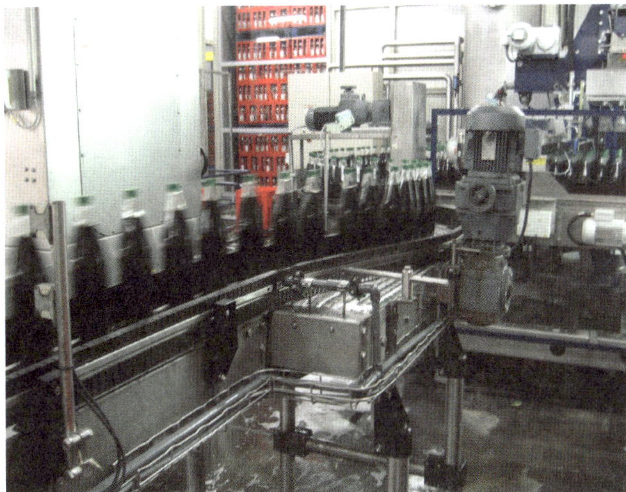

Bottling Line 2004

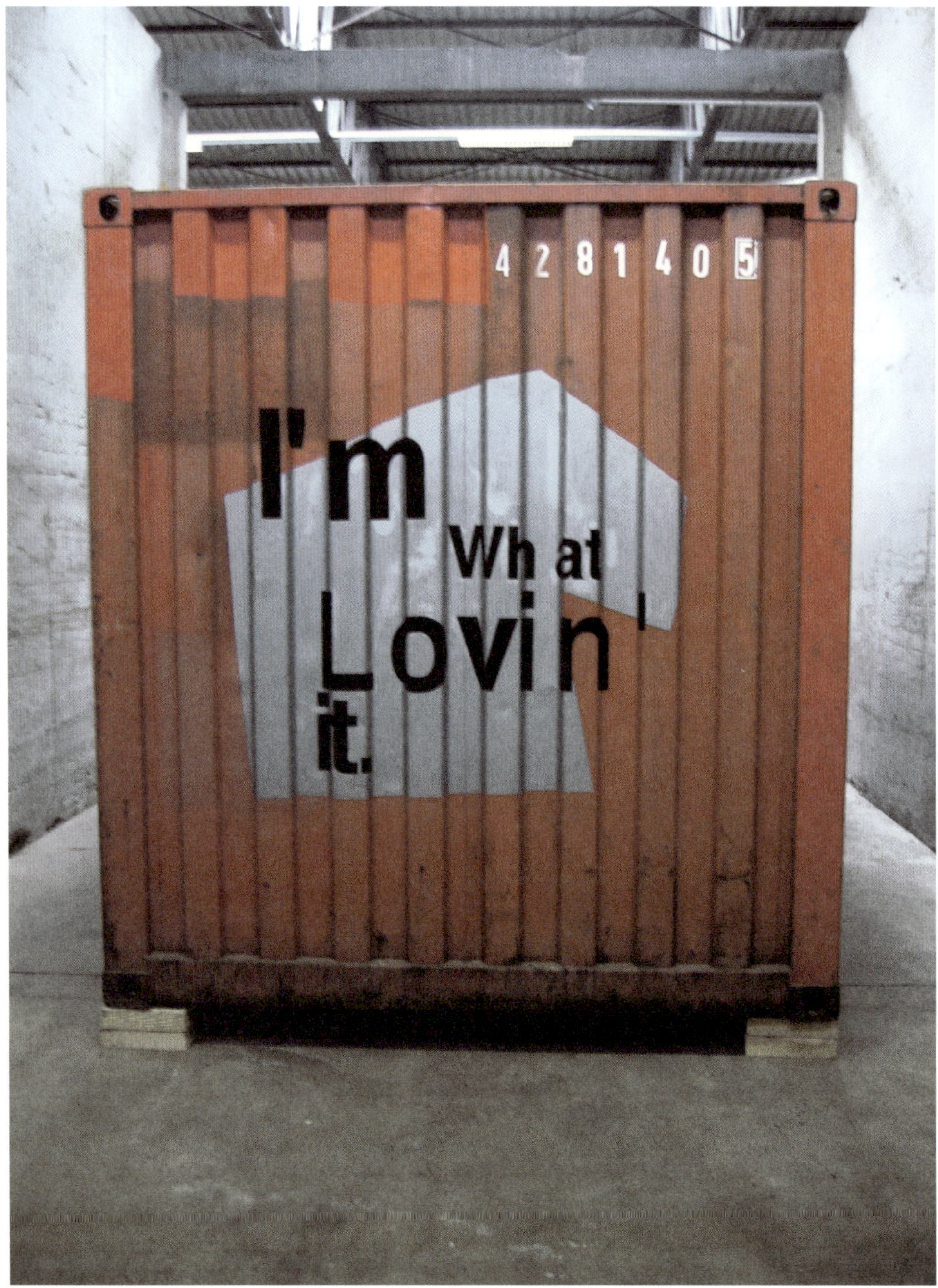

Cola Container 2004
Installation view, Extra City Center for Contemporary Art, Antwerp, Belgium

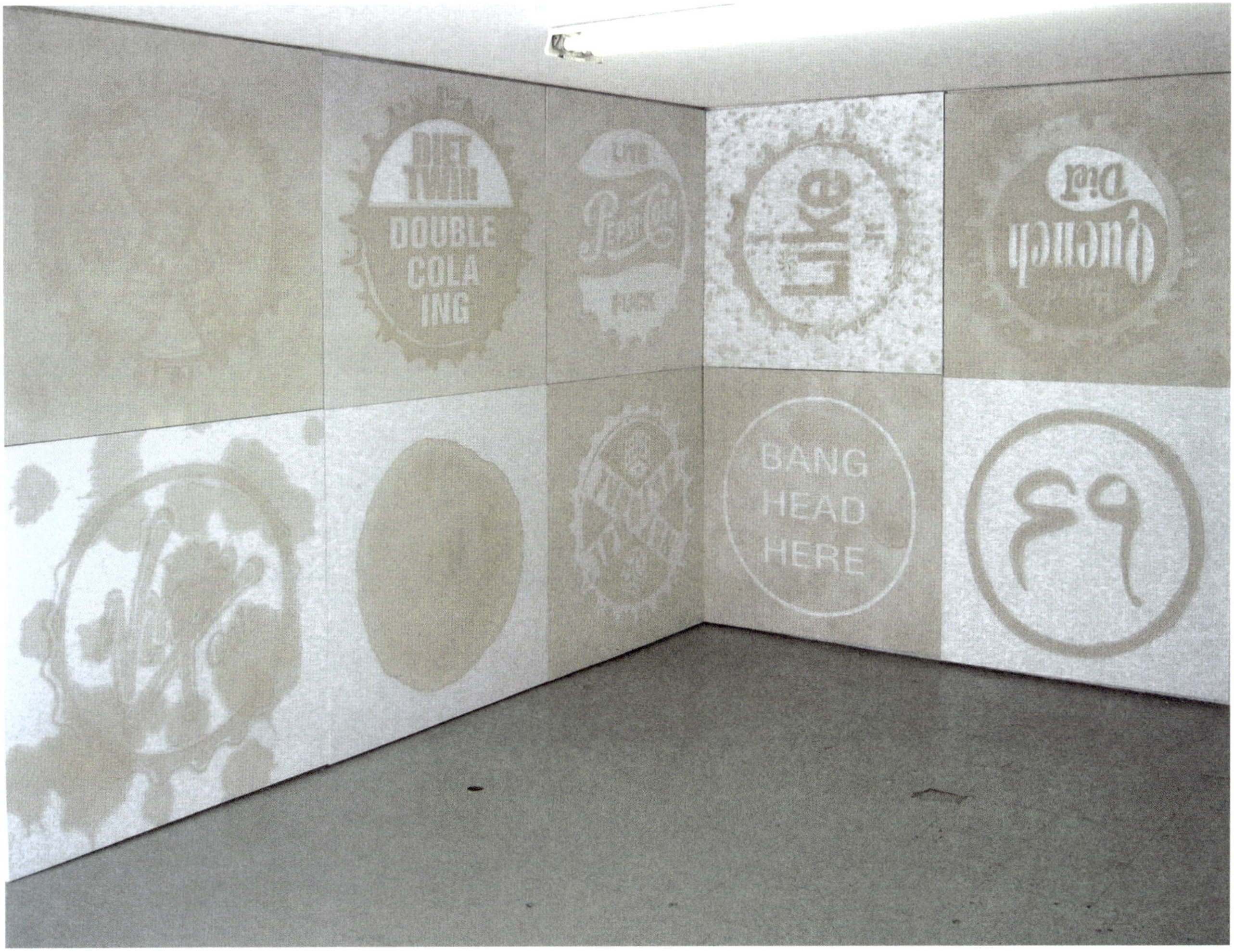

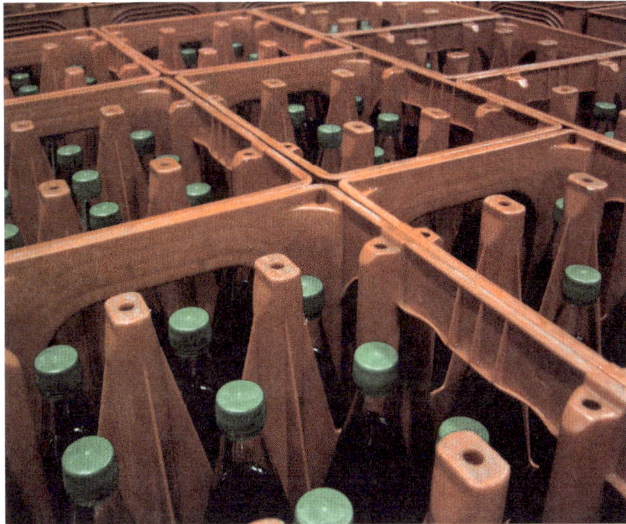

Long and Skinny 2005
Installation view, Maccarone, Inc., New York City

My Cola Lite 2004
detail

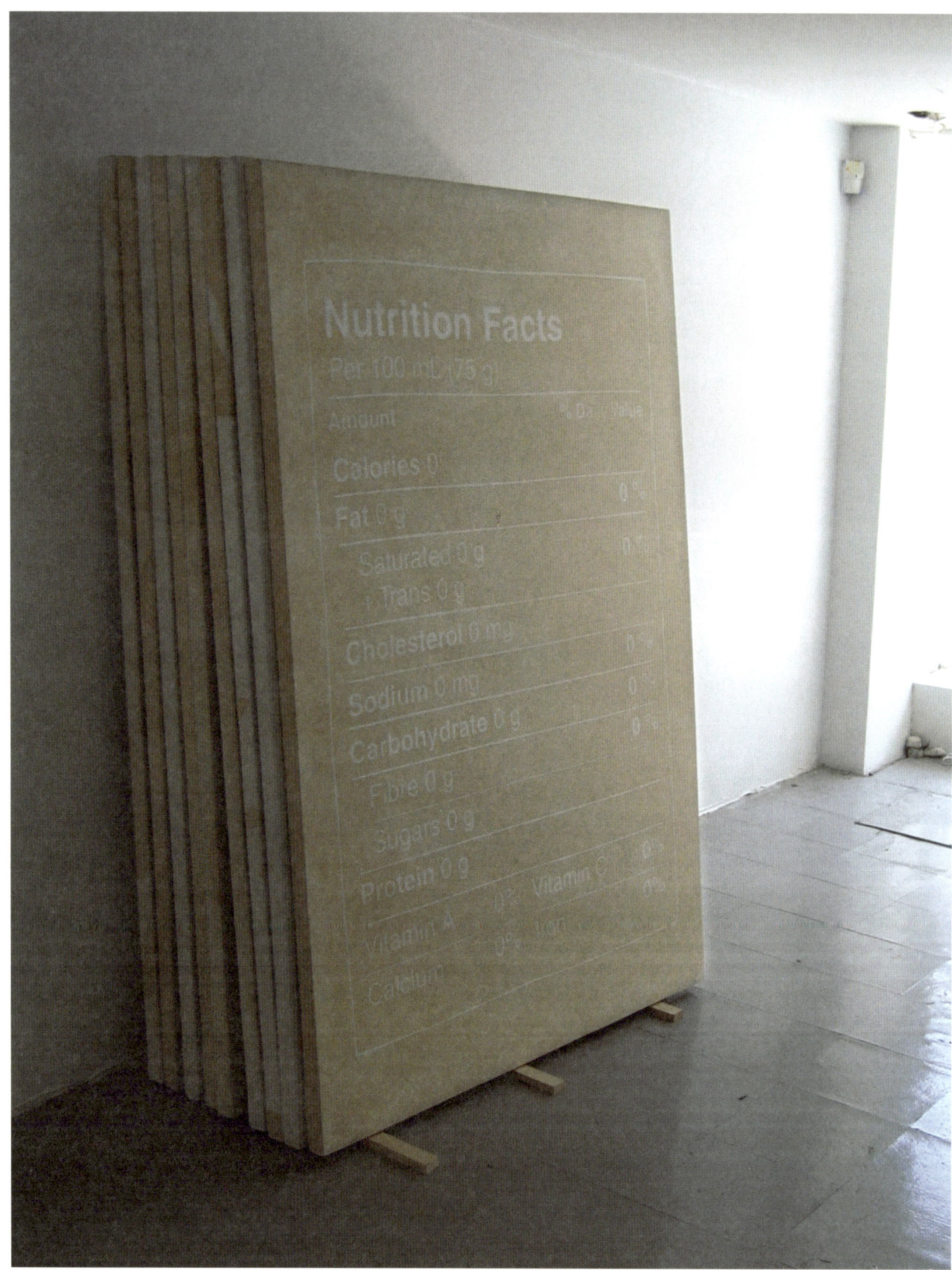

Cola Painting Stack 2005
Installation view, Maccarone, Inc., New York City

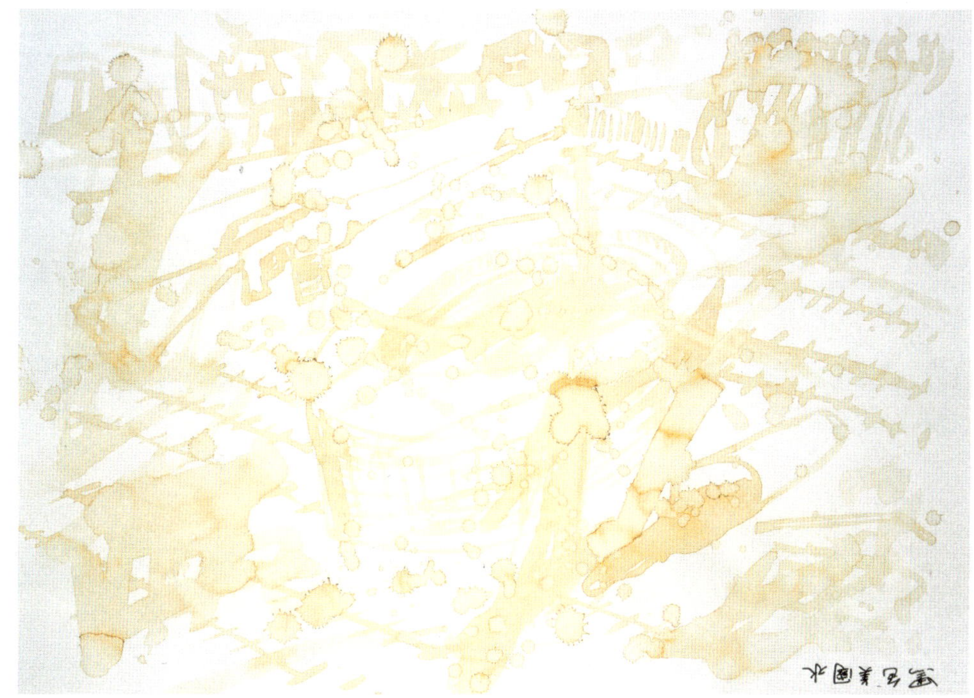

Stadium 2004

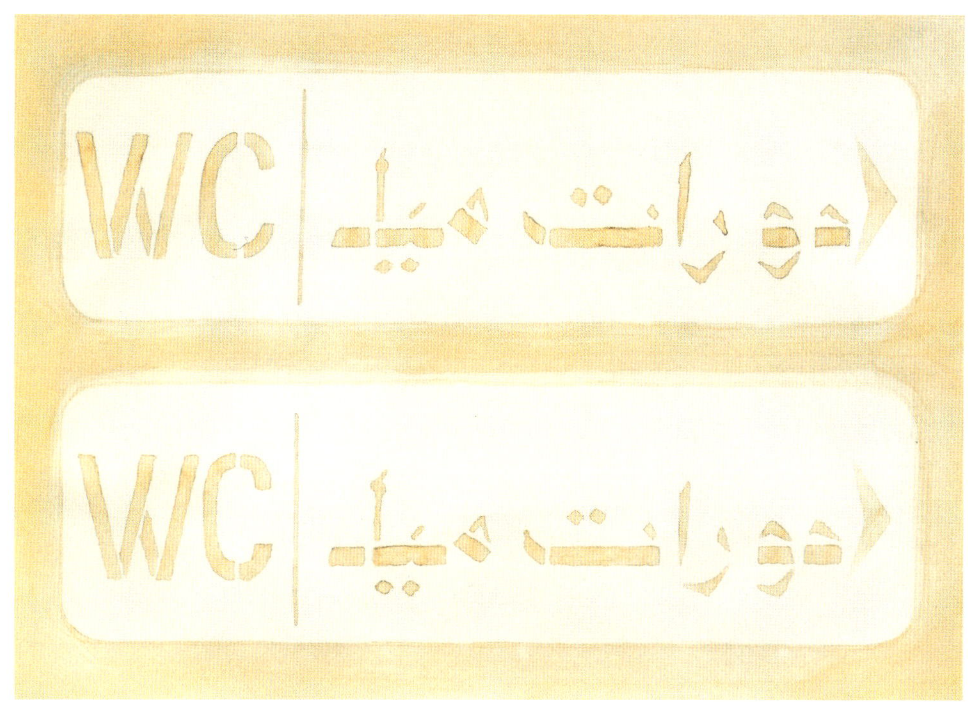

WC 2005

Long and Skinny 2 2005

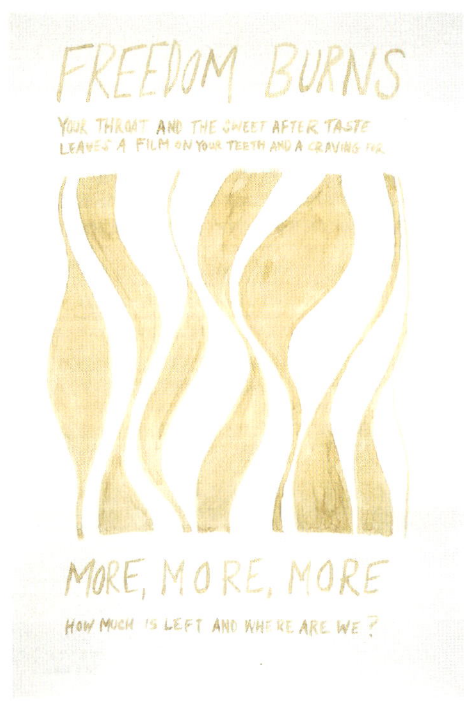

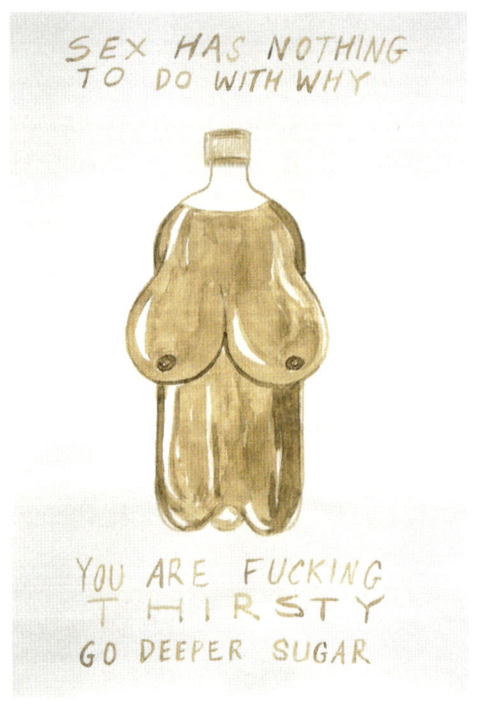

Freedom Burns 2004

Sex has Nothing 2004

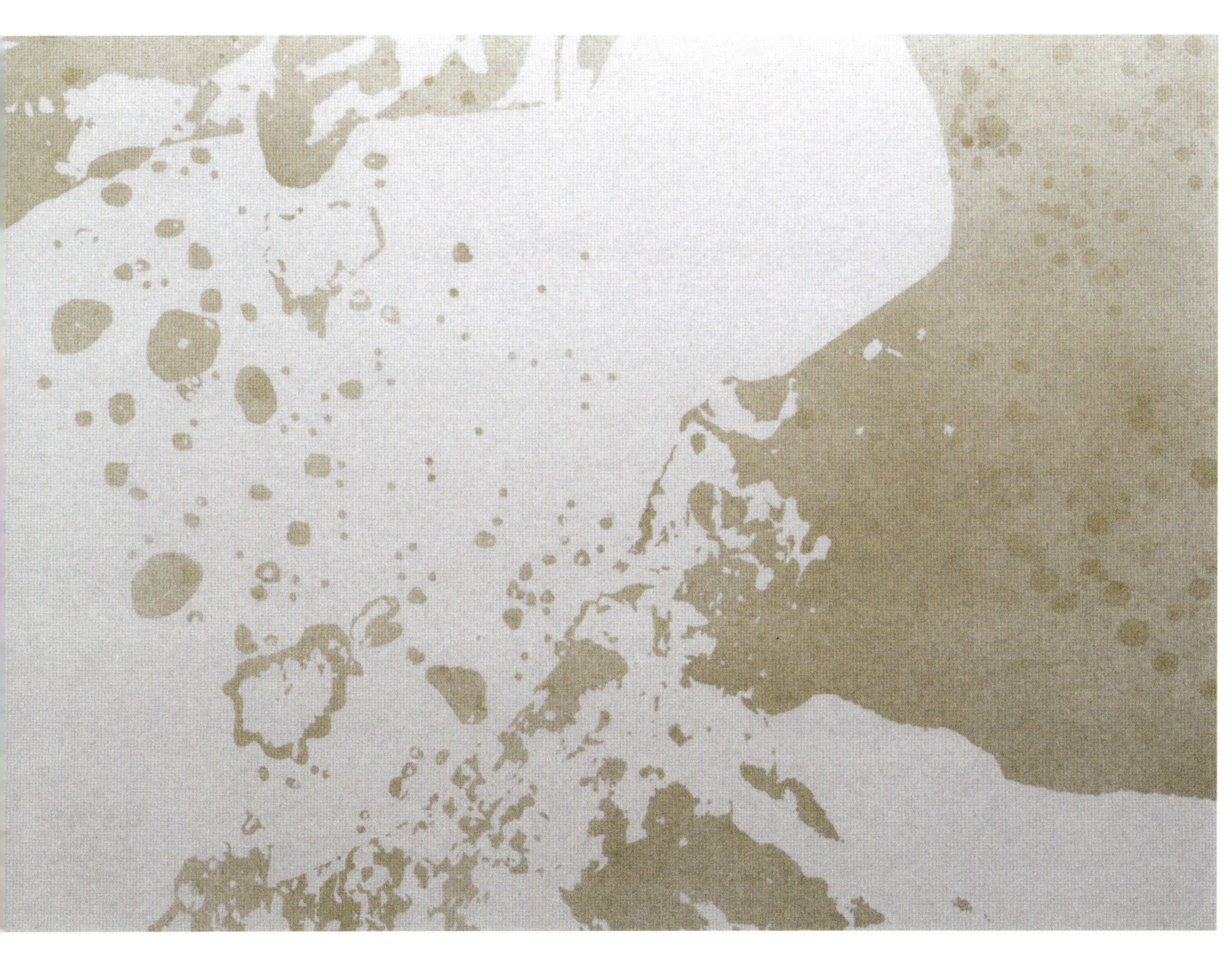

Heaven and Hell study 2004

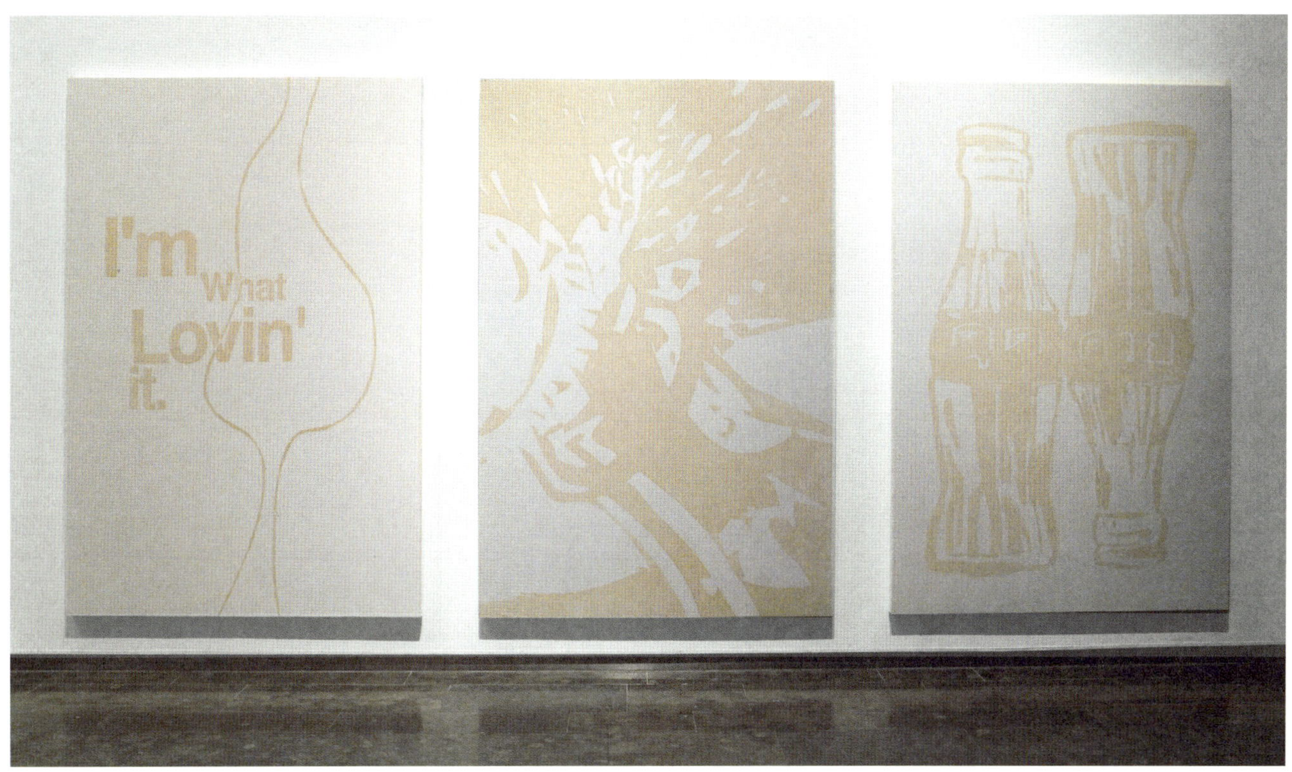

Positive What Lovin it, Explosion 1, Thai Sucky Fucky 2005
Installation view, Astrup Fearnley Museum of Modern Art, Oslo, Norway

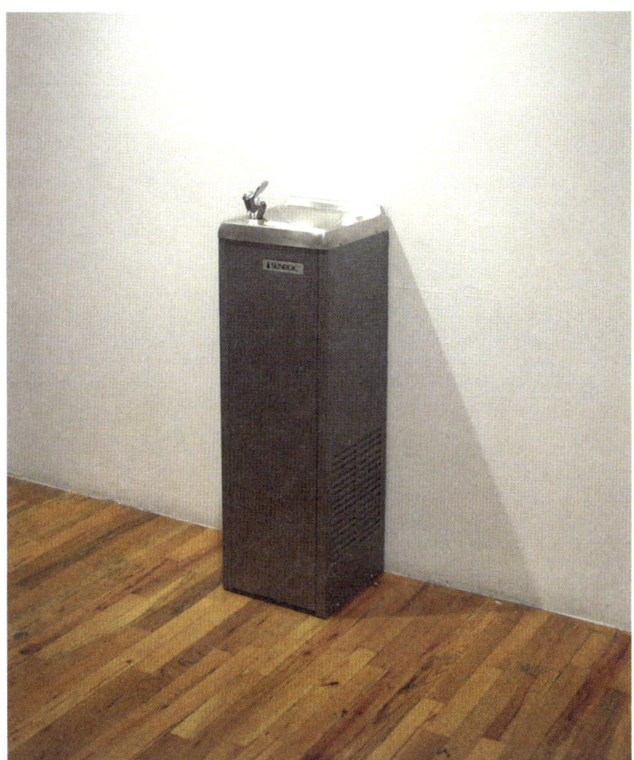

Cola Fountain 2007
Installation view, Artists Space, New York City

Negative Burst 2005

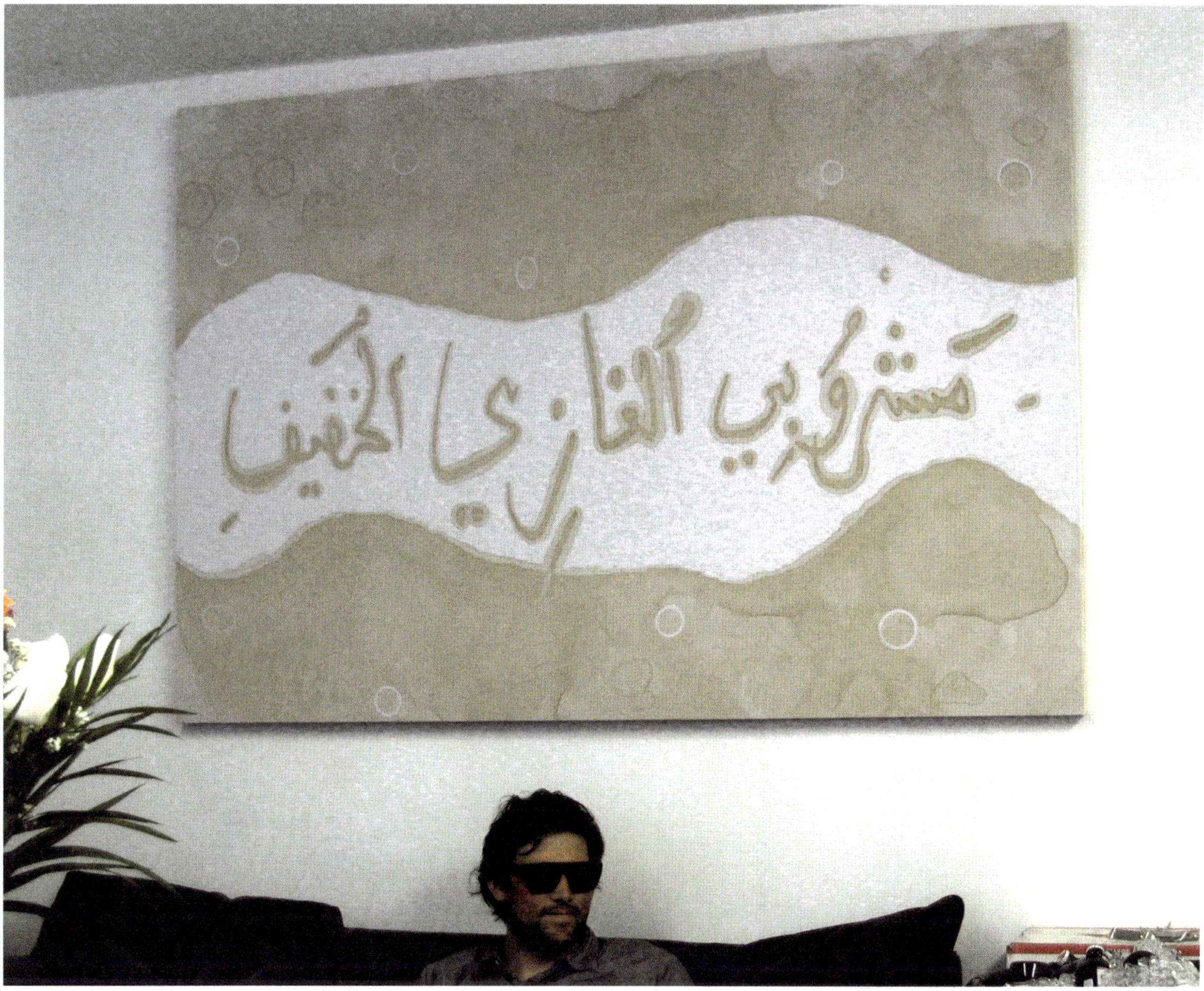

My Arabic Cola Lite 2005

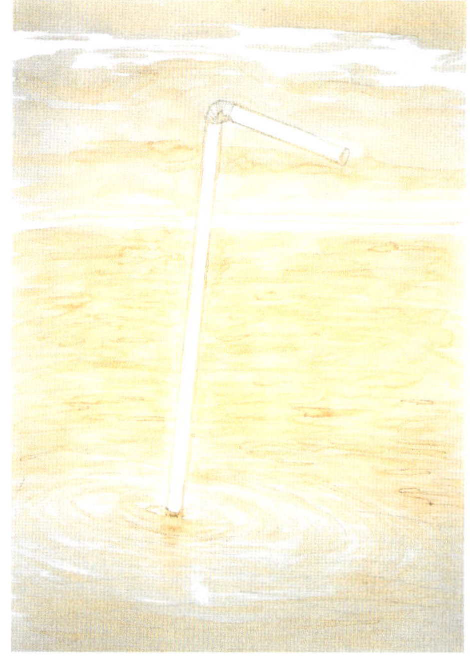

C Scape 2005

Dirty Room 2005

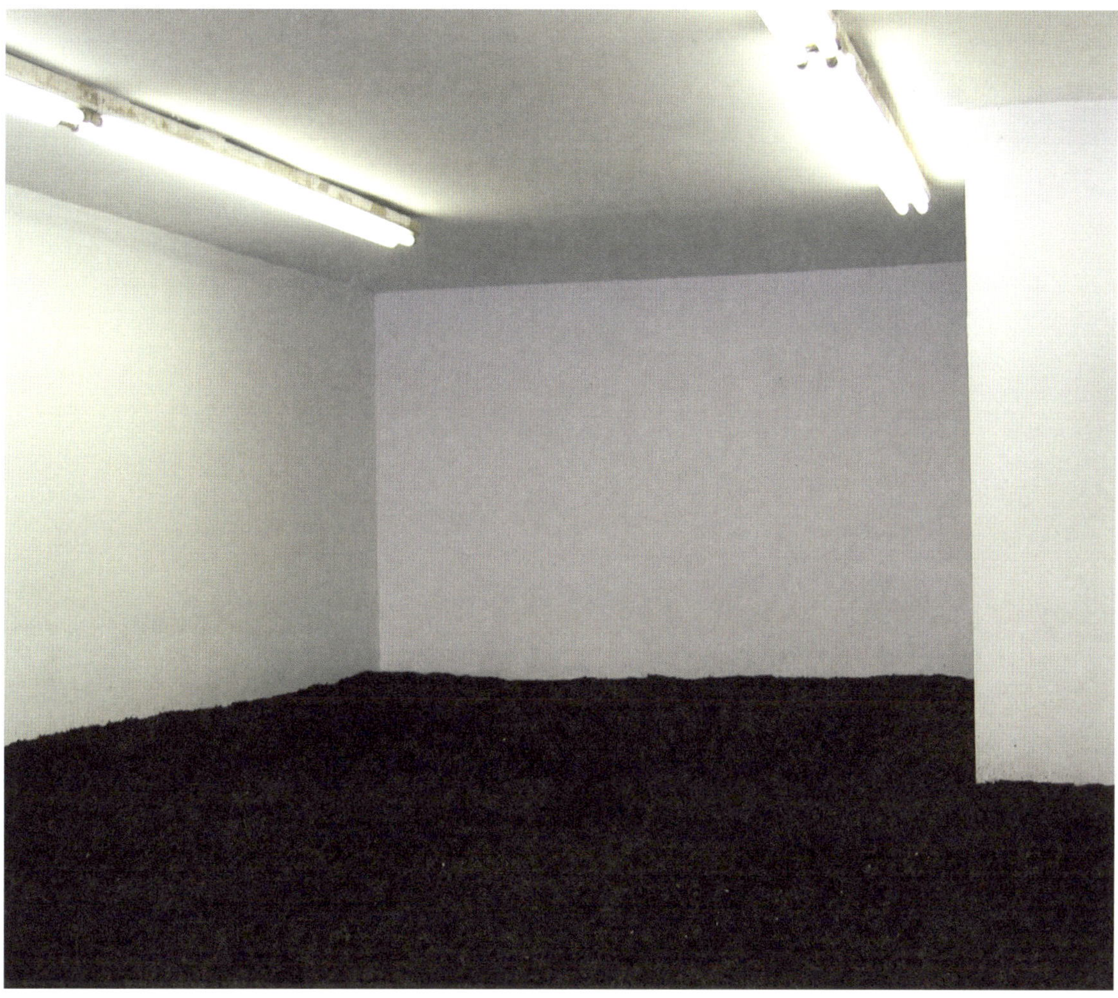

An interior dirt sculpture.
60 cubic yards of dirt (50 cubic meters)
800 square feet of floor space (80 square meters)
30 inch depth (66 centimeters)
Total weight of sculpture 75,000 pounds (30,000 kilos)

This is the first Dirty Room sculpture executed by the artist. The Dirty room material is composed of 50,000 pounds of topsoil from Home Depot and 25,000 pounds of compost from Rikers Island, the world's largest penal colony.

The New York Dirty Room was on view to the public in 2005.
This work was commissioned by the artist.
An alternative version, The Berlin Dirty Room, was shown at the Berlin Biennale in 2006.

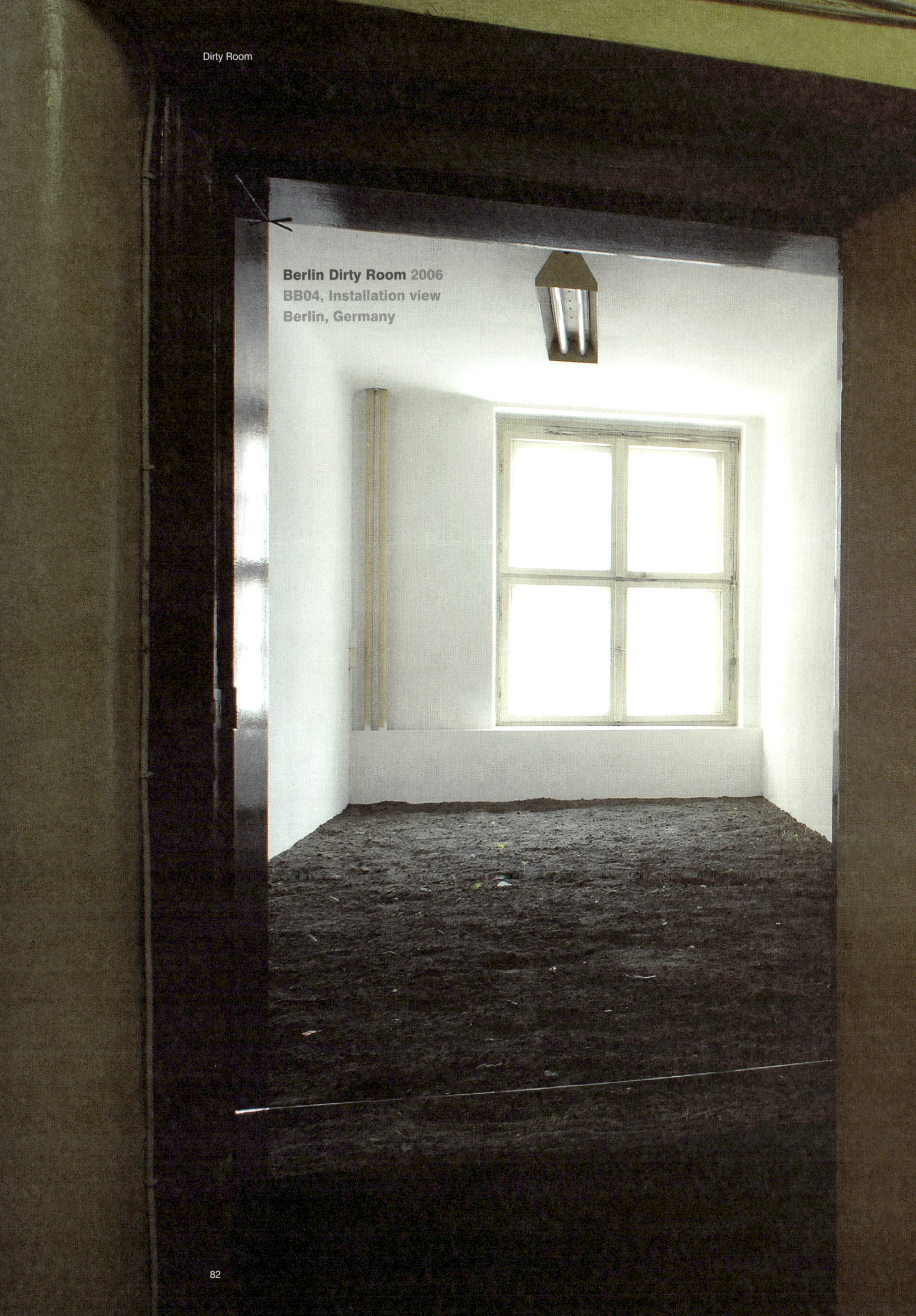

Berlin Dirty Room 2006
BB04, Installation view
Berlin, Germany

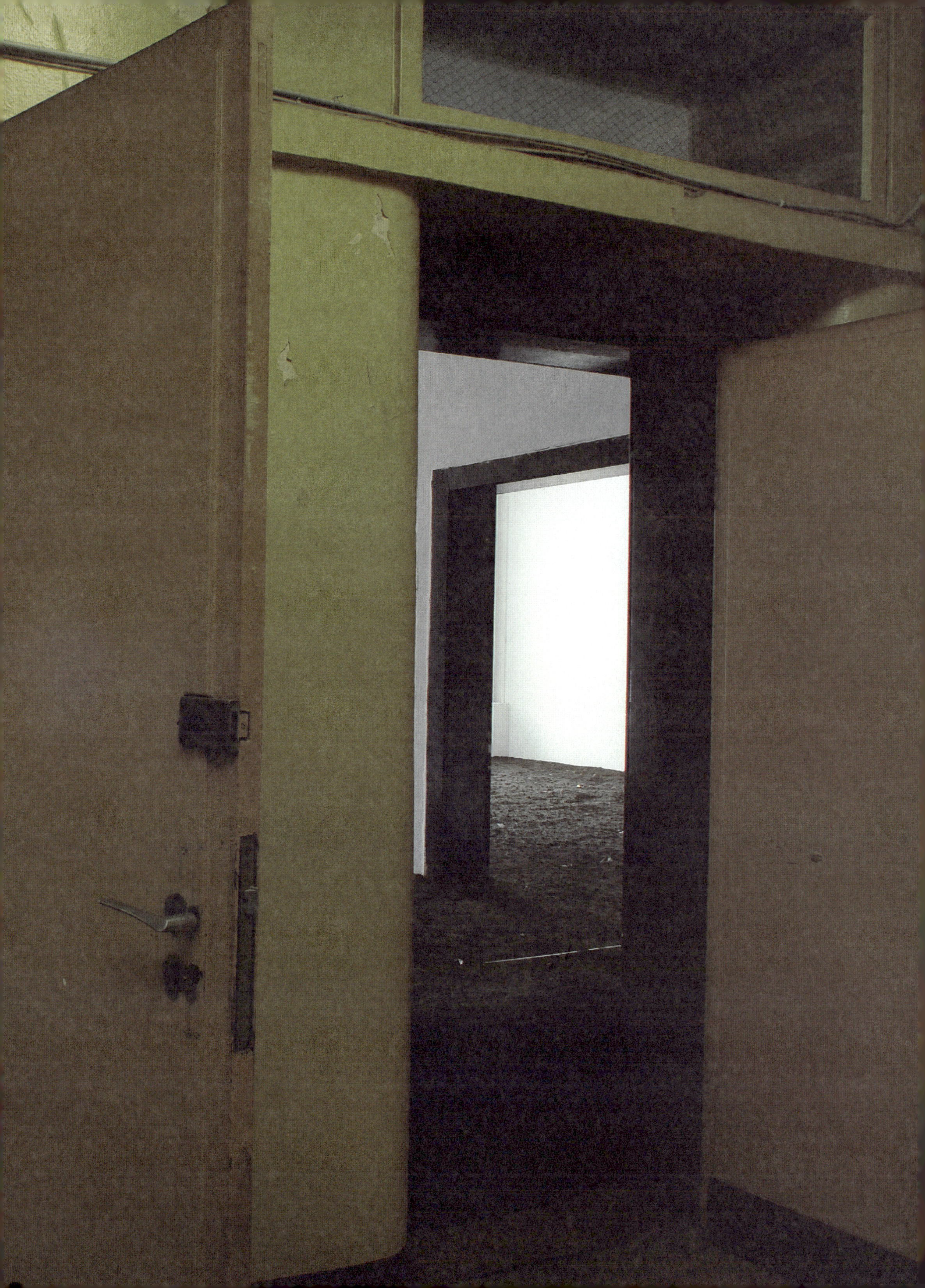

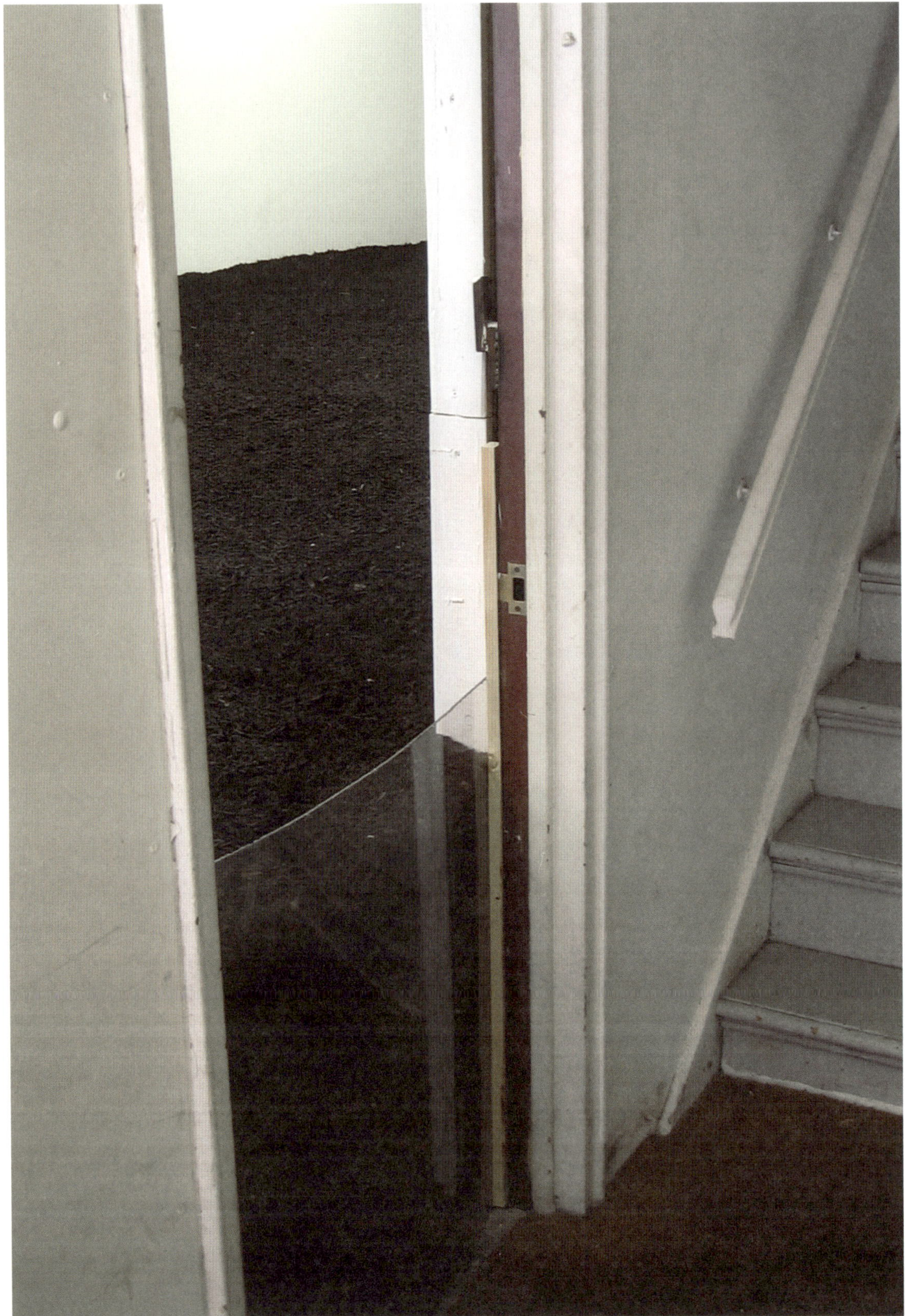

New York Dirty Room 2005
Installation view, Maccarone Inc., New York City

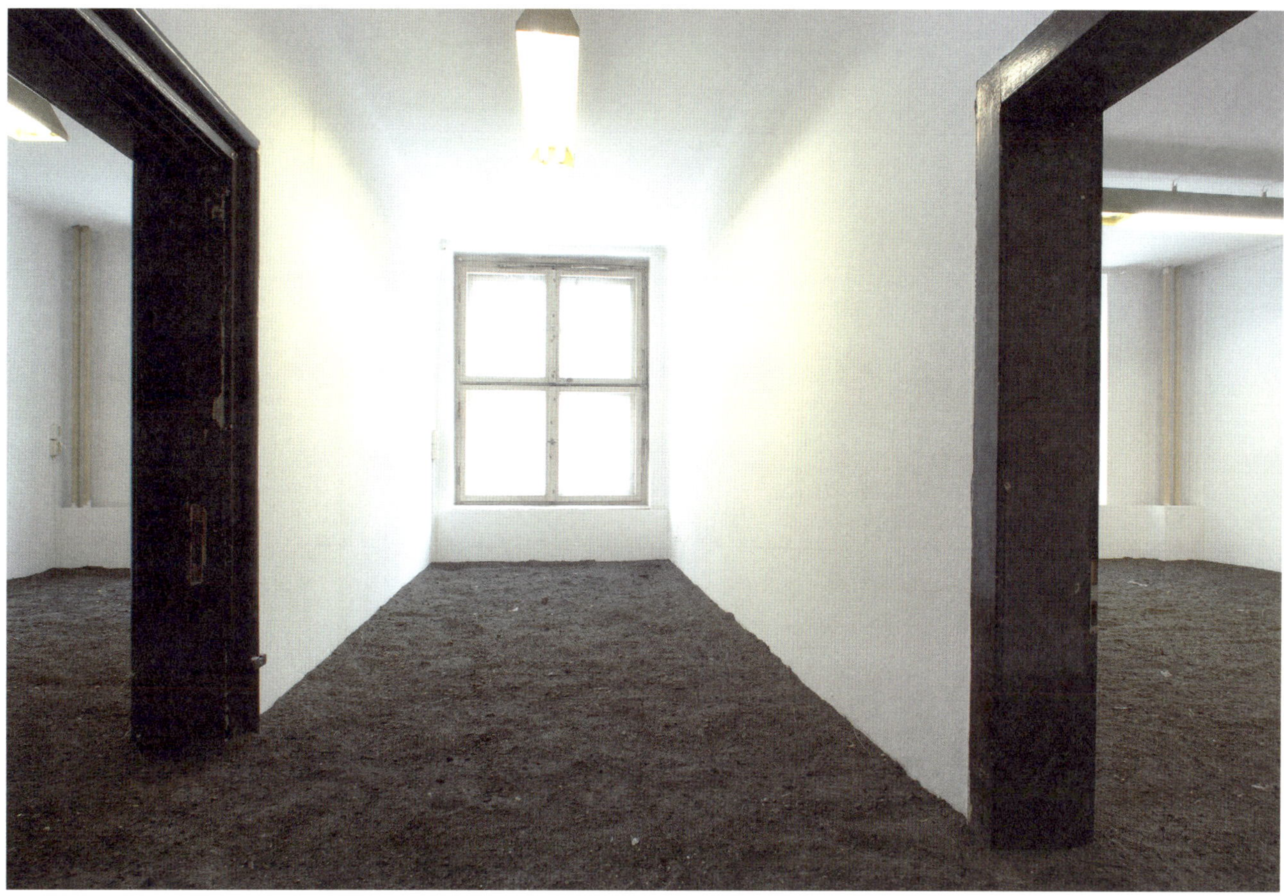

Berlin Dirty Room 2005
Installation view, BB04, Berlin, Germany

Top Cruise 2005

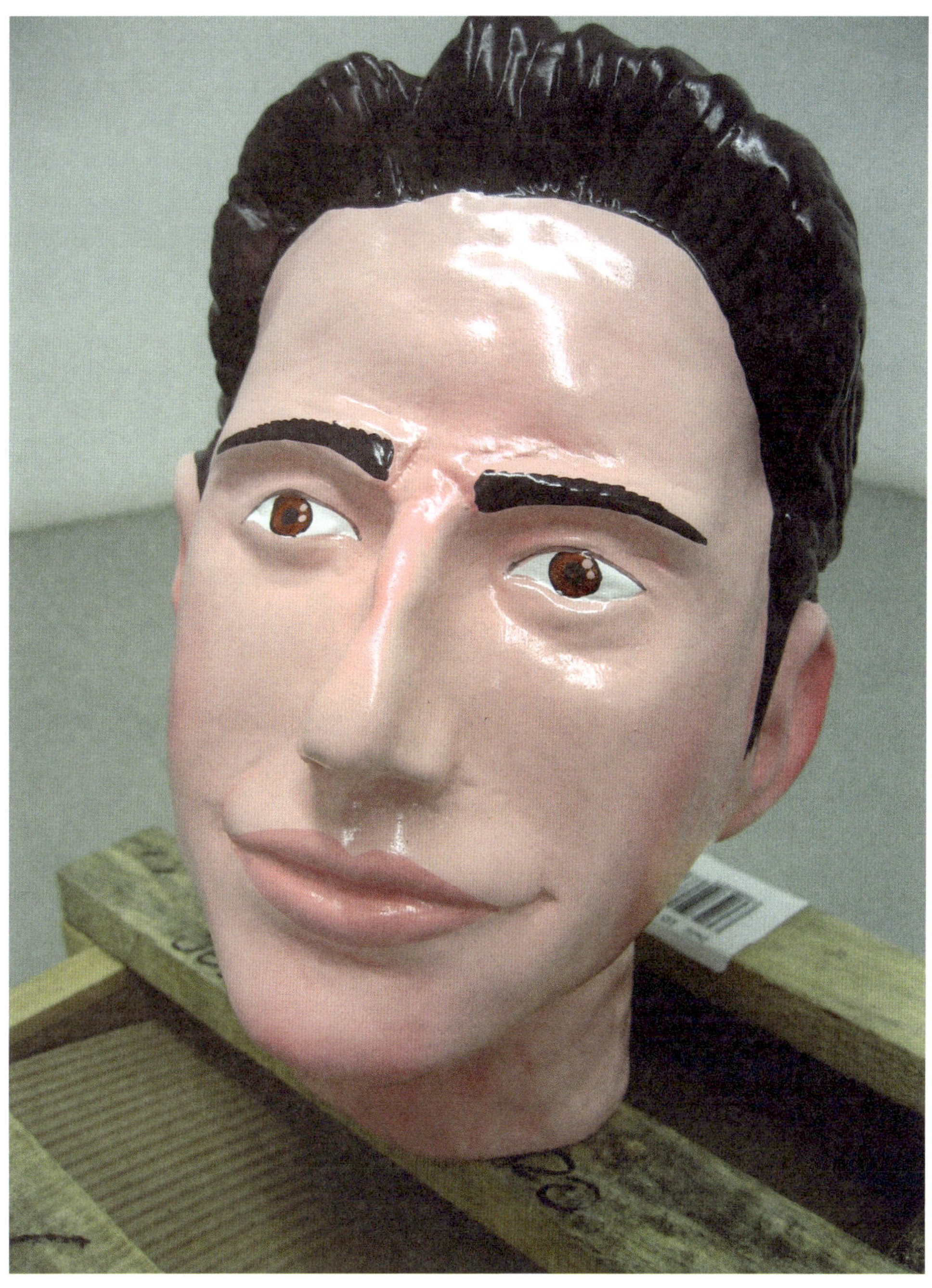

1,000 hand-painted ceramic busts of Tom Cruise were produced for this piece, cast from an original bust of the actor made by the artist.

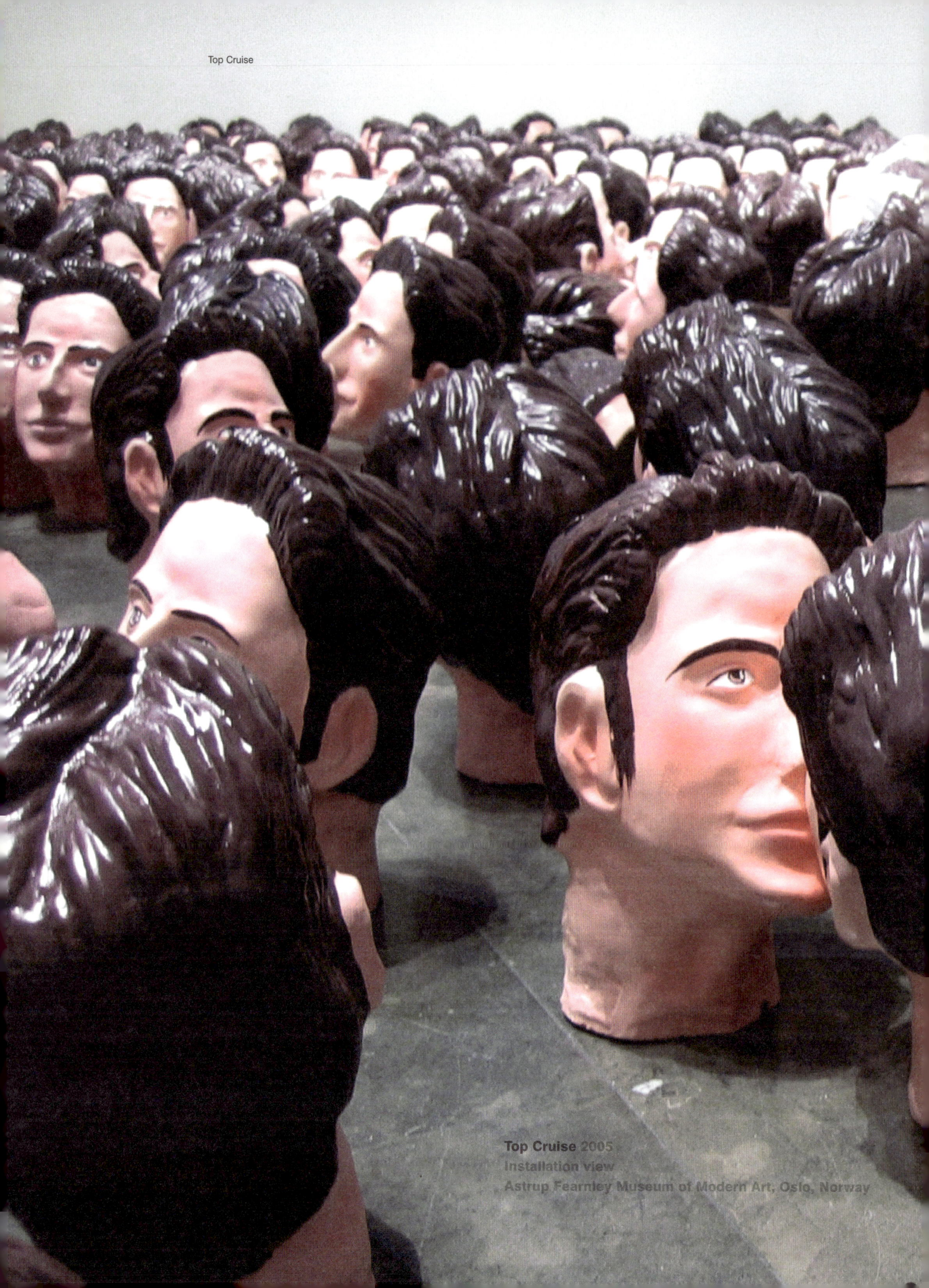

Top Cruise 2005
Installation view
Astrup Fearnley Museum of Modern Art, Oslo, Norway

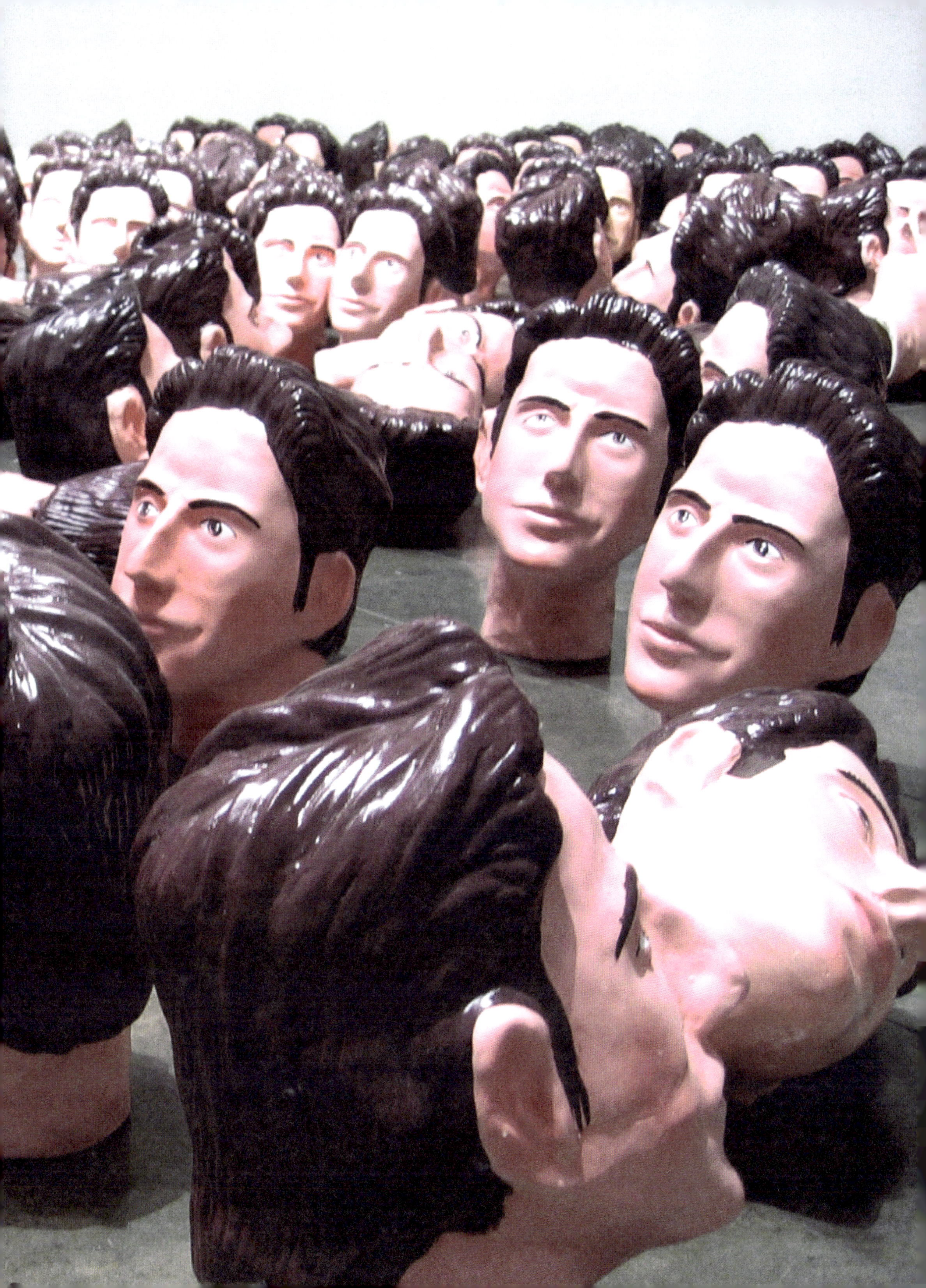

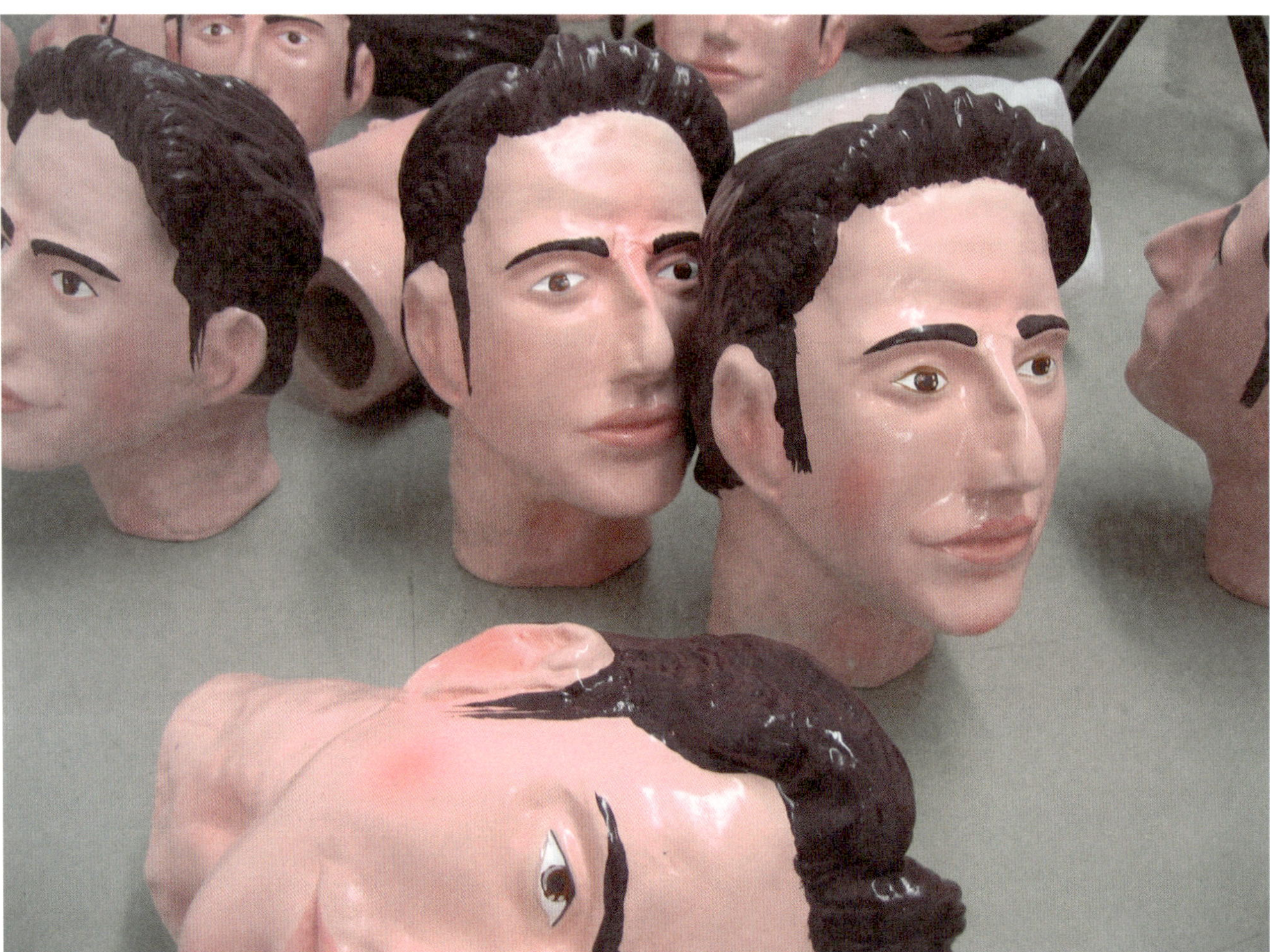

Top Cruise 2005

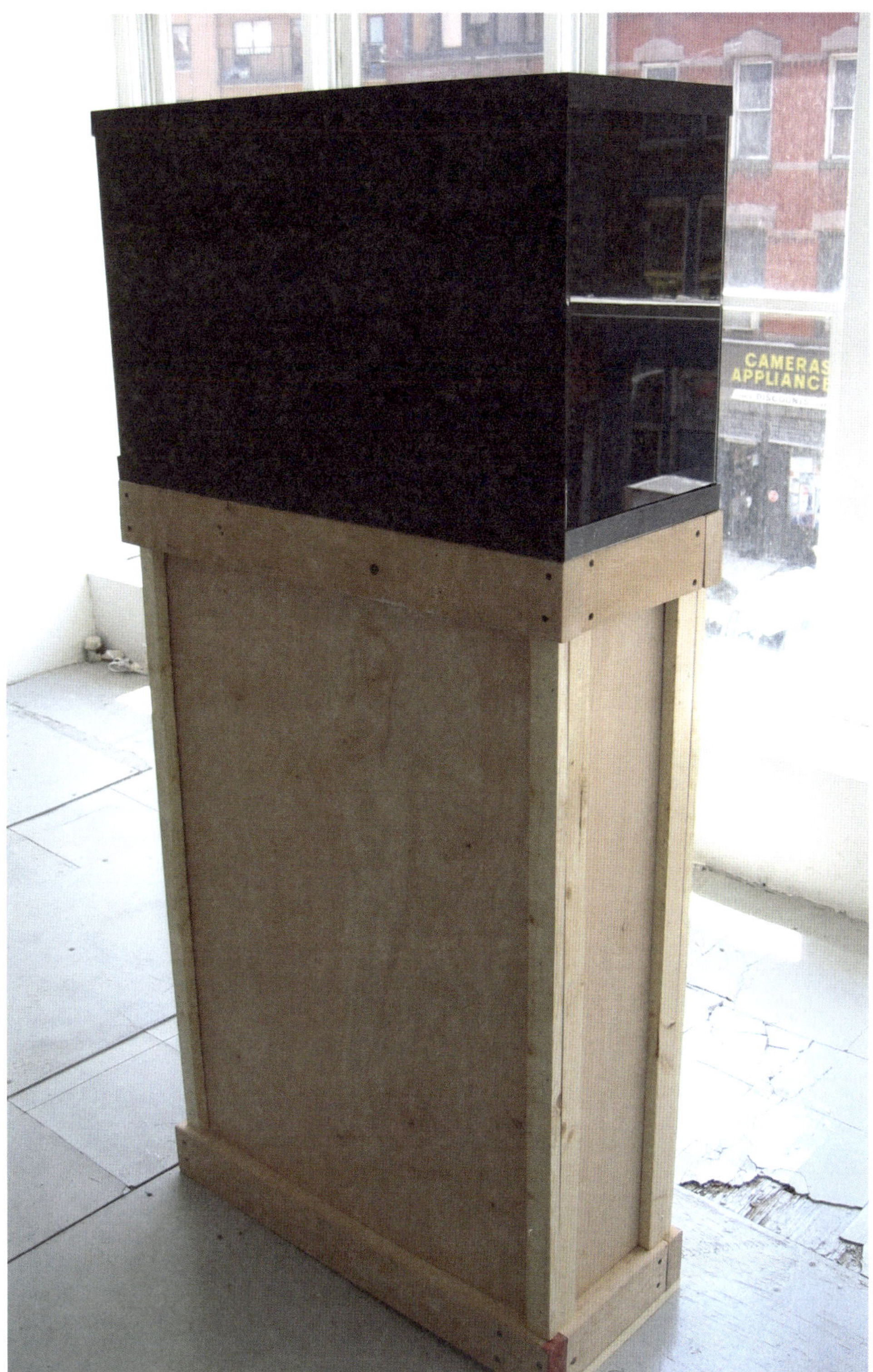

America's Next Top Cruise 2005

Almost Every City In The World 2005

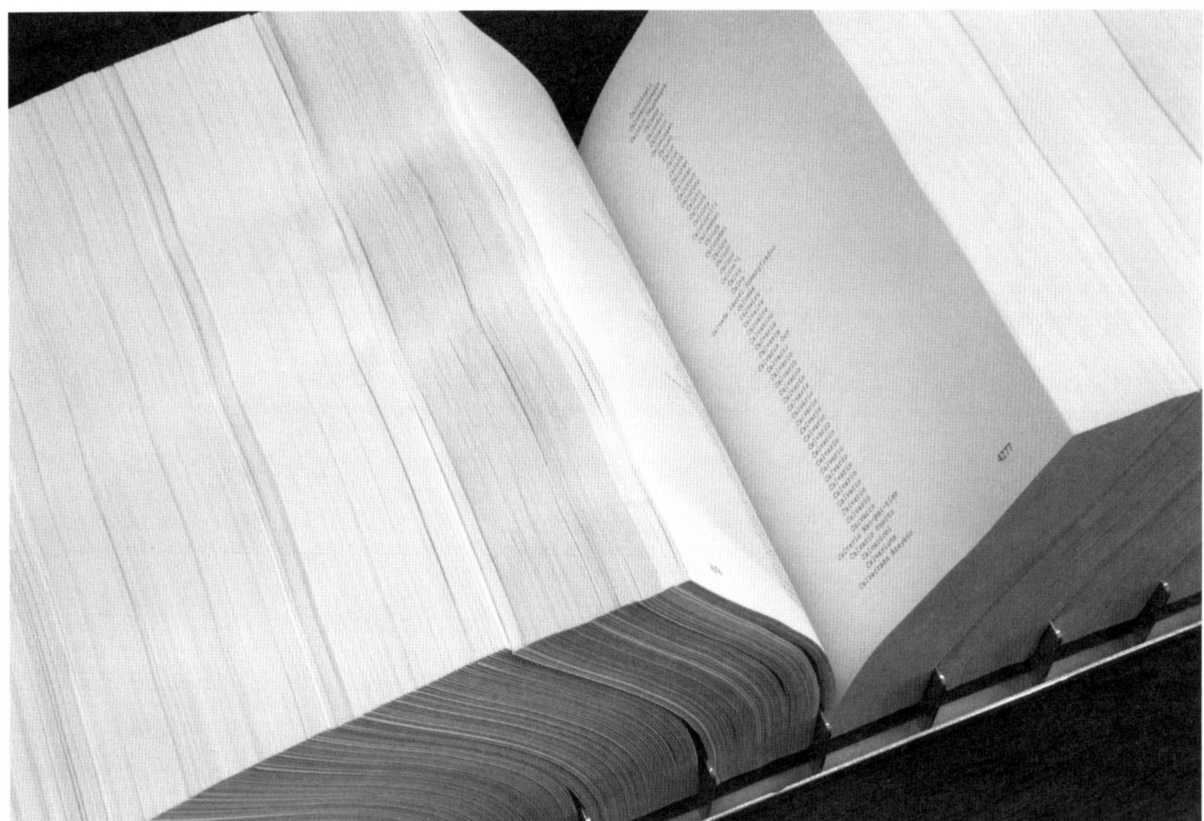

The video is a list of almost every city, town, town, village, or settlement in the world. It has approximately 2,900,000 entries. The alphabetically-listed names are displayed in a continuous scroll, similar to a credit list at the end of a film, with a total running time of over 500 hours. The soundtrack to the video is a one hundred hour long track of film credit scores, which loops more than five times during the projection.

The book is a printed version of this list. It has over 33,000 pages. Printed on A4 paper, its spine measures over 2 meters wide.

Almost Every City In The World (Screenplay) 2006

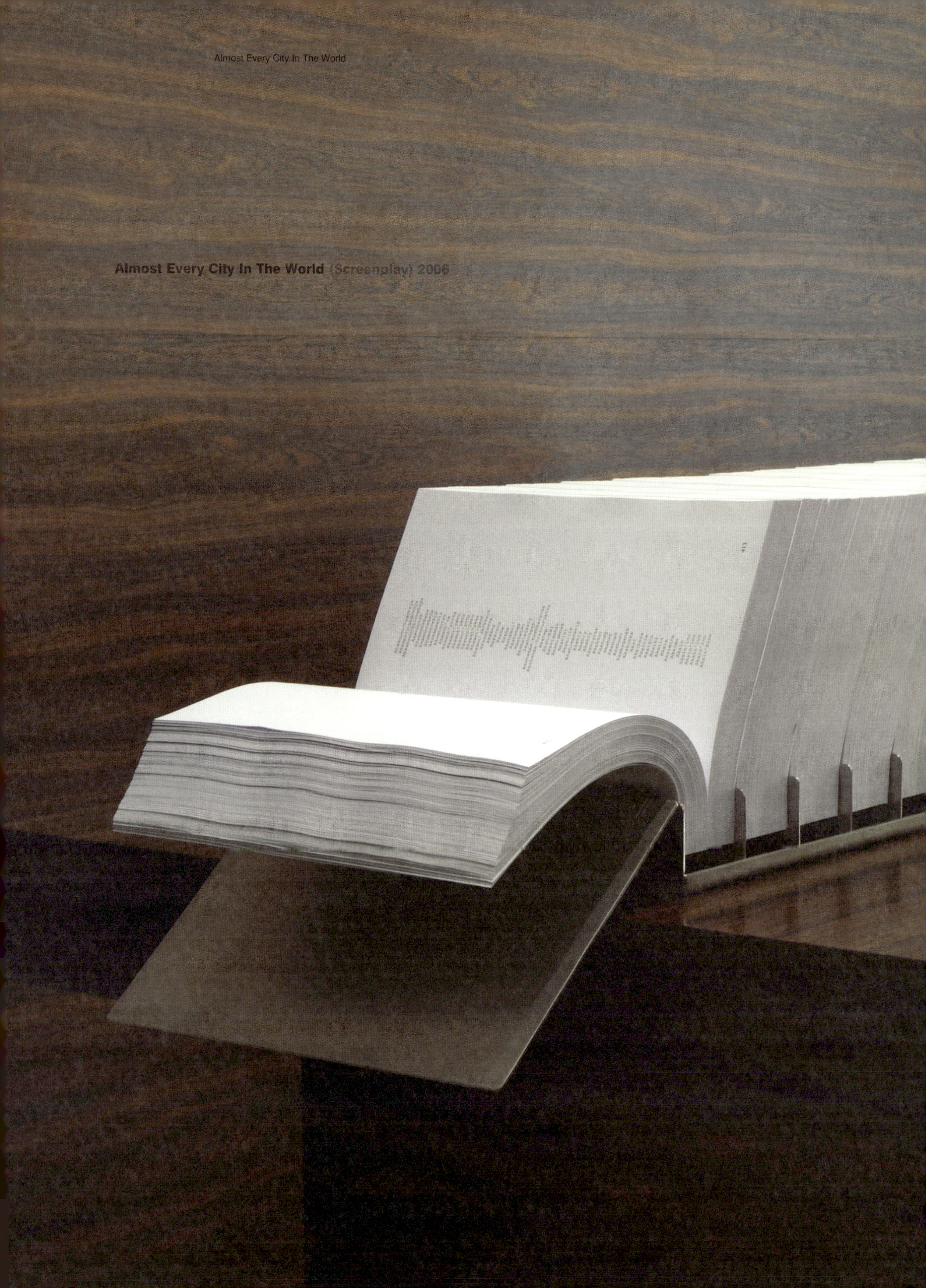

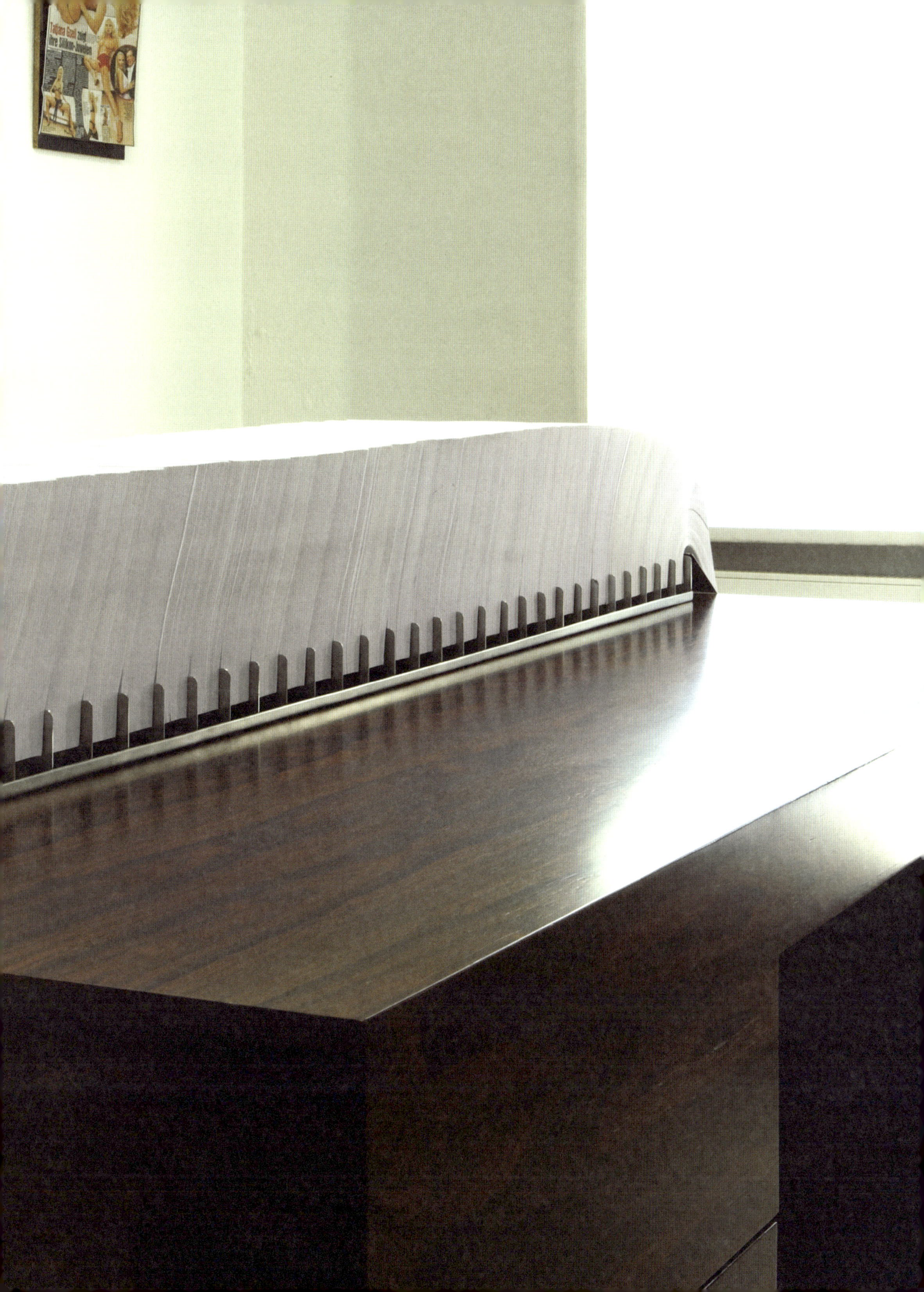

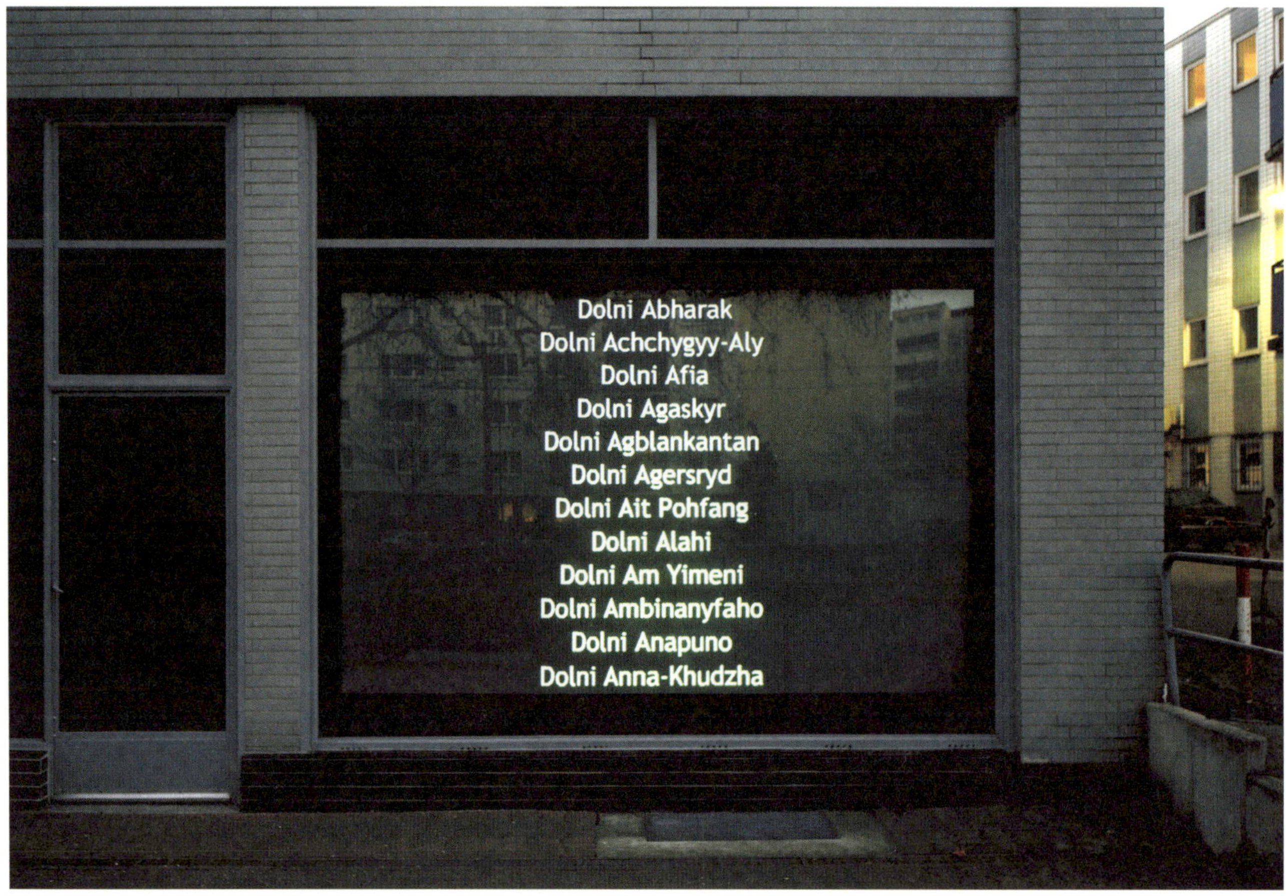

Almost Every City In The World 2006
Outdoor installation view, Galerie Michael Neff, Frankfurt, Germany

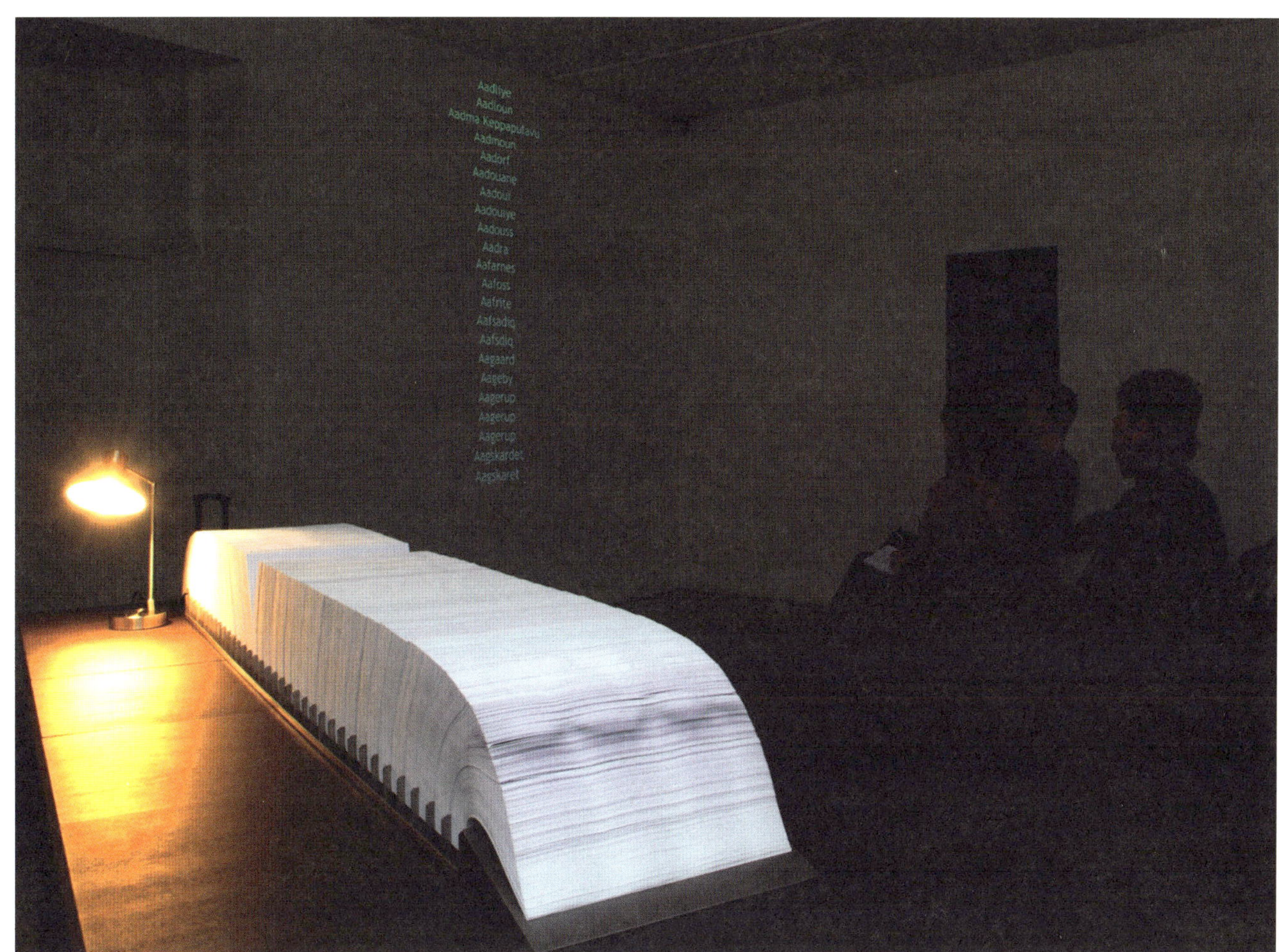

Almost Every City In The World 2006
Installation view, Galerie Georges-Philipe & Nathalie Vallois, Paris

Jacuzzis 1998 –

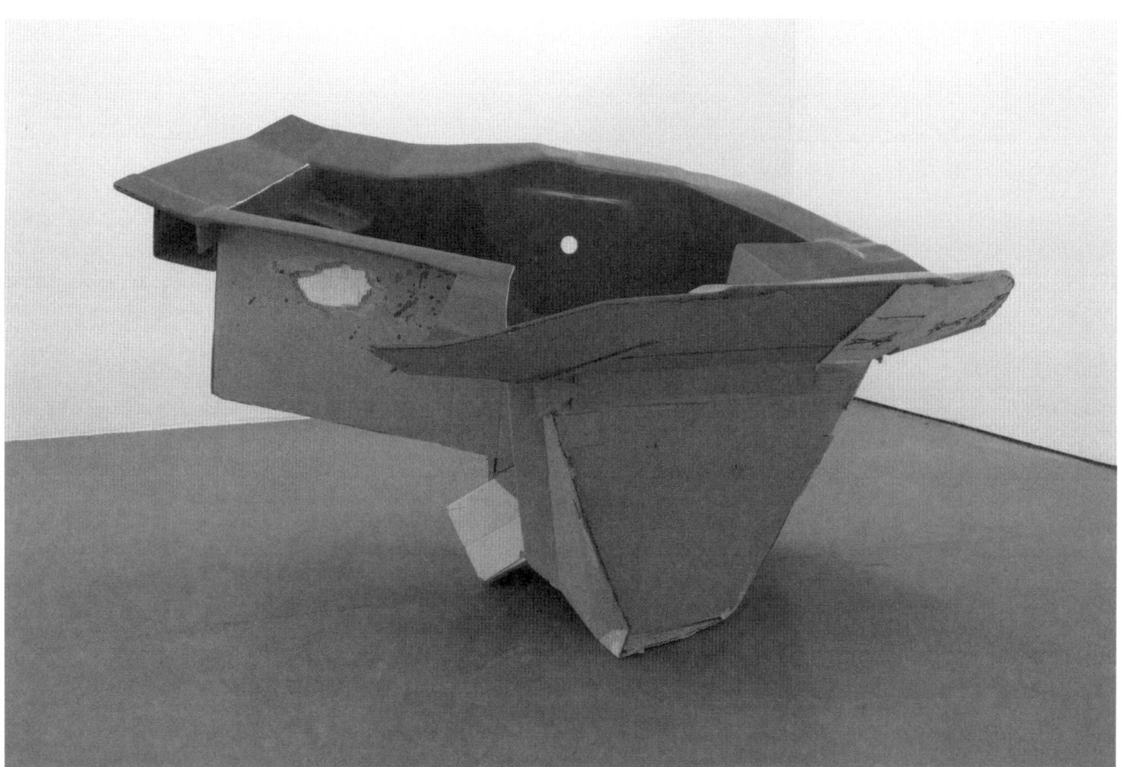

Bouchet's Jacuzzis are first built from cardboard and then coated with fiberglass and painted. The shapes and sizes of the Jacuzzis are derived from crude sketches of shapes designed to hold a human form, though often in eccentric or uncomfortable positions. They function as small scale architectural forms, in which the person can imagine him or herself floating. Though these Jacuzzis are sculptural, they can hold water and be outfitted to function like any commercial jet-water whirlpool. The first Jacuzzis were made in 1998, and Bouchet continues to design and produce them for various celebrities around the world.

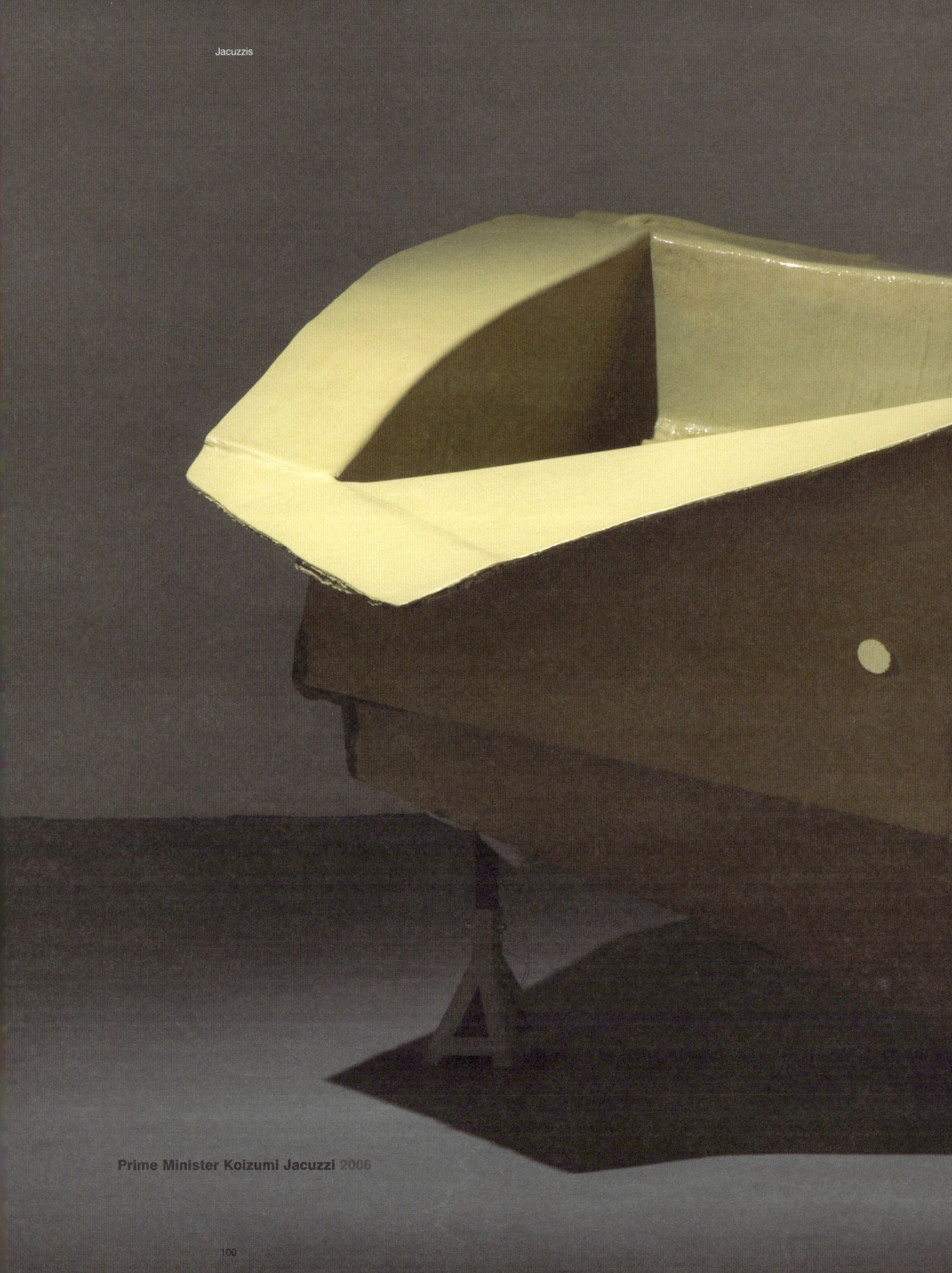

Prime Minister Koizumi Jacuzzi 2006

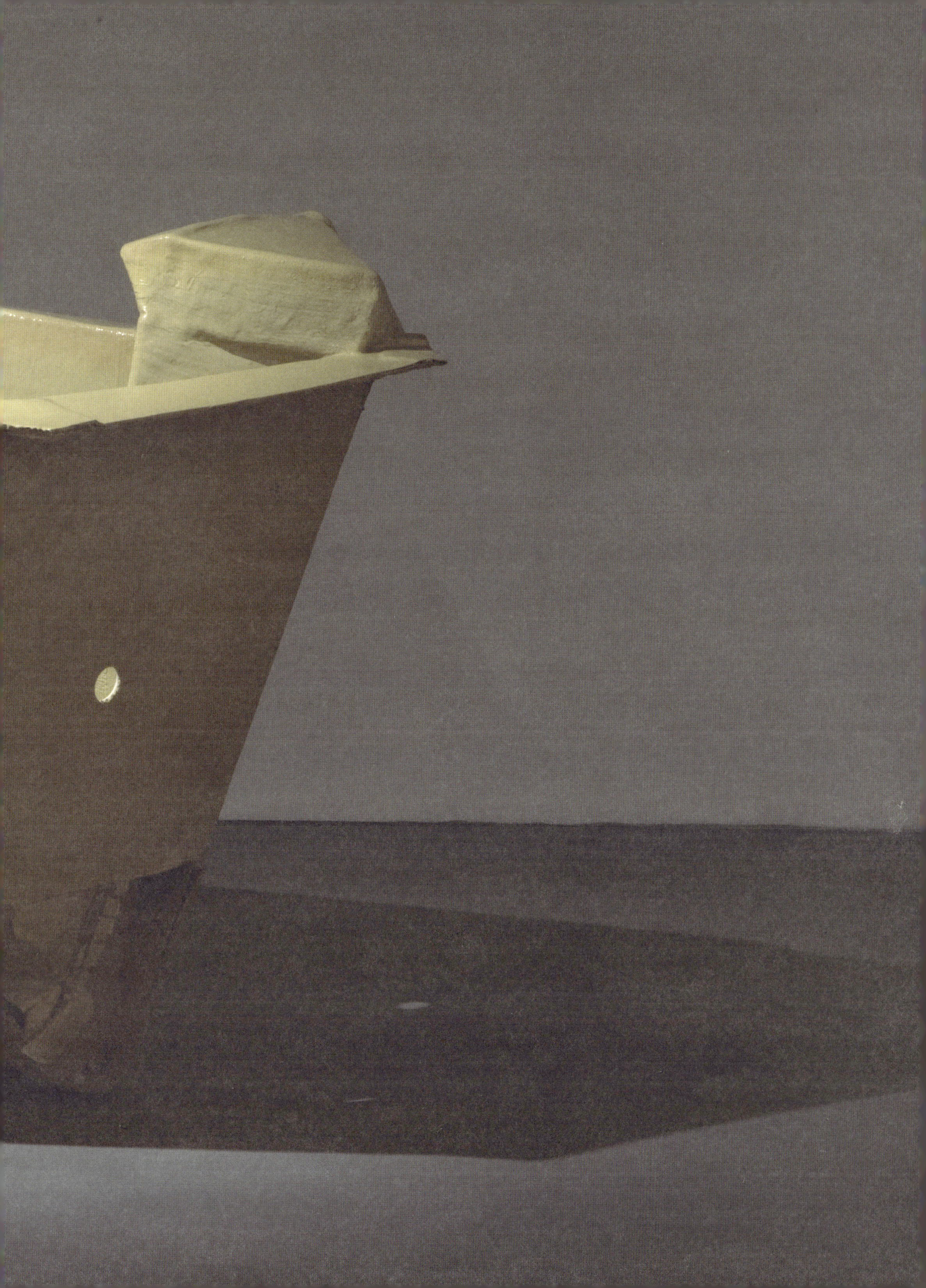

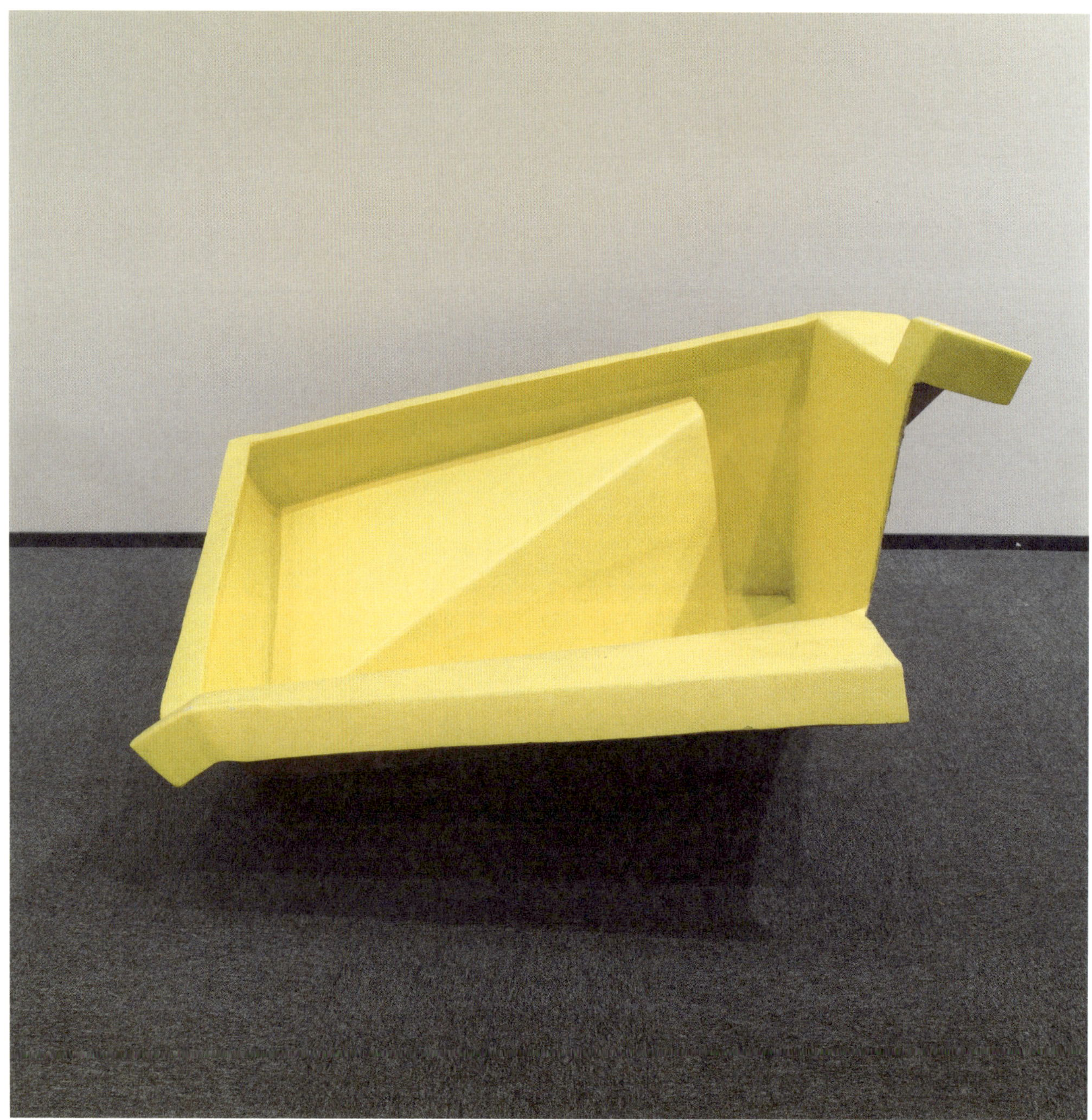

Steffi Graf Jacuzzi 2000

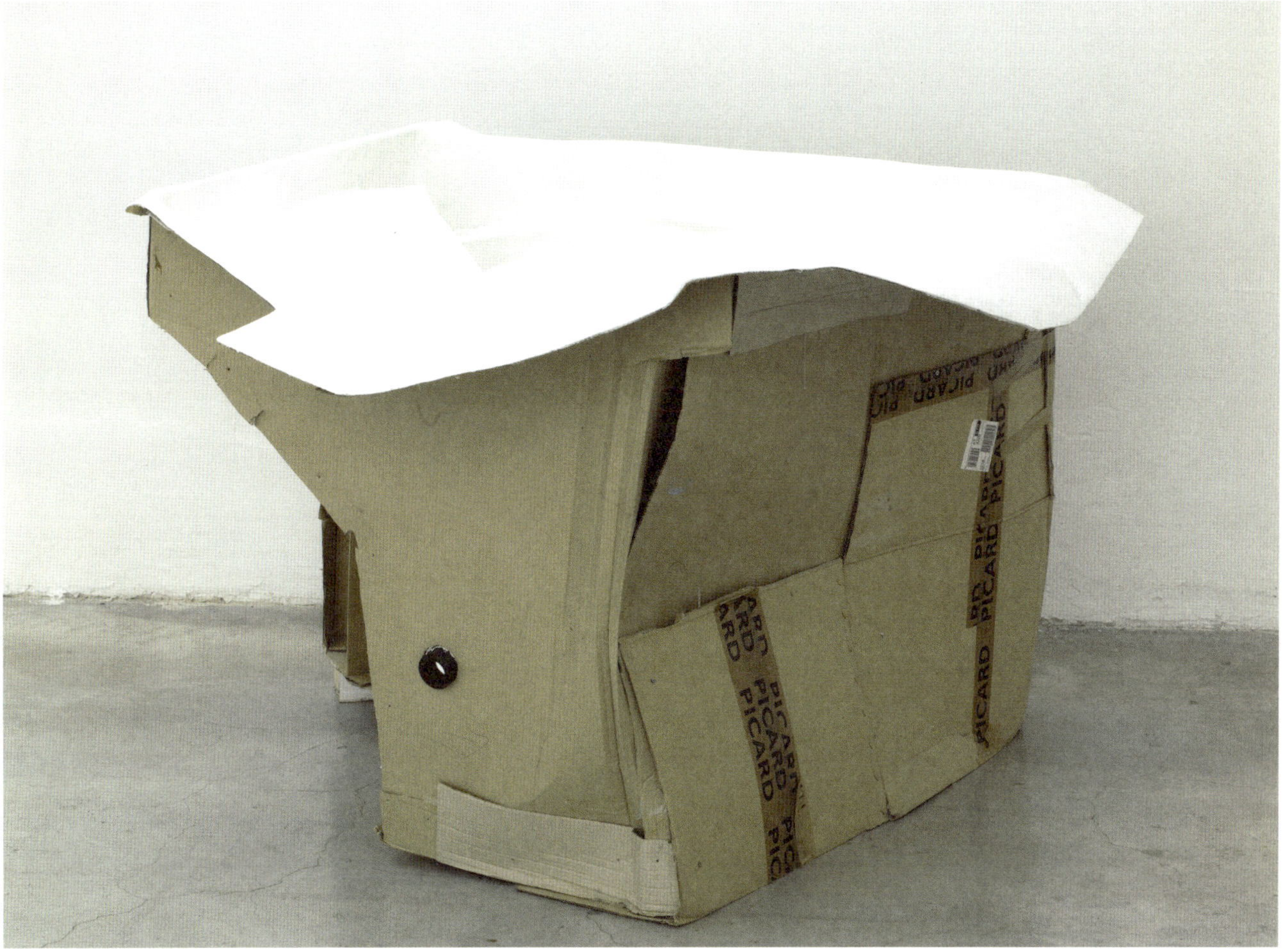

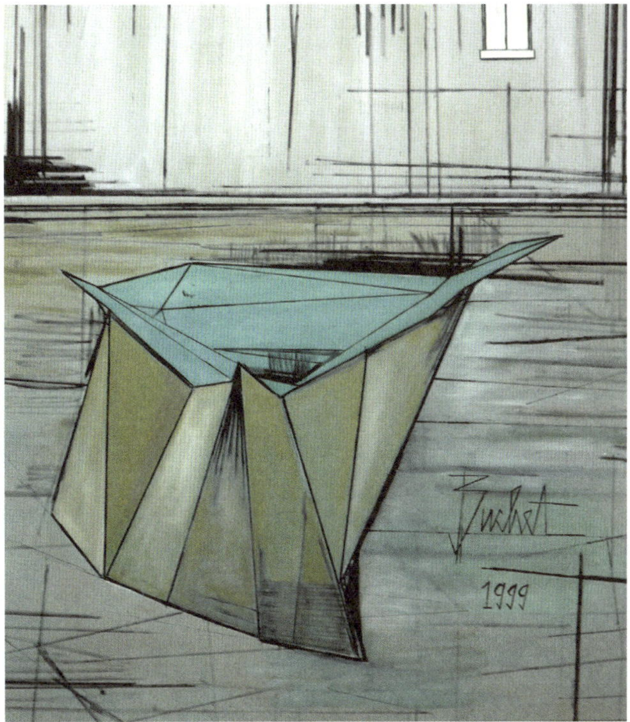

Jude Law Jacuzzi 2005

Ted Turner 1999

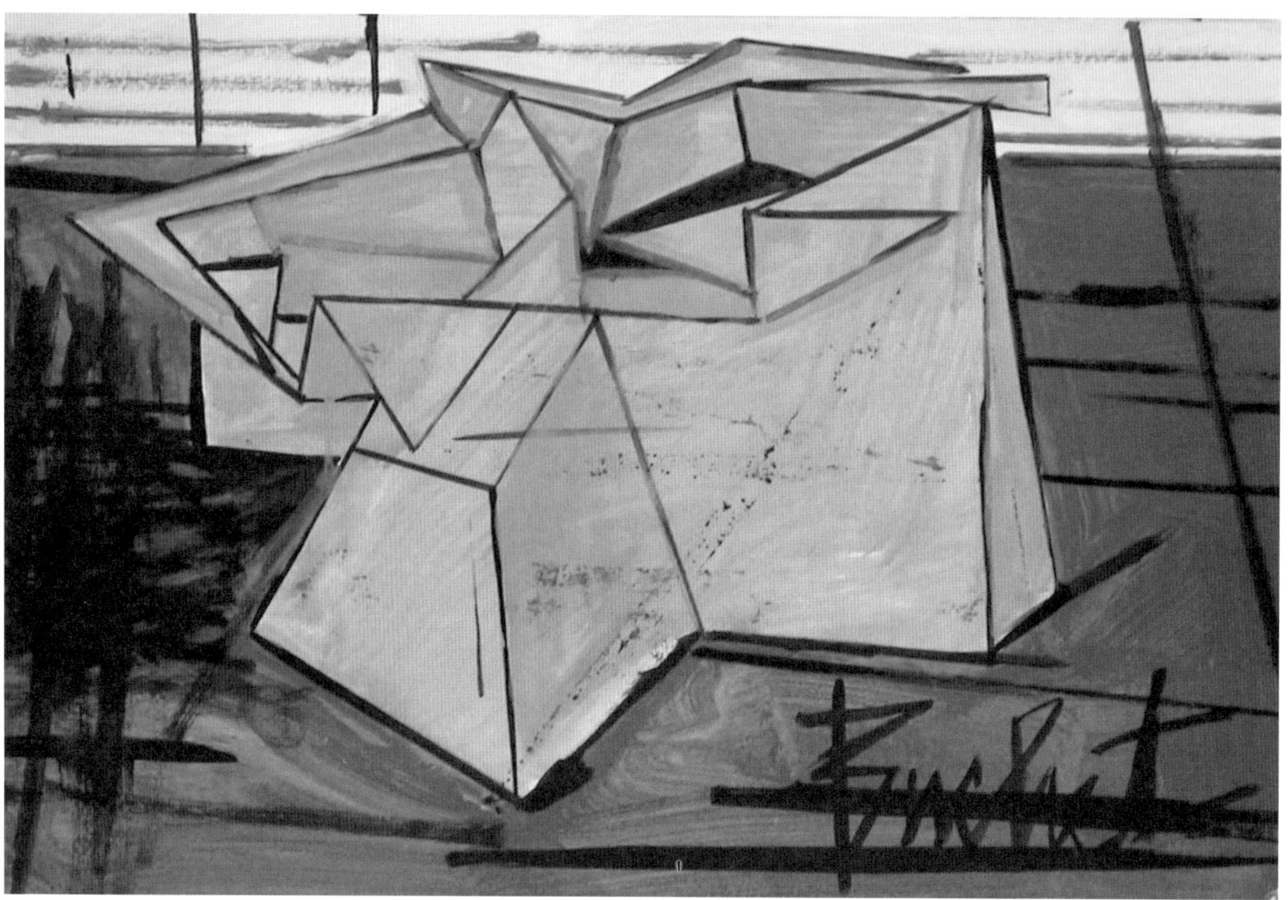

Celine Dion 1998

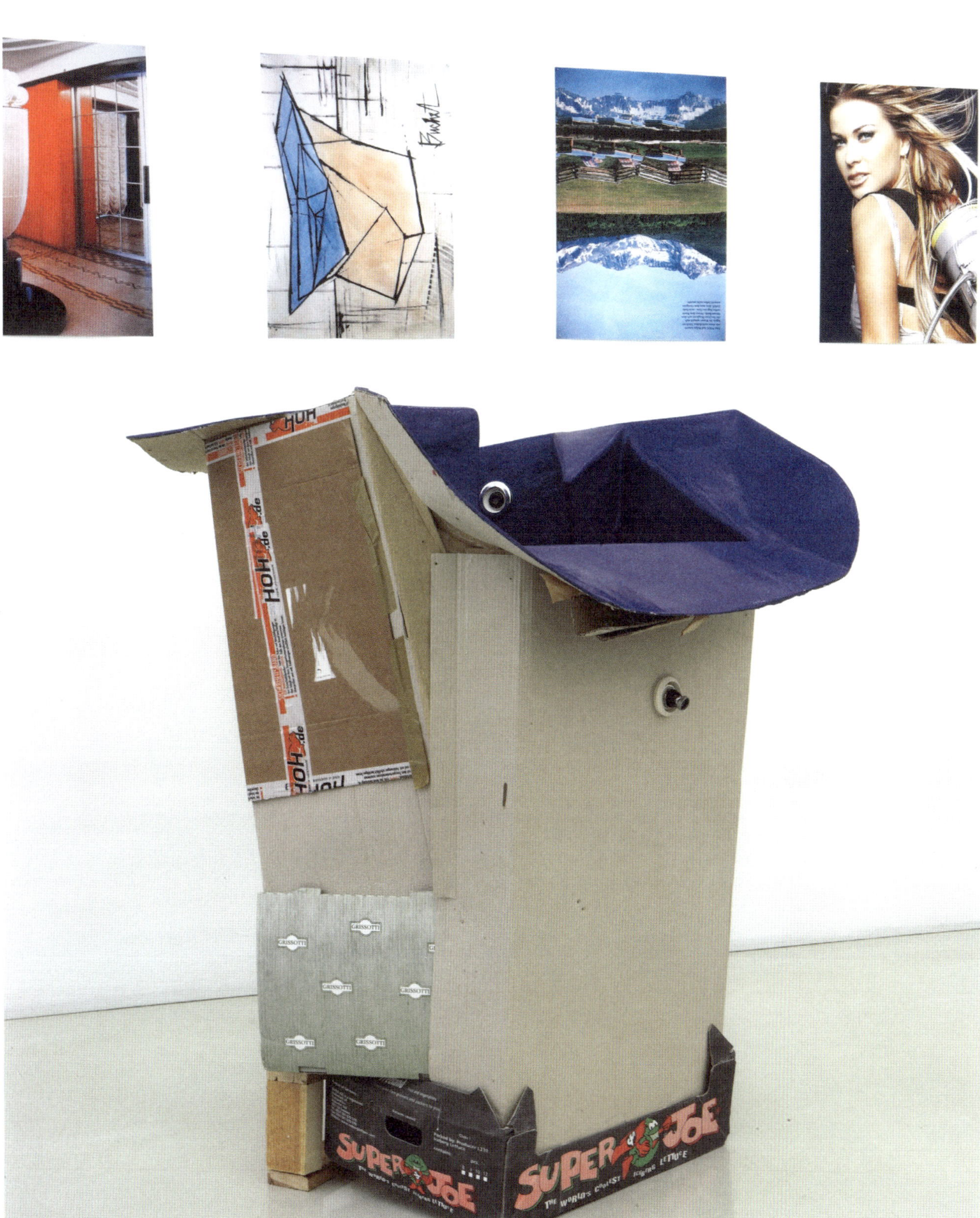

Carmen Elektra Jacuzzi 2005

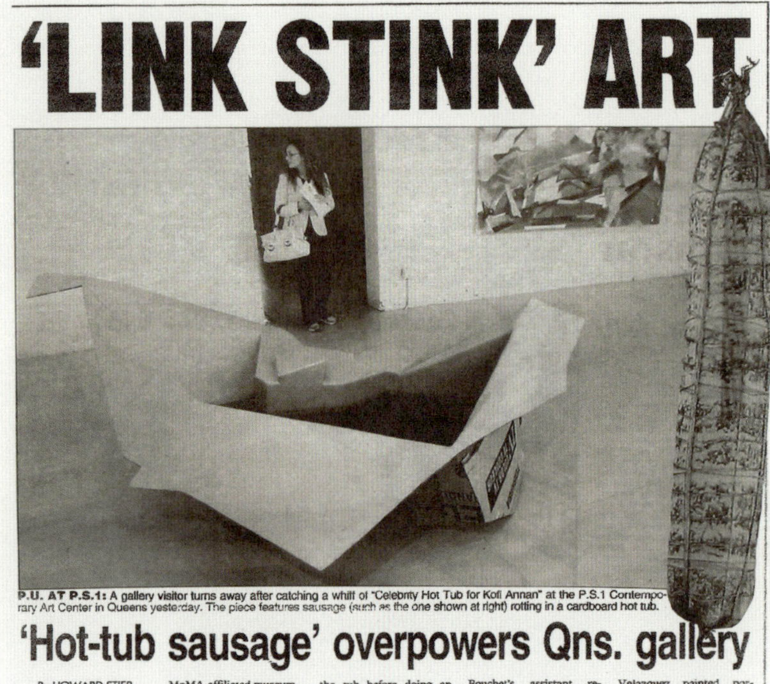

'LINK STINK' ART

P.U. AT P.S.1: A gallery visitor turns away after catching a whiff of "Celebrity Hot Tub for Kofi Annan" at the P.S.1 Contemporary Art Center in Queens yesterday. The piece features sausage (such as the one shown at right) rotting in a cardboard hot tub.

'Hot-tub sausage' overpowers Qns. gallery

By HOWARD STIER

If you think a lot of contemporary art stinks, you haven't smelled anything like a gag-inducing work that has visitors fleeing the current show at P.S.1 Contemporary Art Center in Long Island City.

Artist Mike Bouchet's odorific "Celebrity Hot Tub for Kofi Annan" sculpture — which features a rotting sausage stewing in a tub of noxious water — produces an overwhelming stench that is sickening visitors to the MoMA-affiliated museum.

No warnings are posted at "Greater New York 2005," the current show of emerging New York artists, and museum staffers nod wearily at visitors' complaints.

"The second floor? Sure it's terrible, everyone complains, someone vomited," said a staffer. "It got real bad, we didn't know you had to clean it out. The guards are really mad about this."

On a recent visit, Ista Salazer, 28, a Queens painter, didn't get within 20 feet of the tub before doing an about face, nauseated.

"I'm outta here," she said. "The smell is making the tint peel off my sunglasses."

The sculpture is a full-sized Jacuzzi fashioned from cardboard, loaded with capocollo, and left to ferment.

After installing the work, Bouchet took off for Germany, where he recently moved, without leaving instructions for maintaining the work.

Finally, after six weeks, Bouchet's assistant replaced the water and sausage, and the odor went away — but only briefly.

"It should be in a room by itself," said Williamsburg photographer Tanyth Berkeley, 35, whose portraits of young women hang steps away from the tub. "He knew this was going to happen. I mean you put a piece of meat in open water, it's going to rot."

Reached for comment in Switzerland, Bouchet, 34, compared himself to the Old Masters. "As much as Velazquez painted portraits of his royal patrons, I am making works for contemporary celebrities," he wrote in an e-mail.

When pressed, he admitted, "I assumed that the salami would probably emit odor."

The show remains open through Sept. 22.

Fans of Bouchet can also catch a whiff of his work at Chinatown's Maccarone Inc. gallery, where he has mixed tons of soil and composted human waste generated by Rikers Island inmates.

THE NEW YORK POST   June 3, 2005

NY Post Article 2005

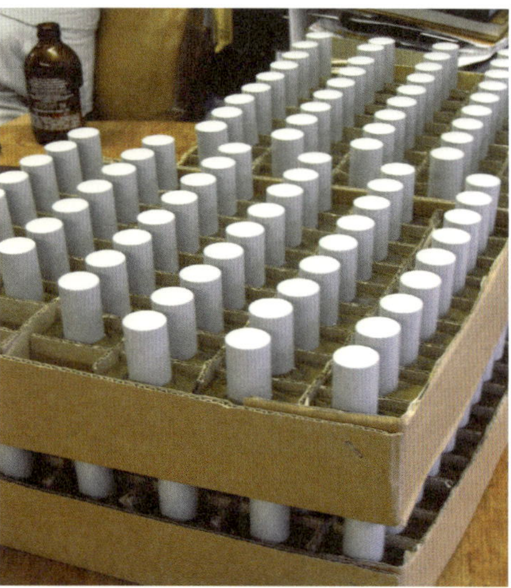

Kofi Annan Sweet Cappacola Water 2005

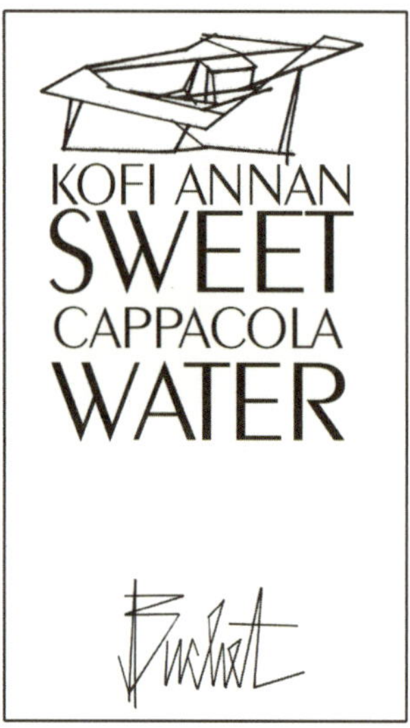

**Kofi Annan Sweet Cappacola Water
Label Design** 2005

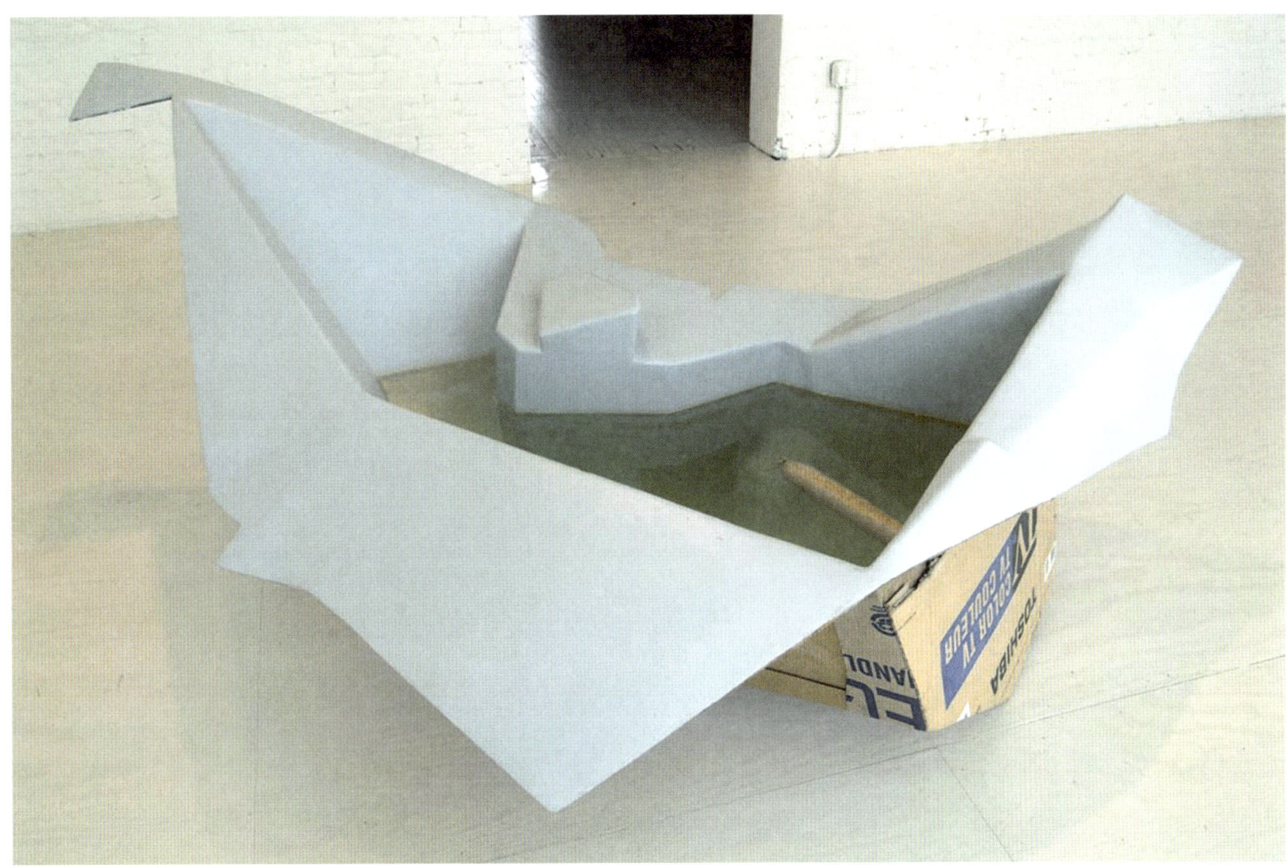

Kofi Annan Jacuzzi 2003
Installation view, P. S. 1, New York City

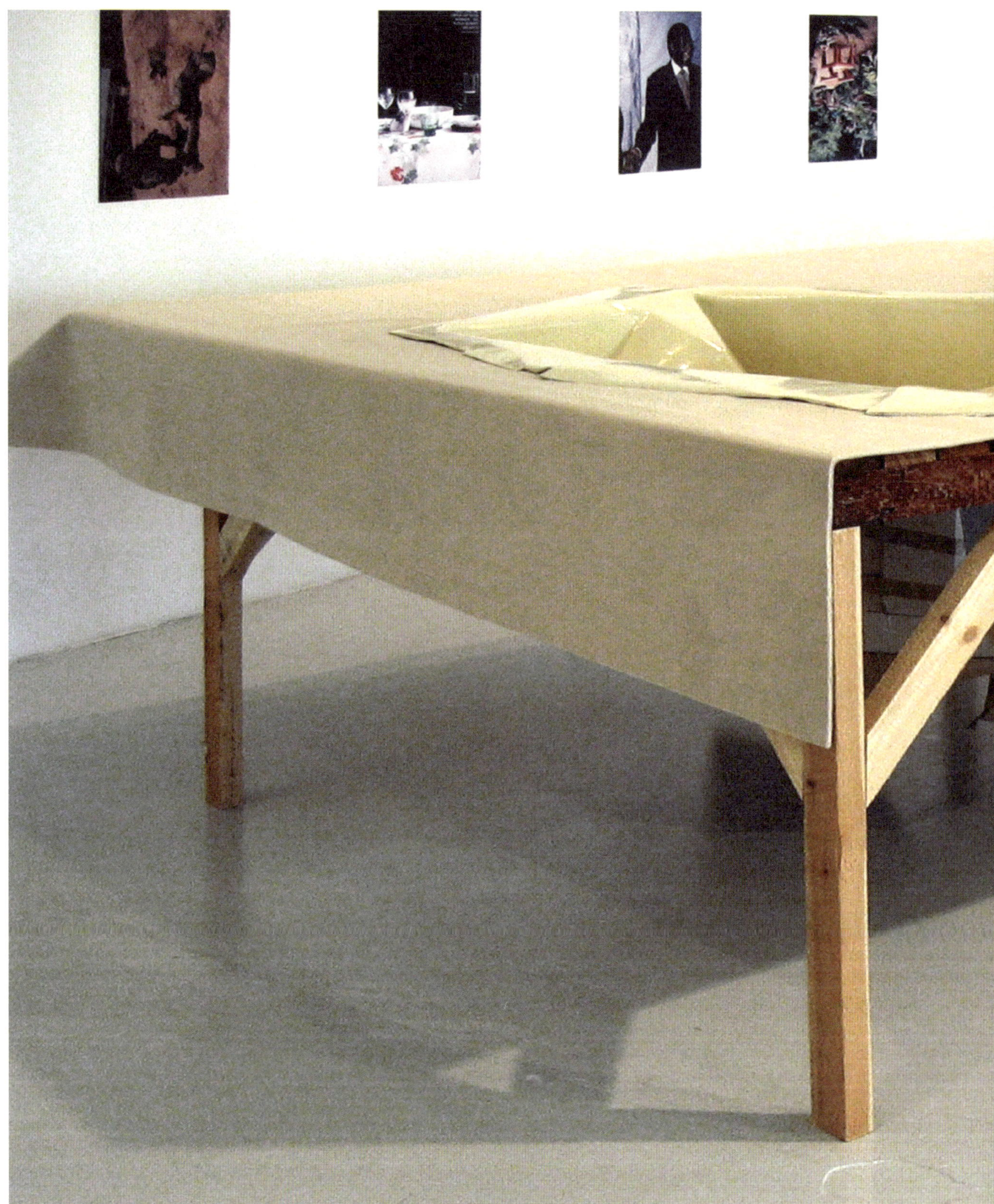

Tatjana Gsell Jacuzzi 2005
Installation view, Kunstraum Innsbruck, Austria

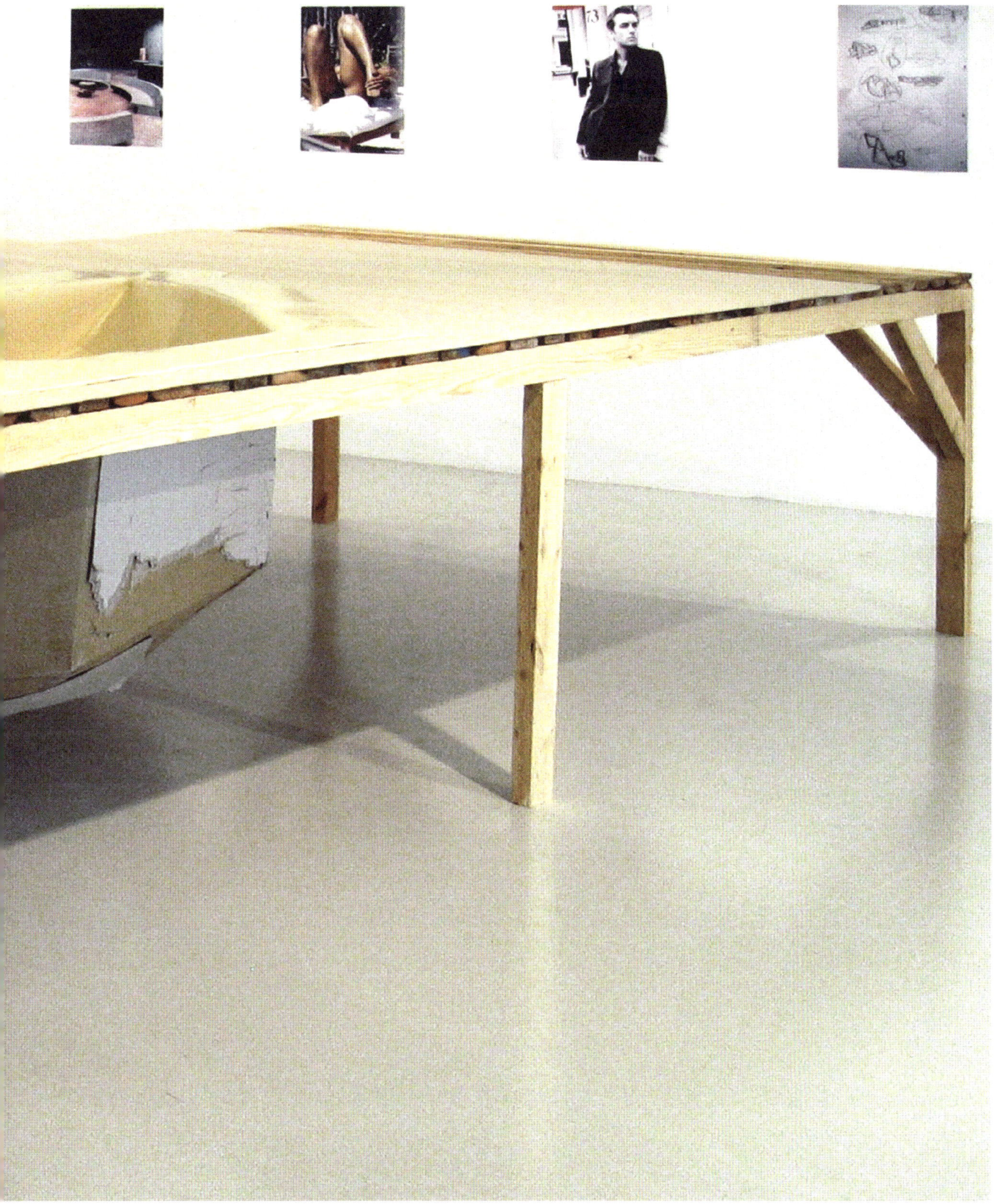

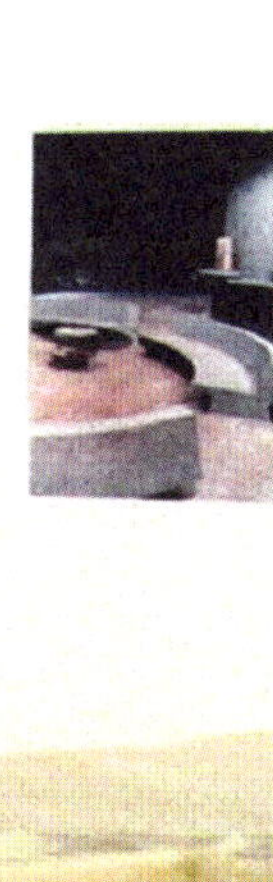
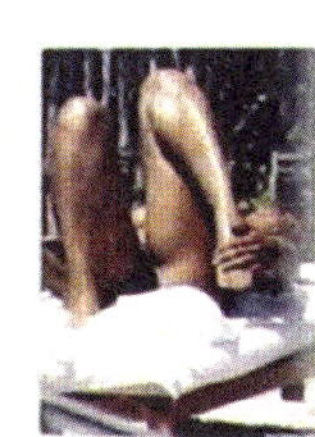
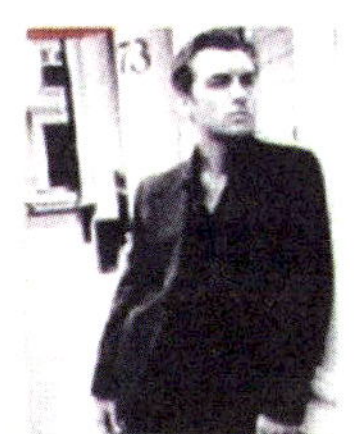
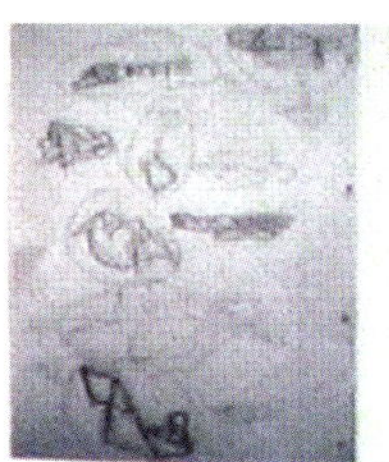

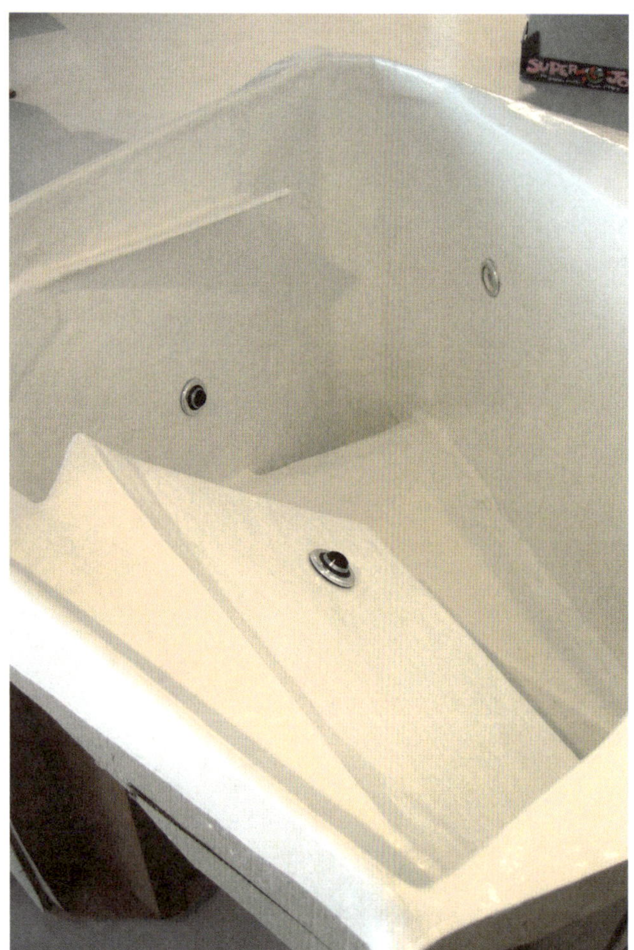

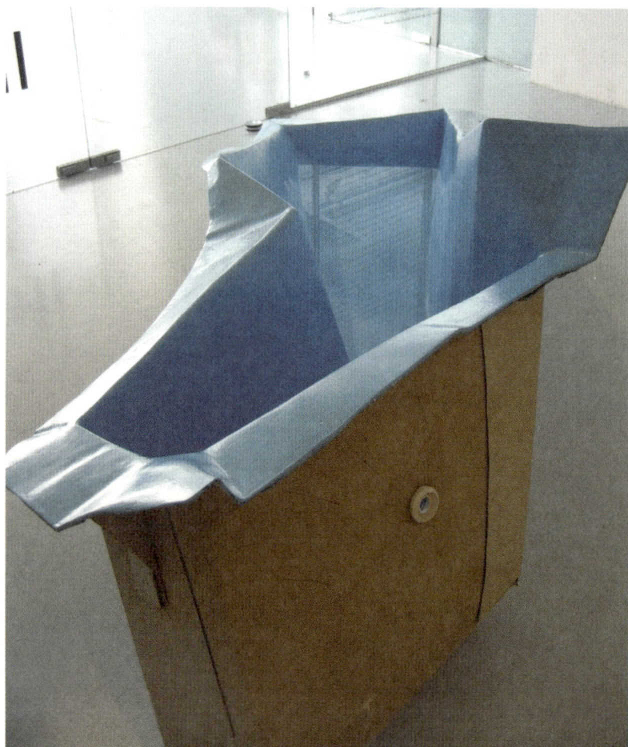

Jack Welch Jacuzzi 2005

Jude Law Jacuzzi 2005
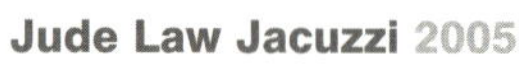
Interior detail

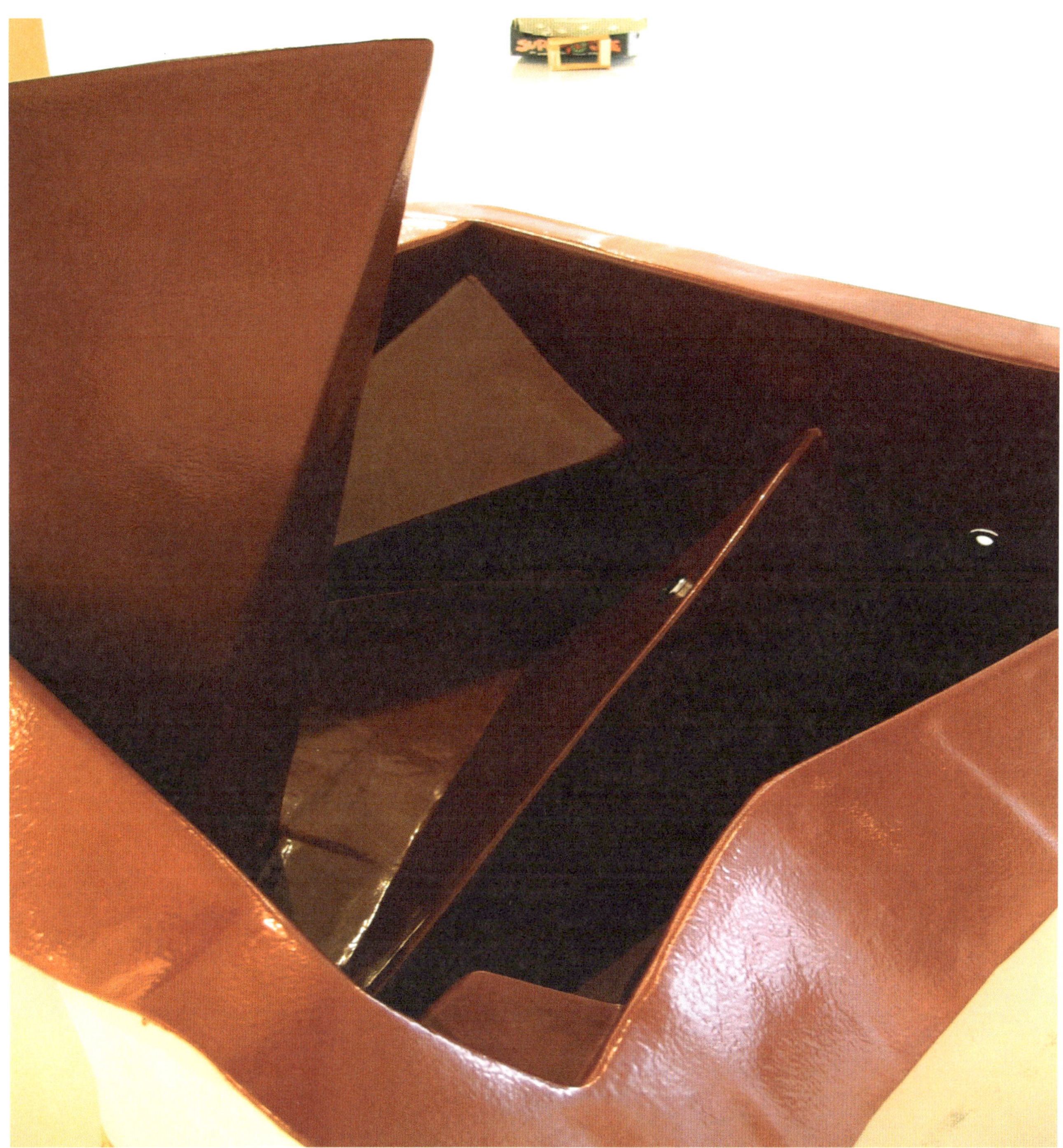

Robert Mugabe Jacuzzi 2005
Interior Detail

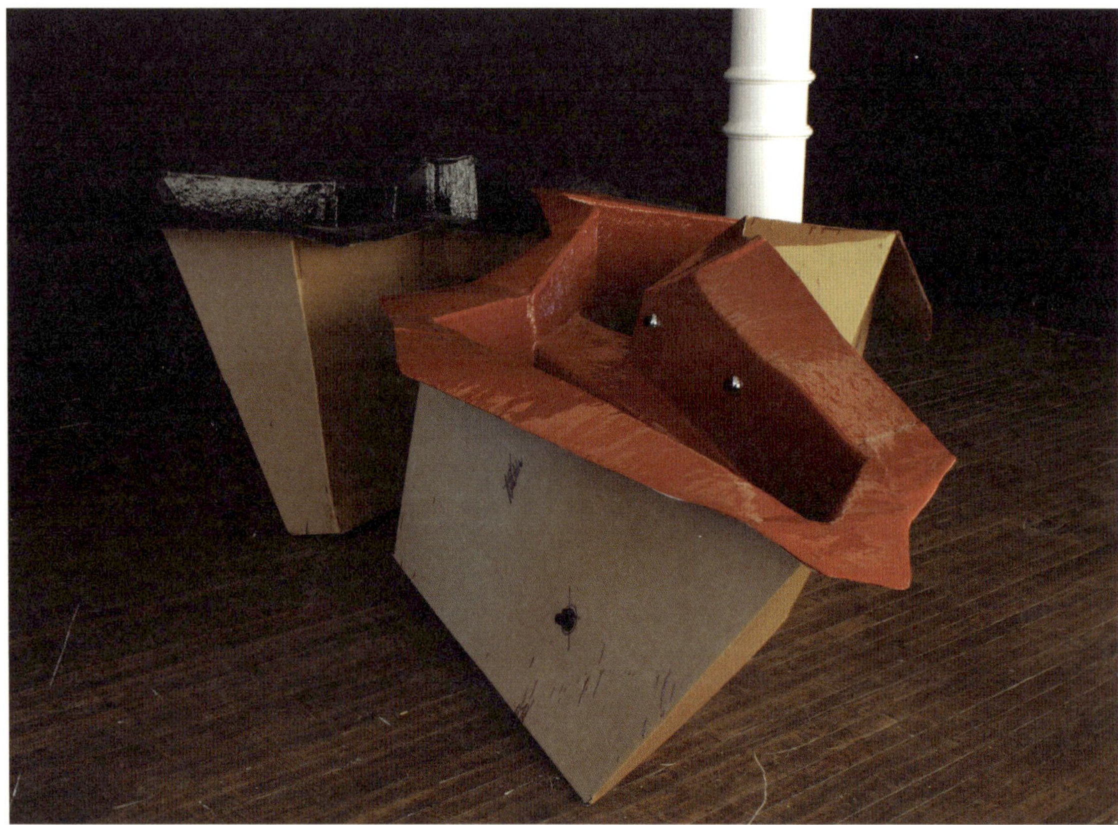

Banks/Khadaffi Jacuzzi (left), Derek Jeter Jacuzzis (right) 2006
Installation view, Swiss Institute, New York City

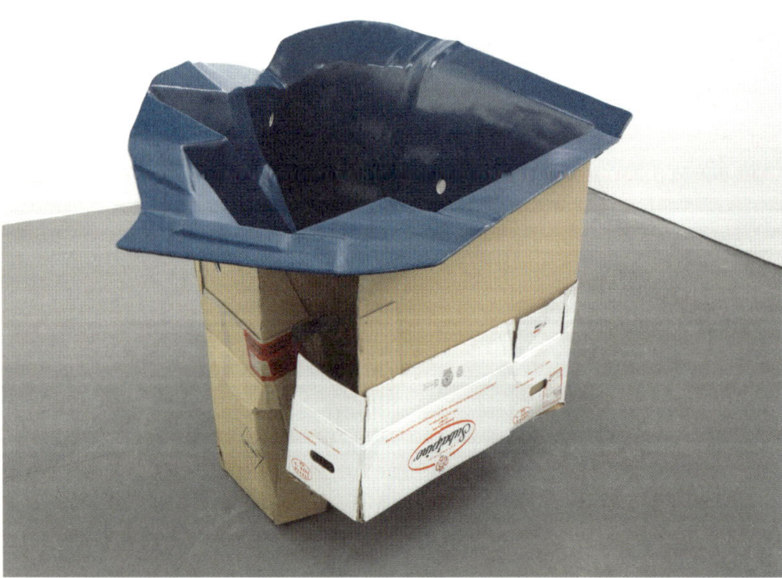

Lionel Ritchie Jacuzzi 2007

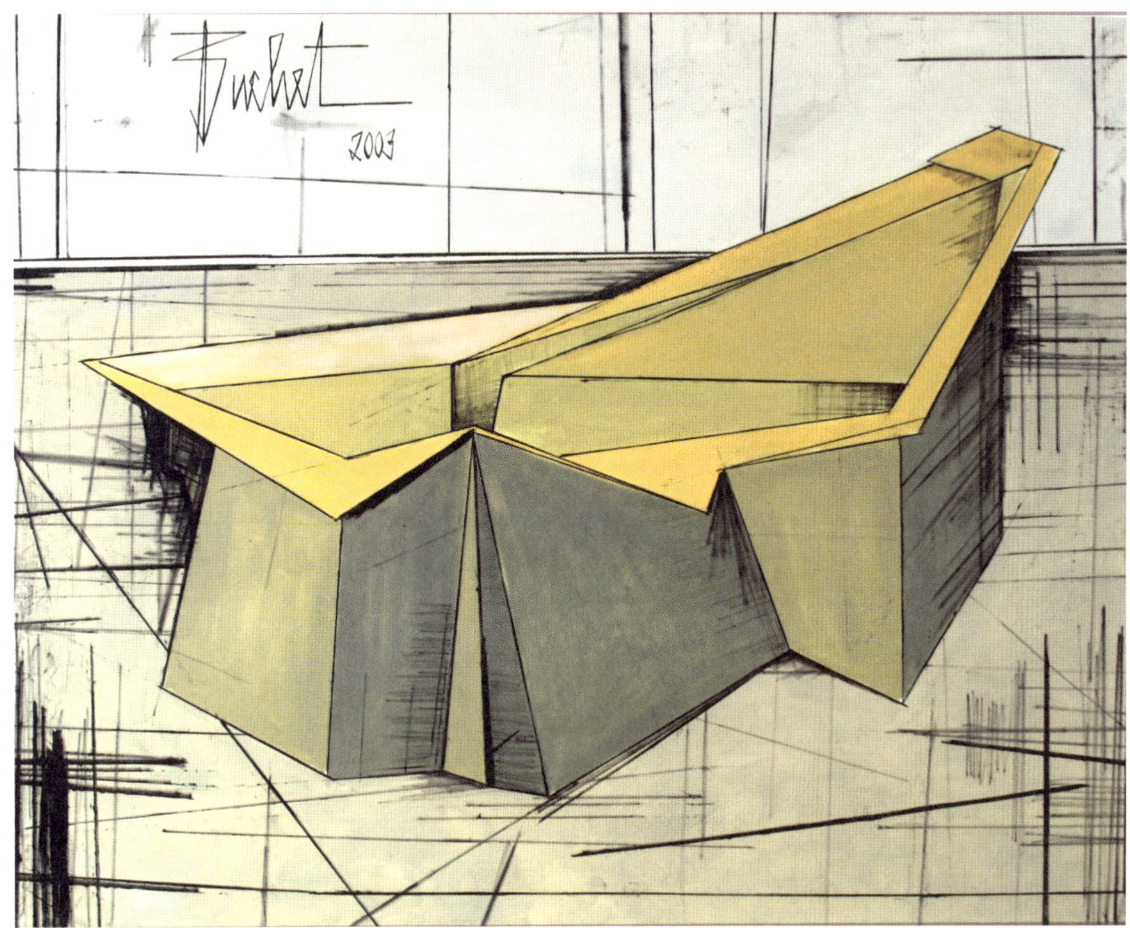

Carly Fiorina 2003

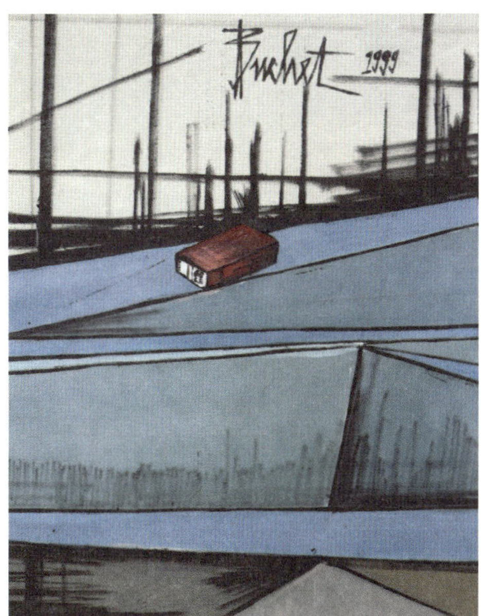

S. Penn 1999

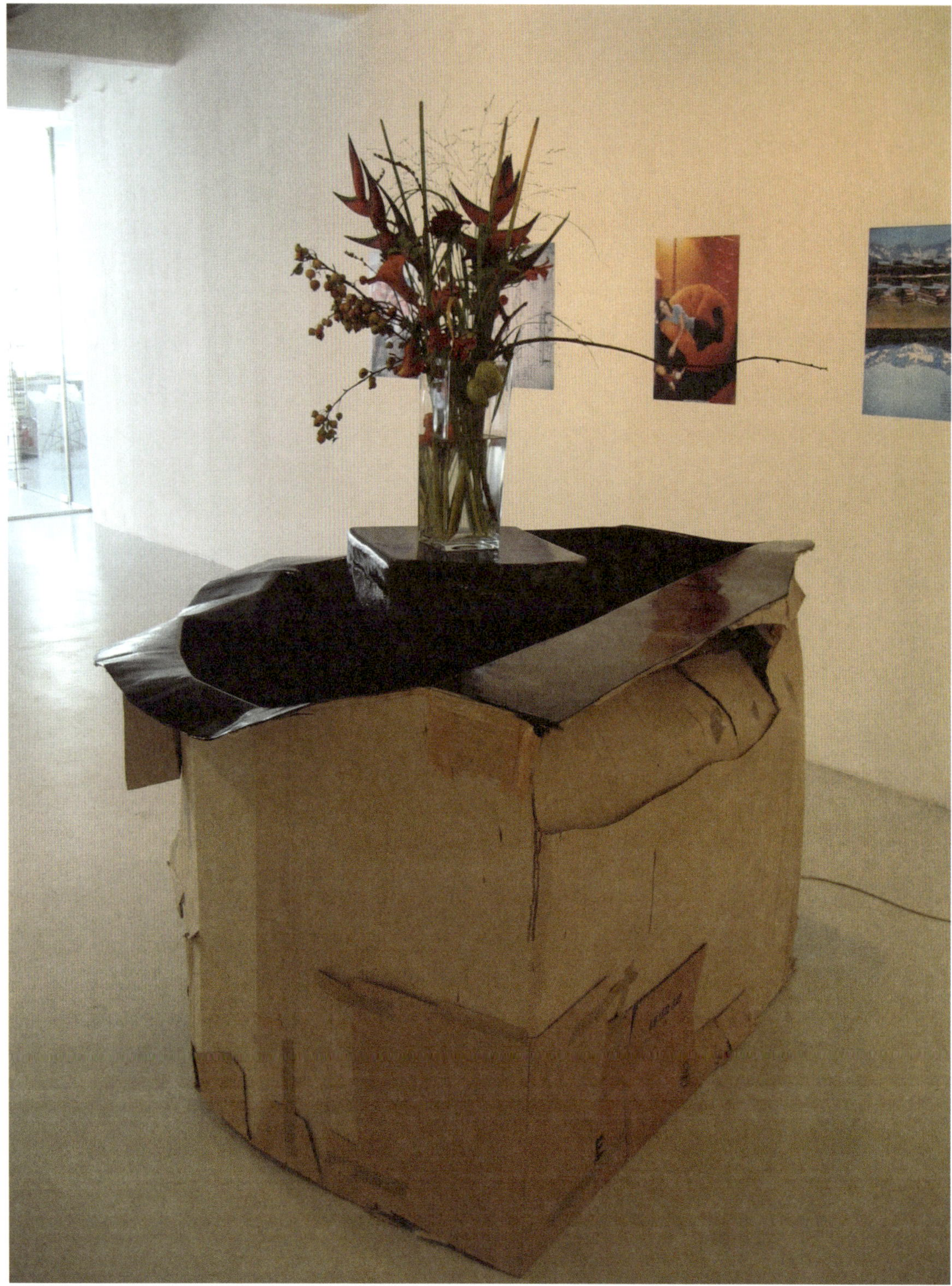

K. Lagerfeld Jacuzzi 2006
Installation view, Kunstraum Innsbruck, Austria

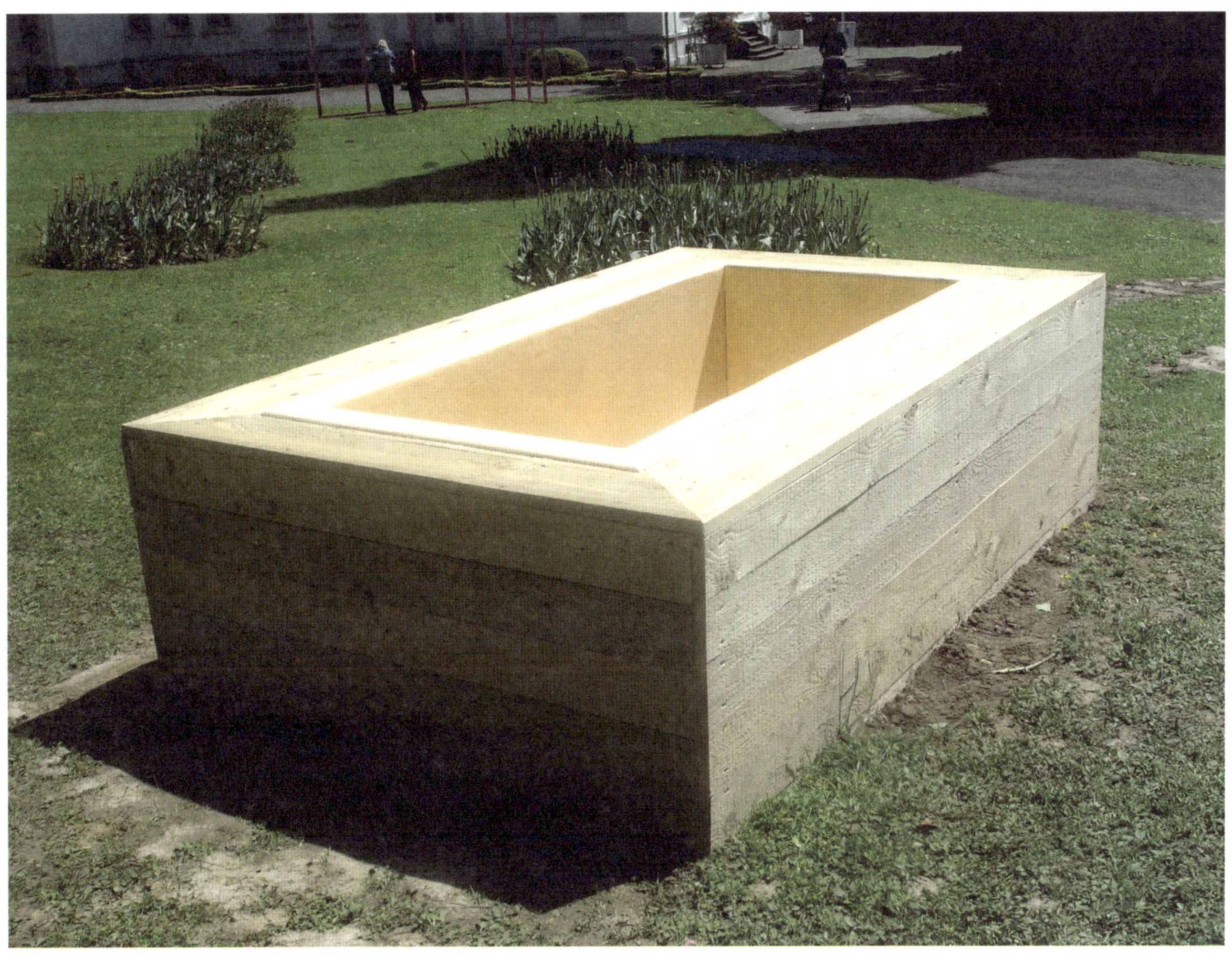

Schwarzenegger Jacuzzi 2006
Installation view, K.F.L., Skulpturenpark, Lahr, Germany

Tapestry Cartoons 2005 –

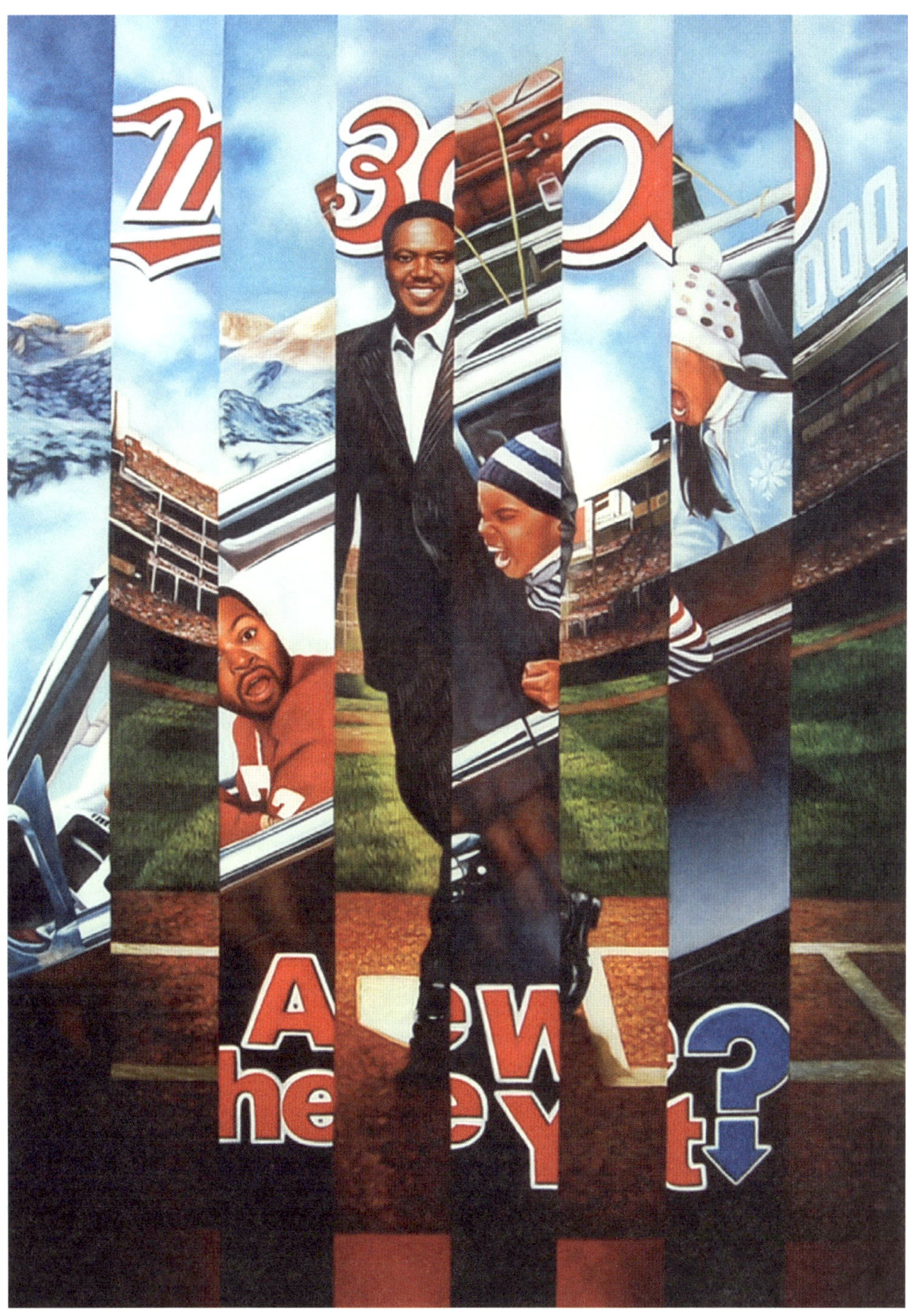

These tapestry cartoon oil paintings, produced by professional painters, are enlarged copies of collages made by the artist. Bouchet makes these collages using original feature film posters.

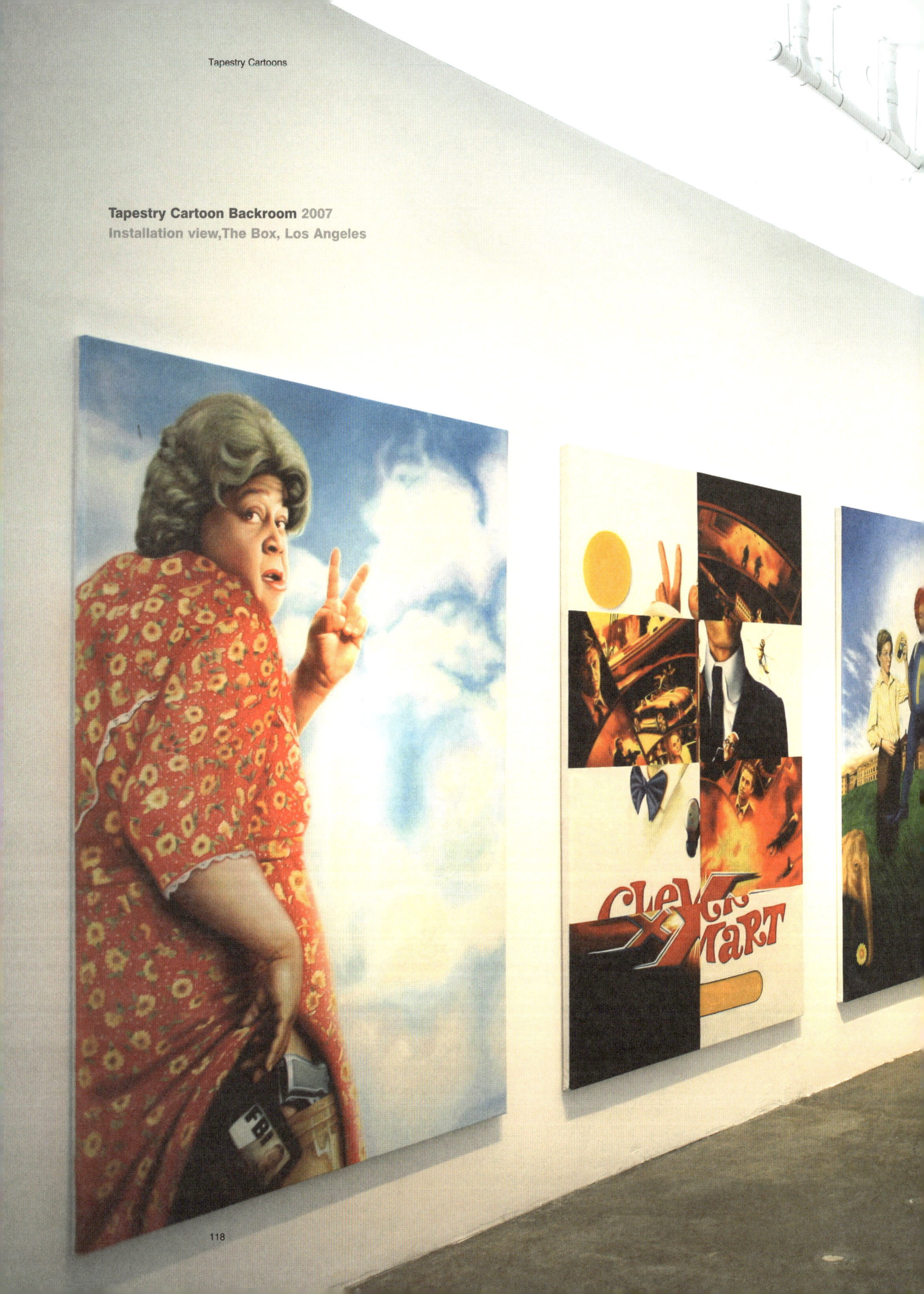

Tapestry Cartoon Backroom 2007
Installation view, The Box, Los Angeles

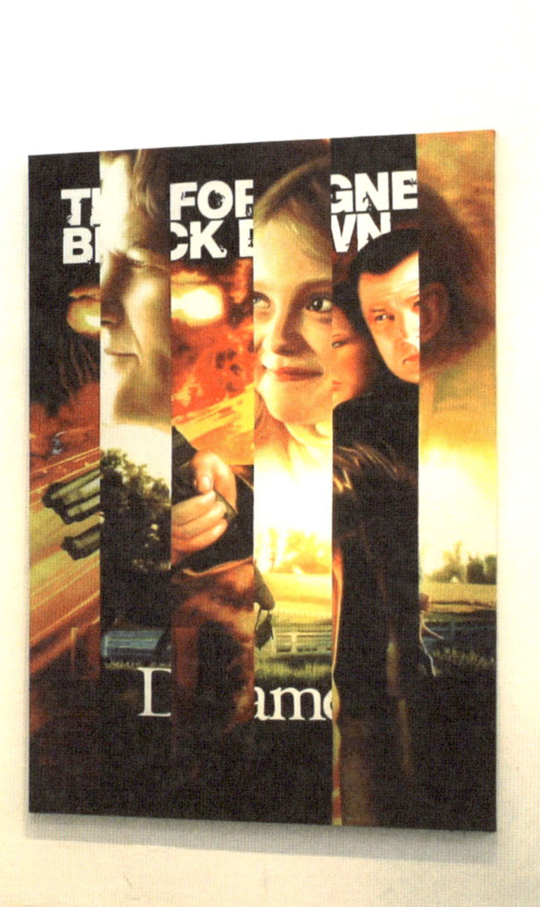
TH FOR GNE
B CK B WN
D amo

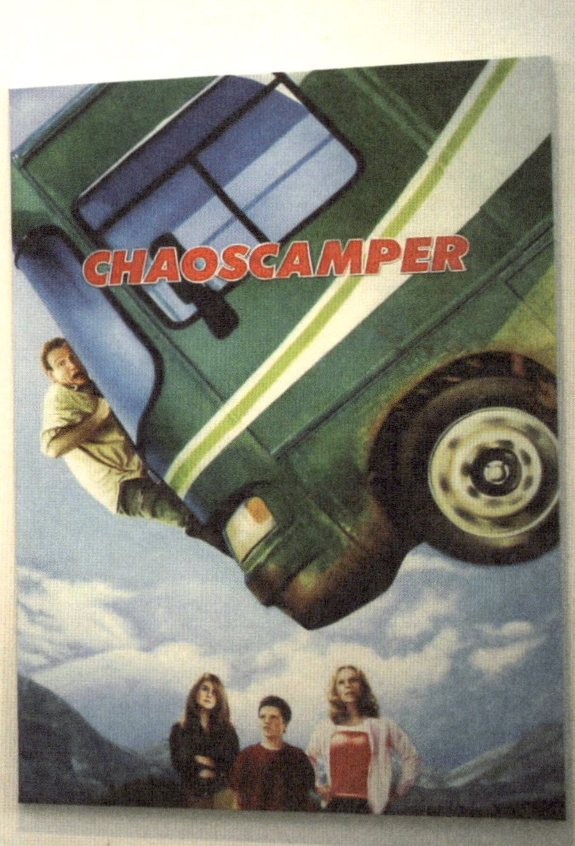
CHAOSCAMPER

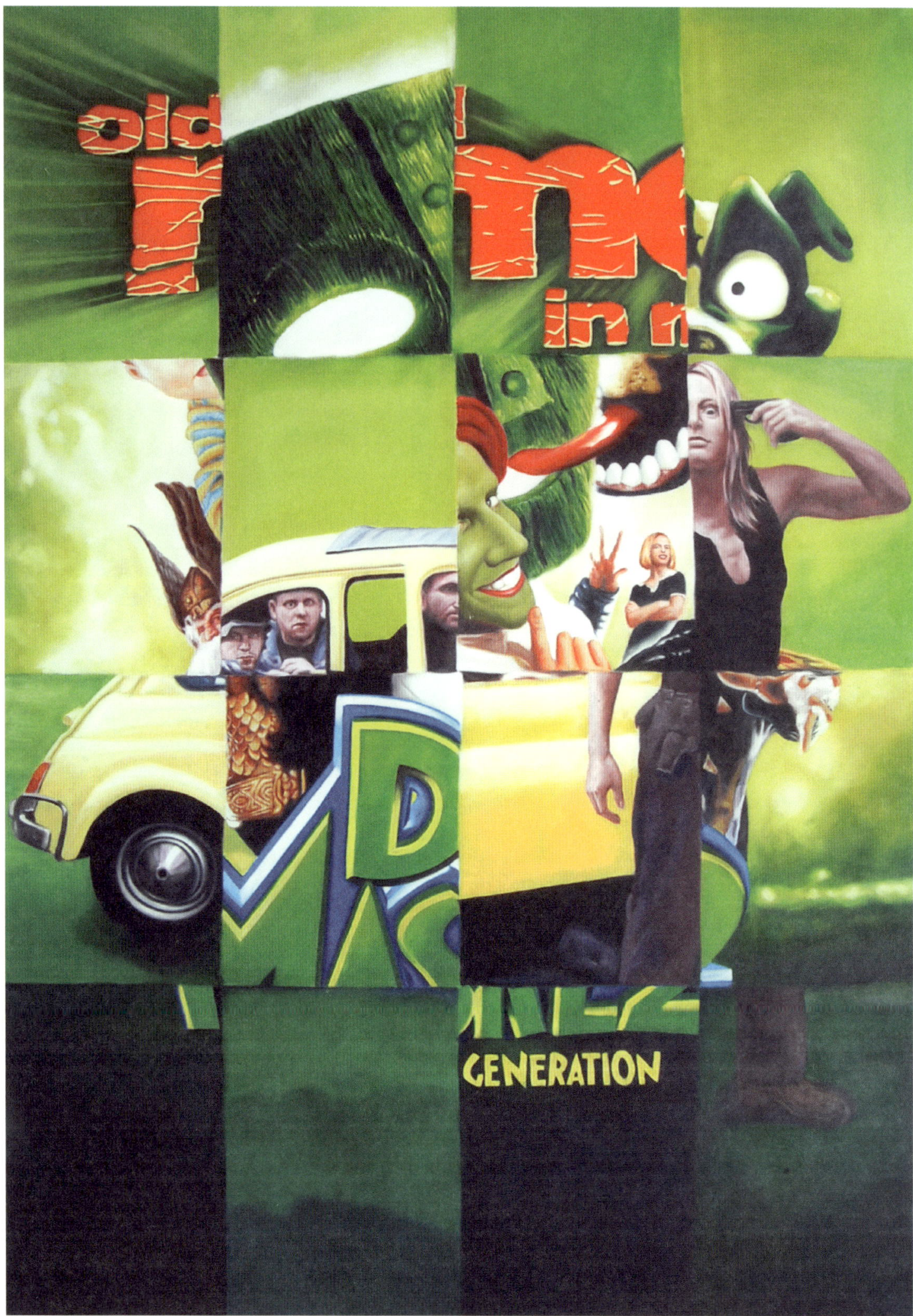

Green Mask 2006

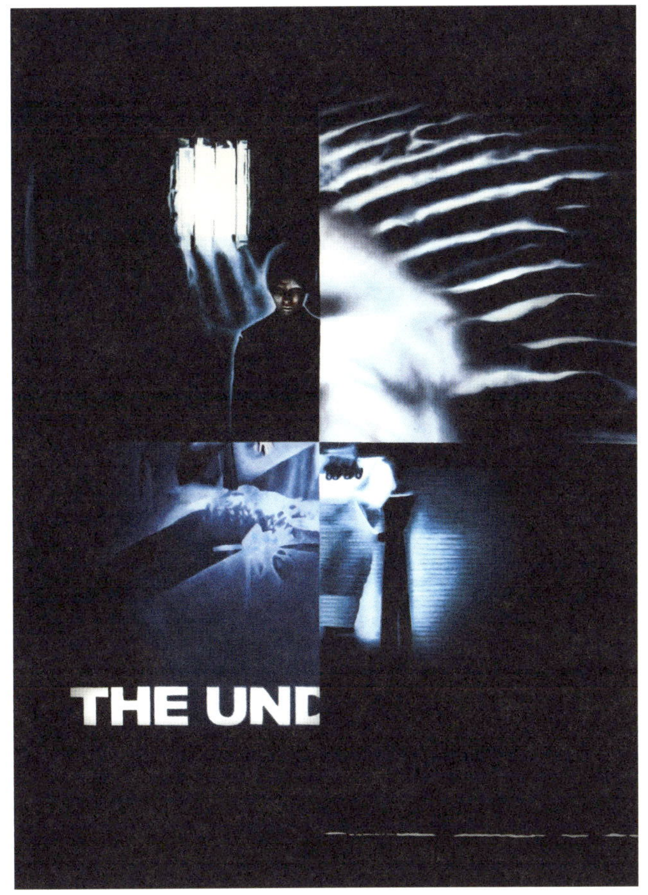

Cool Kids 2006

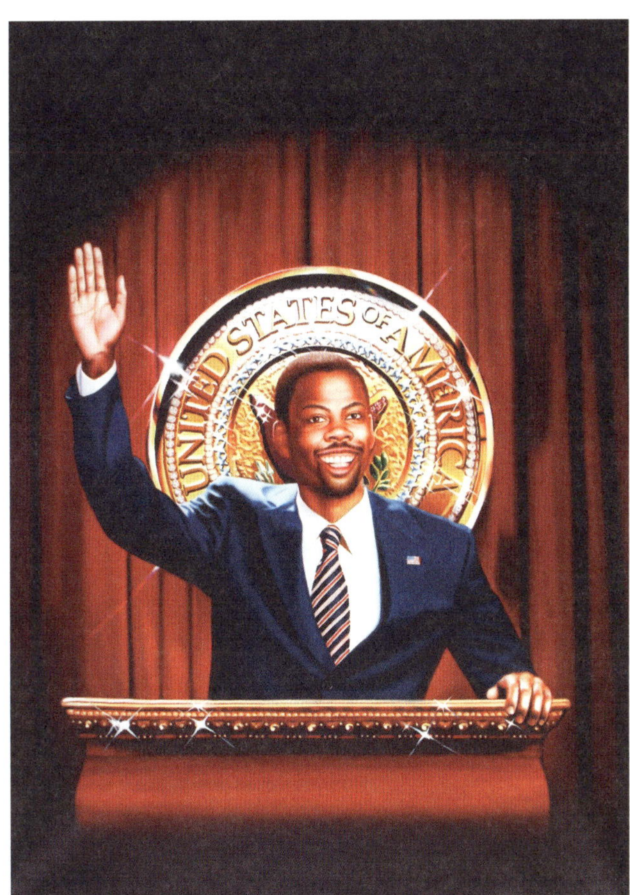

Black President 2006

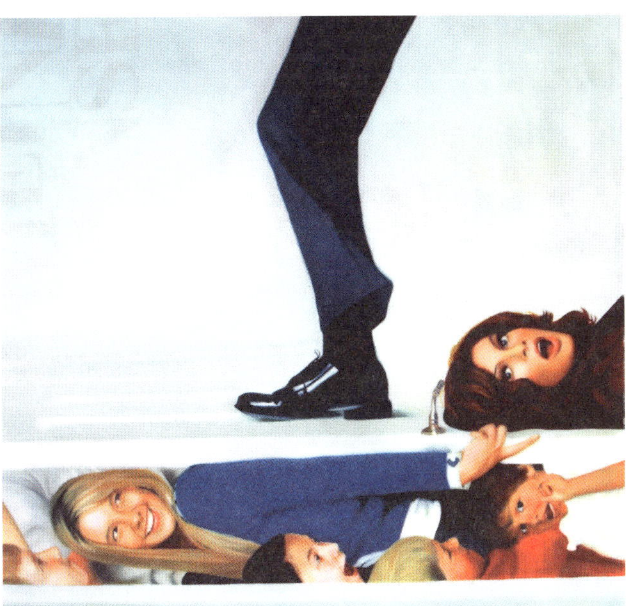

Family Foot 2008

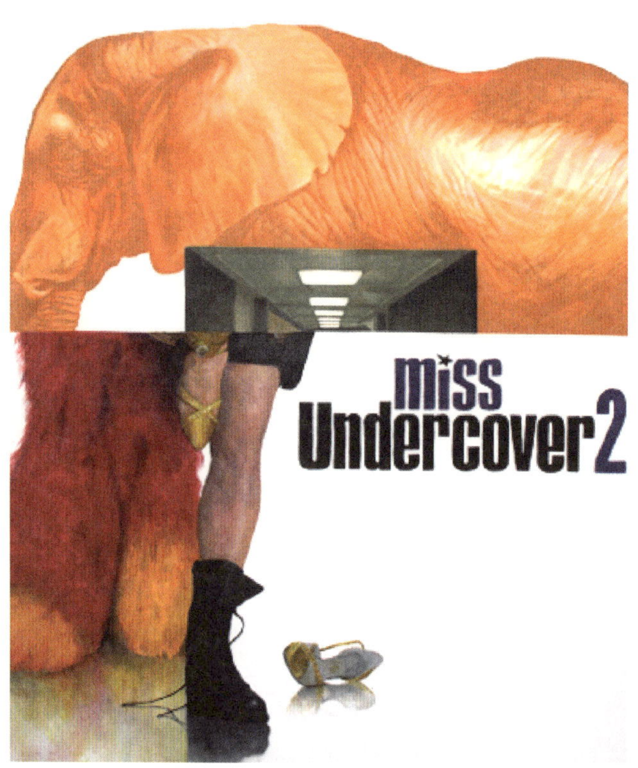

Elephant Miss Undercover 2 2006

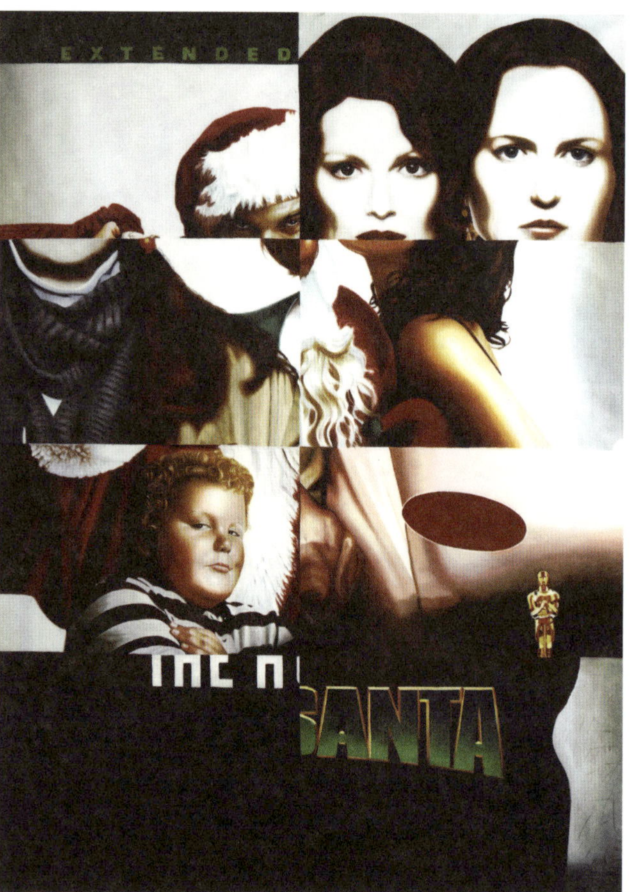

Extended Bad Hours 2006

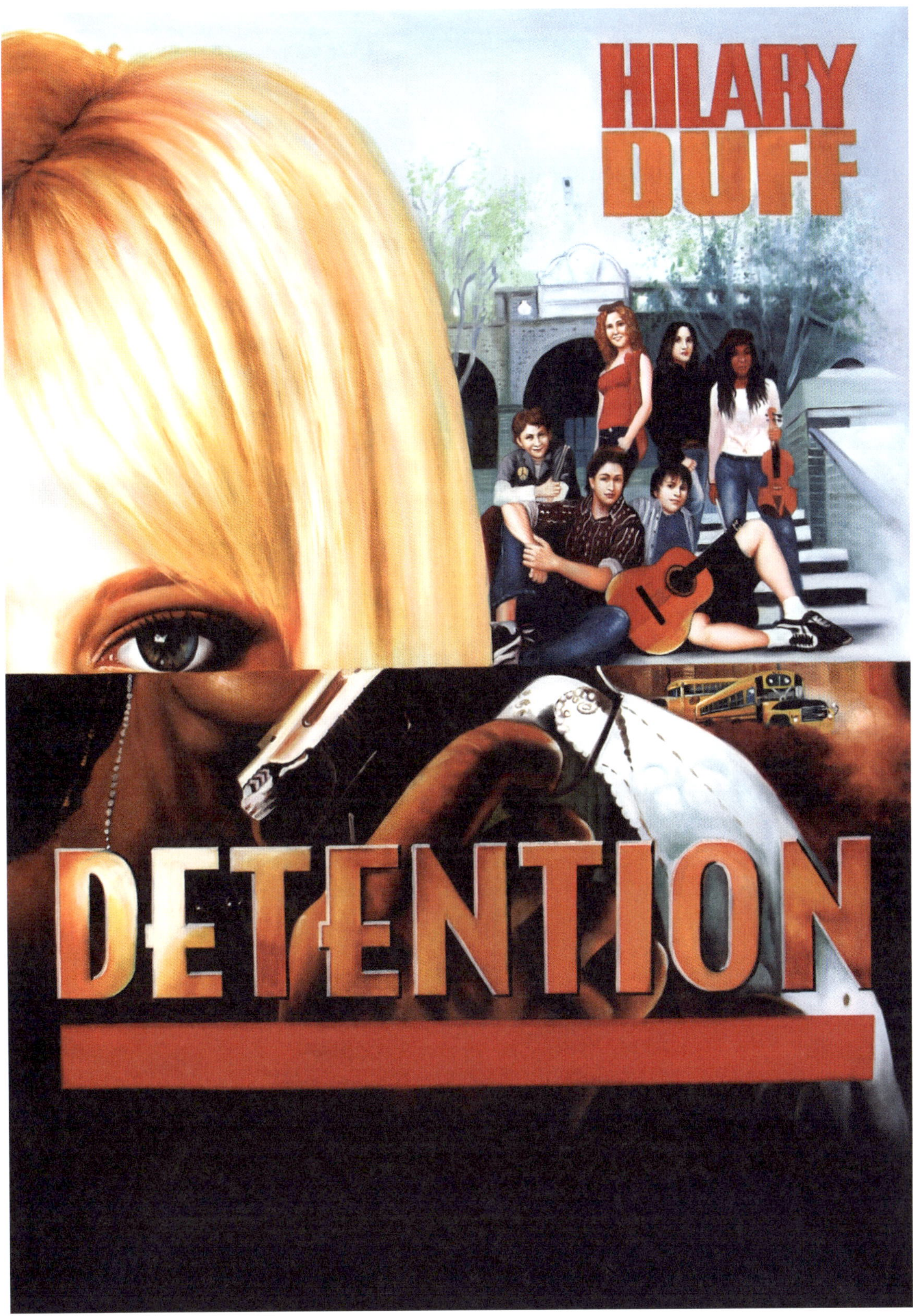

Duff Detention 2006

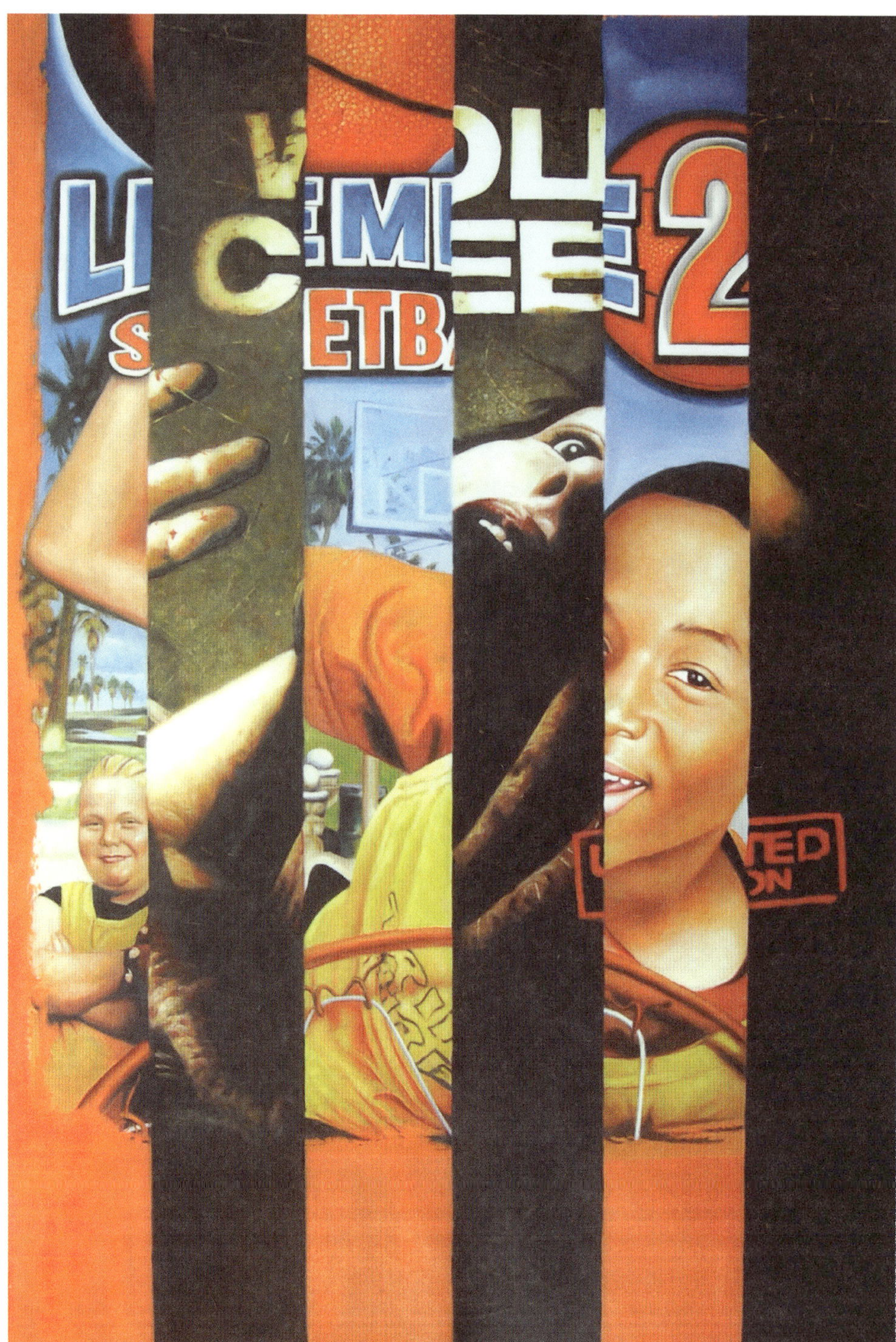

Triple Wolf Ball 2007

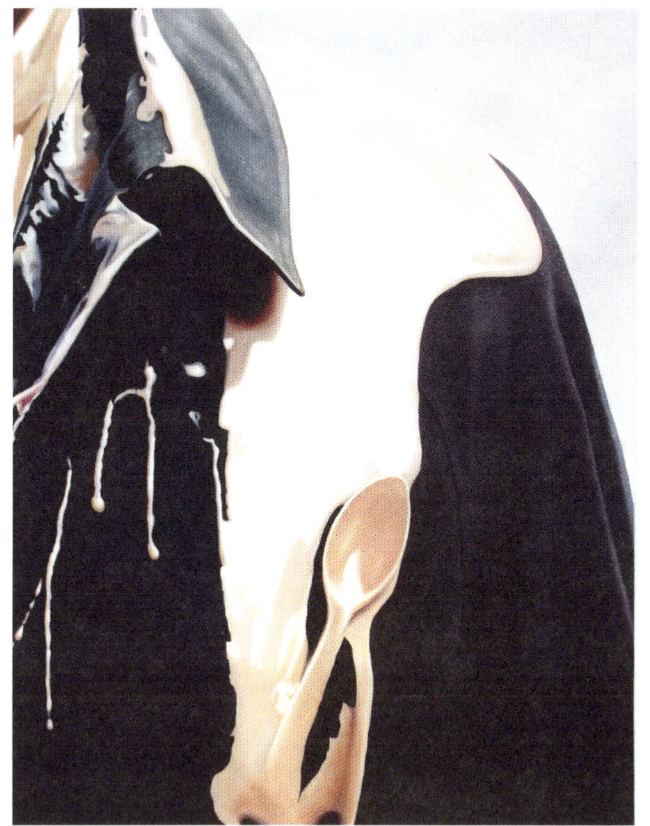

Spill 2007

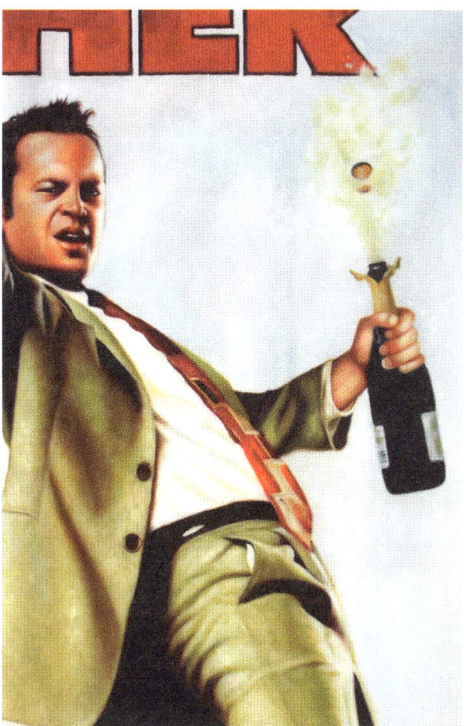

Release 2008

Peer Pressure 2008

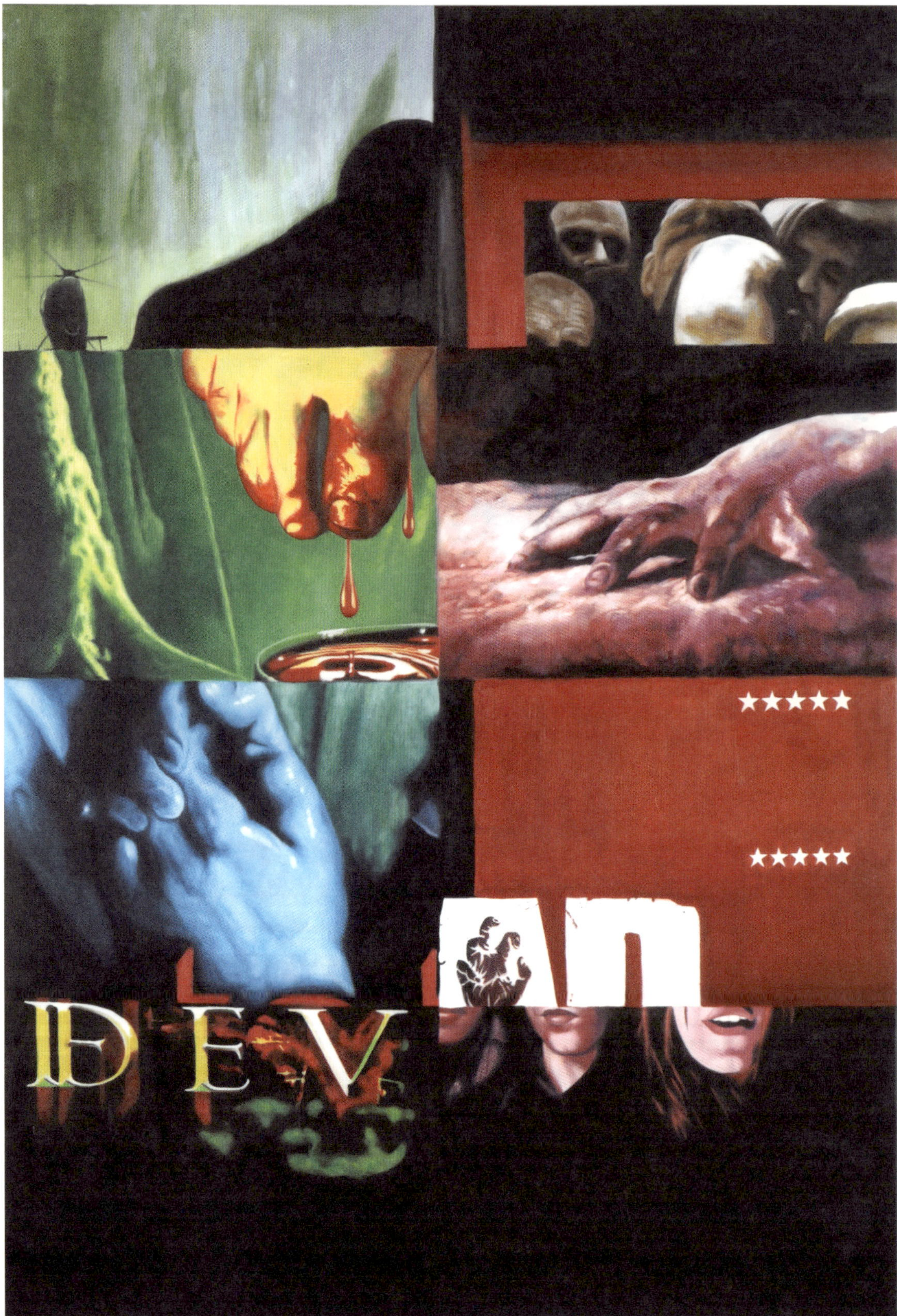

Red Green Six 2006

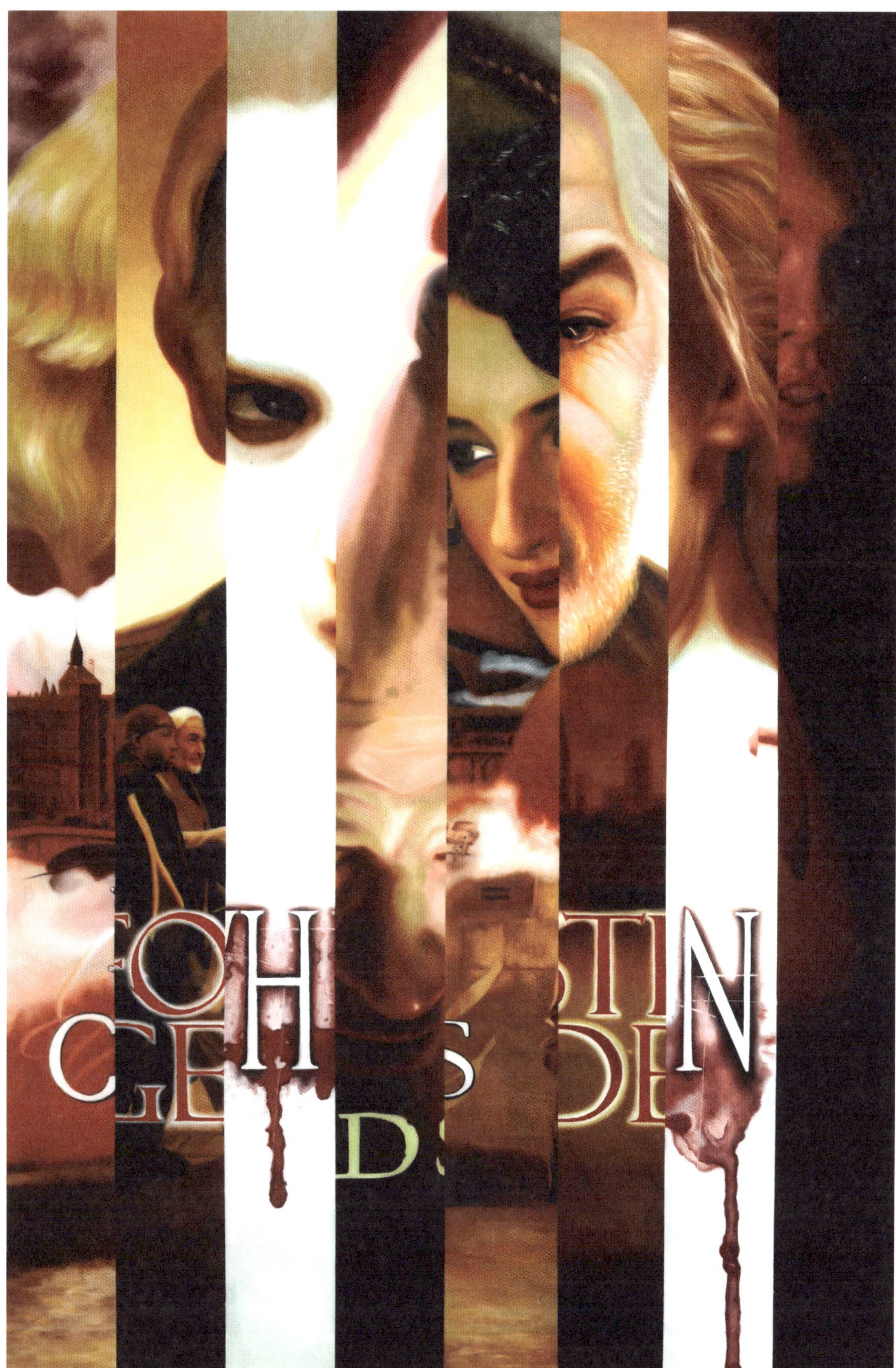

HeadForestChildSkin 2005

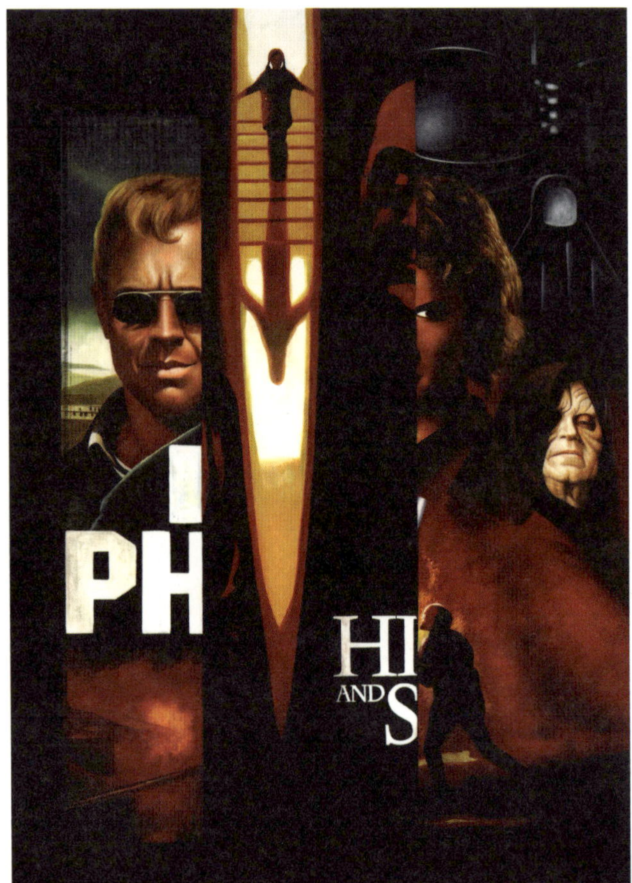

Dark Lords 2006

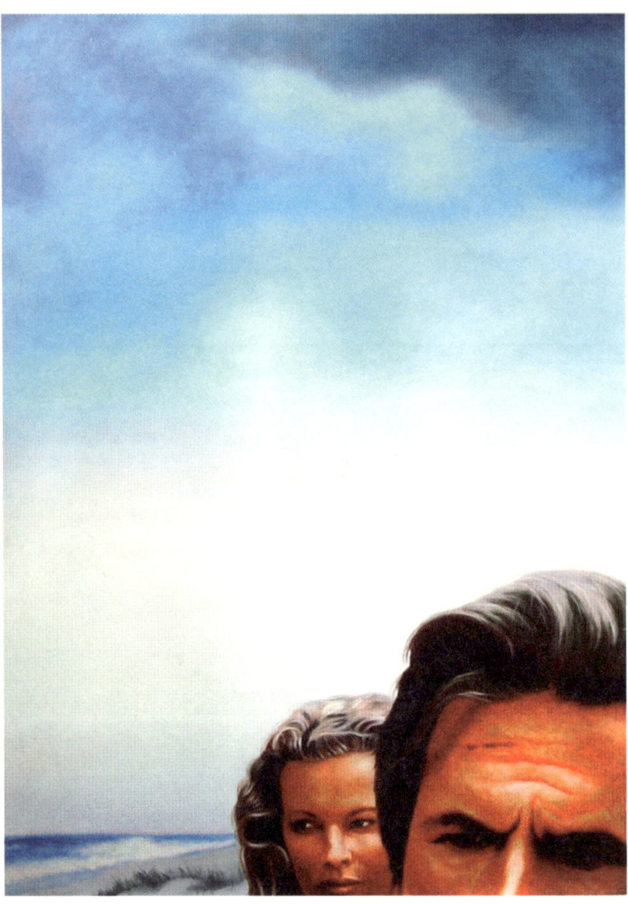

Door In The Floor 2007

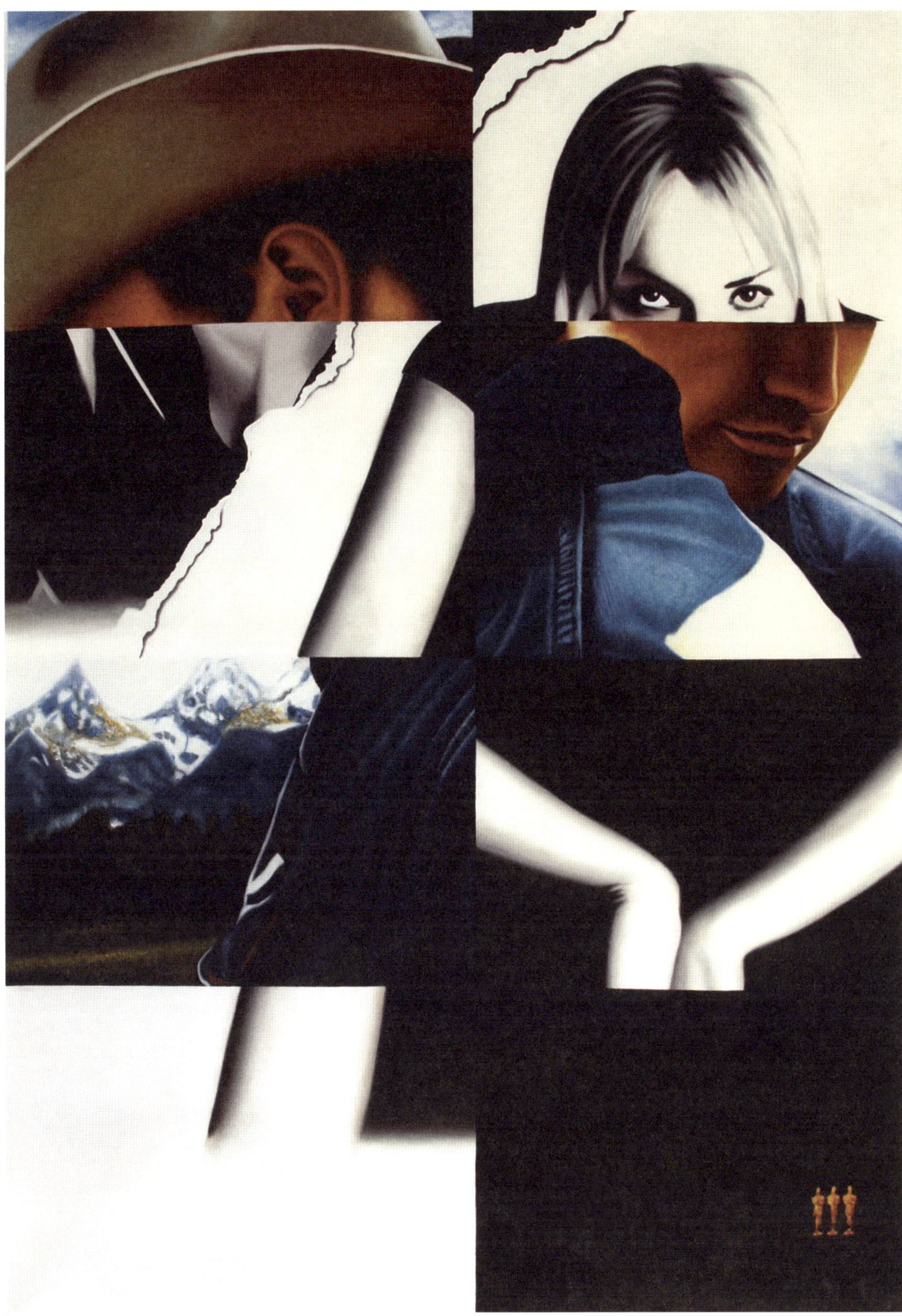

Broke Instinct 2008

Fat Slices and Conscious Primers 2007

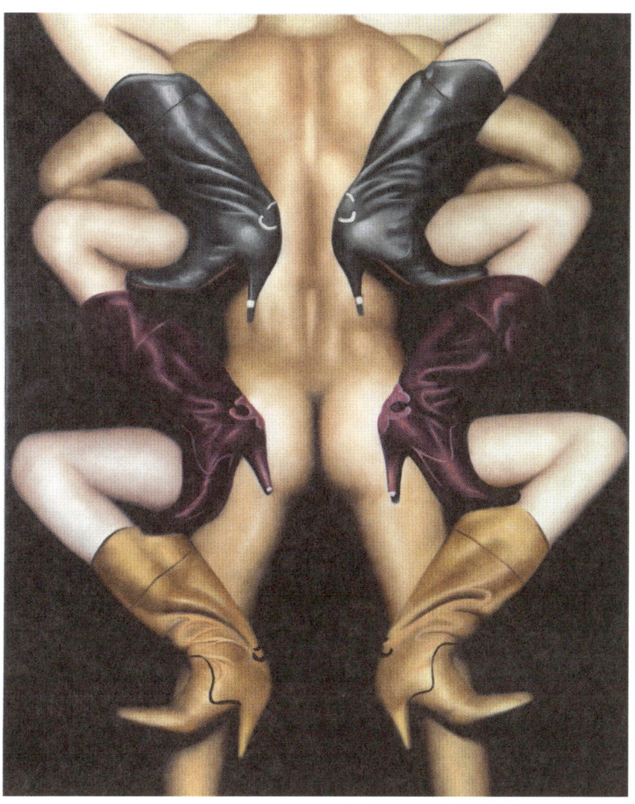

"The title of this body of work addresses two popular topics in Behavioural Psychology today: Thin Slicing and Unconscious Priming. Thin Slicing involves the close monitoring of a subject's facial expressions, palm humidity, body language and temperatures in order to determine the way in which rapid cognitive actions and decisions are made. Unconscious Priming is the process by means of which unconscious motives impact the conscious decision-making process. This work attempts to dwell in the liminal space between consciousness and unconsciousness, the space from which habitual or spontaneous actions arise. It specifically targets the way in which the sexual energies of teen and young adult populations the world over are being channeled, observed, and even „farmed" in popular culture.

As with the participants of the dating shows screened in black and white slow motion, these are generations whose spontaneous actions, including mannerisms of speech and gesture, are shaped and molded by a complex layering of cultural influences. Moreover, rather than assert control over them, popular media incites them towards types of behavior strikingly similar to those espoused by Wilhelm Reich and his followers, a figure whose impact on contemporary culture is well-known. In that respect, the spectacle that is youth in our time is one whose underlying philosophy bears a striking affinity to some of the more radical social, aesthetic, and sexual experiments of the previous century. The difference is that while the latter sought emancipation by means of these experiments, we are content to engage with them solely as entertainment, and to be lulled by them into an increasingly complacent acceptance of „the way things are." In that respect, inasmuch as these processes are unconsciously primed, what they circumvent is not simply our awareness, but also our capacity for reflection and critical thought, as well as the capacity for making other, less spontaneous, yet ultimately far more liberating decisions."

The installation consisted of a 3x3 meter bed, with a hole in its center, through which one could watch muted, slowed-down edits of episodes of popular teenage dating shows. Around it were a series of text pieces, consisting of disconcertingly sober layouts of lyrics from popular rap and R&B songs, as well as several commercially produced paintings, employing imagery that was conceptually related to the other works in the show.

Fat Slices and Conscious Primers 2007
Installation view, MC, Los Angeles

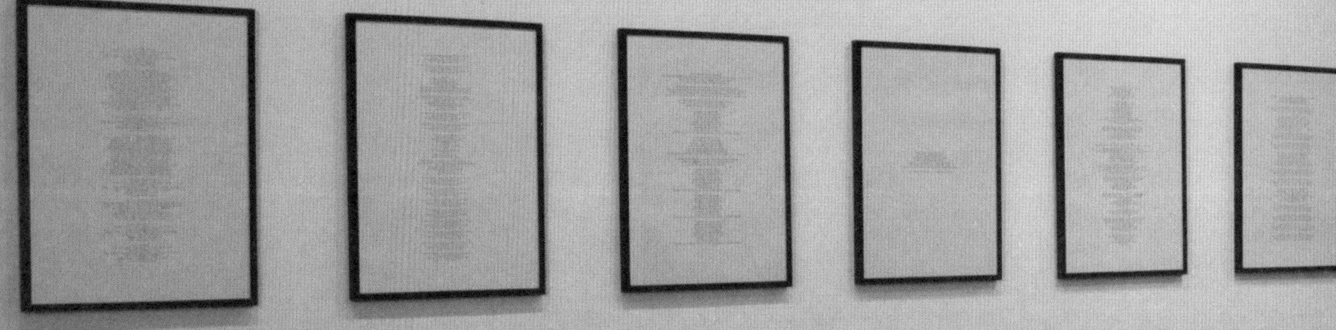

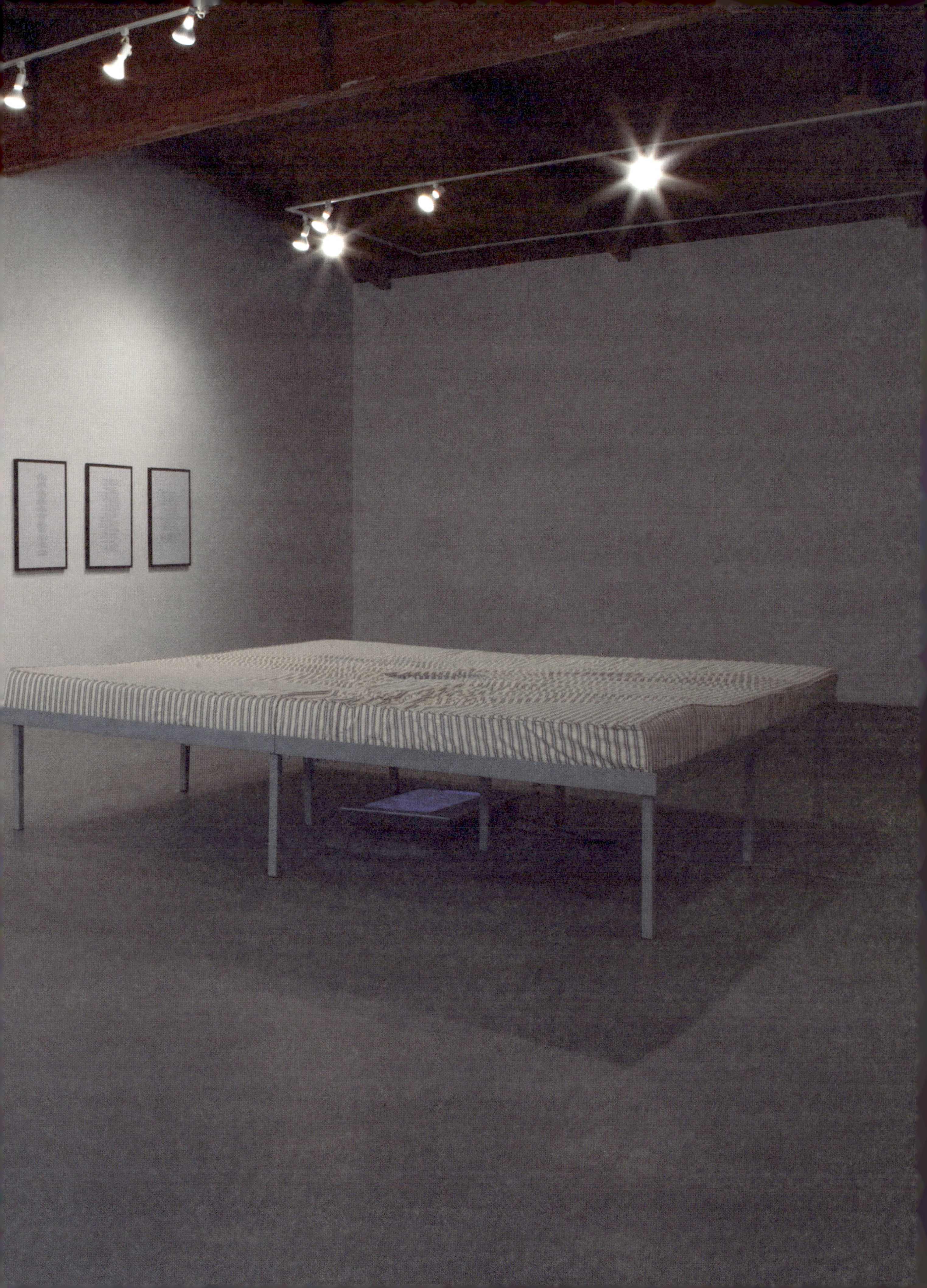

Convict...convict...convict
Convict...music
And you know we up front

I see you winding and grinding up on that pole
I know you see me looking at you and you already know
I wanna fuck you, fuck you, you already know
I wanna fuck you, fuck you, you already know girl

Money in the air as more fell grad you by your coat tail
Take you to the motel, ho sale, don't tell, won't tell
Baby said I don't talk Dogg but she told on me, oh well
Take a picture with me, what the flick gon' do
Baby stick to me and I'ma stick on you
If you pick me then I'ma pick on you
D-O-double G and I'm here to put this dick on you
I'm stuck on pussy and your's is right
Rip ridinin' them poles and them doors is tight
And I'ma get me a shot for the end of the night
Cuz pussy is pussy and baby ya pussy for life

I see you winding and grinding up on that pole
I know you see me looking at you and you already know
I wanna fuck you, fuck you, you already know
I wanna fuck you, fuck you, you already know girl

Shorty I can see, you ain't lonely
Handful of niggaz and they all got cheese
So you looking at me now what's it gonna be
Just another tease far as I can see
Trying to get you up out this club
If it means spending a couple dubs
Throwing bout thirty stacks in the back make it rain like that cuz
I'm far
from a scrub
And you know my pedigree
Ex-dealer use to move 'phetamines
Girl I, spend money like it don't mean nothing
And besides I got a thing for you

I see you winding and grinding up on that pole
I know you see me looking at you and you already know
I wanna fuck you, fuck you, you already know
I wanna fuck you, fuck you, you already know girl

Mobbin' through club in low pressin'
I'm sittin' in the back in the smoking section (Just smoking)
Bird's eye, I got a clear view
You can't see me but I can see you (Baby I see you)
It's cool we jet the mood is set
Ya pussy is wet, you rubbin' your back and touchin' your neck
Ya body is movin' ya humpin' and jumpin' ya titties is bouncin'
(Yeah)
You smilin' and grinin' and lookin' at me

Girl and while your looking at me
I'm ready to hit the Caddy right up on the patio
Move the patty to the Caddy
Baby you got a fatty the type I like to marry
Wanting to just give you everything and that's kind of scary
Cuz I'm loving the way you shake your ass
Bouncing, got me tipping my glass
Lil' mully don't get caught up too fast but I got a thing for you

I see you winding and grinding up on that pole
I know you see me looking at you and you already know
I wanna fuck you, fuck you, you already know
I wanna fuck you, fuck you, you already know girl

I see you winding and grinding up on that pole
I know you see me looking at you and you already know
I wanna fuck you, fuck you, you already know
I wanna fuck you, fuck you, you already know girl

I Wanna Love You 2007

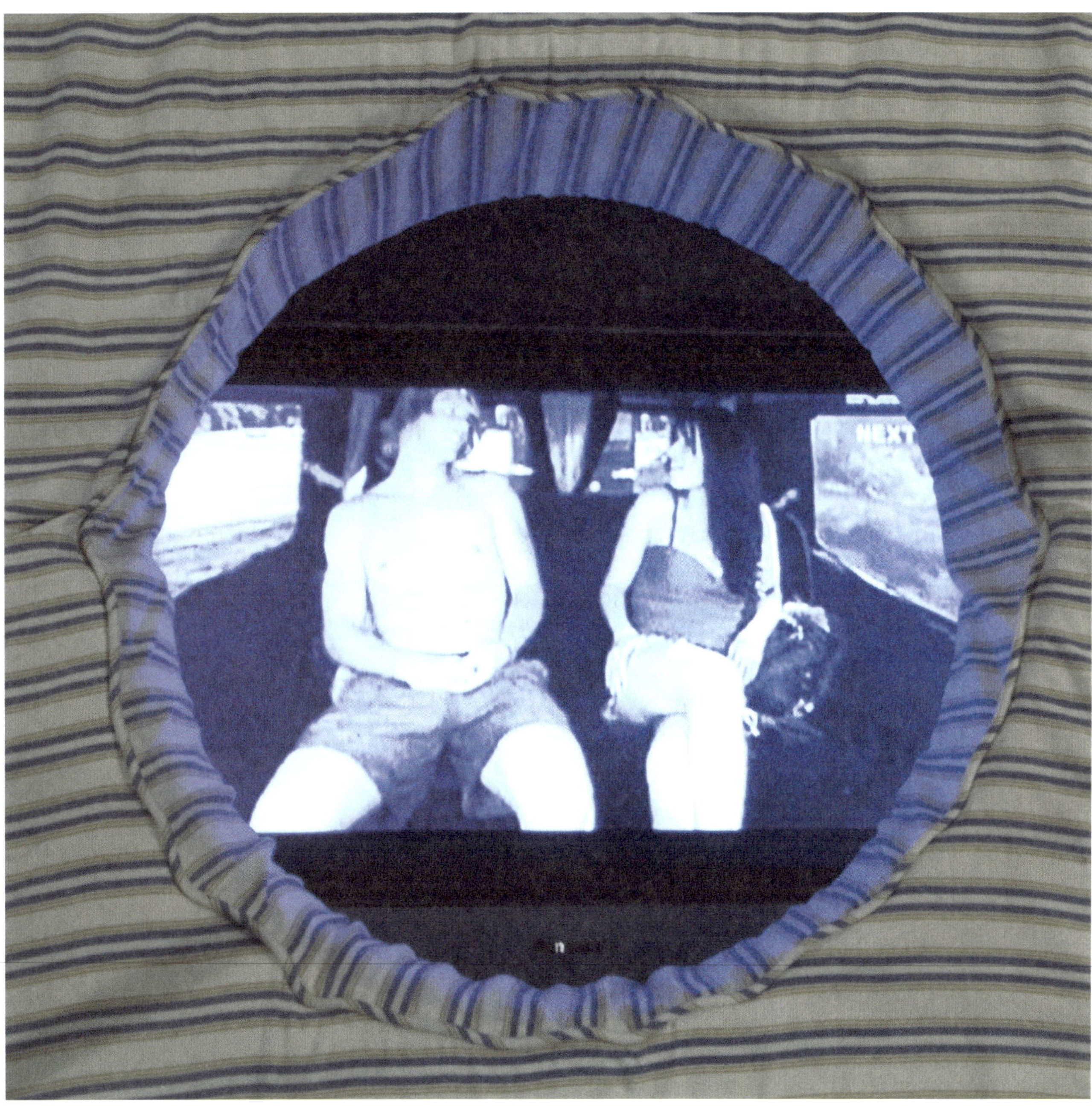

Video Bed 2007
Detail view

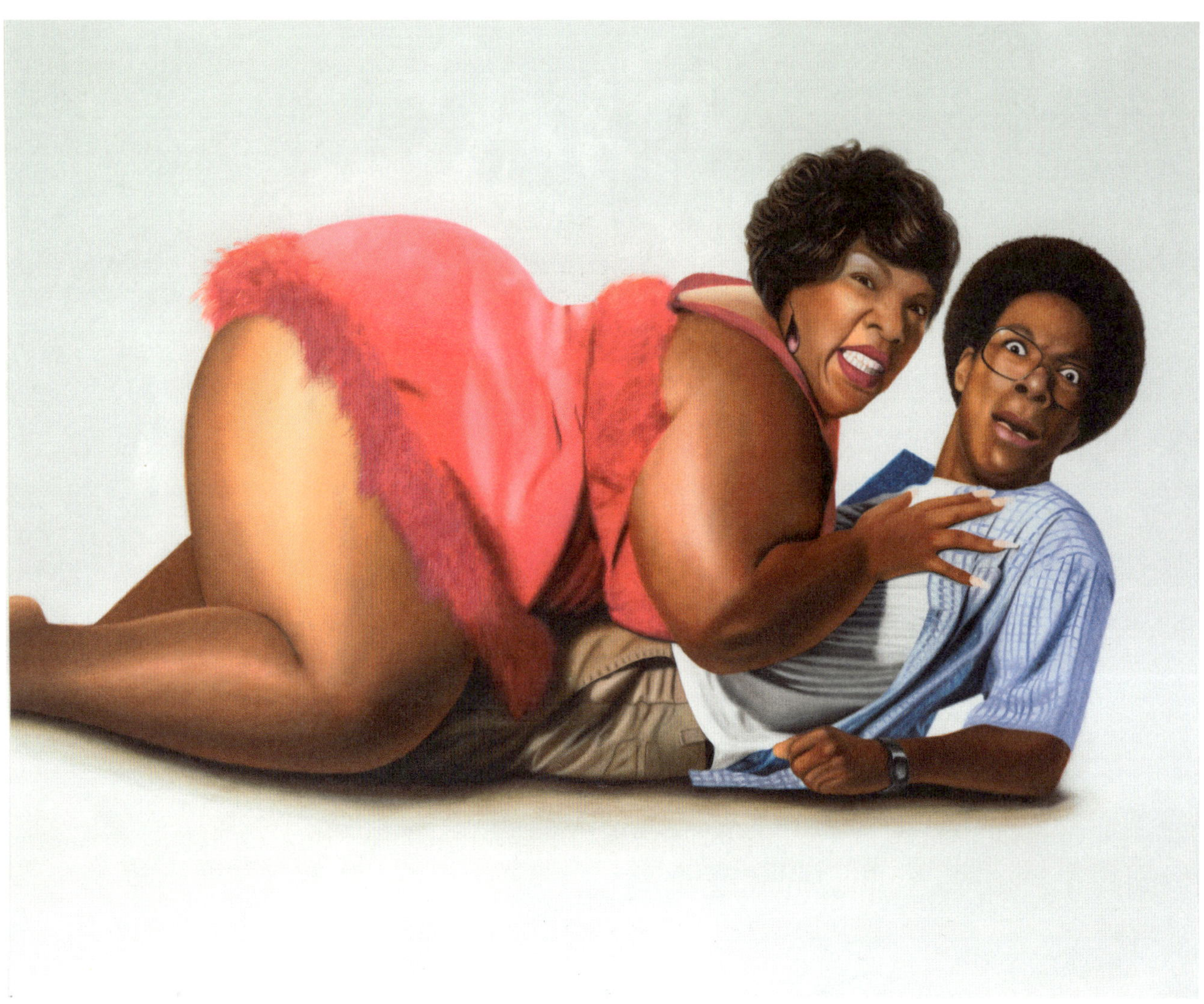

Eddie on Ediie 2007

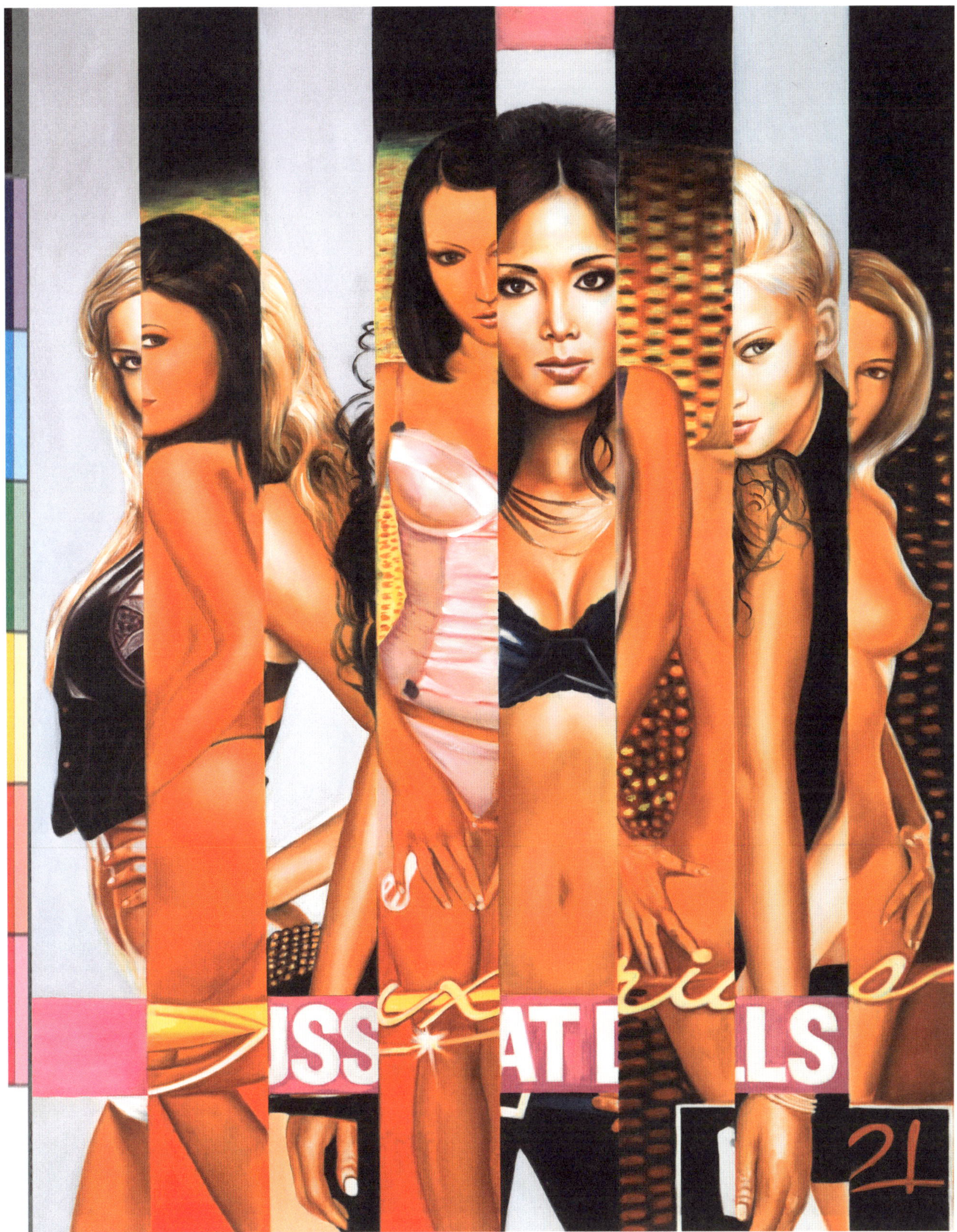

Blonde and Brunette Stares 2007

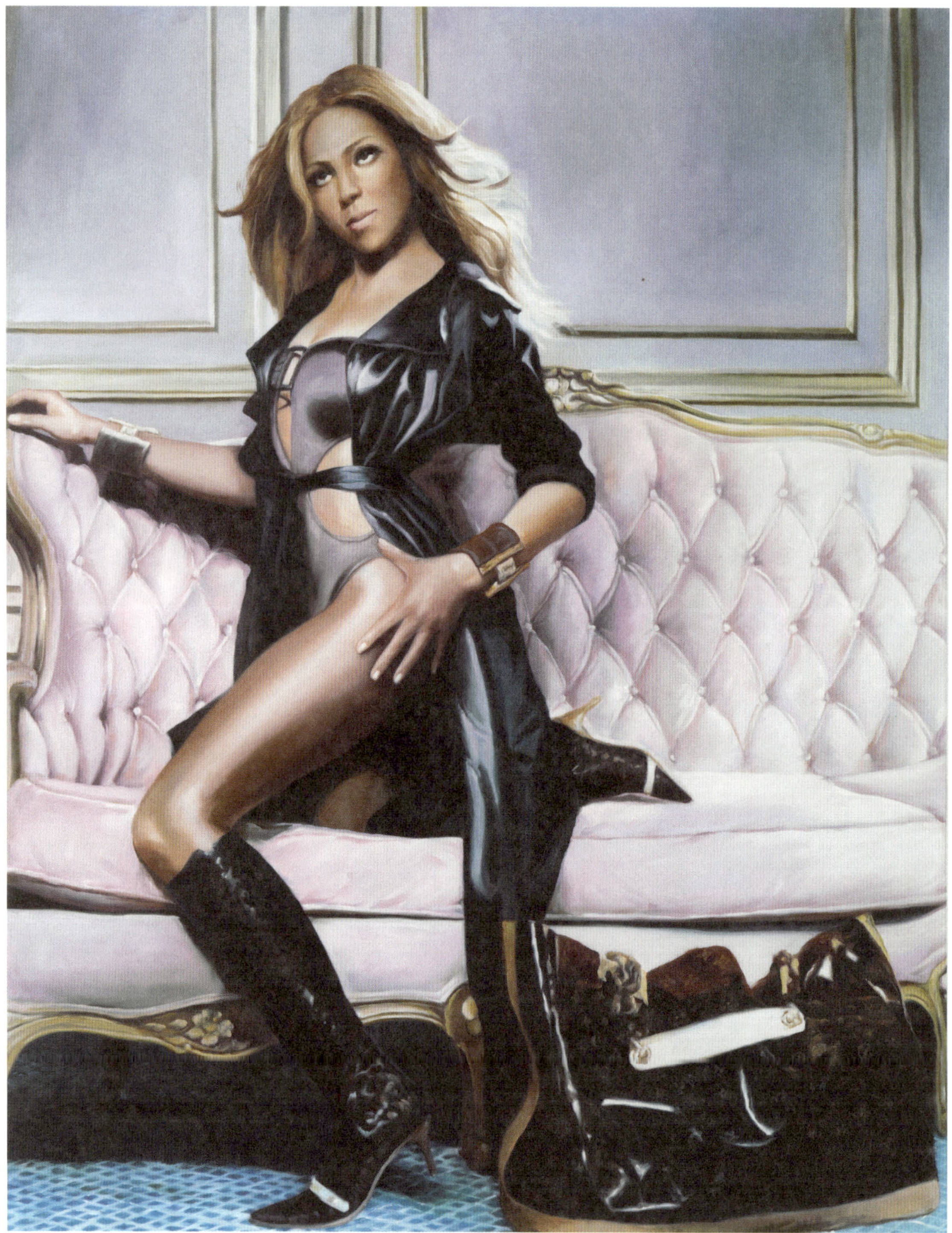

Kim on Pink Couch 2007

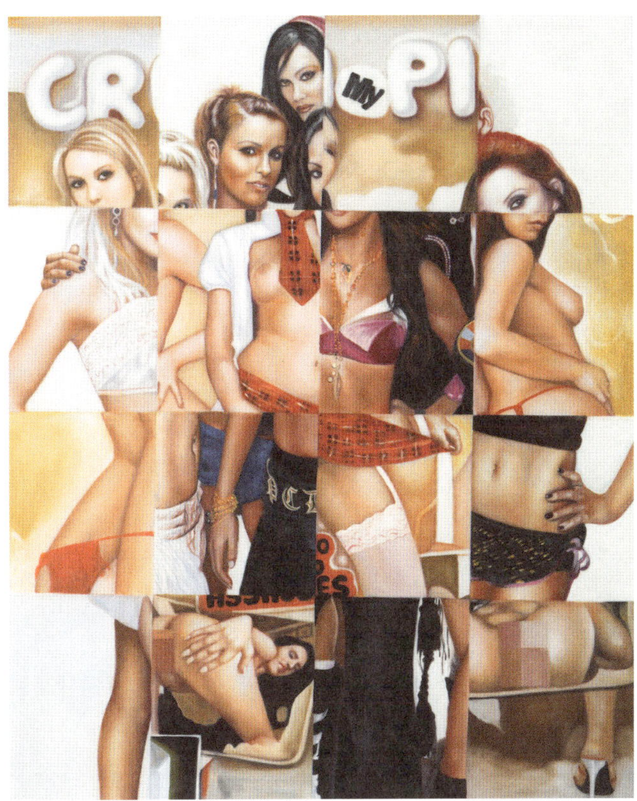

CreamMyPussyCats 2007

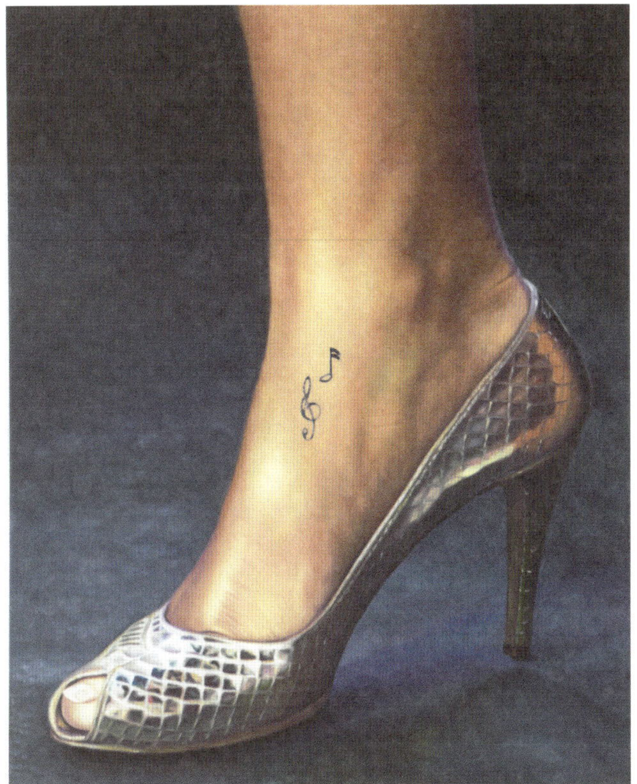

Rihanna's Ankle on Blue 2007

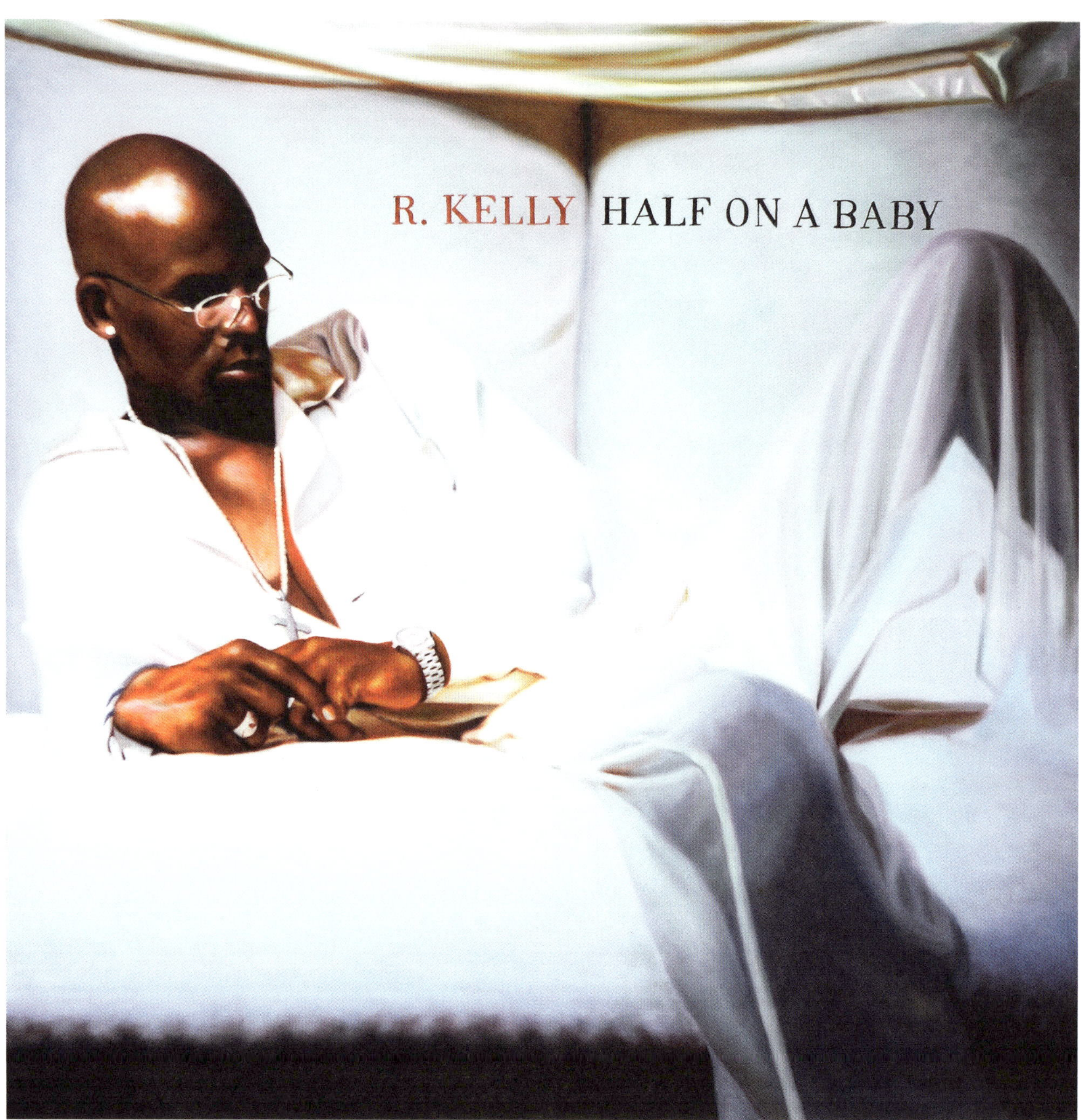

Half On A Baby 2007

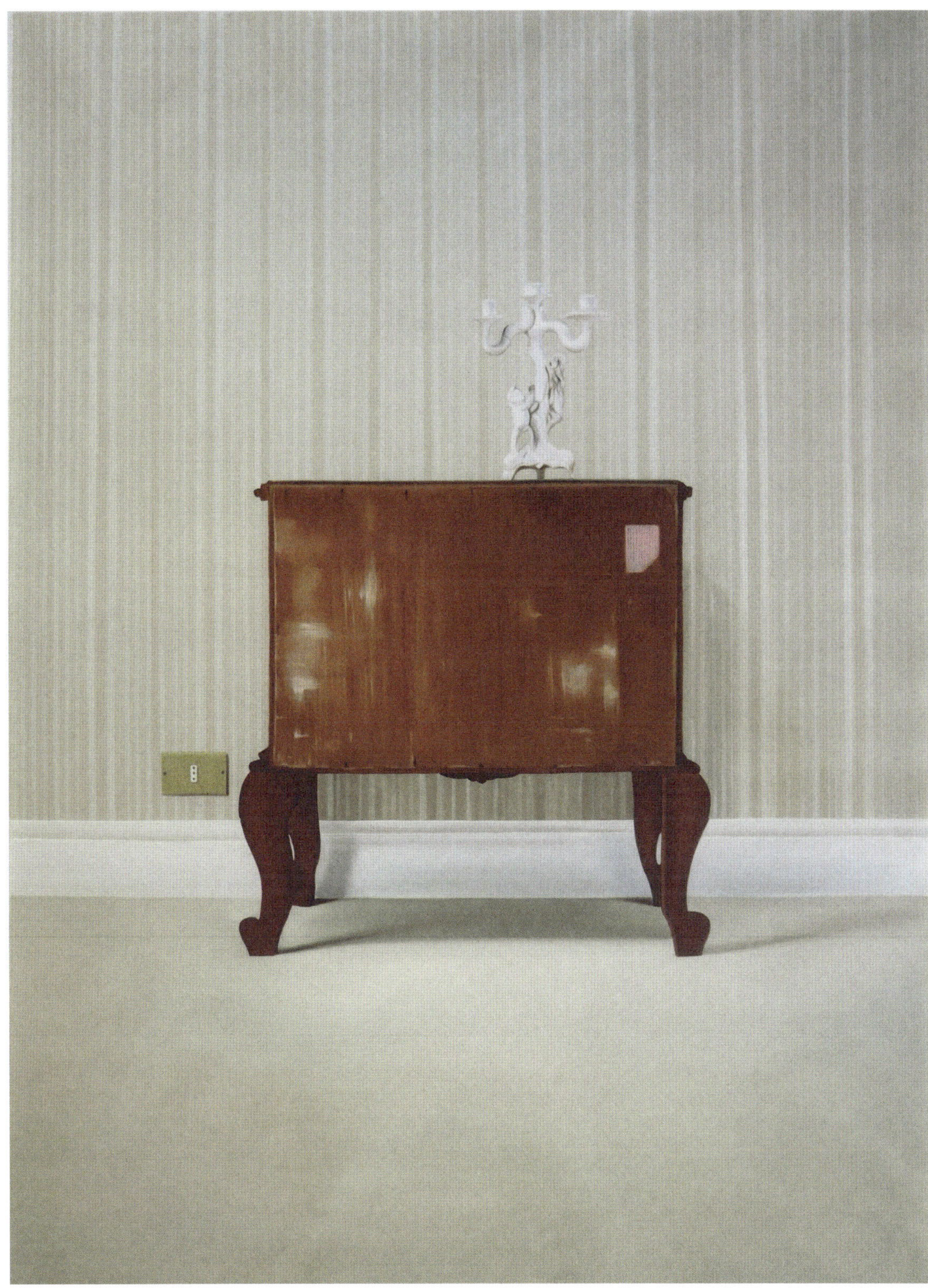

Enjoy The Backside (Dresser) 2008

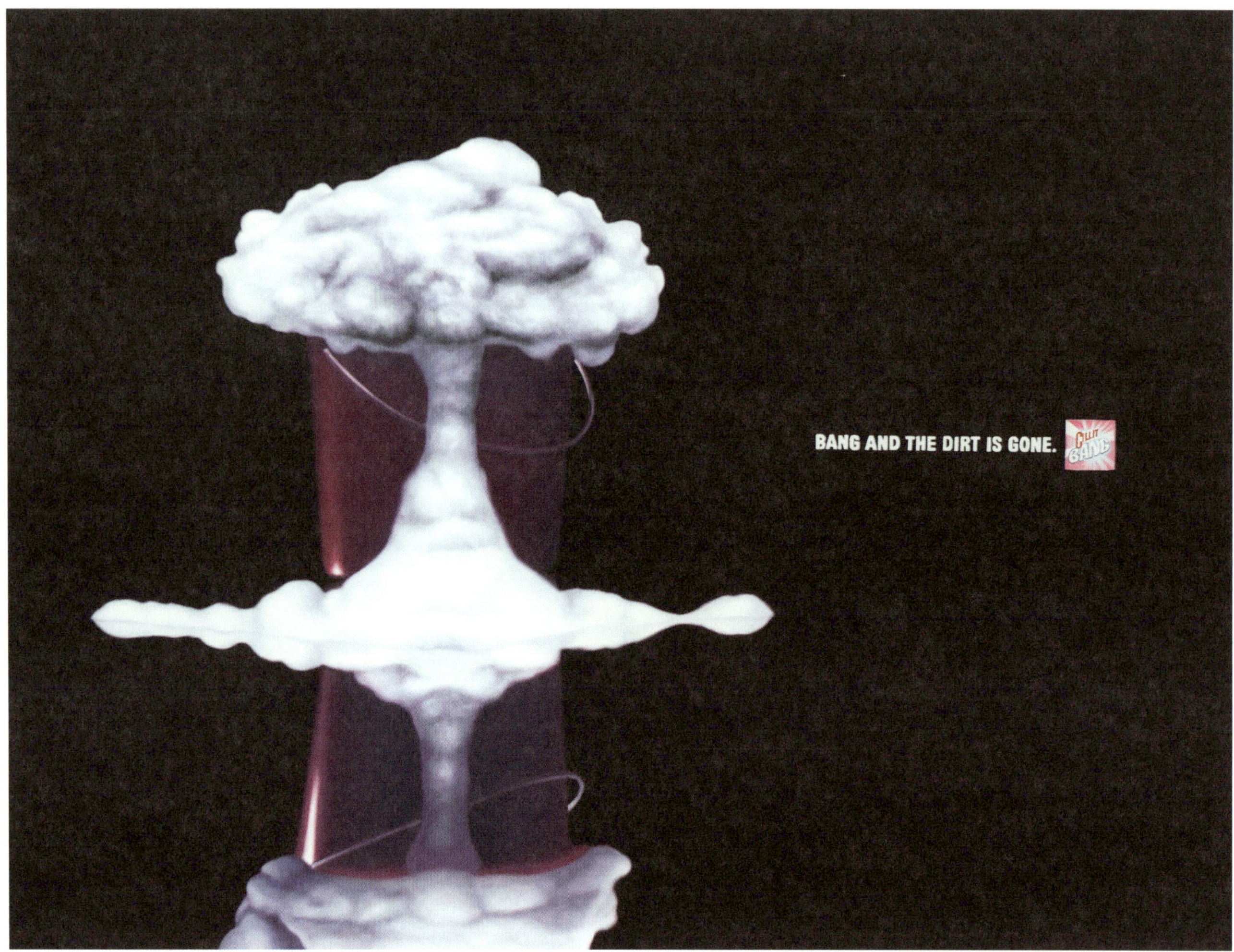

Bang And The Dirt Is Gone 2007

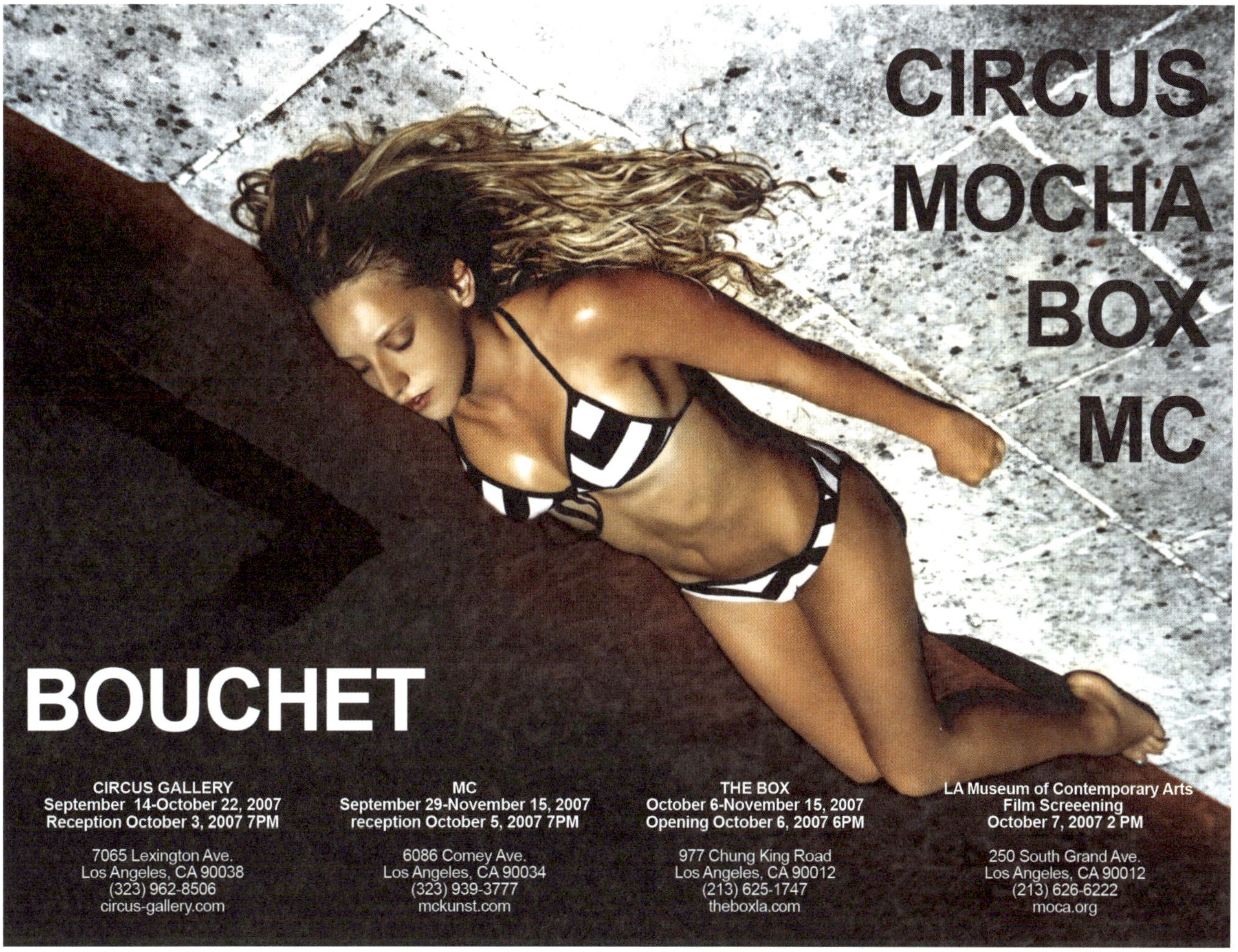

CIRCUS
MOCHA
BOX
MC

BOUCHET

CIRCUS GALLERY	MC	THE BOX	LA Museum of Contemporary Arts
September 14-October 22, 2007	September 29-November 15, 2007	October 6-November 15, 2007	Film Screeening
Reception October 3, 2007 7PM	reception October 5, 2007 7PM	Opening October 6, 2007 6PM	October 7, 2007 2 PM
7065 Lexington Ave.	6086 Comey Ave.	977 Chung King Road	250 South Grand Ave.
Los Angeles, CA 90038	Los Angeles, CA 90034	Los Angeles, CA 90012	Los Angeles, CA 90012
(323) 962-8506	(323) 939-3777	(213) 625-1747	(213) 626-6222
circus-gallery.com	mckunst.com	theboxla.com	moca.org

Exhibition Poster 2007

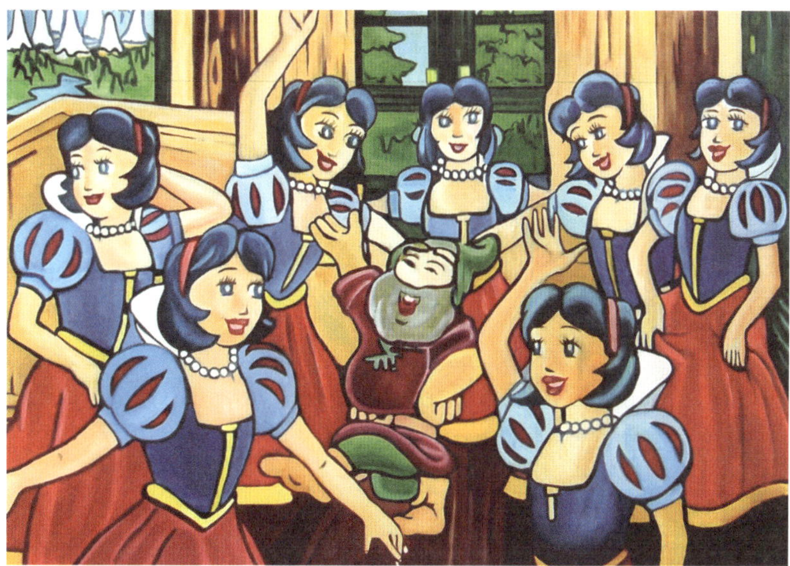

Lucky Dwarf 2008

Reaction Time 2007

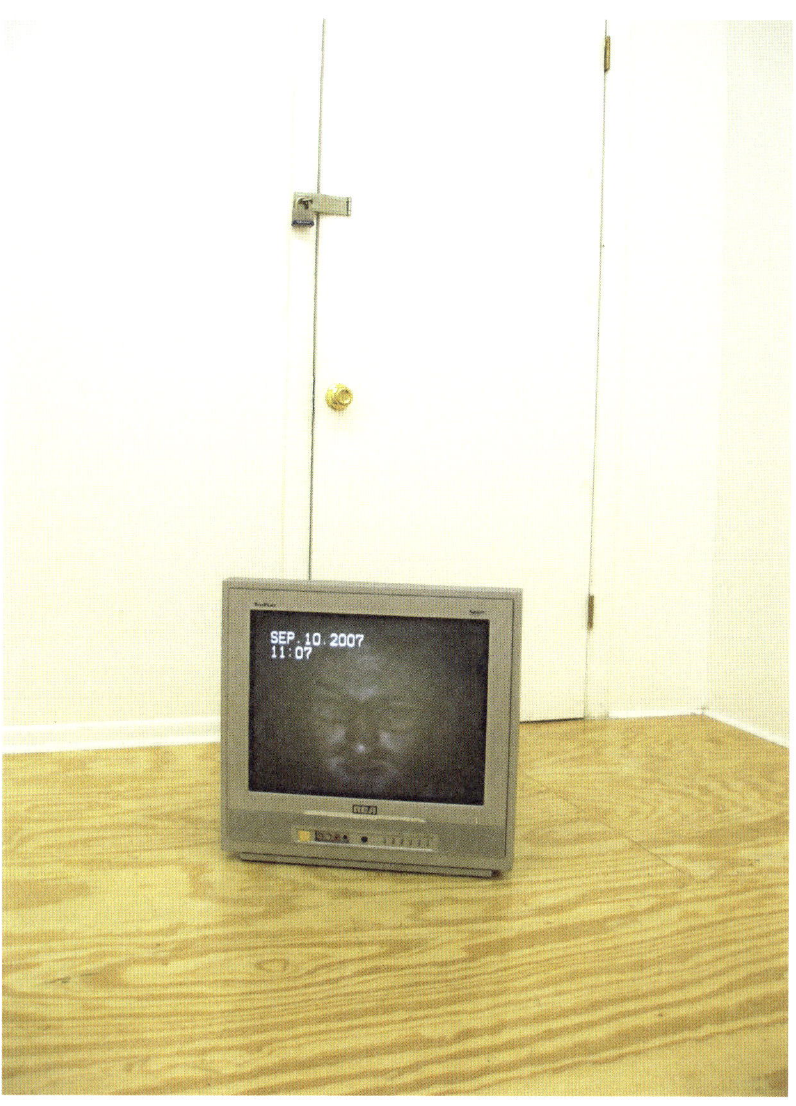

This work was originally made in 1998, in a small rented space above the Circus of Books adult bookstore on Sunset Blvd, in Los Angeles. For one of many pieces he staged there, he locked himself into a closet for 24 hours and watched movies, with a video camera zoomed in on his face. A monitor on the floor just outside the door displayed the image coming from the video camera, and played the sound from the movies he was watching. He left the door to the space and the door to the building open, with a sign displaying his name on the street. The viewer entered to find the image of Bouchet's face being screened to the soundtrack of the movie he was watching, while the artist himself remained hidden behind a padlocked door.

Nearly ten years later Bouchet remade this action in the Circus Gallery, located quite literally in the center of Hollywood, California. In the traditional sense of a Hollywood "remake" or "made for drama" presentation, Bouchet hired a look-a-like actor to repeat his original action, in this new, but identically titled work.

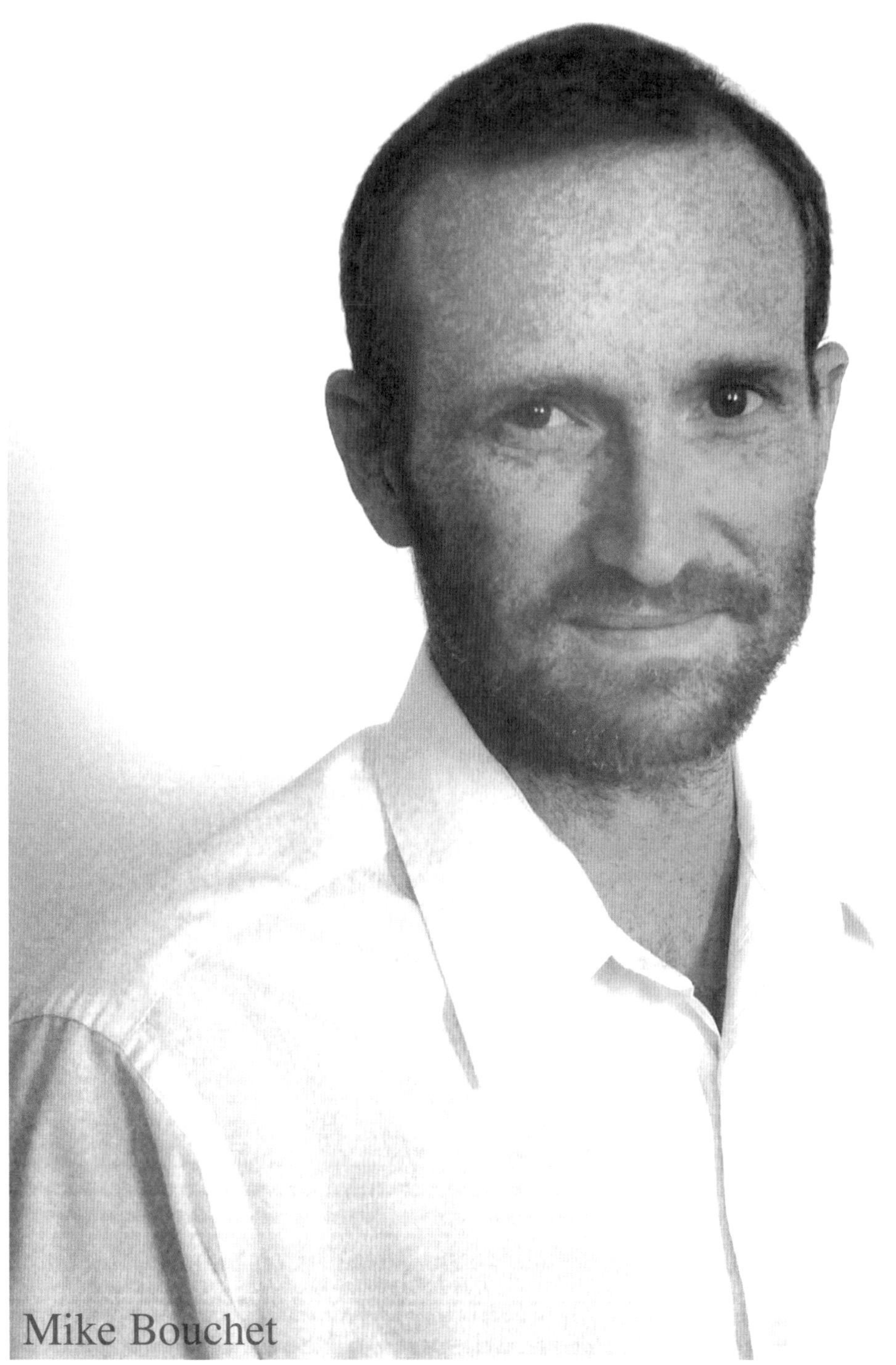

Mike Bouchet

Reaction Time 2007
Artist's Head Shot

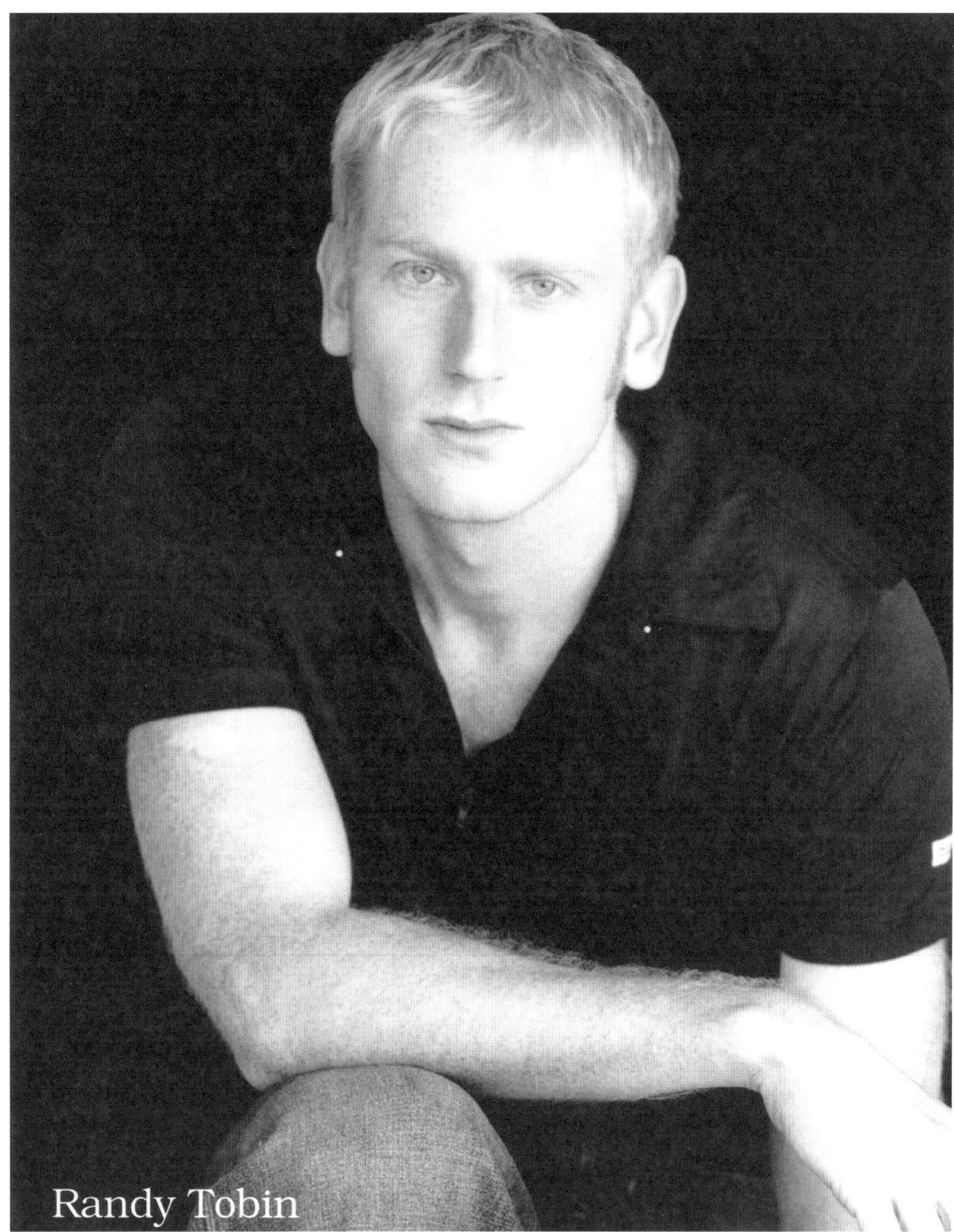

Randy Tobin

Reaction Time 2007
Actor's Head Shot

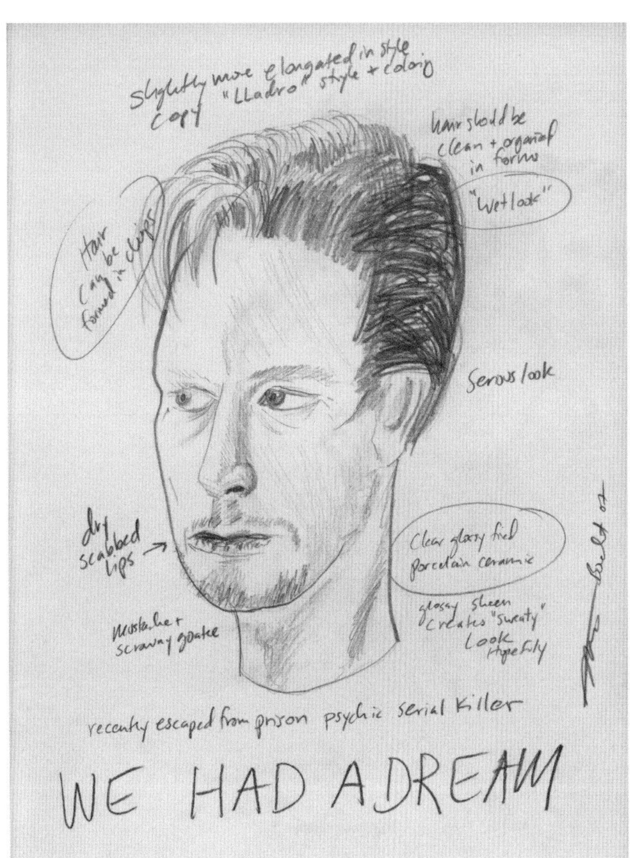

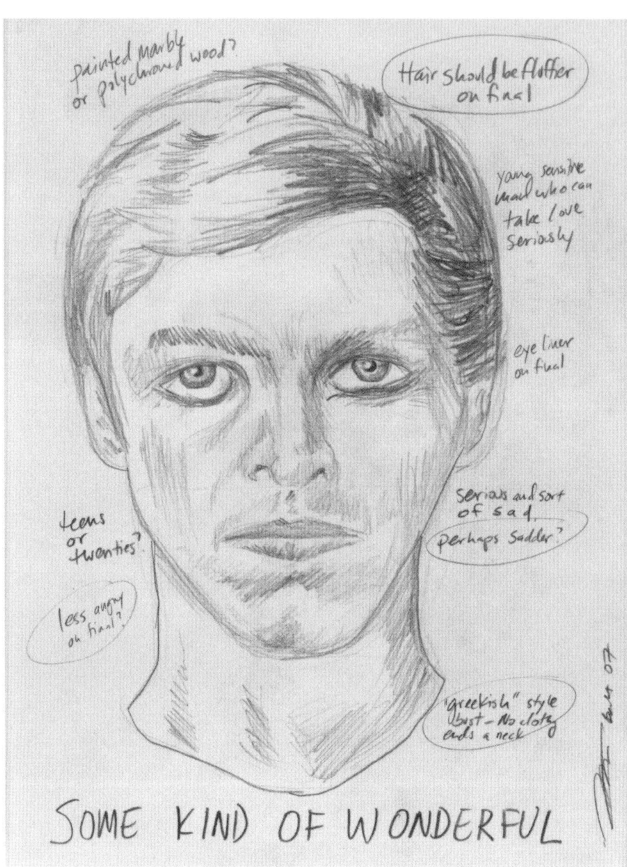

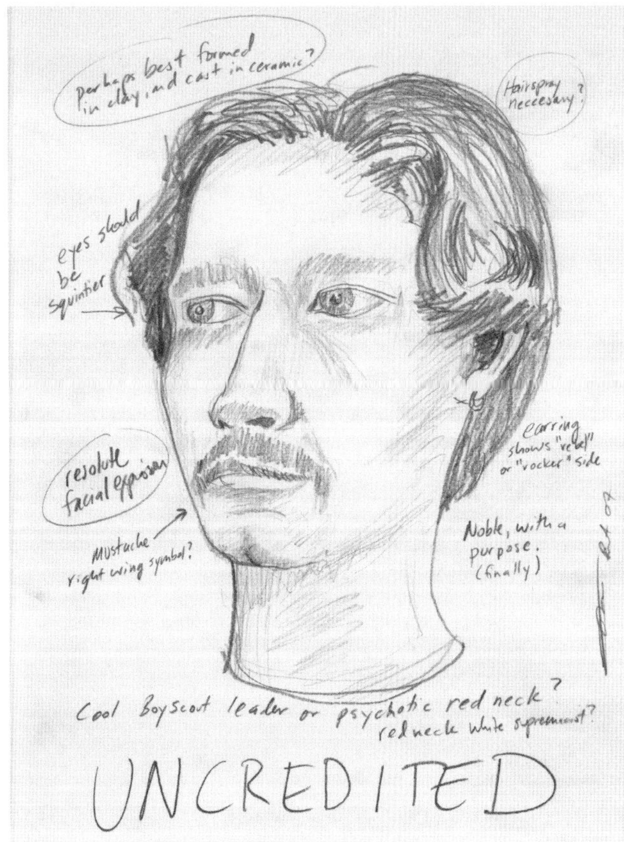

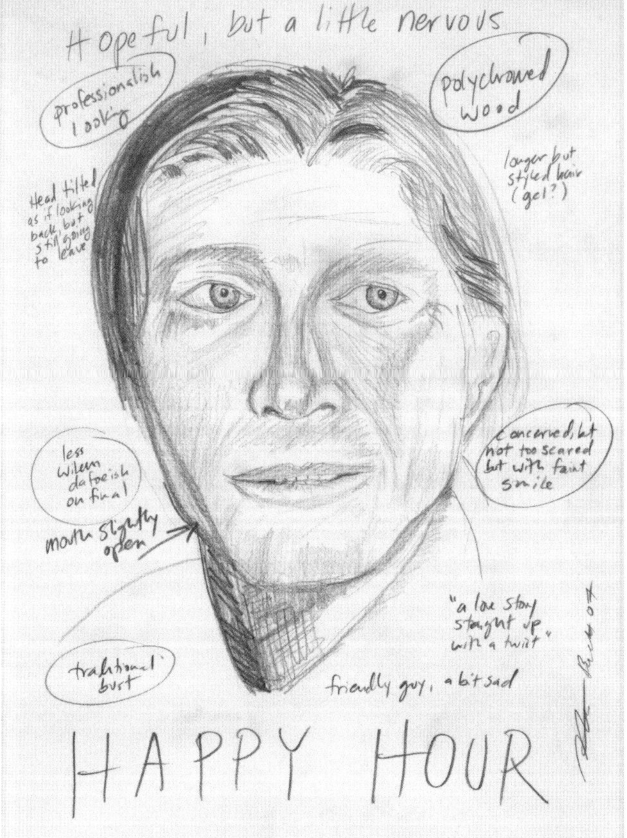

FBI ID drawings 2007

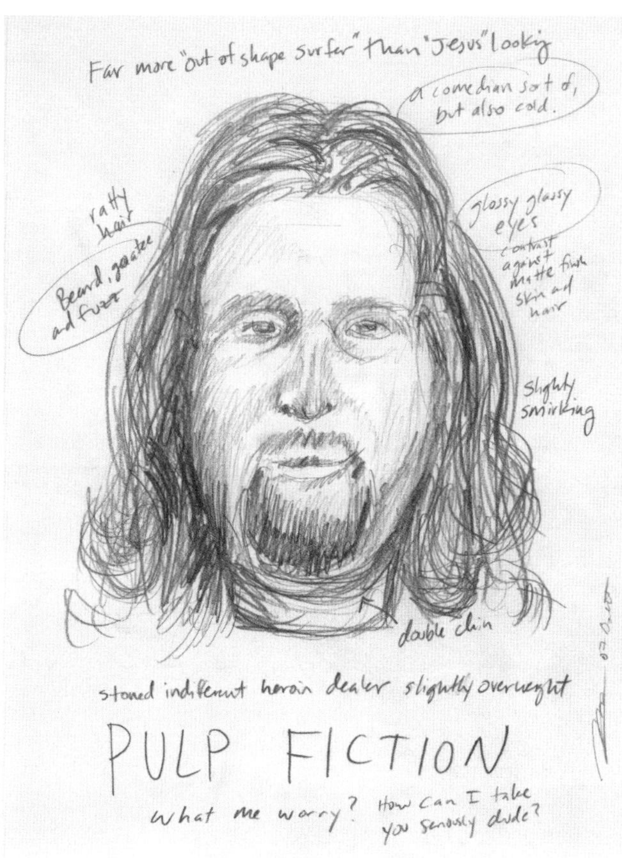

Far more "out of shape surfer" than "Jesus" looking
a comedian sort of, but also cold.
ratty hair
Beard, goatee and fuzz
glossy glossy eyes
contrast against matte finish skin and hair
Slightly smirking
double chin
stoned indifferent heroin dealer slightly overweight
PULP FICTION
what me worry? How can I take you seriously dude?

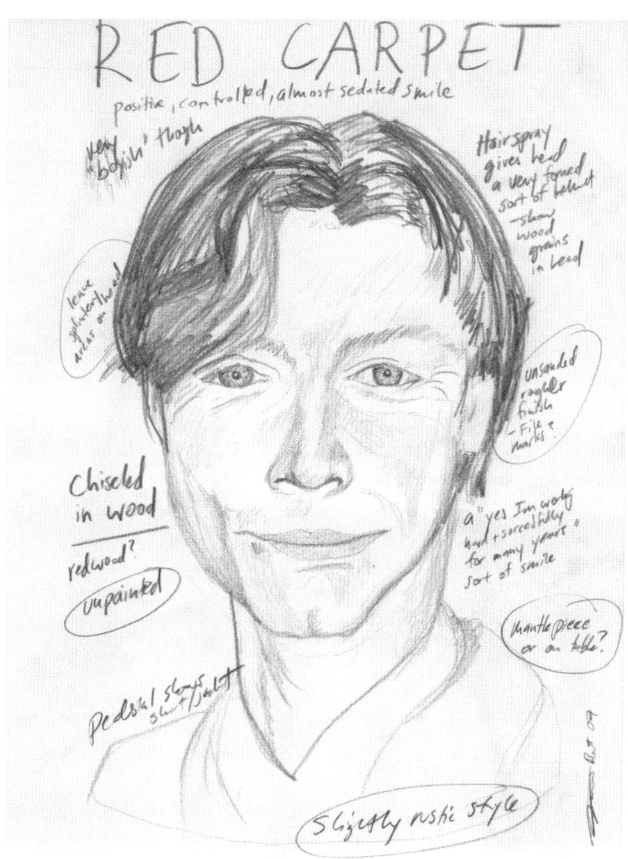

RED CARPET
positive, controlled, almost sedated smile
very "boyish" though
Hairspray gives head a very formed sort of helmet — show wood grains in head
leave splinter/wood areas on
unsanded rougher finish — File + marks
Chiseled in wood
redwood?
unpainted
a "yes I'm working hard + successfully for many years" sort of smile
mantlepiece or on table?
Pedestal shows shirt/jacket
Slightly rustic style

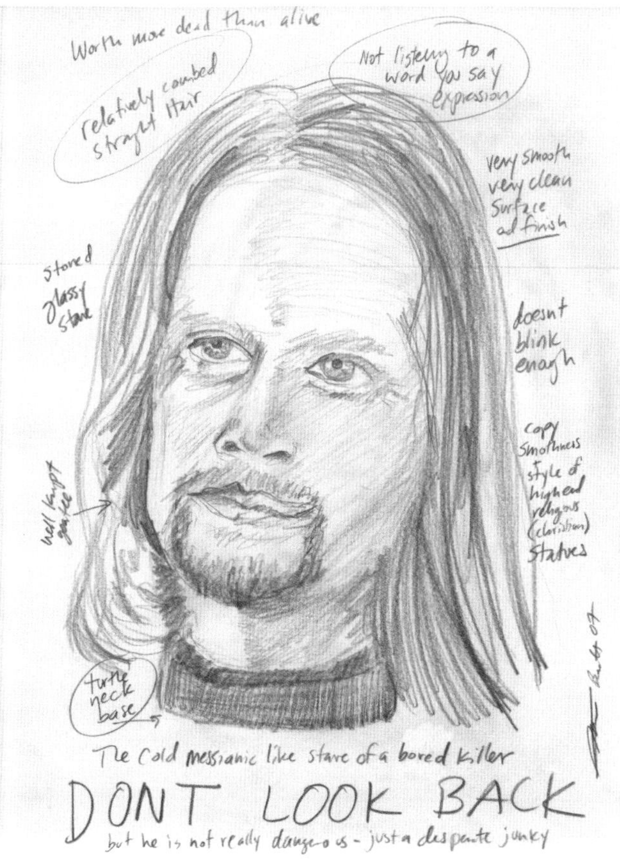

Worth more dead than alive
relatively combed straight hair
Not listening to a word you say expression
very smooth very clean surface and finish
stoned glassy stare
doesn't blink enough
copy smoothness style of high end religious (christian) statues
well kempt goatee
turtle neck base
The cold messianic like stare of a bored killer
DONT LOOK BACK
but he is not really dangerous - just a desperate junky

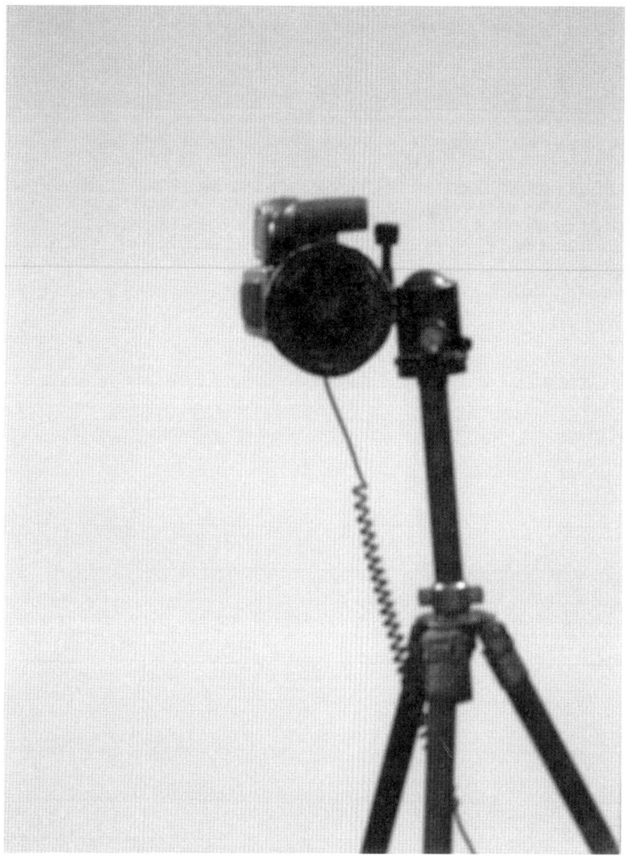

Peter Jennings Film Festival 2006

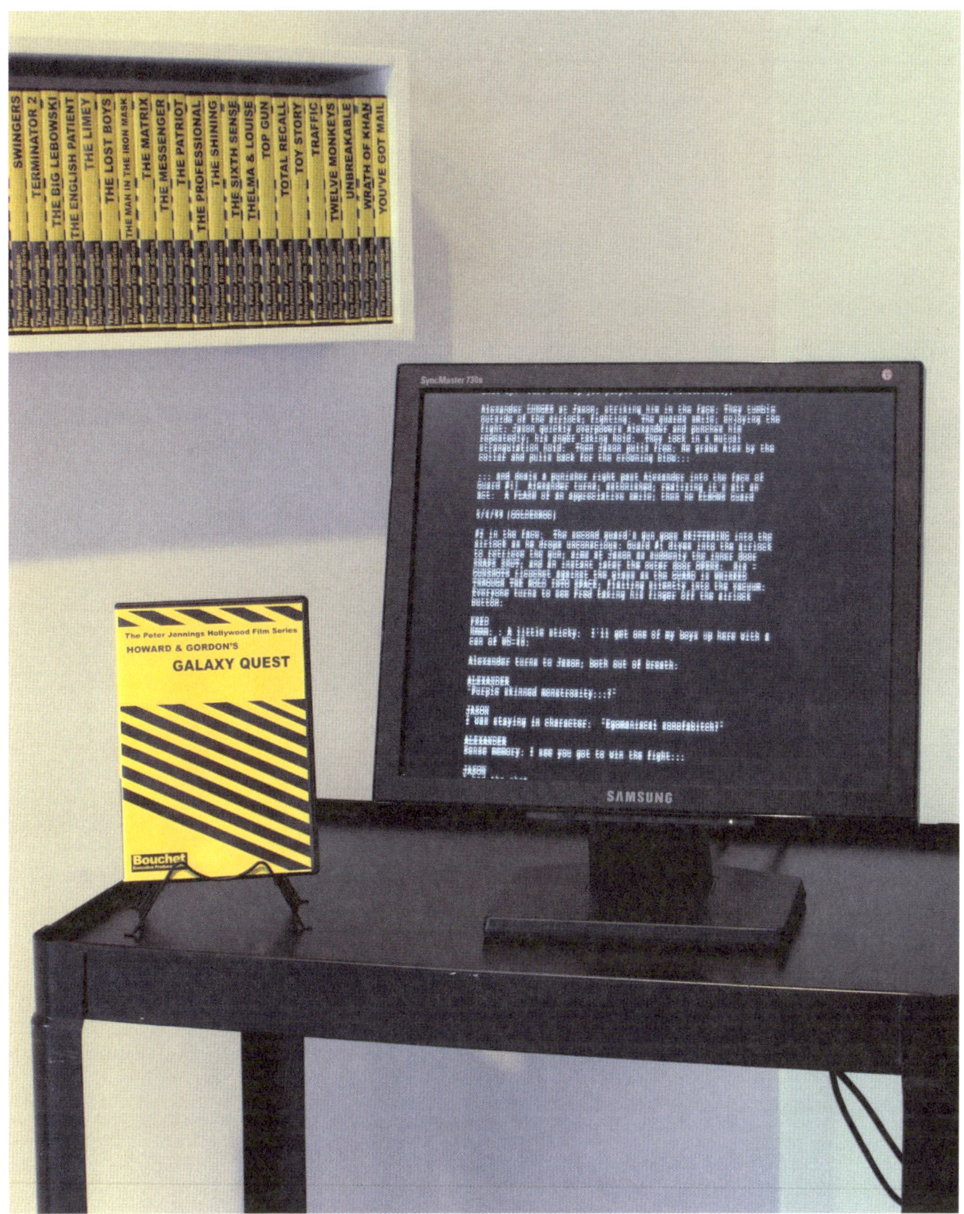

A collection of 103 videos, also titled "Films for Readers". The script of each movie scrolls like the credits usually viewed at the end of a film. Thus, the entire film can be read.

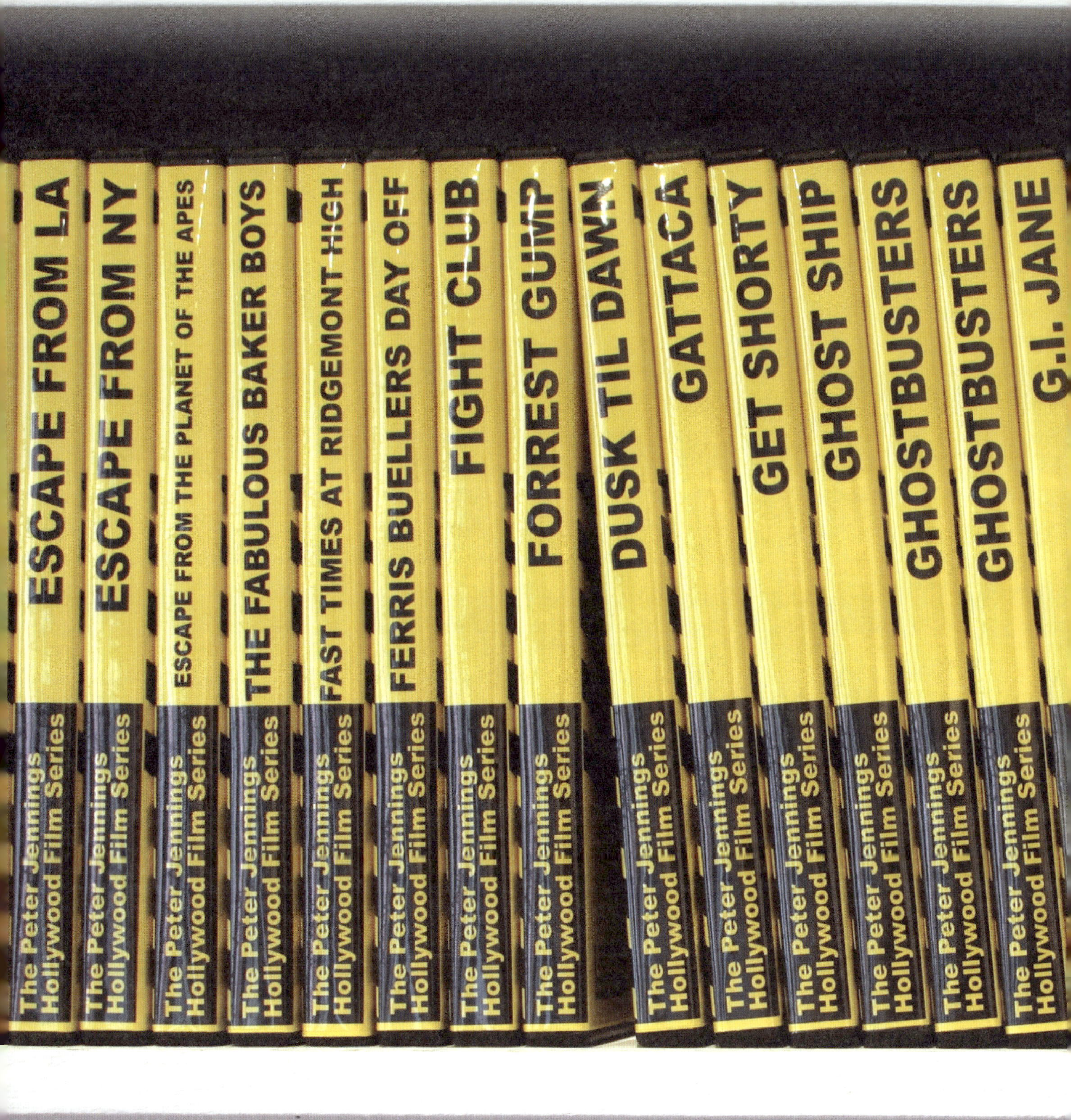

Peter Jennings Film Festival 2007
103 DVDs

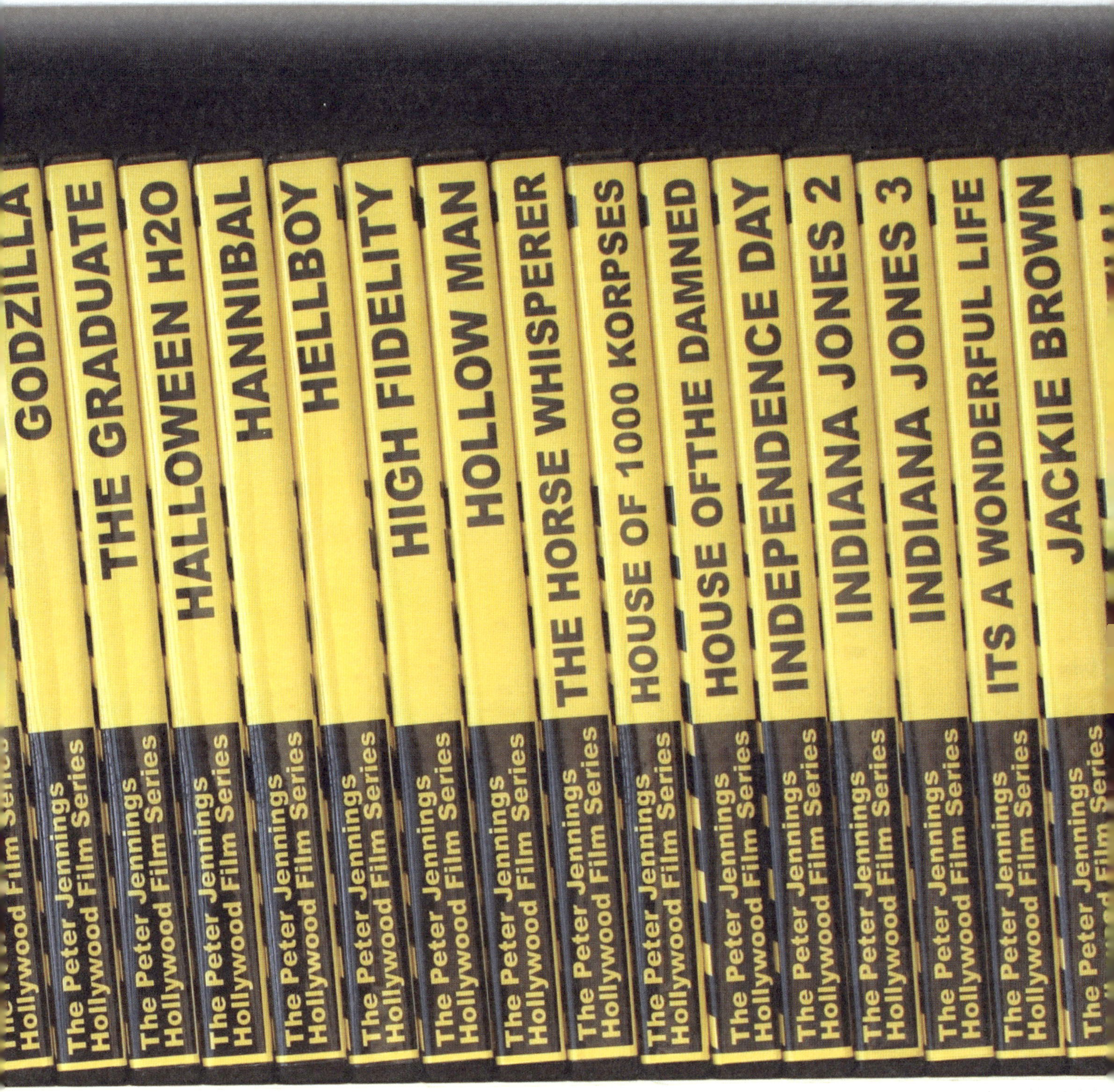

GODZILLA

THE GRADUATE

HALLOWEEN H2O

HANNIBAL

HELLBOY

HIGH FIDELITY

HOLLOW MAN

THE HORSE WHISPERER

HOUSE OF 1000 KORPSES

HOUSE OFTHE DAMNED

INDEPENDENCE DAY

INDIANA JONES 2

INDIANA JONES 3

ITS A WONDERFUL LIFE

JACKIE BROWN

The Peter Jennings
Hollywood Film Series

Guggenheim Toilet 2006

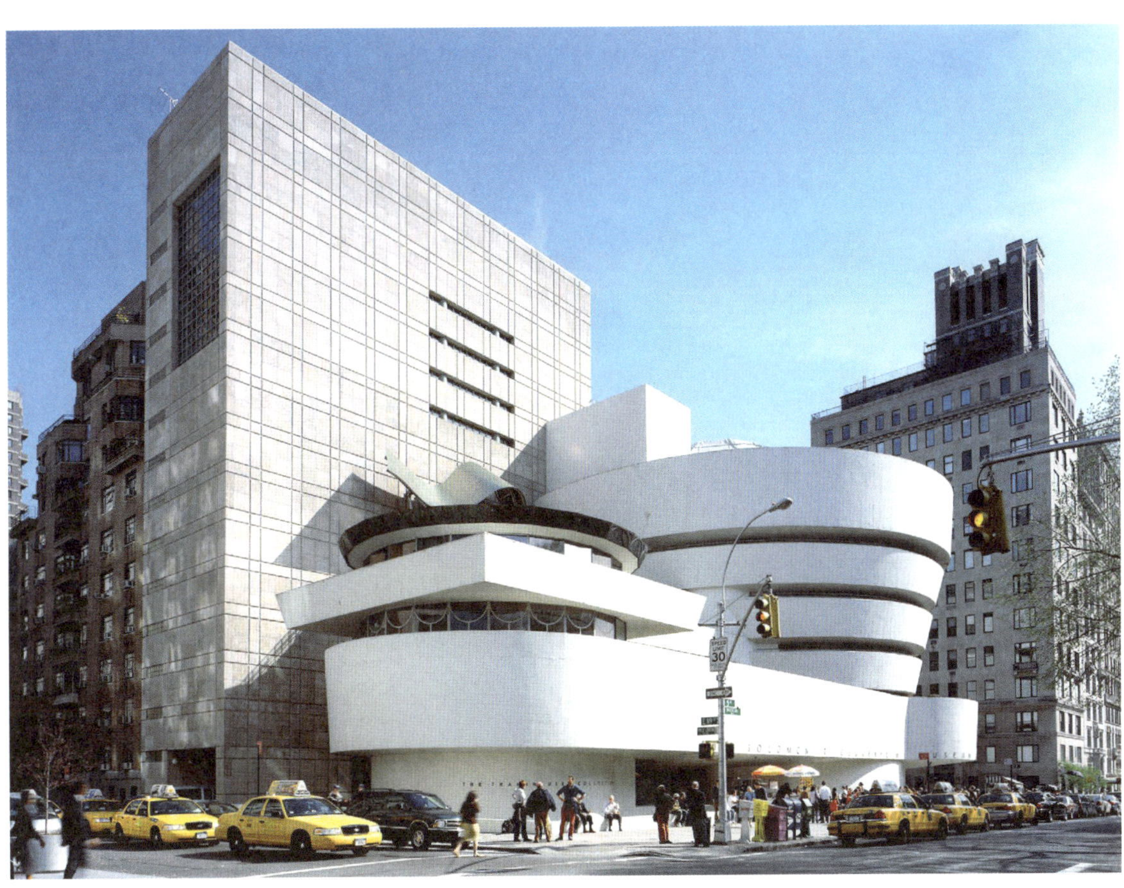

A fully functioning ceramic toilet that is modeled after Frank Lloyd Wright's Solomon R. Guggenheim Museum located at 1071 Fifth Avenue in New York City.

Guggenheim Toilet 2006

SpaceBags/Next 2006

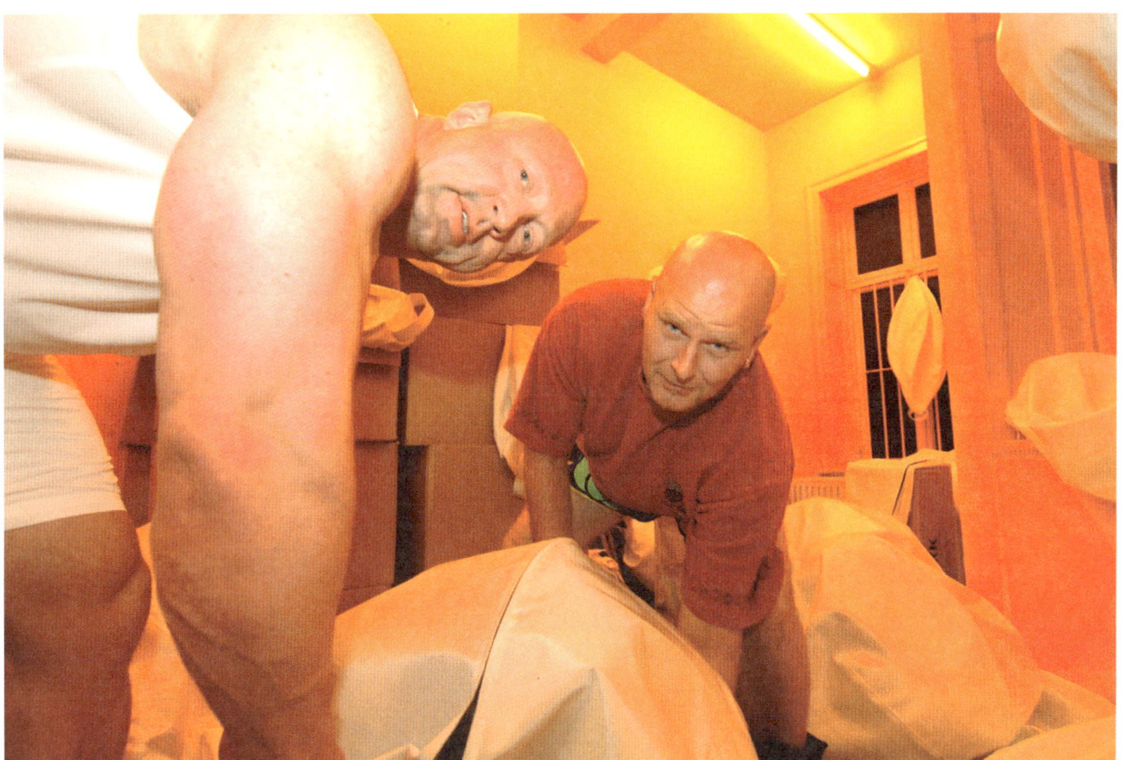

This artwork consisted of two components – a sculpture and a play. The exhibition took place in an abandoned storefront in Hamburg, Germany.

The sculpture titled "SpaceBags" consists of 500 white vinyl bags. The bags are 1 meter diameter spheres, sewn from thick white pleather with a zipper that runs top to bottom and handles sewn onto either end. The bags are modeled after the NASA "Johnson Personal Rescue Enclosures", and are designed to hold a human being curled up inside with an oxygen cannister. The bags are to be used in the event of air loss on the space shuttle, as there are too few actual space suits to accomodate the entire crew. Boxes of the bags were stacked in the space, which was painted yellow. In addition, the windows were blackened out, and a large floor-to-ceiling mirror was installed along one of the walls in an effort to virtually expand the space.

The play is based on the transcribed dialogue of an episode of the television program "Next". The actors rehearsed and performed the lines of the popular MTV dating program in the bags. Weightlifters acted as the stagehands, carrying the actors (in bags) to and from their designated stage positions. The stage consisted of two mattresses taped together in the middle of the room, and a row of seats off to the side of the room. The play was performed in front of a live audience.

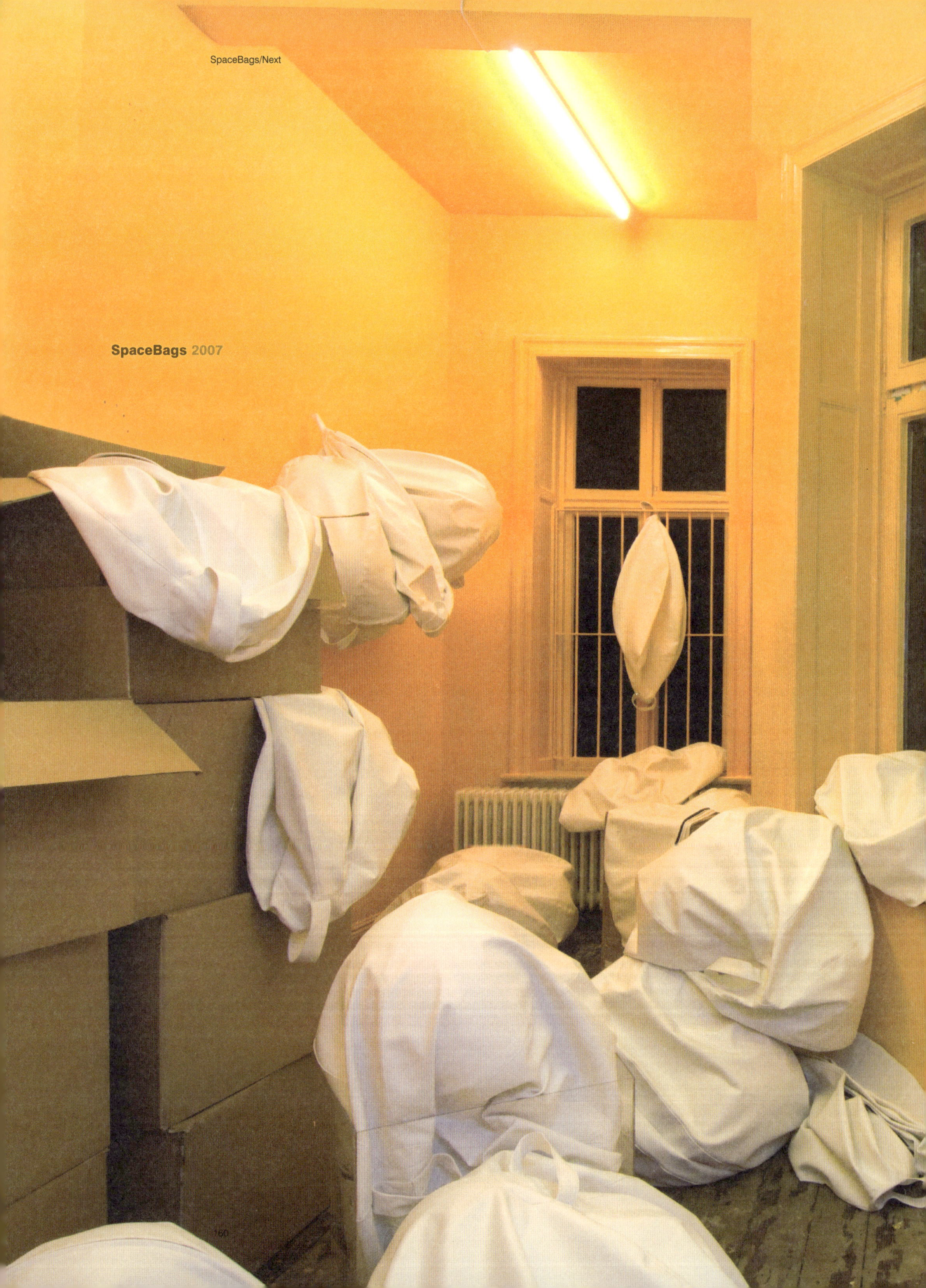
SpaceBags/Next
SpaceBags 2007

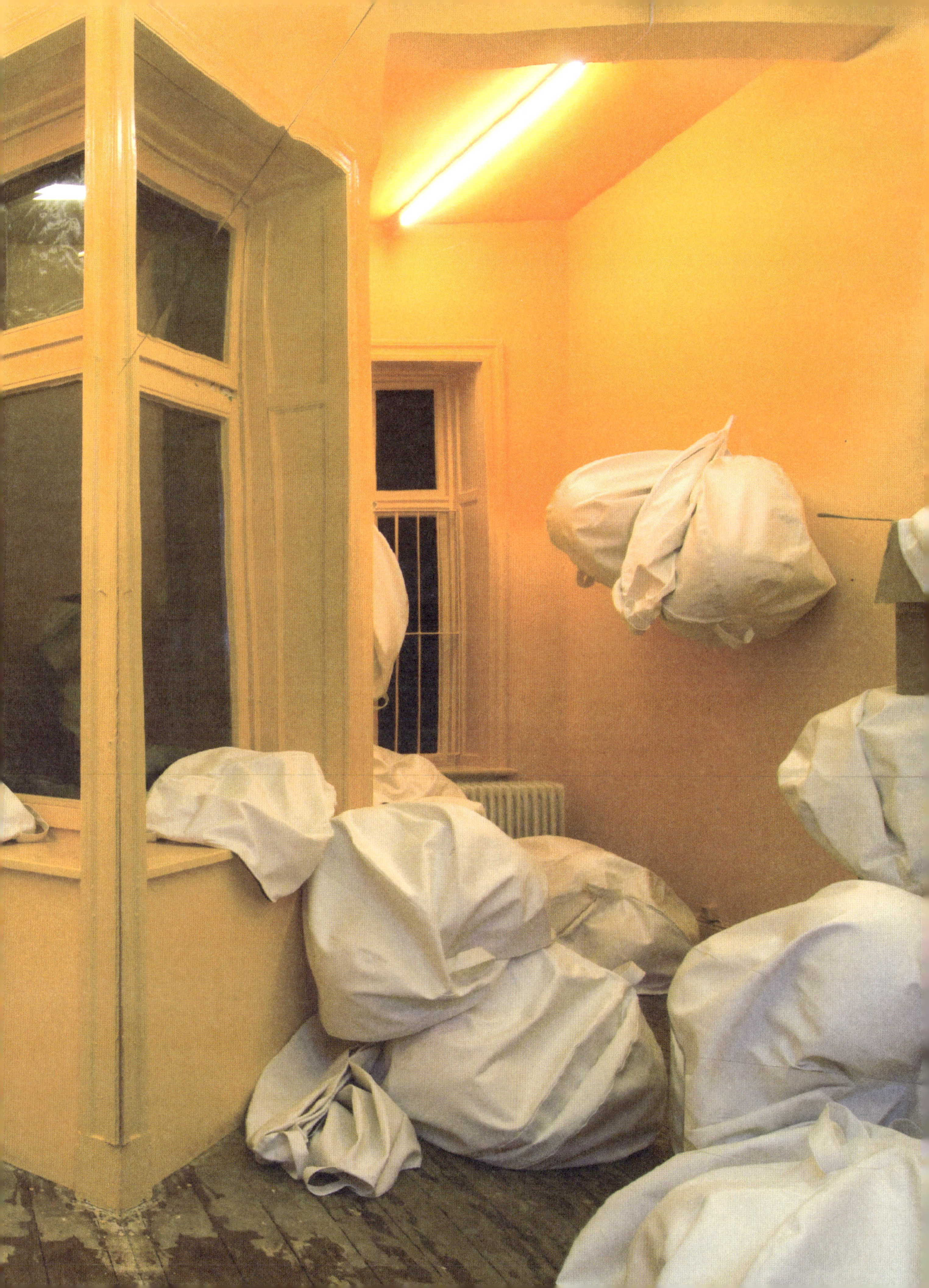

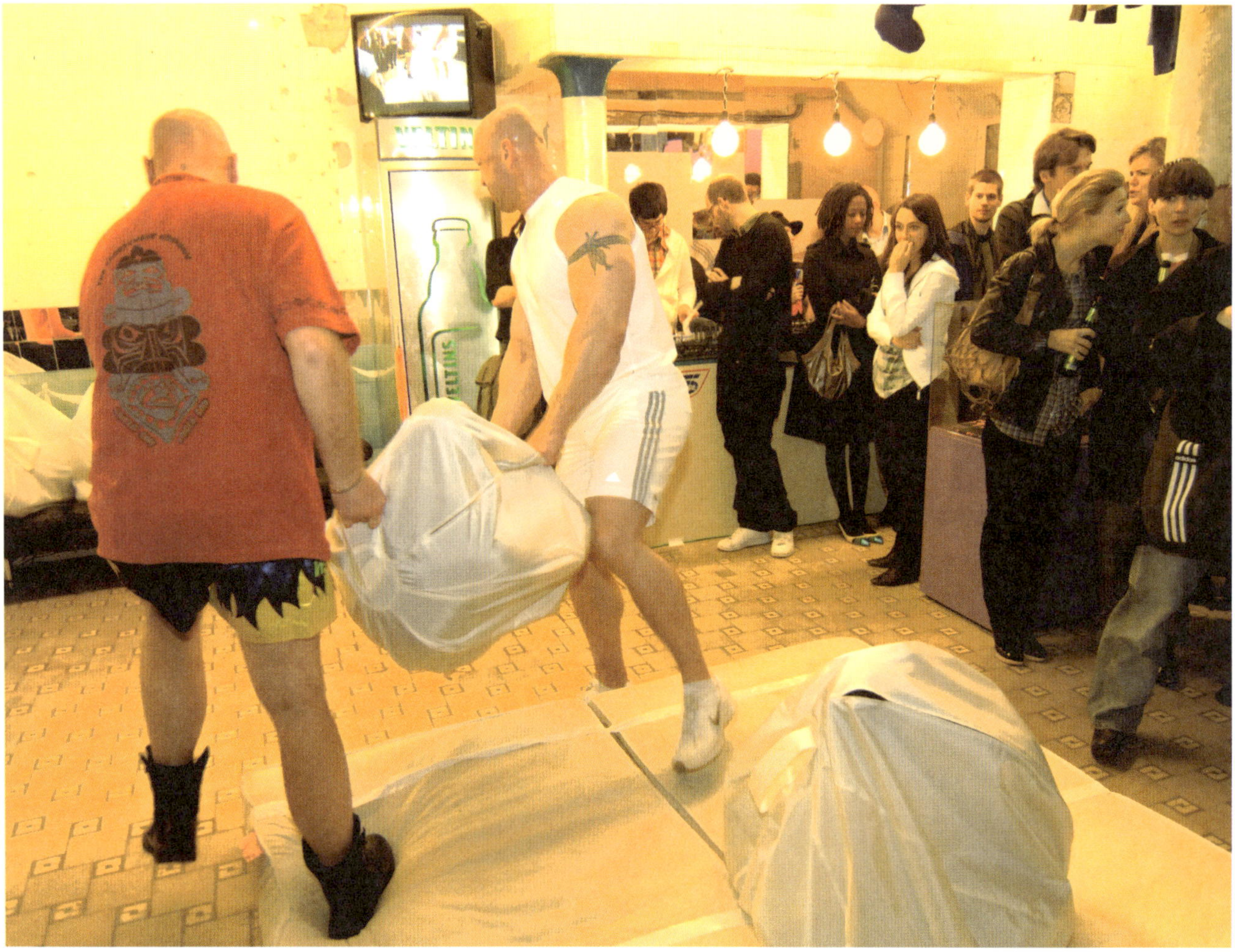

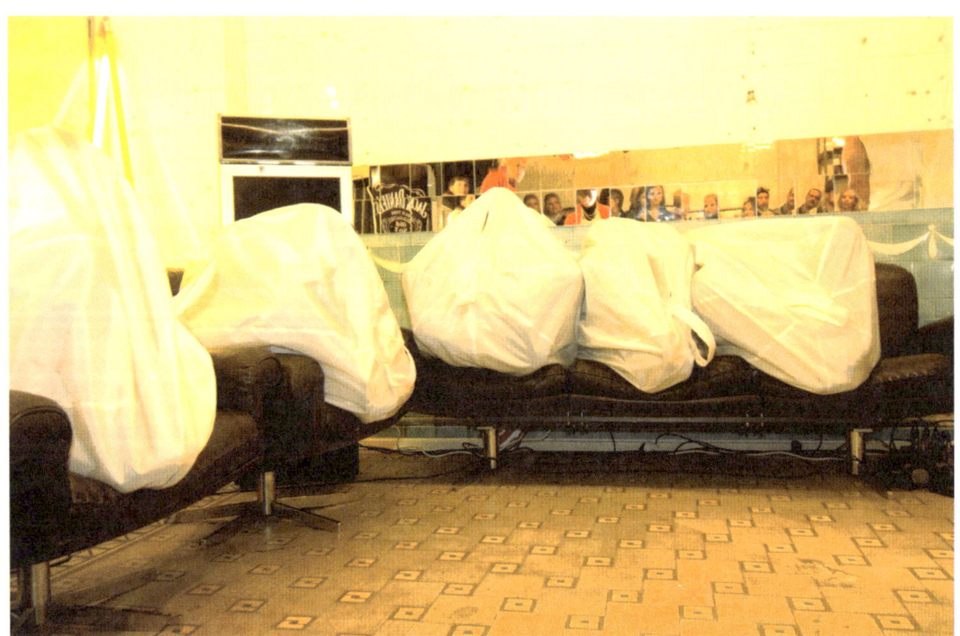

Next 2007
Theatrical still

Next 2007
Theatrical still

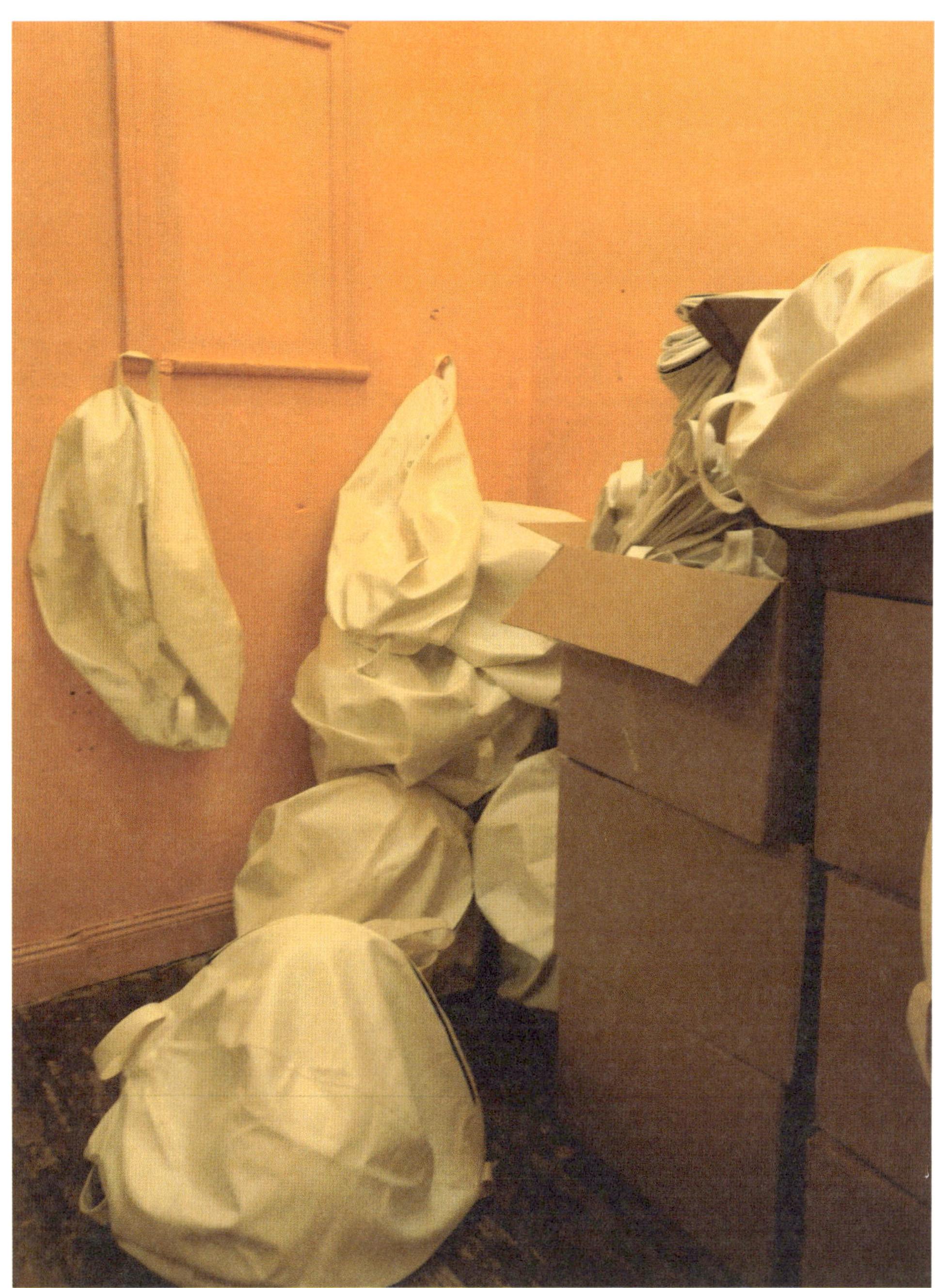

SpaceBags 2007
Installation detail

Canburger 2008

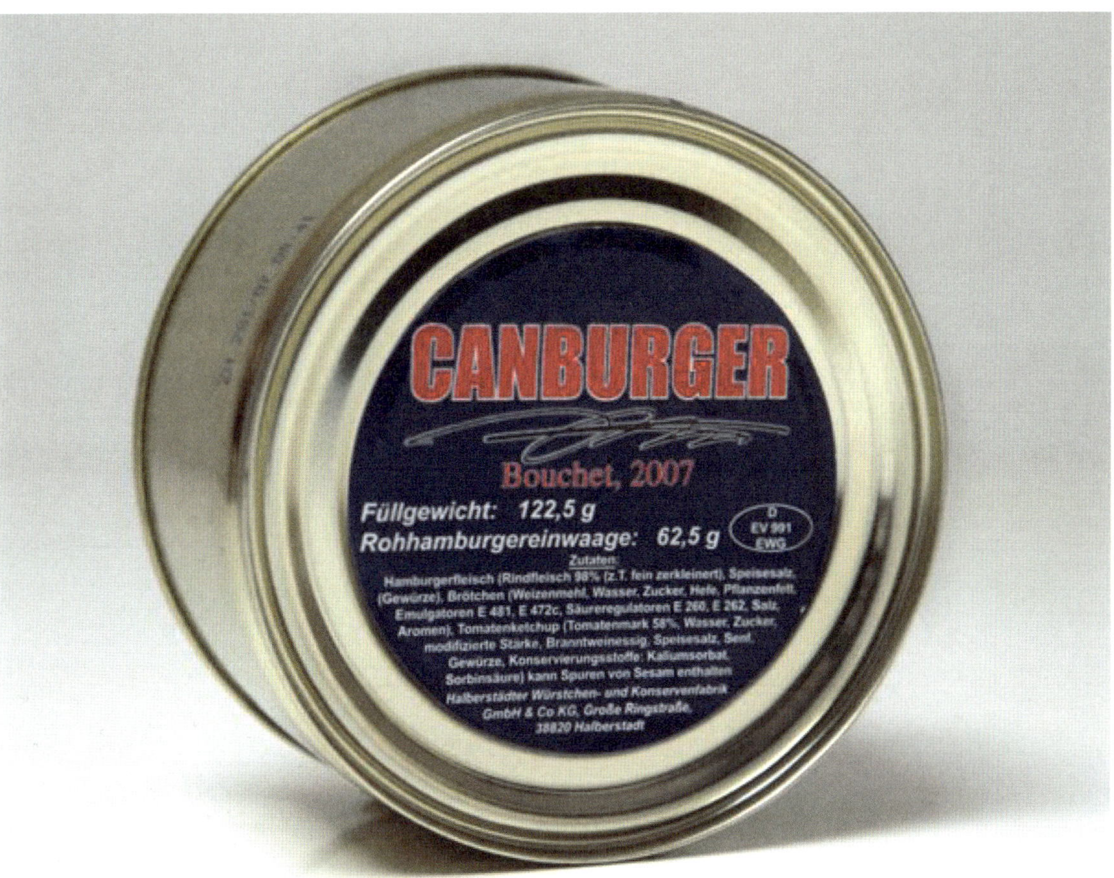

The central element of the **CANBURGER** exhibition are the 10,000 canned burgers which the artist produced for this sculpture. Working with a meat canning company in Germany, Bouchet has developed a hamburger in a can, with a shelf life of two years. The hamburger is sandwiched between two buns, has tomato catsup and mustard already on it, and has a pull top lid for easy opening.

In the month of December, 2007, Bouchet placed a stand offering free samples of the **CANBURGER** at the Marché des Enfants Rouges in Paris. This public market was created under Louis XIV and is the oldest public market in Paris.

The **CANBURGER** is a starting point for a larger investigation into some of the more manifest issues involved in one of the worlds most popular food items. Bouchet also generated sculptures and large paintings for this body of work that touch upon some of the more deep-seated issues surrounding food production and consumption in today's world, from fast-food restaurants to canned military rations and survivalist movements.

While the large-scale photo-realistic paintings of hamburgers take fetishistic food photography to its grotesque limits, the bronze hamburger sculpture (and shiny metallic hamburger cans) also take the current trend for what can be called "spectacular materiality" to its uncomfortable extreme.

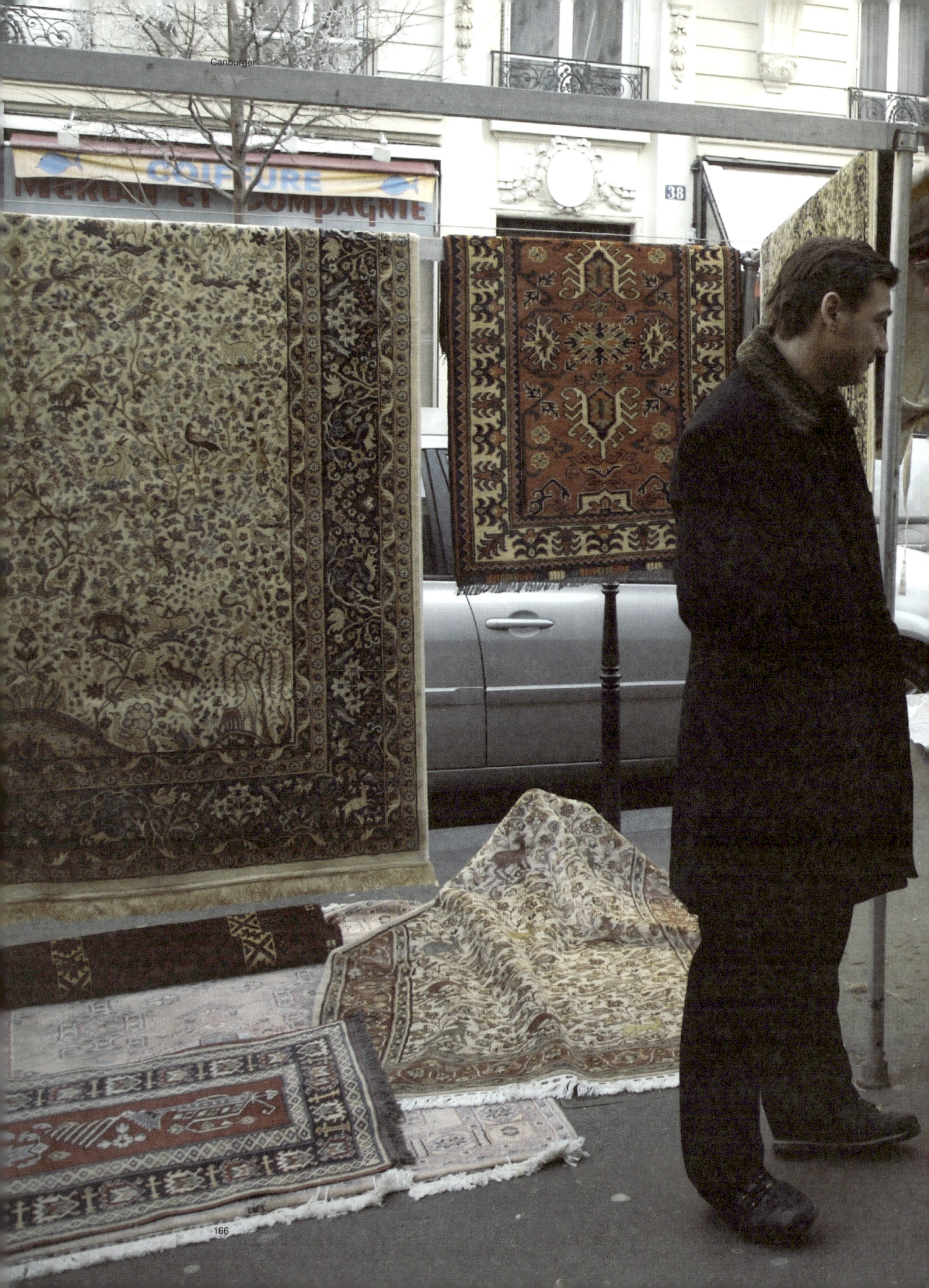

Canburger
COIFFURE
MERIAT ET COMPAGNIE
38

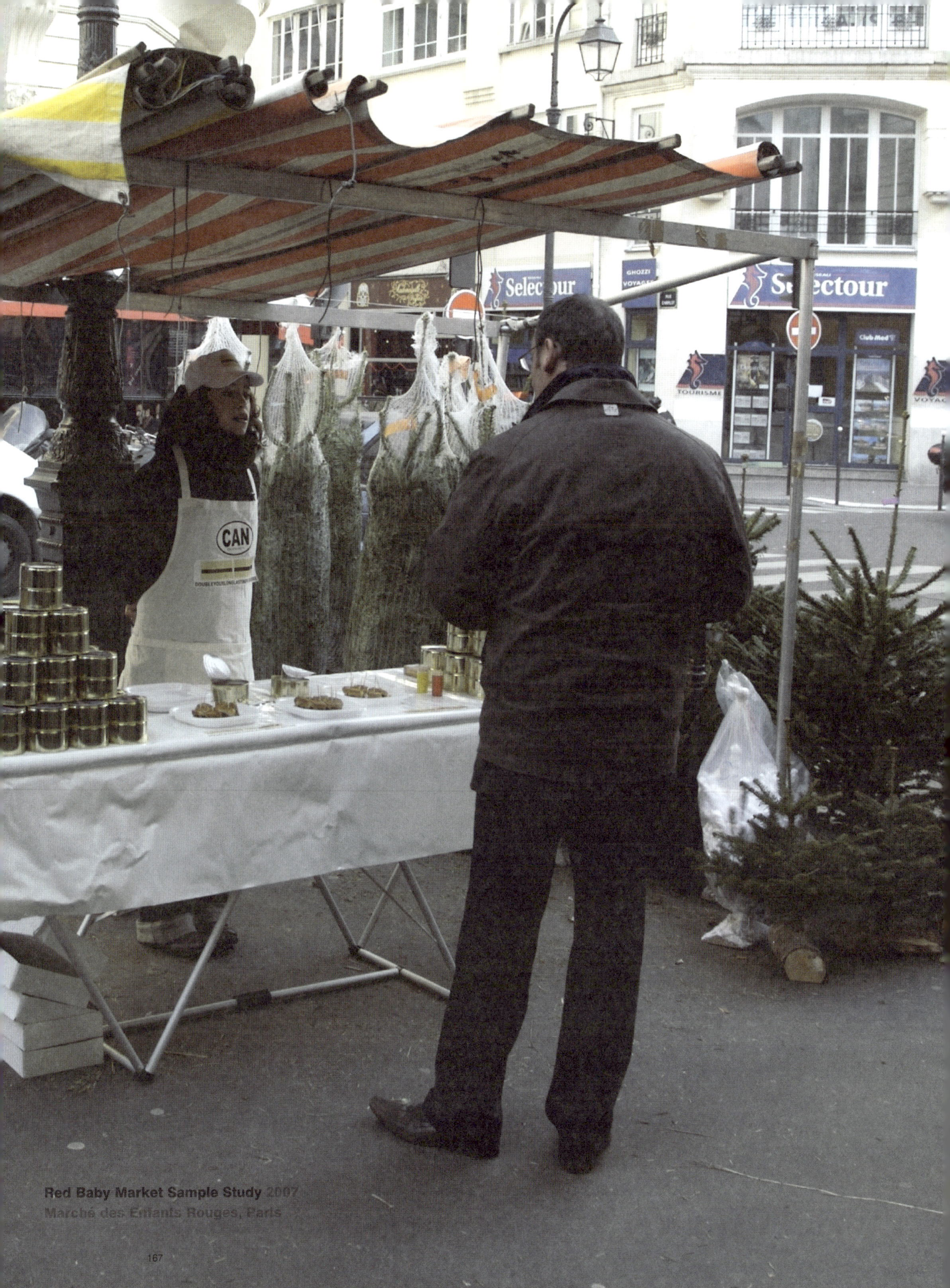

Red Baby Market Sample Study 2007
Marché des Enfants Rouges, Paris

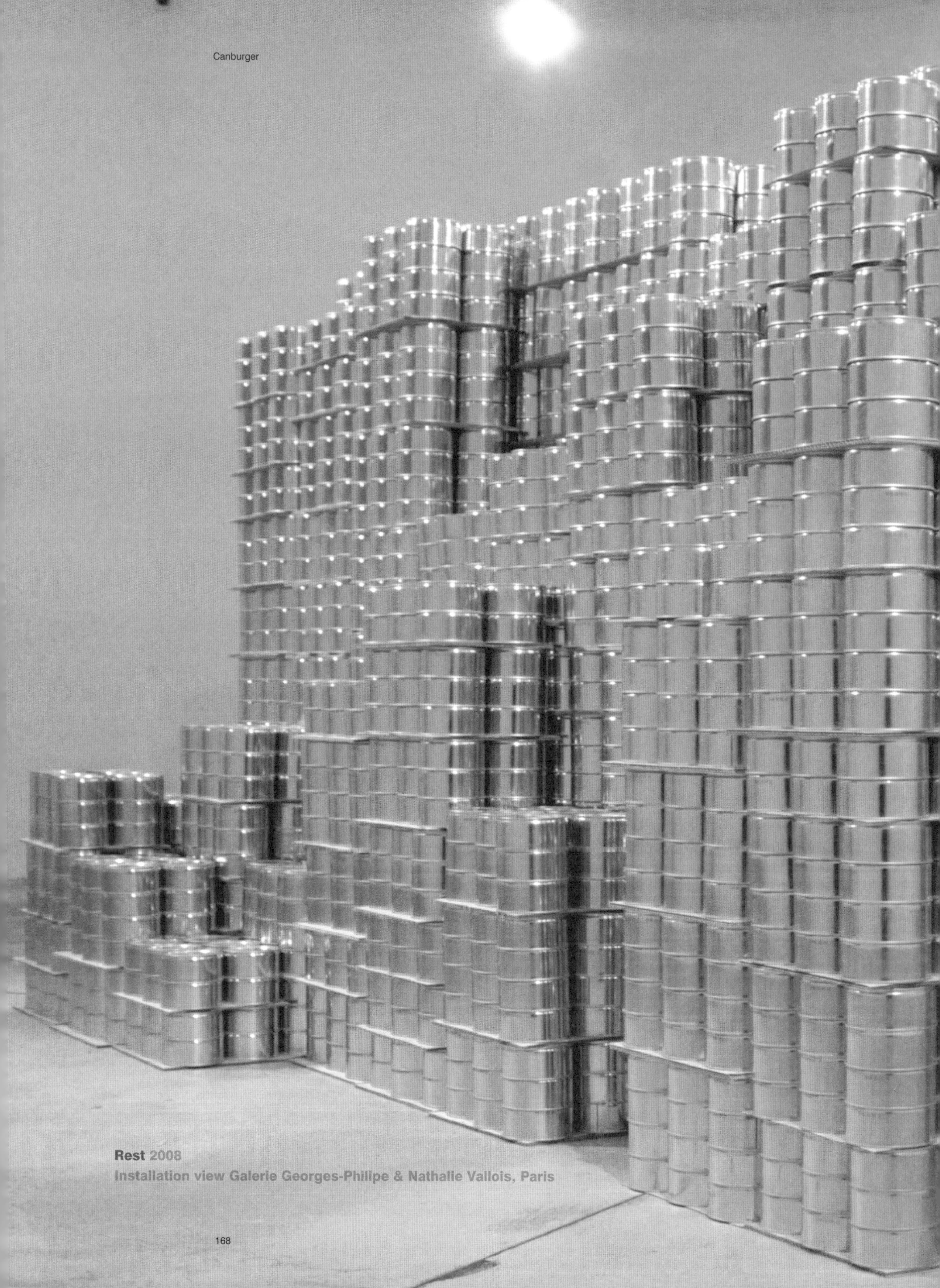

Canburger

Rest 2008
Installation view Galerie Georges-Philipe & Nathalie Vallois, Paris

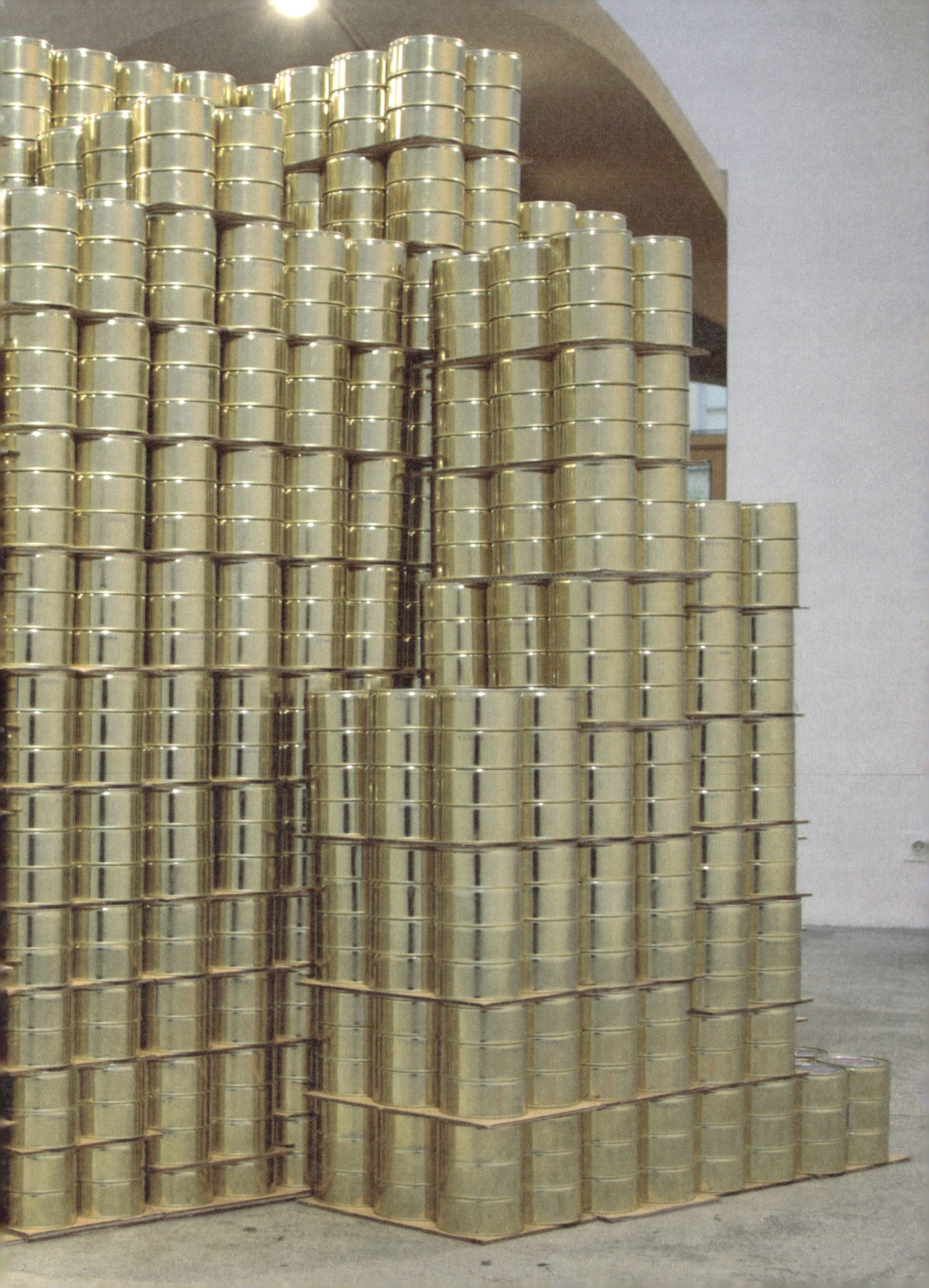

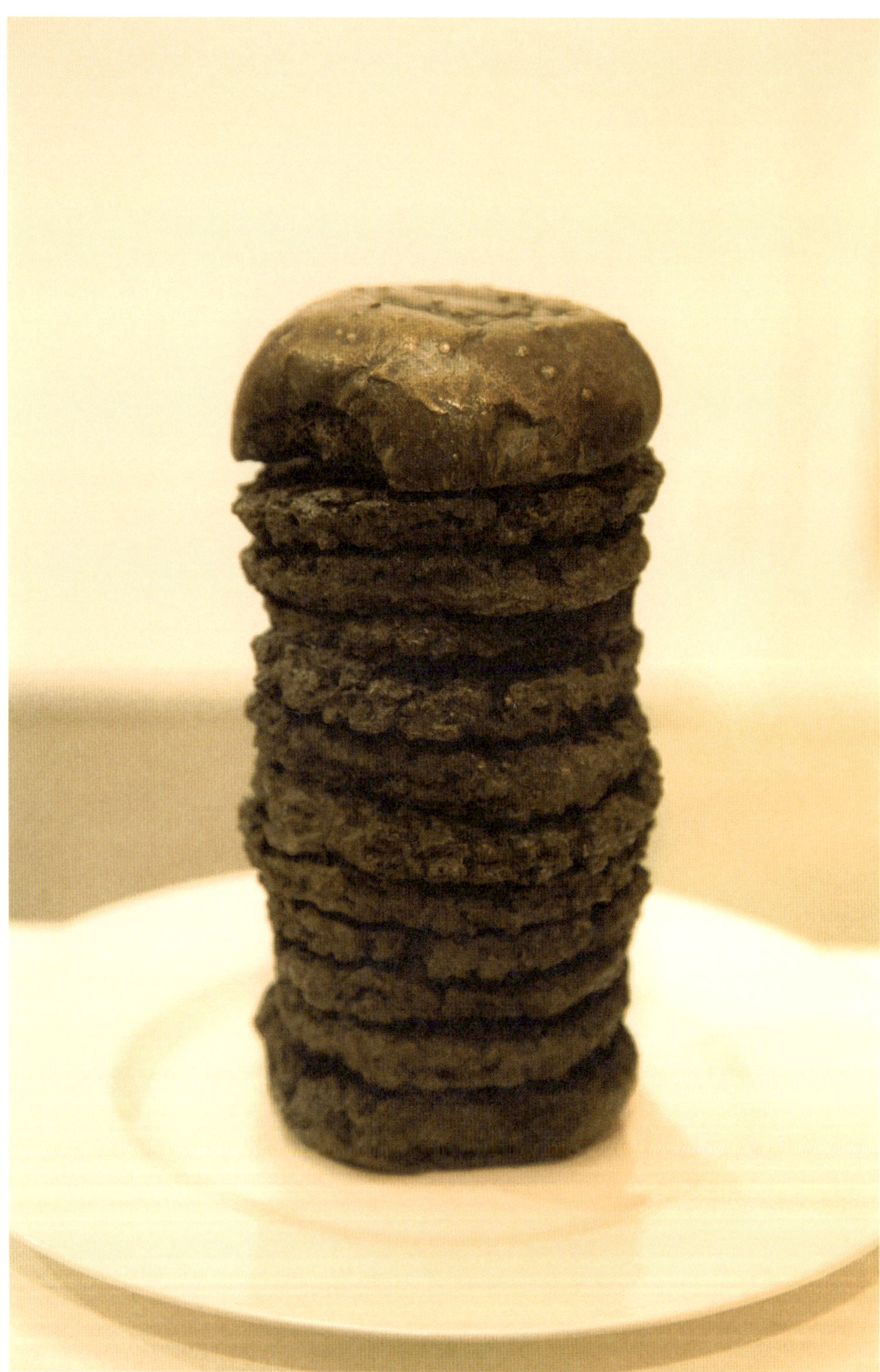

DecaBurger 2007

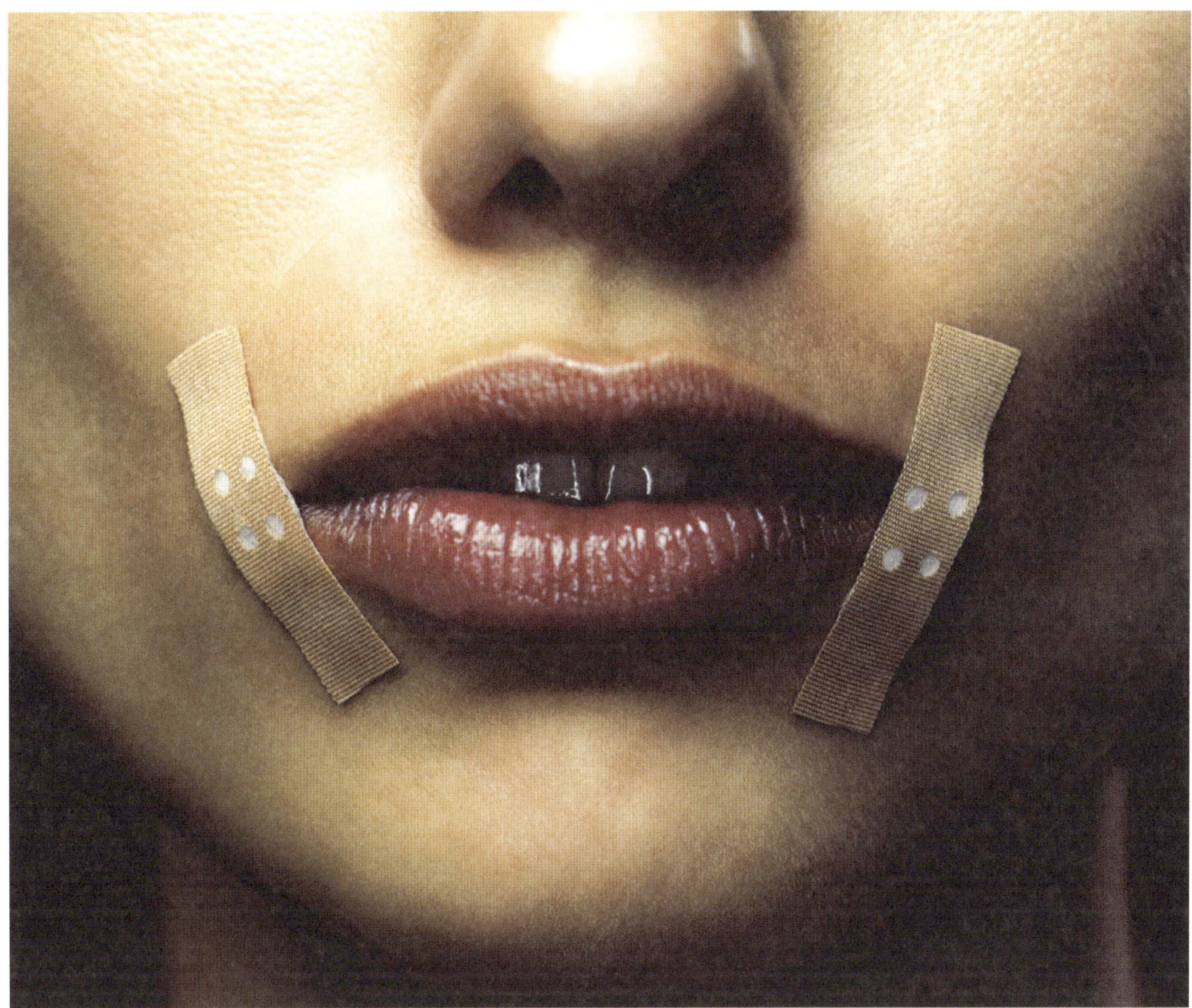

Tear 2007

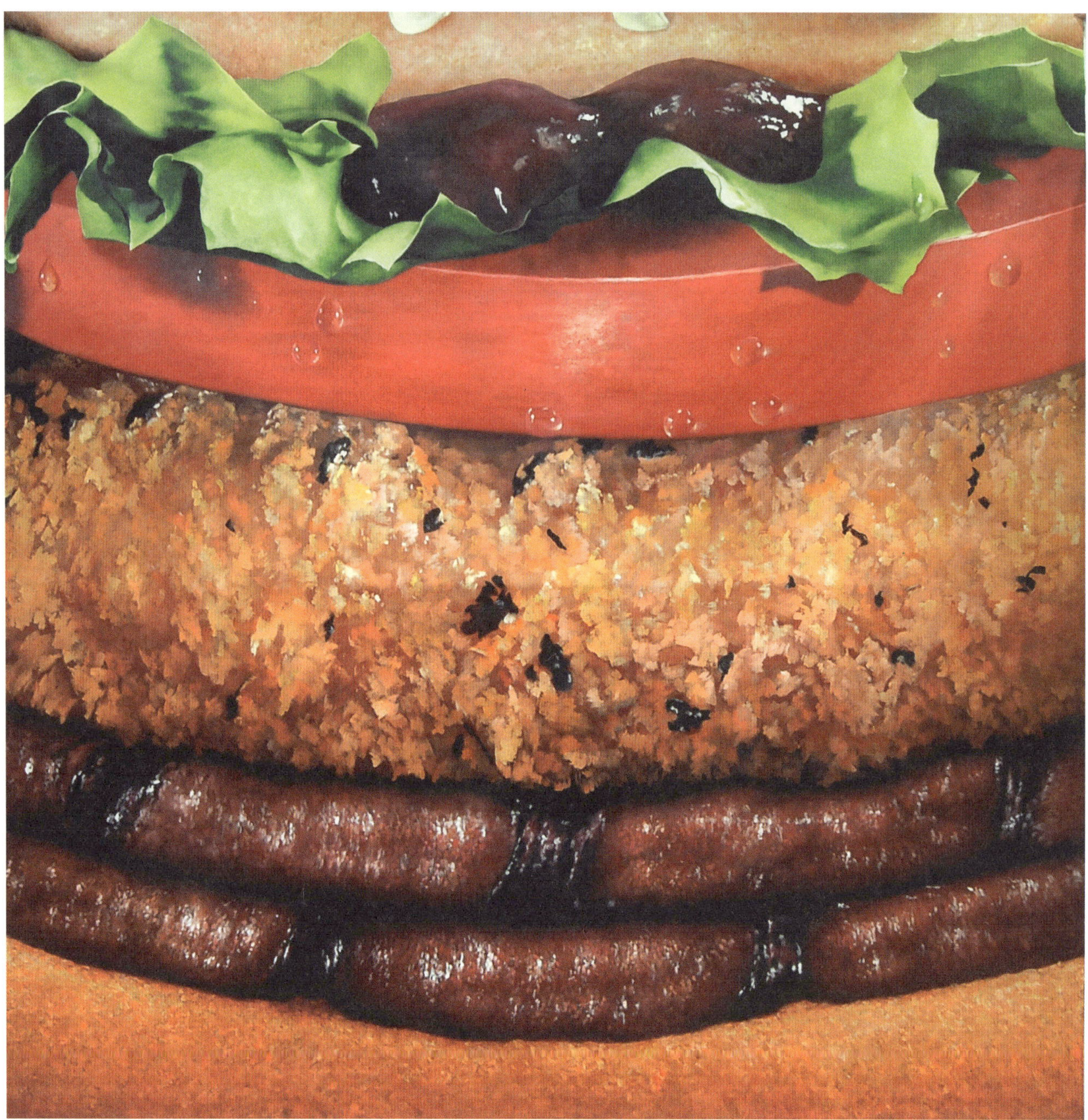

Rocky Mountain Cheese 2008

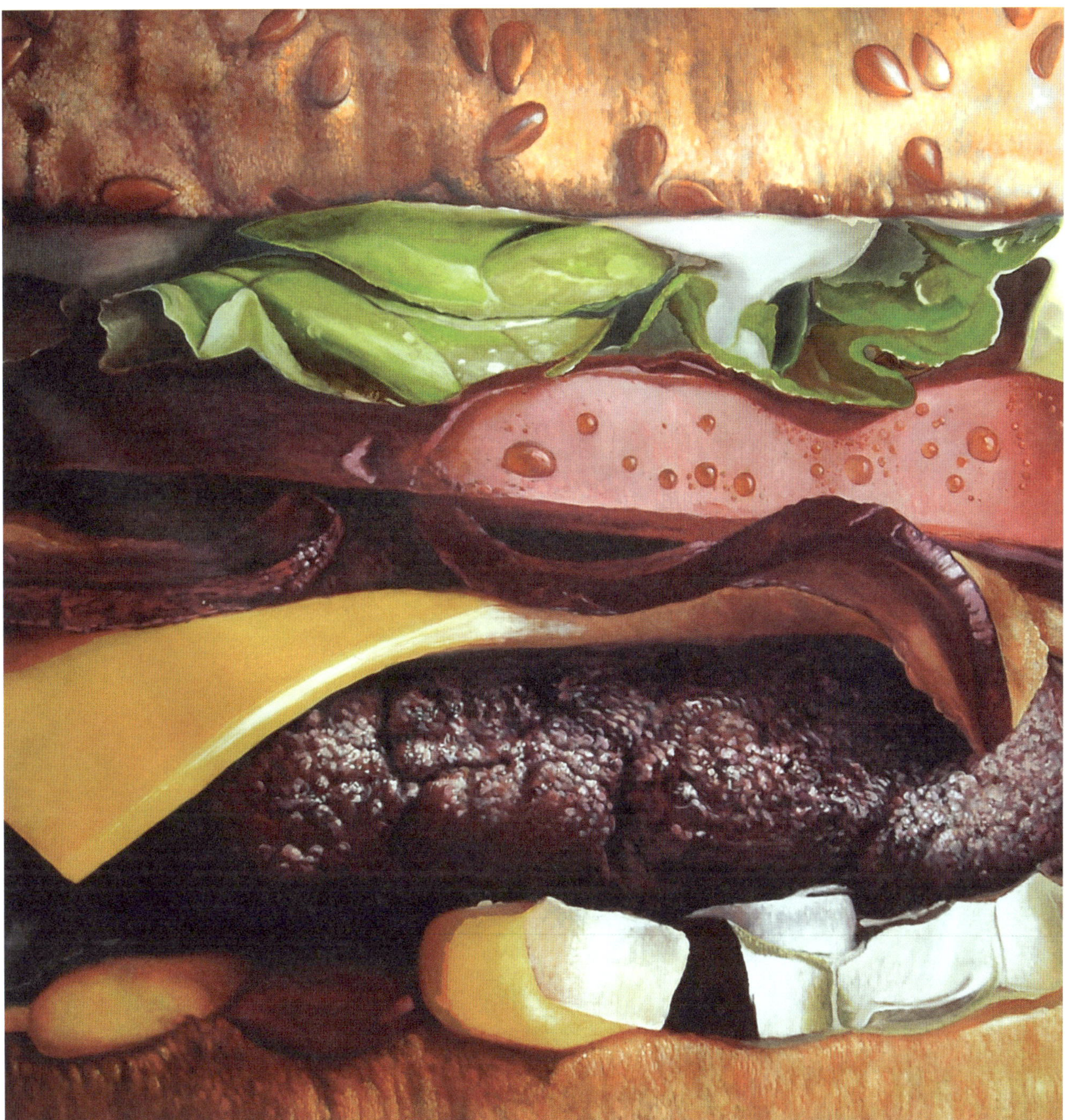

Teen 2008

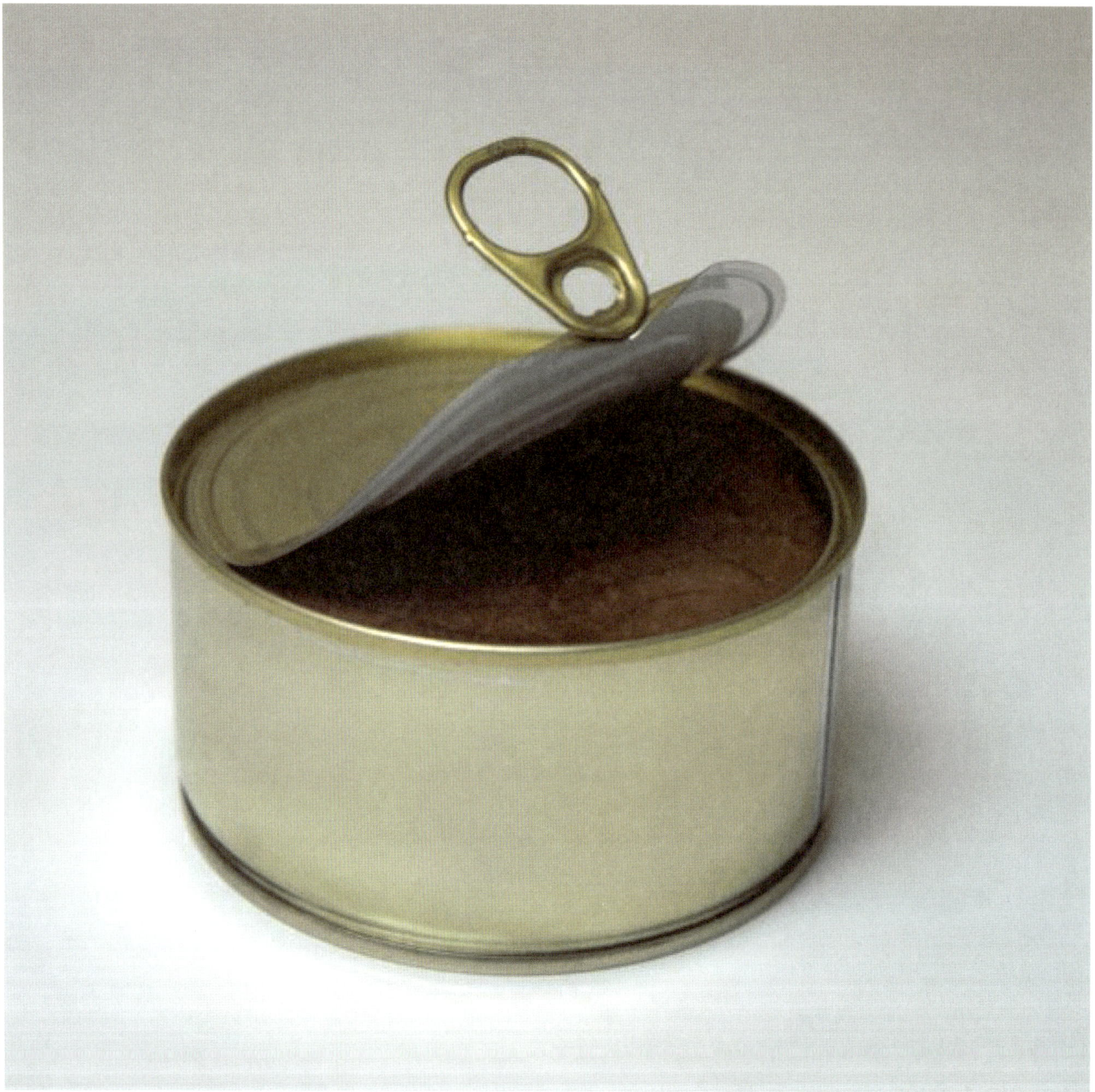

Canburger (opened) 2007

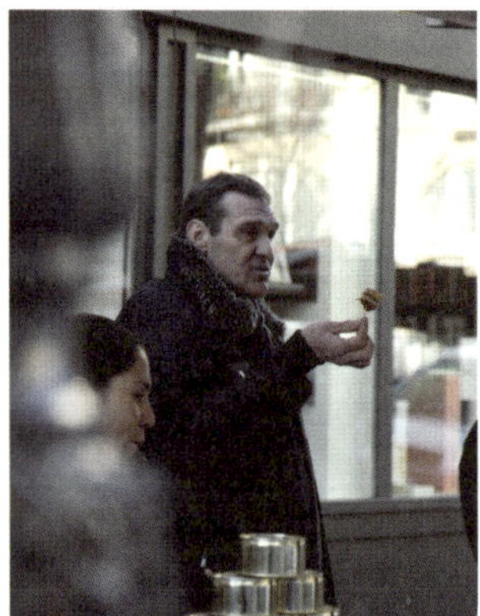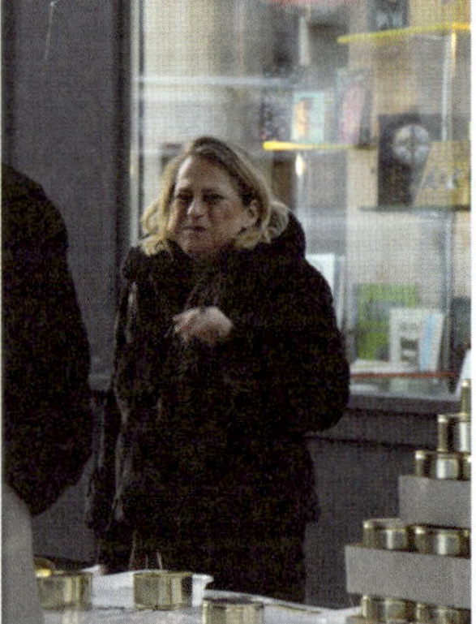

Red Baby Market Sample Study, Paris 2007

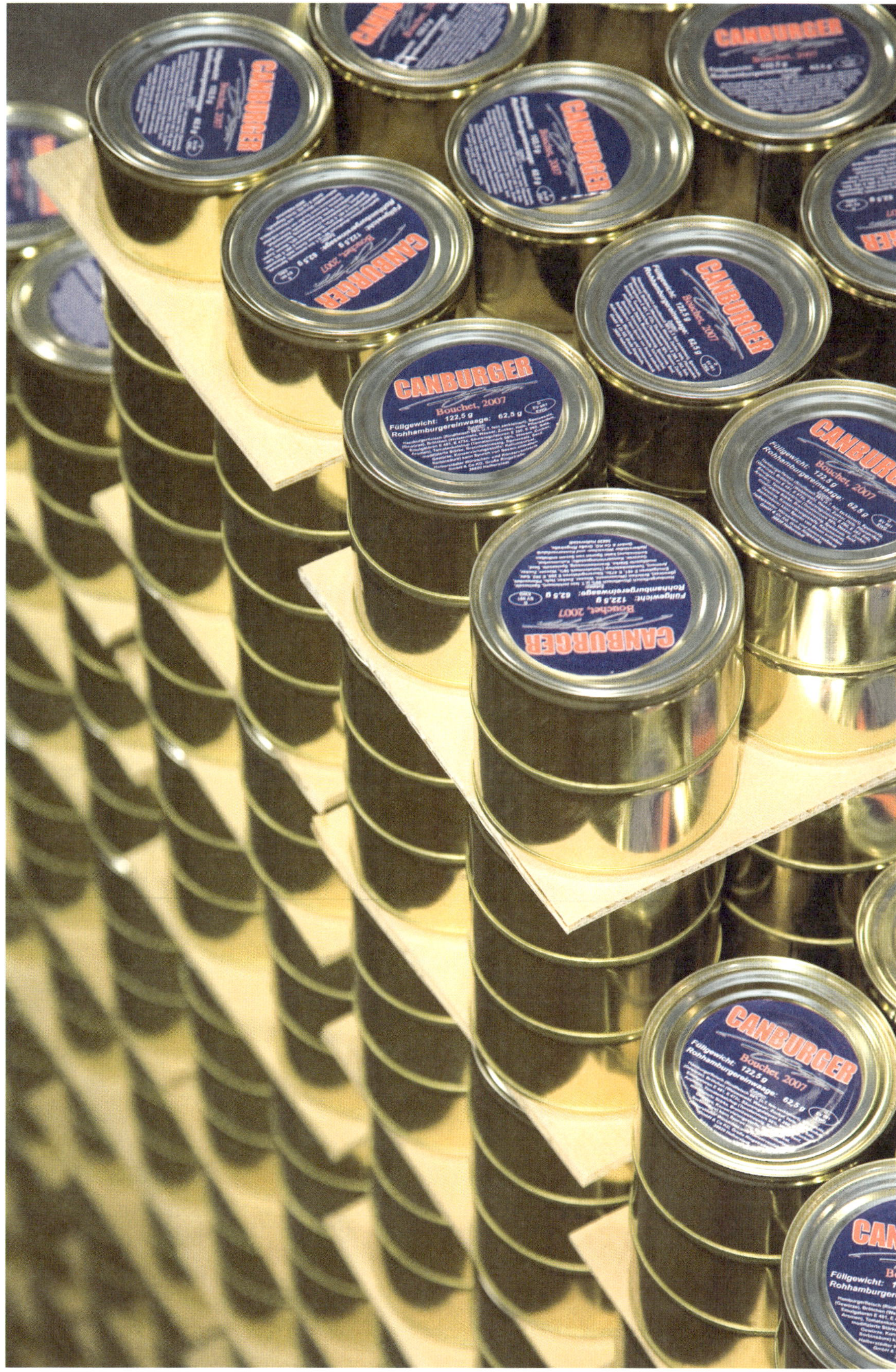

Rest 2008
Detail view

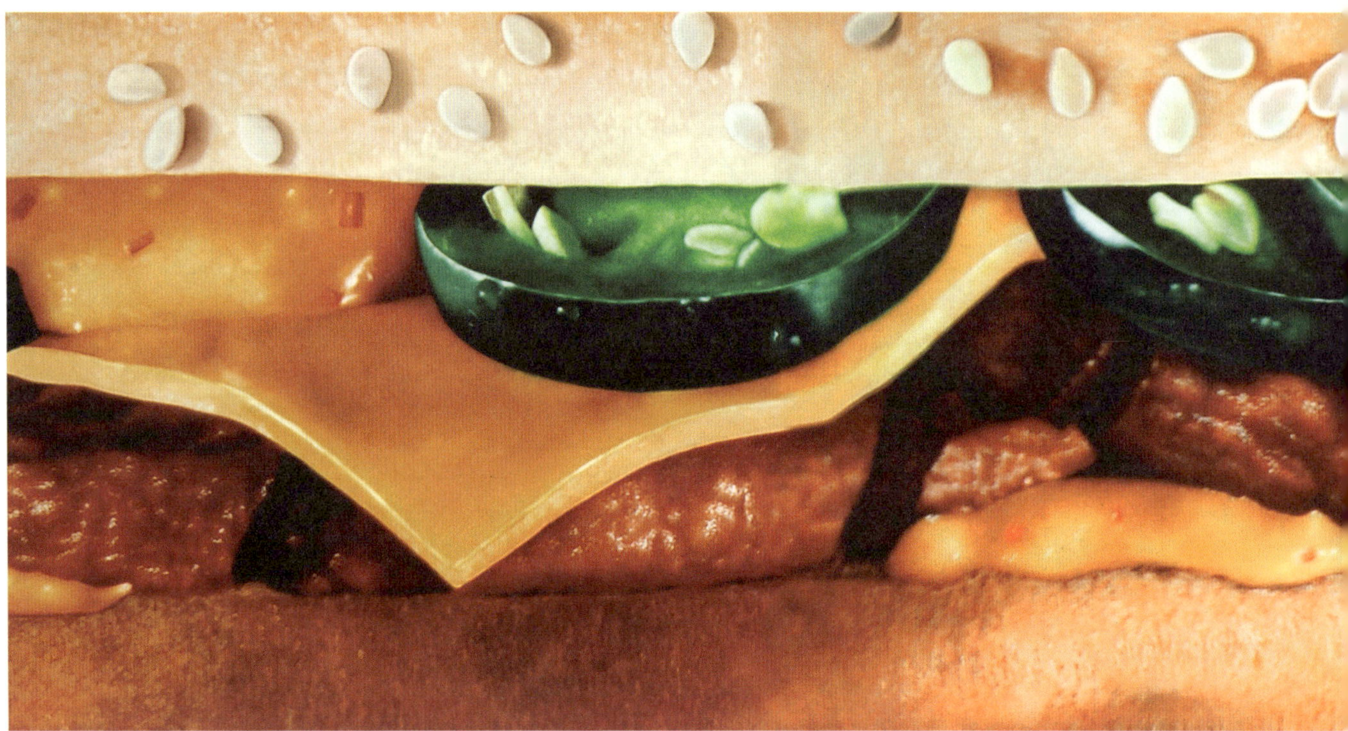

Triple Chili Cheese 2007

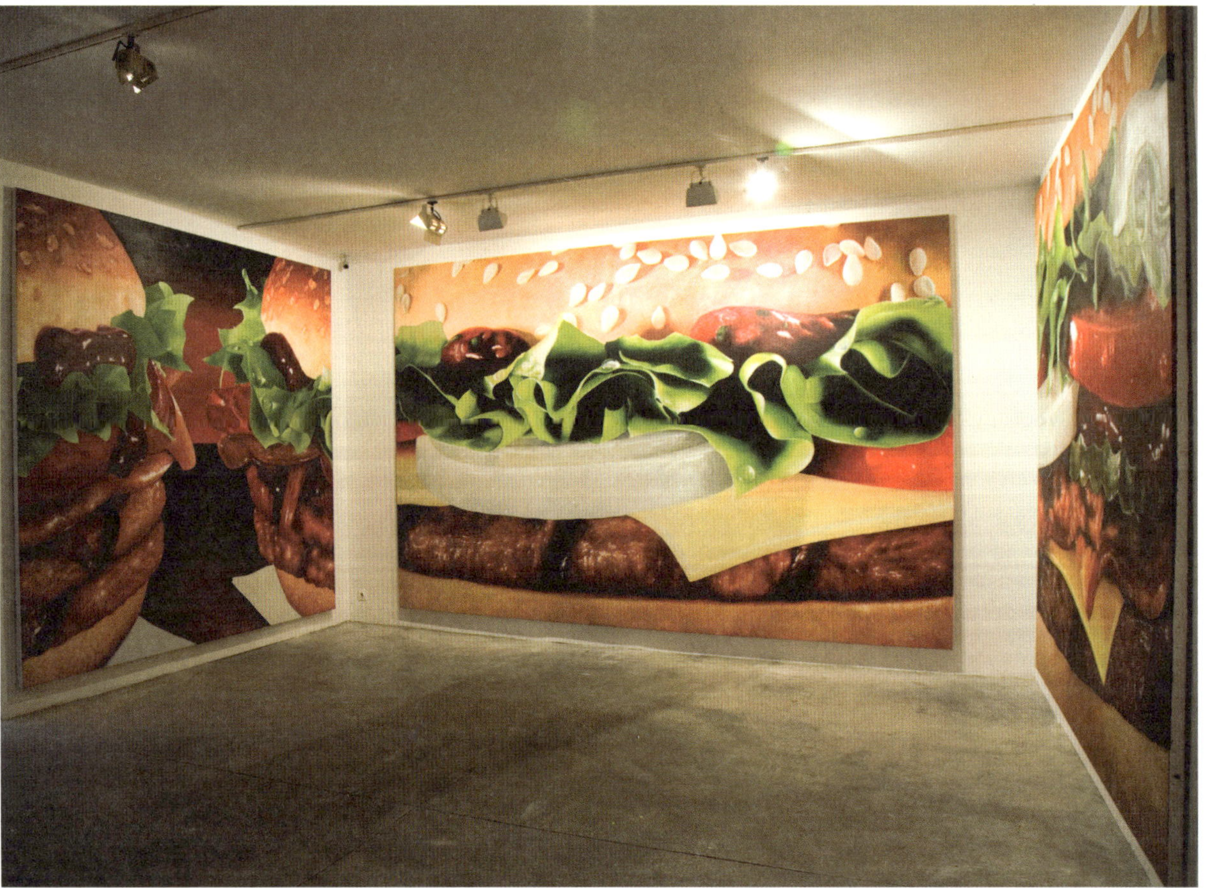

DBL DBL BBQ BBQ, Italian Summer, Everything 2007
Installation View Galerie Georges-Philipe & Nathalie Vallois, Paris

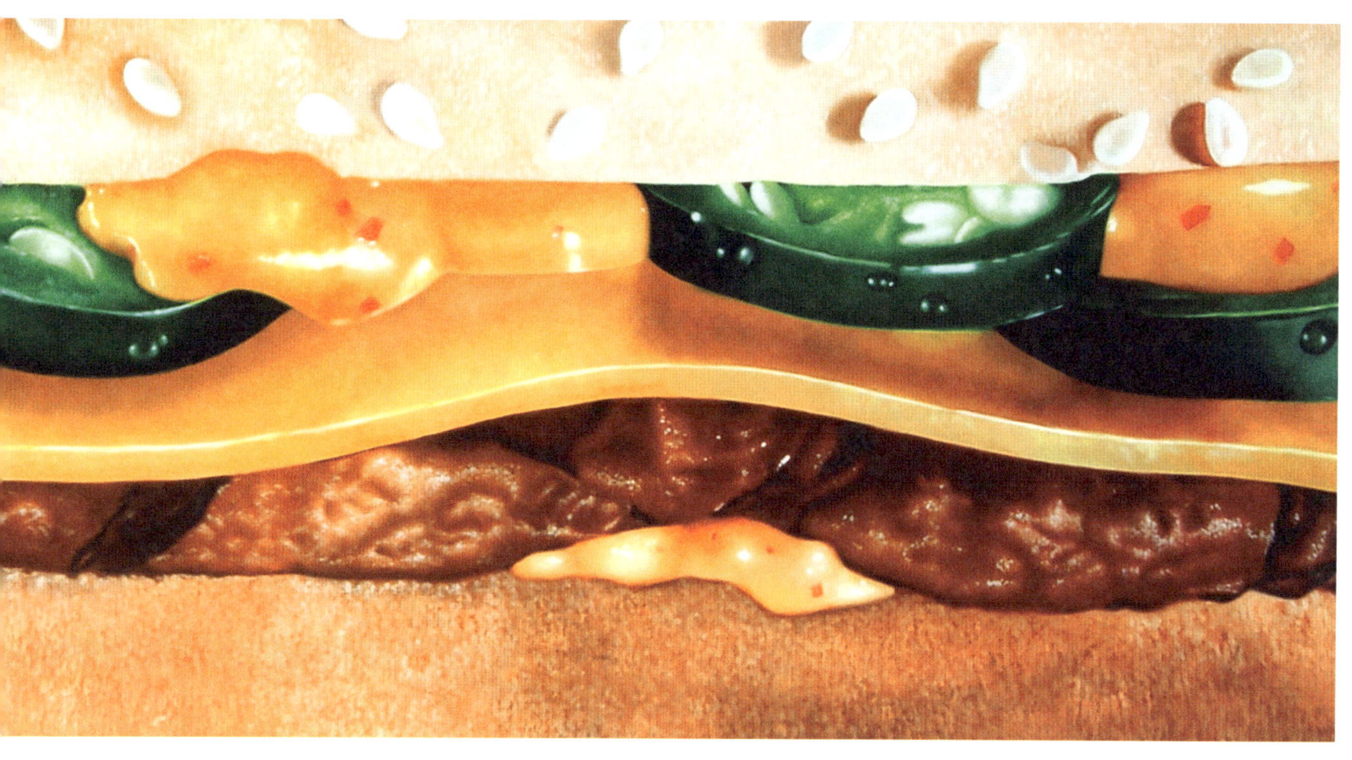

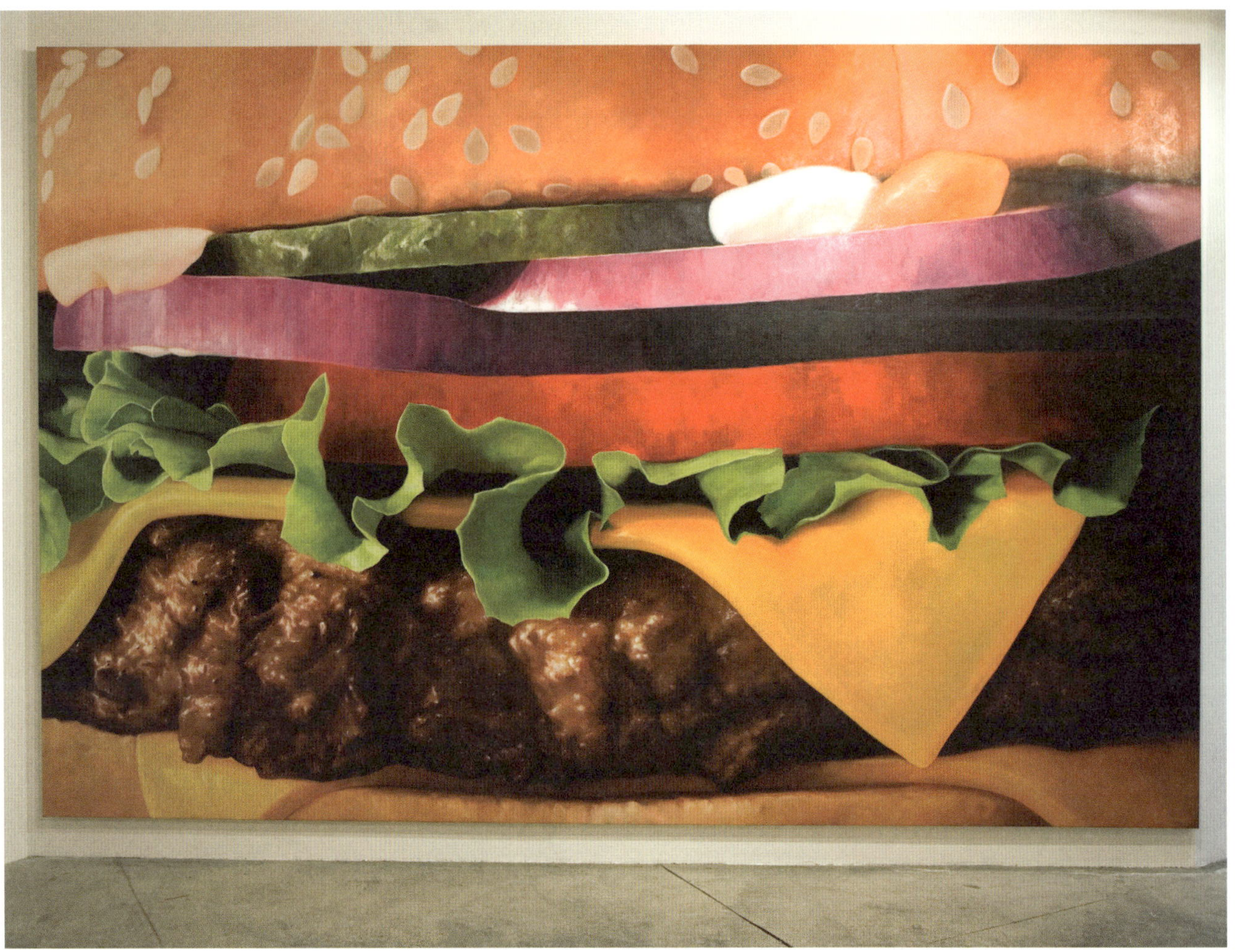

Angus 2007

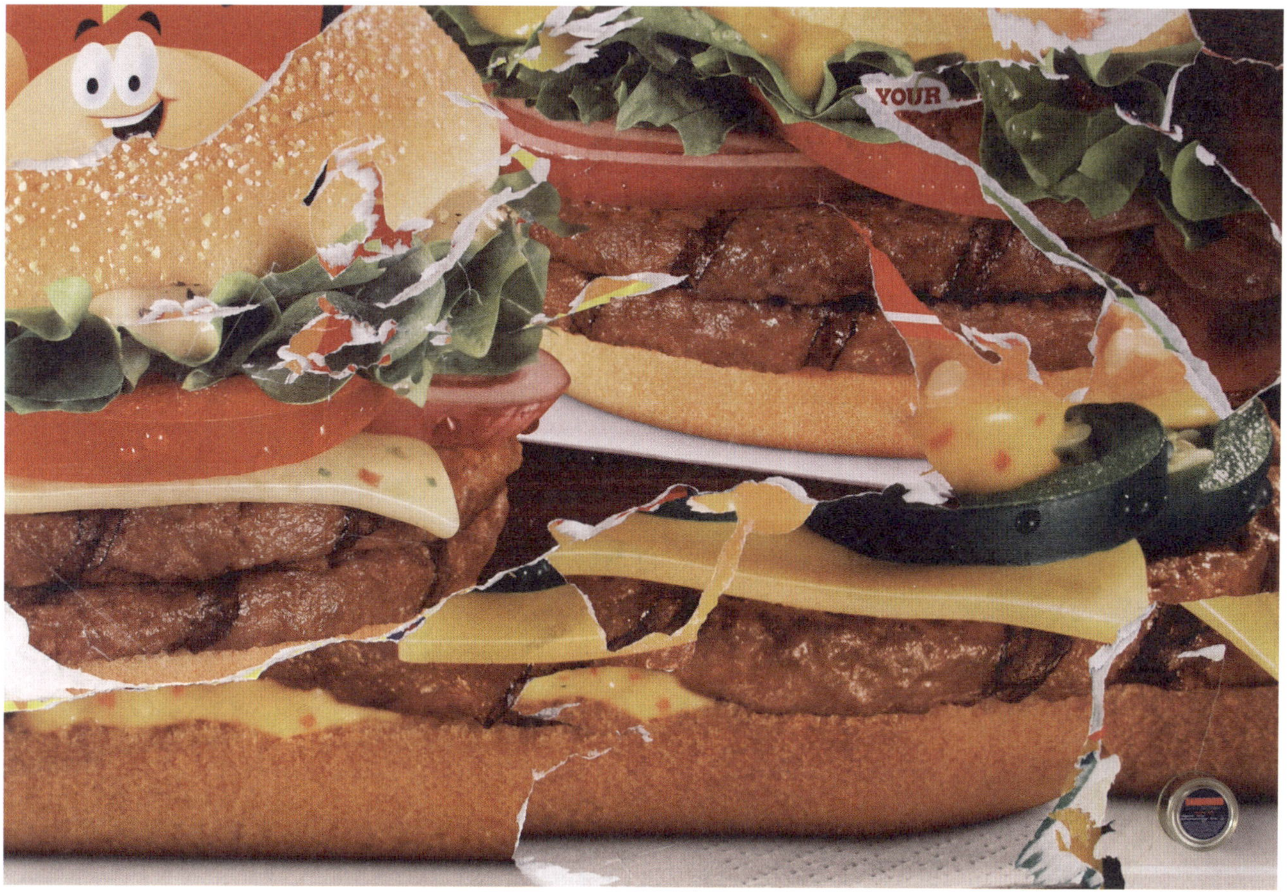

Happy Pile 2008

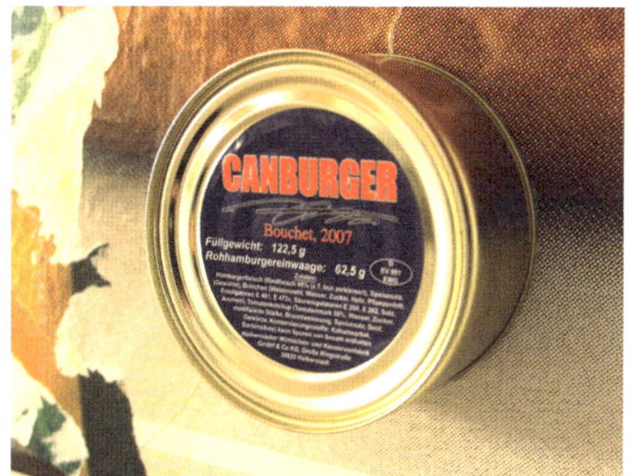

Happy Pile (detail) 2008

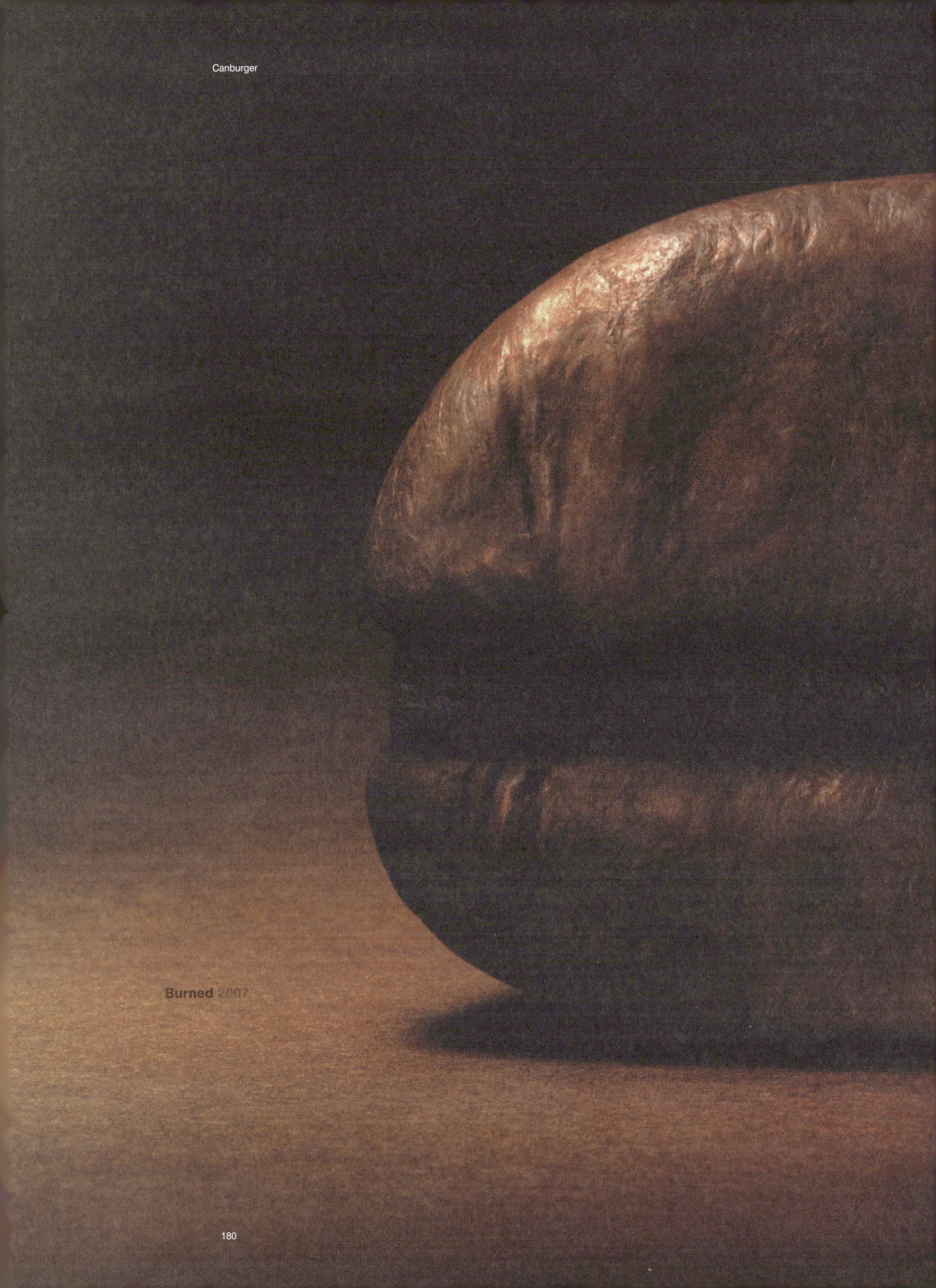

Burned 2007

Beyond the Action-Image: Mike Bouchet's Schizophrenic Time Machine
By Colin Gardner

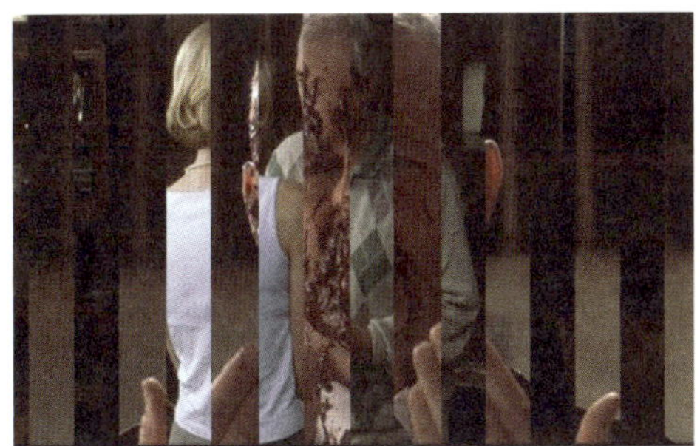

Mile Drive 2008 video still, TRT: 137 min.

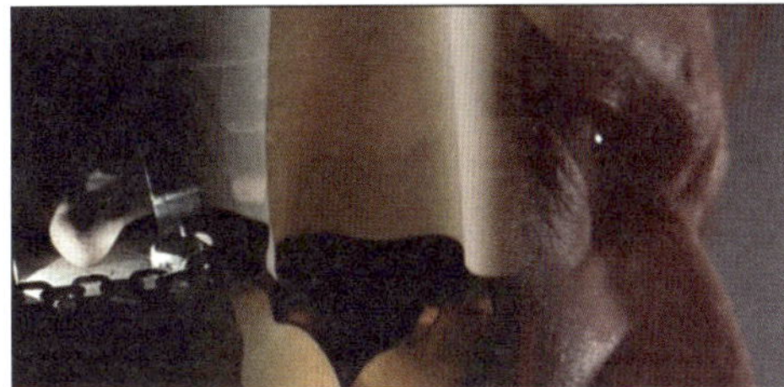

Hard Pie 3 2008 video still, TRT: 94 min.

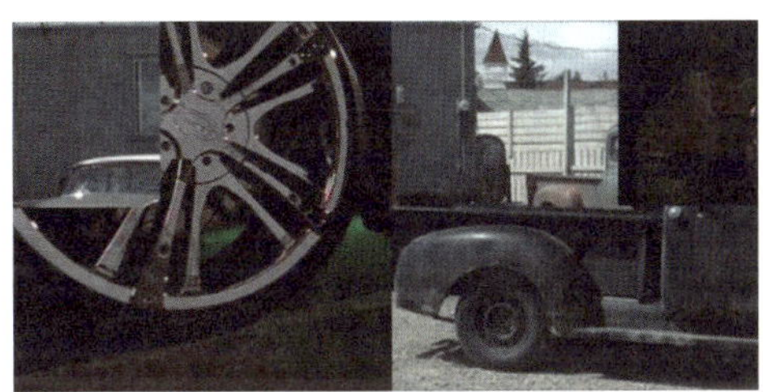

2 Furious for Mountains 2008 video still, TRT: 96 min.

"Sometimes it is necessary to restore the lost parts, to rediscover everything that cannot be seen in the image, everything that has been removed to make it 'interesting'. But sometimes, on the contrary, it is necessary to make holes, to introduce voids and white spaces, to rarify the image, by suppressing many things that have been added to make us believe that we were seeing everything. It is necessary to make a division or make emptiness in order to find the whole again." – Gilles Deleuze

Mike Bouchet and Orson Welles might seem, at first glance, to be strange conceptual bedfellows but they have one fundamental formal tenet in common: the foregrounding of false movement and continuity all the better to accentuate the immanent presence of direct time within the cinematic image. In *Filming Othello* (1978), his documentary on the making of his 1952 Shakespeare adaptation, *The Tragedy of Othello: The Moor of Venice*, Welles bemoaned the project's tight budgetary constraints and the constant need to improvise, whether through the utilization of found sets, perpetual globe-trotting from location to location, and a radically discontinuous shooting schedule. "Iago steps from the portico of a church in Torcello, an island in the Venetian lagoon, into a Portuguese cistern off the coast of Africa," he notes. "He's across the world and moved between two continents in the middle of a single spoken phrase. That happened all the time. A Tuscan stairway and a Moorish battlement are both parts of, what in the film, is a single room. Roderigo kicks Cassio in Massaga and gets punched back in Orgete, a thousand miles away. Pieces were separated not just by plane trips, but by breaks in time. Nothing was in continuity." Of course, as is typical of films driven by causal action and character psychology, the final edit helps to smooth out such spatio-temporal anomalies and irrational cuts to provide at least a modicum of narrative continuity, what Gilles Deleuze, in his Peirce-ian taxonomy of the cinema, calls the action-image, a cinema ruled by the sensory-motor schema. However, Welles's own looming presence as a self-reflexive master of cinematic fakery – remember *F for Fake!* - guarantees that we are also fully aware of this false movement as well as the autonomous visual and sound images (opsigns and sonsigns) that it makes possible.

In contrast to Welles's often vain struggle with his producers to construct a coherent final narrative from broken fragments, Bouchet approaches false movement from the other end of both the narrative and budgetary spectrum. In his "*New New Age Film Festival*" (2008) – a collection of forty feature length "films" (technically theatrically projected videos) screened over the course of a five week schedule in a traditional film festival programming format – and his recent widescreen magnum opus, *16x9 Action Film* (2007), Bouchet begins with the completed films (usually medium-to-high budget commercial Hollywood "product") and then proceeds to edit them together in various spatial combinations so that the hegemony of the action-image (and its concomitant clichés) is undermined through a combination of formal fragmentation and audio-visual overdetermination. For example, most of the forty films in the "*New New Age Film Festival*" are binary constructions, where two different films – often with complementary or dialectically opposed narrative content (e.g. a blaxploitation comedy and a psychological drama; a Bernie Mac baseball film paired with an historical epic about the Battle of Thermopylae) - are conjoined using a wide variety of video and audio effects. These include conventional split screen (50-50 bifurcation, more elaborate alternations of between three and sixteen vertical panels, polygonal or spiral "banding"), super-imposition and the straightforward swapping of the audio and visual source material. Each combination is then trimmed in length so that both films begin and end at exactly the same time, as if edited for a commercial television time slot (once again, we are reminded that time is also money). Far from creating an abstract viewing experience in which affect and psychology are drained out of the new narrative multiplicity, the films allow for a wide variety of emotional and conceptual responses, particularly in relation to non-linear temporality. Plotlines, although stretched and strained, are still relatively easy to follow, despite the constant interference and disruption of the simultaneous image and audio tracks. This has much to do with Hollywood's formulaic adherence to the three-act structure of conventional realism, so that certain plot twists and narrative crescendos tend to coincide and overlap from film to film, producing a mutually reinforcing composite narrative structure. However, despite this centripetal tendency, our highly developed multi-tasking perceptual skills also allow us to discover and exploit new narrative contiguities and (dis)continuities, a sensory-motor schizophrenia that discloses latent sub-texts on different planes or sheets of memory that become raw material for a more creative narrative line-of-flight in which time itself emerges as the dominant formal trope of a new, ever-changing Whole.

In *Little Men* (2008), for example, Bouchet presents a straight superimposition of Keenan Ivory Wayans' infantile comedy, *Little Man* (2006) with Bennett Miller's Oscar-nominated *Capote* (2005), the story of Truman Capote's research into the 1959 Clutter Family killings in Holcomb, Kansas for his best-selling "non-fiction novel," *In Cold Blood*. On a superficial level, Bouchet's title draws an obvious allusion to the two films' lowest common denominator, namely the small stature of their respective leads. Little Man's entire joke revolves around a 2-foot-6-inch tall ex-con named Calvin (Marlon Wayans' shaved head "grafted" on the body of a nine year old boy), who commits a jewel robbery with his dimwitted sidekick, Percy (Tracy Morgan) but accidentally drops his loot – the Queen Diamond – into the purse of a Chicago suburbanite, Vanessa Edwards (Kerry Washington). Inspired by the equally brain-challenged prompting of his hoodlum boss, Walker (Chaz Palminteri), Calvin attempts to retrieve the diamond by disguising himself as a baby and getting Percy to drop him off as an abandoned child on the doorstep of Vanessa and her husband, Darryl (Shawn Wayans). Calvin's corollary in Capote is the 5' 3" eponymous writer himself, and Bouchet has considerable fun collapsing the two identities together in a series of composite scenes where Capote's literary but affected, high-pitched Southern drawl segues with Calvin's street-wise, hip-hop bravado to create a strange mutant form that is both man and child, black and white, gay and straight, linked ultimately by the fact that both men are, in their different ways, con artists striving to scam their way into procuring their prize – the Queen Diamond and the ultimate confessional piece of literature. This physical and psychological connection is forged by often serendipitous and accidental visual coincidences, such as a high angle down on Capote lying in bed superimposed on a similar shot of Calvin in his cot, creating an almost perfect eyeline match. This structural and formal connection is cemented seconds later when Calvin is "abandoned" on the Edwards's doorsteps at the exact moment that Capote appears on the doorstep of Alvin Dewey, the investigating sheriff (Chris Cooper), painting both as devious supplicants with a secret agenda.

However, there is a third "little man" in Capote – the crippled and stunted Perry Smith (Clifton Collins Jr.) – who, along with Dick Hickock (Mark Pellegrino), was responsible for the brutal killings. On an obvious level, the composite narrative connects Smith with Capote, drawing out the writer's less than innocent fascination with his subject, not only in terms of a writer attempting to befriend his protagonist in order to gain a deeper insight into his background and the underlying causes of his latent violence (only to abandon him once the seemingly endless appeals process delays the completion of his book), but also a less than subtle homosexual attraction. Bouchet's juxtaposition expresses the latter in almost slapstick terms when we see the two handcuffed killers being taken into custody and Capote's almost hypnotic exchange of glances with Smith. This is superimposed on a childish prank as Calvin yanks hard on the nose of one of the Edwards' friends, taking him off

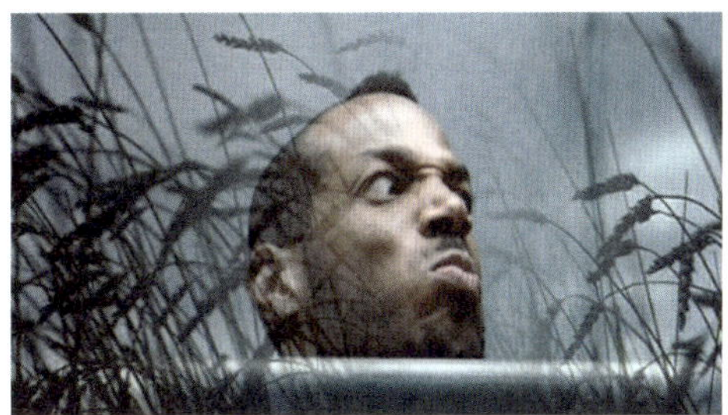

guard and pulling him forwards, thereby physically manifesting what Capote is thinking and feeling as he watches Smith from the assembled crowd. This attraction is further reinforced when Capote visits Smith in his jail cell, asking solicitously after his welfare as Calvin takes great enjoyment in breast feeding from one of the Vanessa's girlfriends. In this way, illicit heterosexuality – a man masquerading as a baby - provides an disjunctive affective inroad into a barely concealed homosexual attraction across and between two points of otherwise disparate presents as the identities of the three 'little men' start to mutate and transform across time and space.

On another level, Bouchet's film creates a strong contiguity between Smith and Calvin, particularly during a poignant but also highly ironical scene when the latter (who actually hungers for a hearty breakfast) is being fed baby food by the Edwards at the very same moment that Capote – who fears that the chief protagonist of his story may be dissipating before his very eyes - is feeding Smith the exact same thing in order to nurse him back to life following a hunger strike. Even more heart-wrenching is the films' combined denouement, where Calvin, having turned against Walker, fends off his goons while bouncing around in a baby harness at the very moment that Smith is being strapped into his execution belts minutes prior to his hanging. It is here that the direct time-image emerges most profoundly as a form of "time regained," not only marking the moment that one life begins (as Calvin adopts his new family) and another ends (Smith's execution), but also at the exact instant that art itself is born as a becoming, through the manipulative apprenticeship of Capote the writer, the author of what will become his last novel, *In Cold Blood*, but also Bouchet the filmmaker, that 'forger' of false narratives compiled from the creative investments and machinations of others.

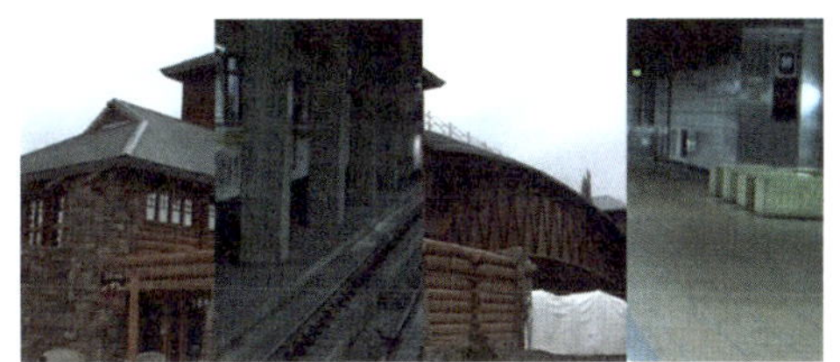

If *Little Men* turns out to be structured around the temporal potentialities of "what will be" through a simultaneity of possible becomings, *Office Job* – a fractured confluence of Michael Mann's *Collateral* (2004) and Alexander Payne's *About Schmidt* (2002) - offers a sober meditation on "what might have been" through the graphic and psychological depiction of parallel universes. Mann's thriller features a hired hitman, Vincent (Tom Cruise), who hijacks a taxi cab driven by Max (Jamie Foxx) in order to carry out a series of assassinations at the behest of Felix, a local Latino gangster (Javier Bardem) during the course of one night in Los Angeles. Collateral's action plays simultaneously with Jack Nicholson's retired widower, Warren R. Schmidt, ambiguously trying to come to terms with his daughter's forthcoming marriage to a dim-witted, albeit sincere loser as well as the realization that his own life has been largely wasted in an alienating marriage and a safely routine, dead-end job working for an insurance company. Schmidt ultimately finds some form of emotional and existential redemption in his long-distance sponsorship of a six year-old Tanzanian boy, Ndugu.

In this case Bouchet resorts to a fourfold vertical "banding" in which the films run alternately across the width of the screen in the combination of *About Schmidt* / *Collateral* / *About Schmidt* / *Collateral*, the films' formal "parallels" also suggesting certain psychological correspondences between the characters themselves. This is borne out by Michael Mann's own published commentary on *Collateral*, where he argues that the film's general theme expresses a clash of ideals between the two main characters. Whereas Vincent represents becoming, living in the moment and improvising his way out of trouble as the need arises, Max is safely sedentary, meticulously planning every move in advance, exemplified by the "Island Limos" company that he plans to establish once his nest egg is complete. Of course, as is typical of all action-image films, characters learn to grow psychologically and transform their situation for the mutual benefit of both the protagonist and the immediate community. *Collateral* is no exception: the extremity of the situation and the resulting violent encounters force Max to become more open to improvisation, culminating in a final shootout on a metro train when he kills Vincent, aided and abetted by his newfound ability to stay calm under pressure and adapt as the circumstances demand. In this respect, Max's psychological and sensory-motor growth is contrasted with that of Schmidt, who represents an older, more calcified version of what Max might have become, had he not encountered Vincent on that fateful night. In contrast, Max and Vincent are more extreme versions of the necessary adaptability that Schmidt is in the process of discovering as he becomes slowly reconciled to his daughter's life choices as well as the emotional gratification offered up by his unconditional generosity to Ndugu.

As in the case of *Little Men*, the film's often stark juxtapositions provide dialectical fodder for a deeper meditation on time, especially concerning matters of life and death. Thus, when Schmidt discovers his wife Helen's dead body sprawled on the floor of their house, Max and Vincent are riding in the cab discussing other forms of death: from the disinterested detachment inherent to the exigencies of Vincent's job as a hired assassin to the pogroms in Rwanda and the dropping of the atom bomb (one recalls Stalin's alleged remark that "One death is a tragedy. A million deaths is just a statistic"). Then as Helen (June Squibb) is wheeled out in a body bag, Max asks Vincent, cynically, "What are you doing? Are you just taking out the garbage?" as if to suggest, via audio-visual contiguity, that Schmidt, isolated in his own time frame, is feeling a less-than-guilty sense of release from his apparent "loss." Even more telling is the film's climax, which utilizes cross-cutting - that staple of the action drama, dating back to the silent features of D.W. Griffith - across and between the respective points of present of the two films to create an ironic commentary on both psychological and narrative catharsis. As in the closing montage of Francis Ford Coppola's *The Godfather* (1972), where the new Don, Michael Corleone takes care of "family business" by systematically executing his enemies at the exact moment of his Godson's christening, Bouchet offers the stark contrast of the drawn-out, violent shootout between Max and Vincent as Schmidt delivers an uncomfortable speech at his daughter's wedding, as if *Collateral*'s visceral tension were creating an objective correlative of Schmidt's internal upheaval.

Of course, the combined narrative doesn't end there. After the nuptials, Schmidt takes to the road in his RV and, accompanied by the voice over narration of his latest letter to Ndugu, he stops by a pioneer museum in the Mid-West and walks through the dioramas featuring the "sooners" and their covered wagons, meditating on his own existential place in the world - "What difference do I make?" – before subsequently lamenting his failure to prevent his daughter's marriage to "That nincompoop." All the while, *Collateral* is unleashing a wave of atavistic violence on the metro train, as Max and Vincent try to outmaneuver each other in a final shootout. The association of classic Western genre tropes with the pioneer dioramas is too obvious to miss, particularly as it suggests a direct correlation between the blatant violence of one scenario with the latent violence of the other, thereby indicting the manifest destiny of American expansionism as yet another variation of the Rwanda massacres. In this way, Bouchet's film jumps across the immediacy of time in the present tense to unleash historical memory (historical materialist time) as a violent becoming toward death.

Whereas the films featured in the "*New New Age Film Festival*" are trimmed to fit a pre-conceived time frame, all the better to disclose a latent temporality – historical and mnemic - within the framework of a displaced and false movement-image, *16x9 Action Film* has a built in "degeneration" that realigns the spectator's response to time as a series of shifting points of present. The feature length video projection consists of 144 action films, ranging from

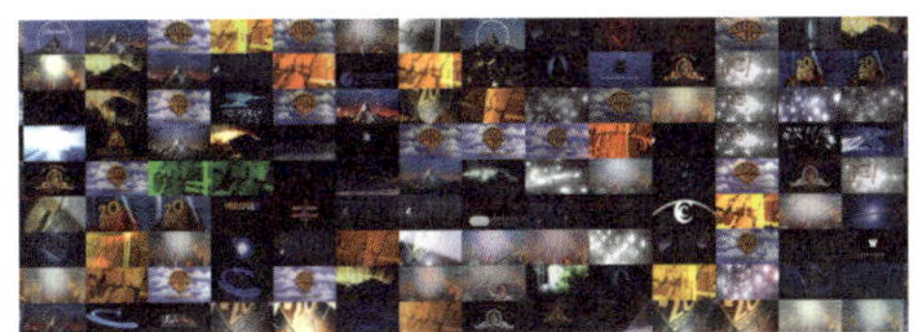

Rambo and *Pulp Fiction* to *Mission Impossible*, which are played simultaneously in a widescreen, rectangular grid (16 films playing across the screen, 9 projected from the top down), much like a gigantic television production room, where the viewer has complete freedom to switch their attention from one image to the next, acting as a surrogate technical "director." In this case, the duration of Bouchet's film is dictated by the length of the feature with the longest running time – 144 minutes – so that as each film reaches its closing credits and ultimately fades to black, its rectangular presence on the larger screen registers as a void or absence. Although the audio component is collaged from all 144 films playing together, creating a cacophony of noise akin to an amplified video arcade, certain soundtracks – most notably the *James Bond* and *Star Wars* themes – tend to emerge from the collective din to act as a recurring and binding leitmotif to the film as a whole.

Echoing *Little Men* and *Office Job*, the film also benefits temporally and thematically from conventional Hollywood action formulas – the films' prevailing three-act structure, pre-credit teasers, recurring audio-visual tropes such as explosions, car chases, stuttering machine guns, skydiving – which help to create a consolidating counterpoint between and across each individual filmic rectangle. Thus, as our eye glides across the surface of the screen, connecting the fragmented points of present that constitute the cinematic grid, we are at the same time able to penetrate selected frames and activate the latent sheets of past (virtual memory) which lay buried within them. In this way virtual and actual, past and present, time and movement, become the basic raw material for a larger narrative becoming that is far greater than the sum of the collective, 144 component parts, producing, in short, a pure multiplicity.

Perhaps even more telling is the film's self-reflexive response to its own built-in durational limits. Almost all of the films seem to end around the two hour mark – another index of Hollywood commercial exigencies, determined by mass-marketing – so that the overall widescreen image's internal "decay" tends to accelerate within a tight, five minute time frame as each filmic rectangle culminates with its closing credits and a punctuating corporate logo. In this way Bouchet reminds us that behind the spectacle of cinematic art lurks the virtual world of money (and time-as-money). In a strange irony, the artist thus works backwards from an extremely expensive finished product (financed by others) to arrive at the exact same point reached by the bankrupt Welles working from the opposite direction via scraps of incomplete scenes in a vain attempt (ultimately financed by himself) to cobble together a "complete" version of *Othello*. In both cases, to quote Federico Fellini, "When there is no more money left, the film will be finished."

Colin Gardner is Professor of Critical Theory and Integrative Studies and Chair of the Art Department at the University of California, Santa Barbara.

16 x 9 Action Film 2007

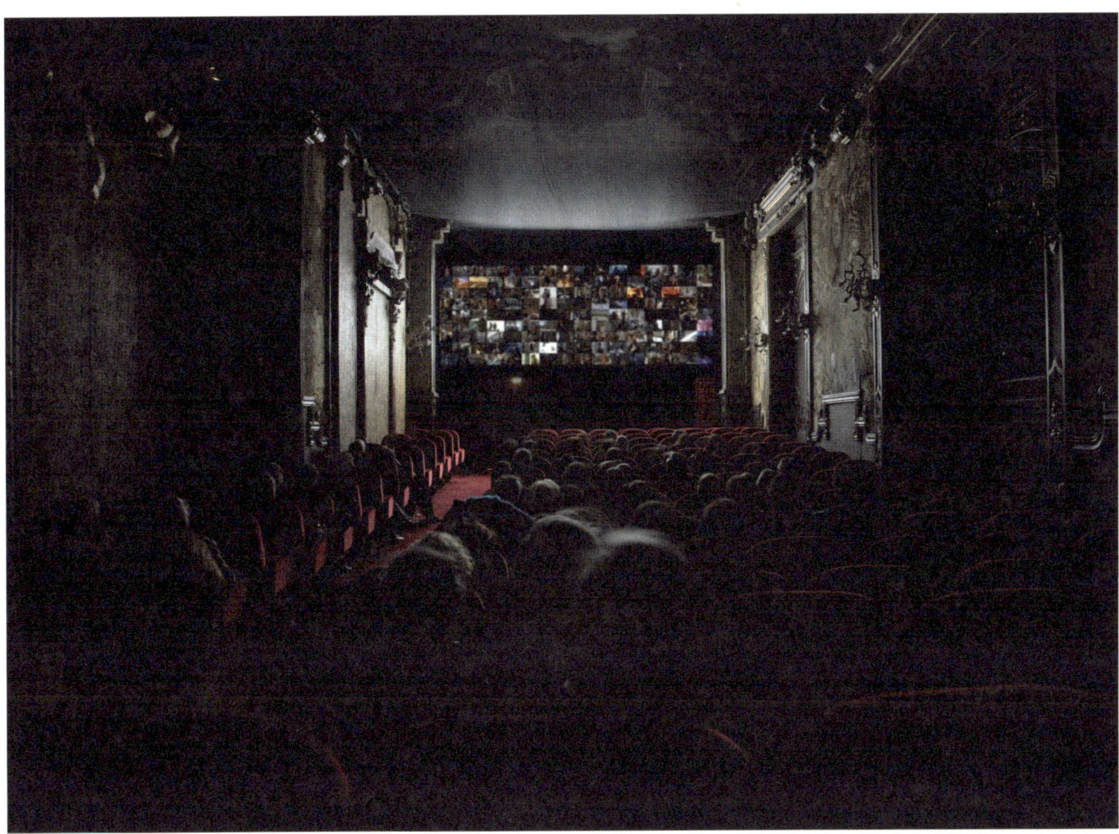

This feature length video projection is composed of 144 "Action" films playing simultaneously. All the films are arranged in a rectangular grid, 16 films across and 9 films down, and the audio is likewise that of all 144 films playing together. The length of the composition is dictated by the length of the film with the longest running time, which is 144 minutes.

The video has been composited at 2K resolution and has been mastered onto D-5 HD tape stock for playback at 35mm film projection resolution. The HD edit masters are timecoded and tailed for projection standards, and the audio is Dolby stereo. The high resolution allows for crisp projections up to 60ft wide.

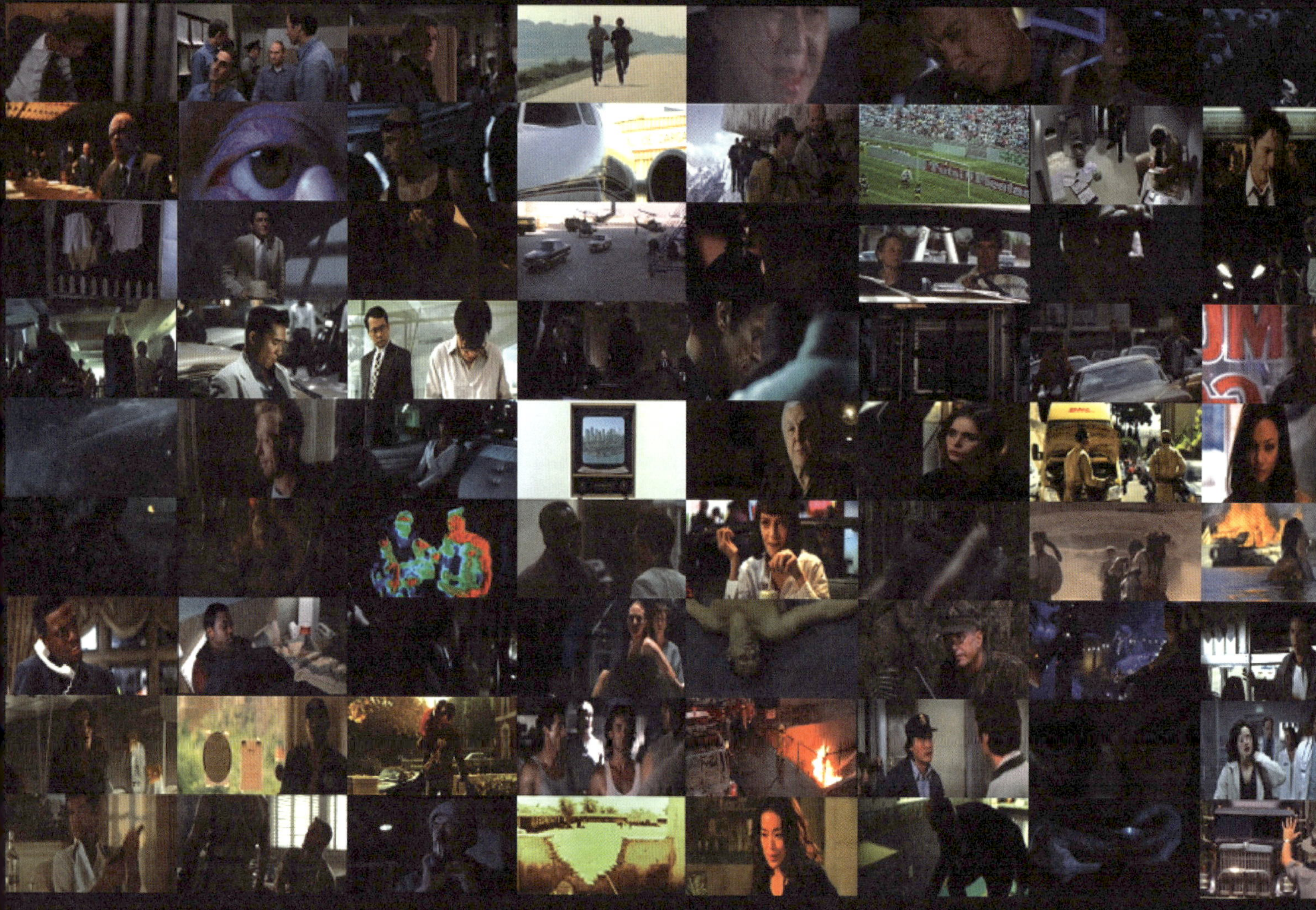

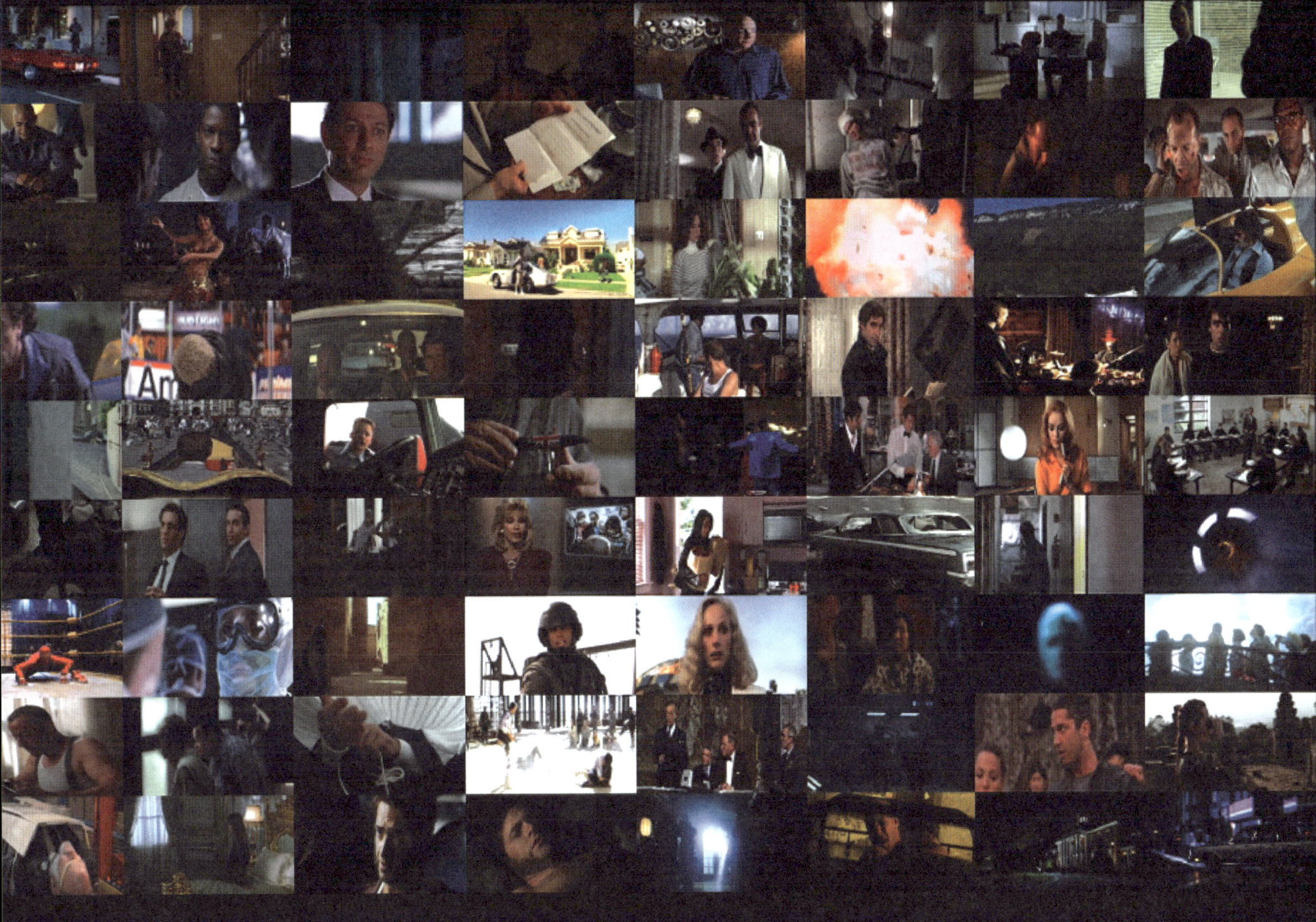

New New Age Film Festival 2008

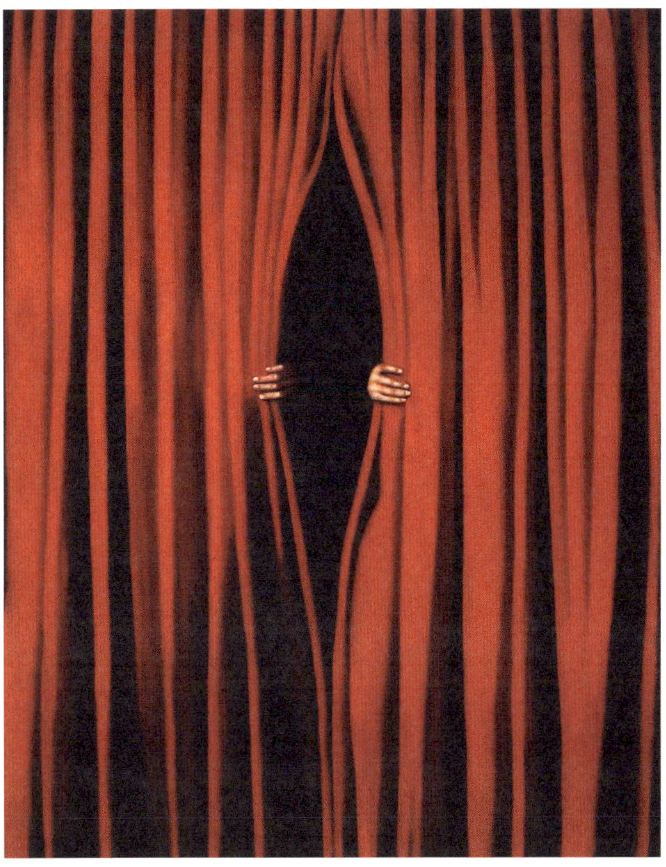

Double Bind: A psychological predicament in which a person receives from a single source conflicting messages that allow no appropriate response to be made.

The New New Age Film Festival, is a classic "Film Festival" of feature length movies the artist has created from compiling existing popular commercial films. 40 films are presented over the course of a 6 week schedule- 3 films per day, (2 on Saturdays) shown twice during this time, allowing for multiple viewings.

The films employ a wide variety of combinations. Most are binary constructions (2 films conjoined), using a variety of split screen and video effects: dissolves, super-impositions and even the simple swapping of audio and video sources. Each film is combined in a method particular to its respective content. The general effect is that the viewer can watch multiple films simultaneously on the same screen. The films cover and multiply a variety of emotional experiences while the Hollywood three-act structure and standardized production techniques keep the films strangely seamless.

Bouchet sees these films as an attempt to exaggerate the "Double Bind" communication rampant in our highly and richly fictionalized visual culture. By conflating multiple emotional states, a psychological effect is created that reveals both the highly manipulative effects of films, as well as their both "over the top" and simple absurdity. Divorce of reality, non plausibility, and cognitive dissonance all dovetail into our newly acquired ability to perceive and cultivate this low level schizophrenia. The modern film-viewing mind has become both keenly attuned to and insulated from this waking hypnosis.

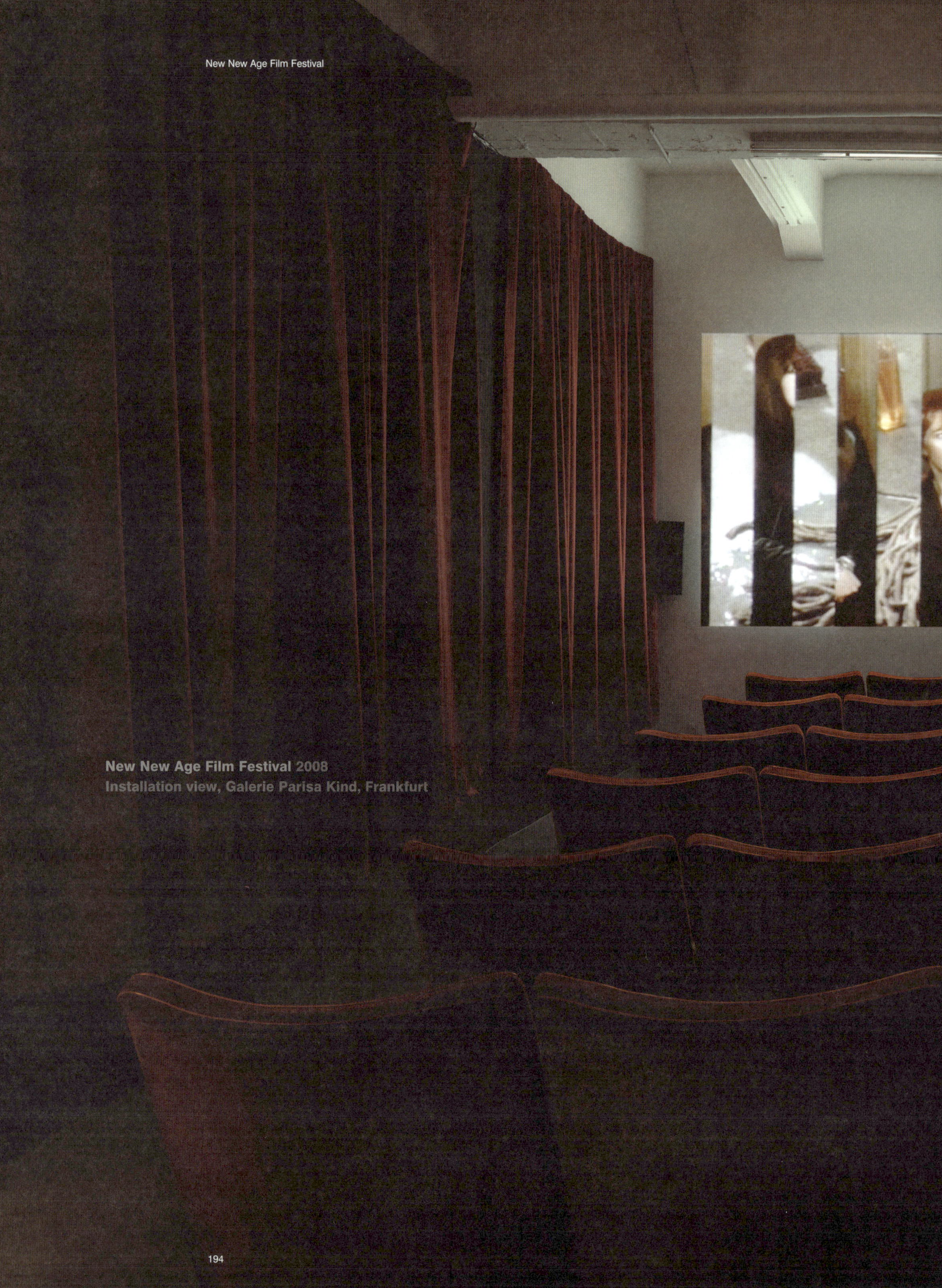

New New Age Film Festival 2008
Installation view, Galerie Parisa Kind, Frankfurt

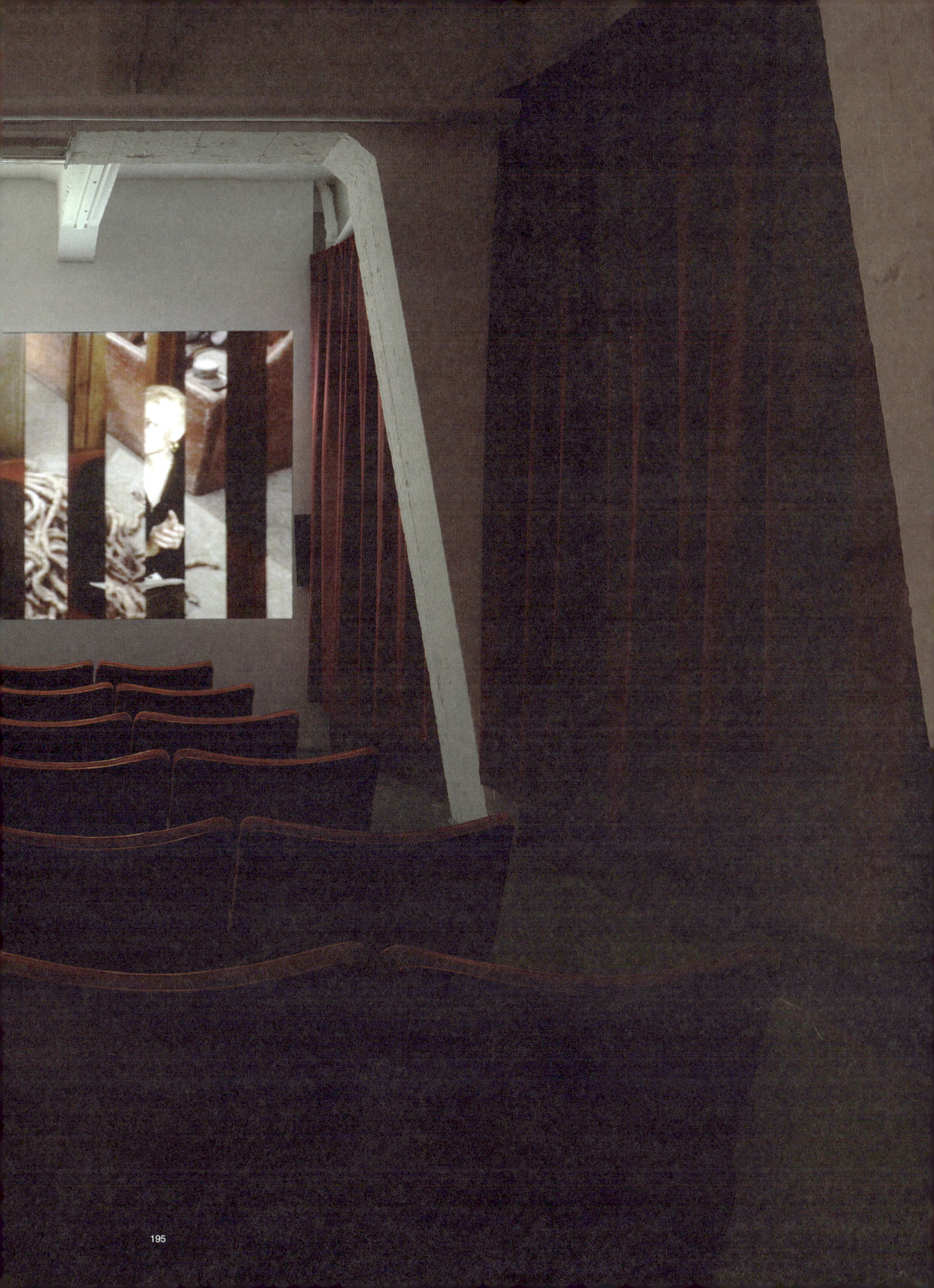

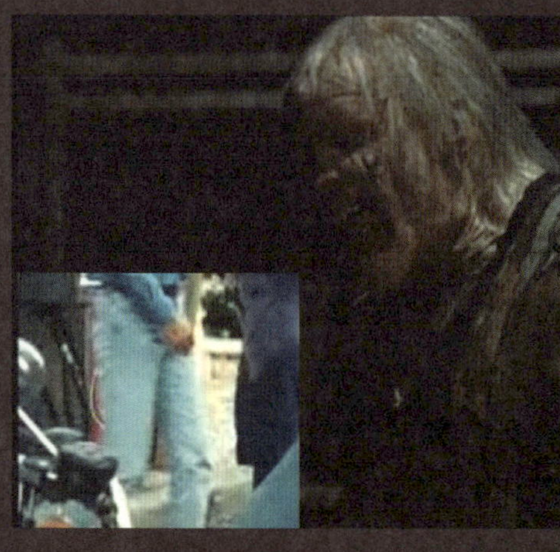
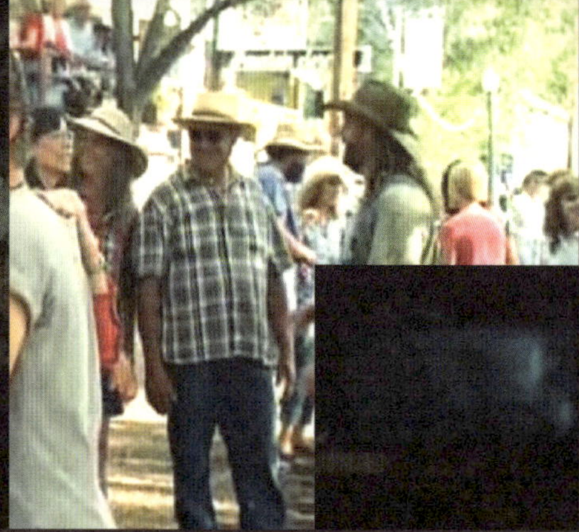

Hill Hogs 2008
Video still
TRT: 93 minutes

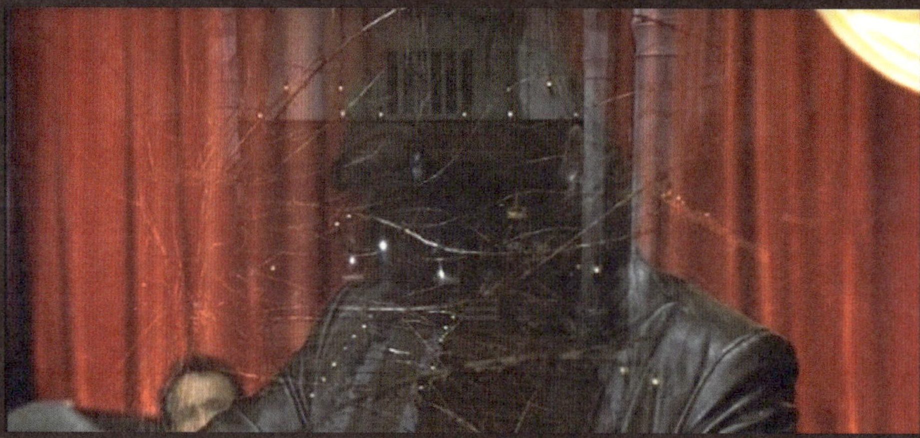

Dark and Silent 2008
Video still
TRT: 93 minutes

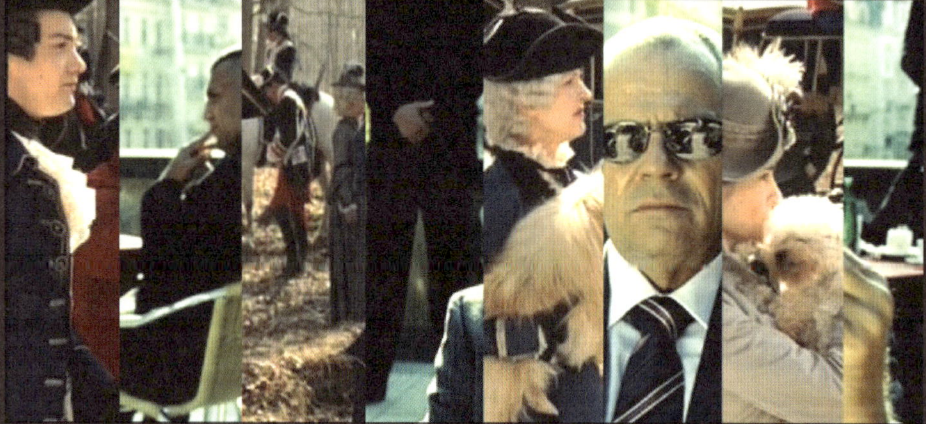

Female European Travels 2008
Video still
TRT: 93 minutes

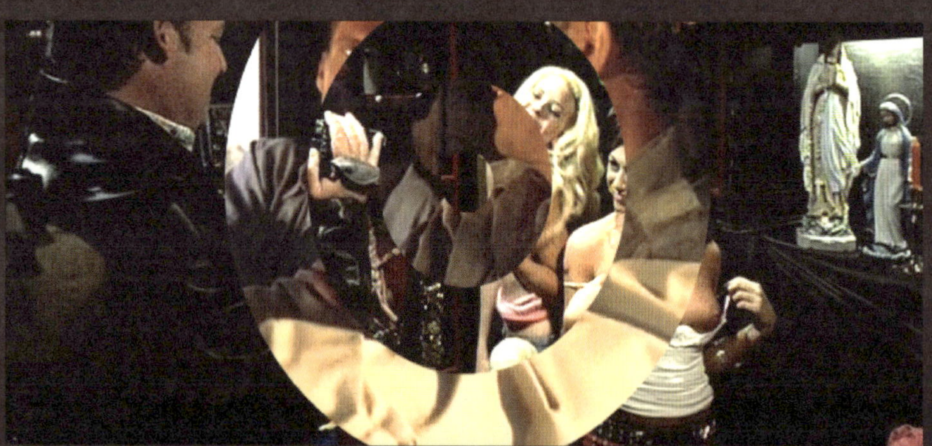

Swamp Patient 2008
Video still
TRT: 93 minutes

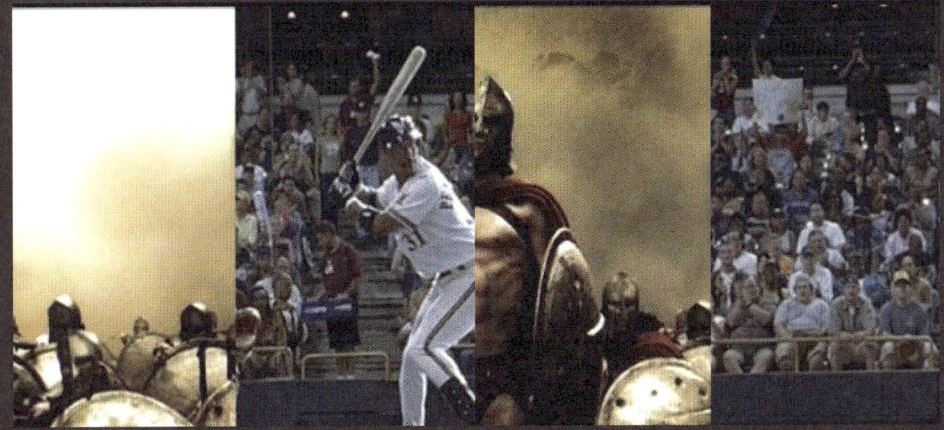

Mr 300,000 2008
Video still
TRT: 93 minutes

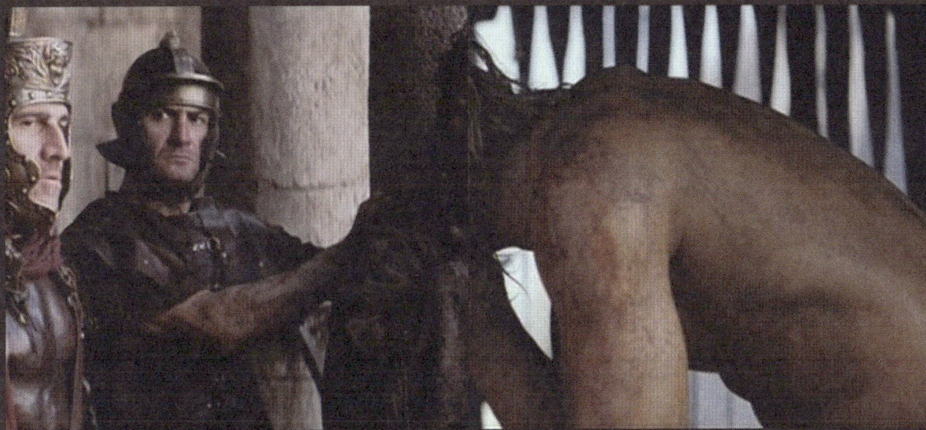

The Passion of Troy 2008
Video still
TRT: 93 minutes

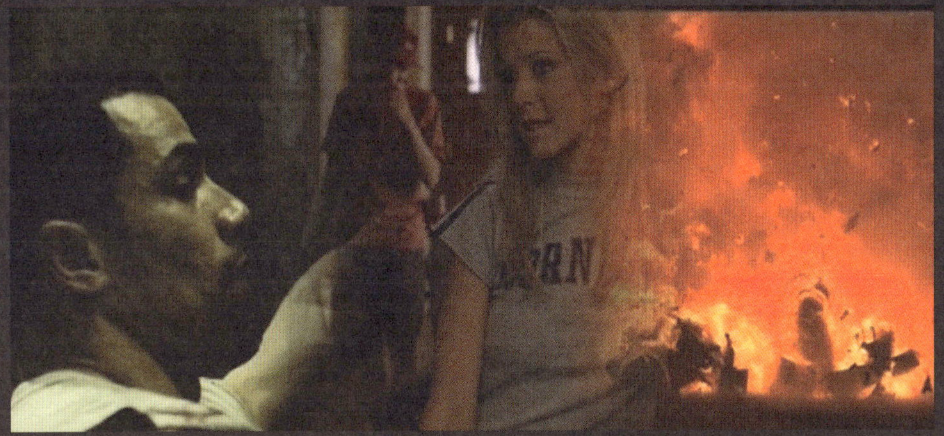

Hard Pie 2008
Video still
TRT: 93 minutes

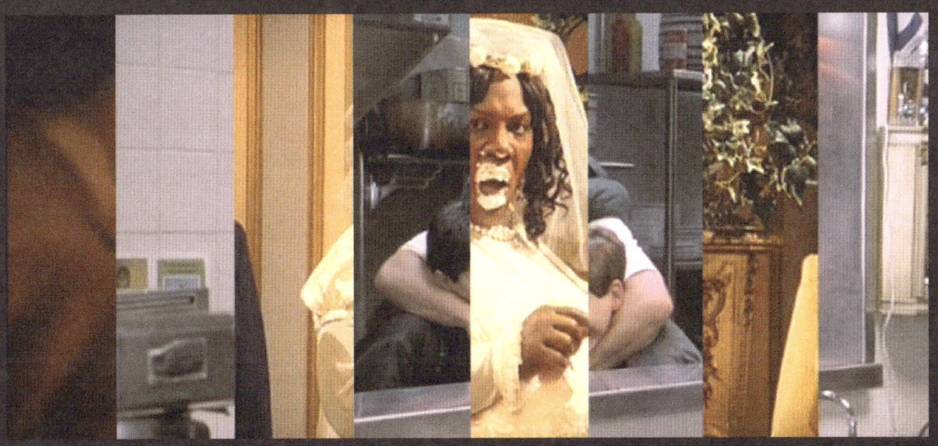

Wedding Troubles 2008
Video still
TRT: 93 minutes

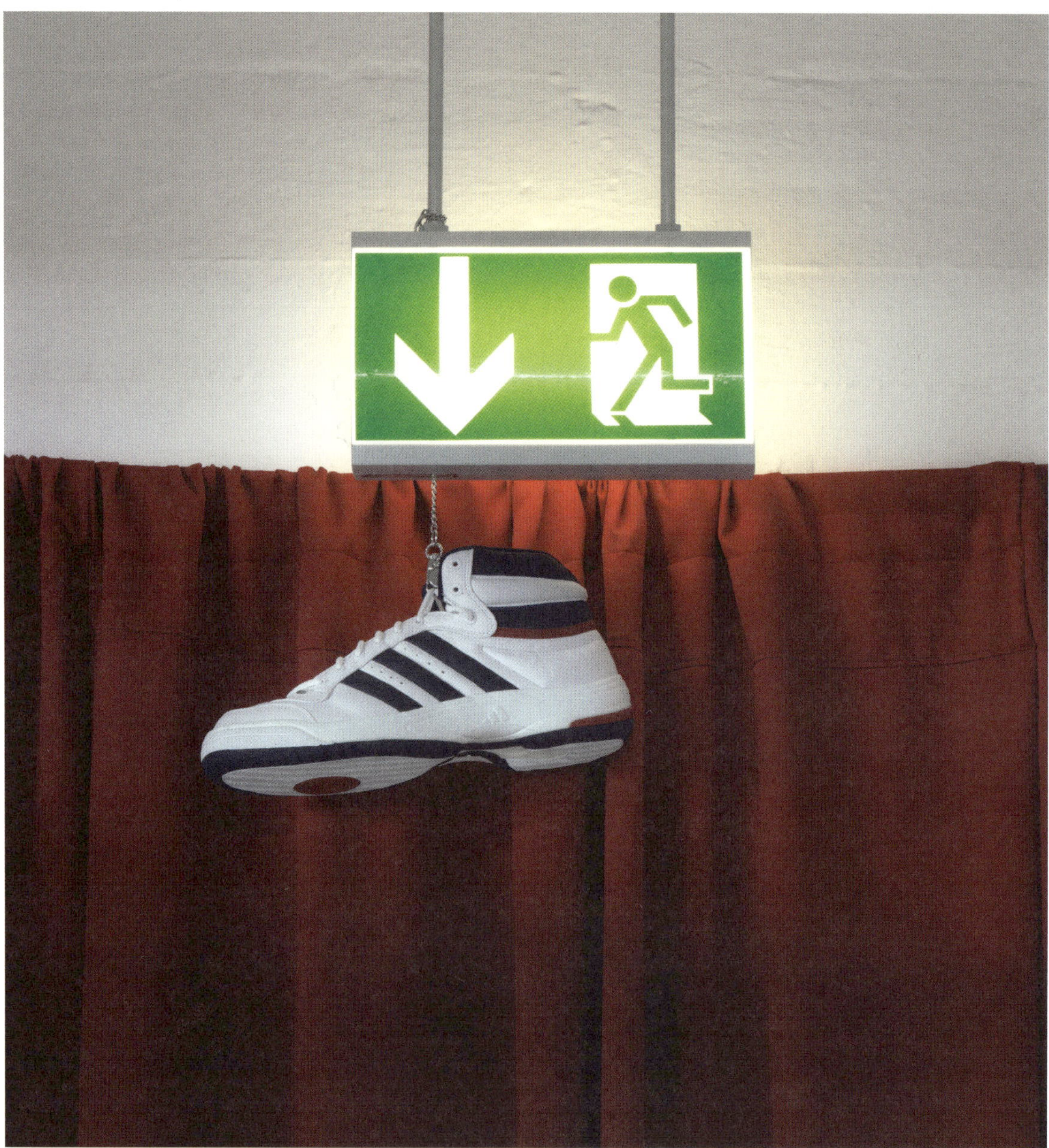

First One Wins Illuminated Theater Exit Sign 2008

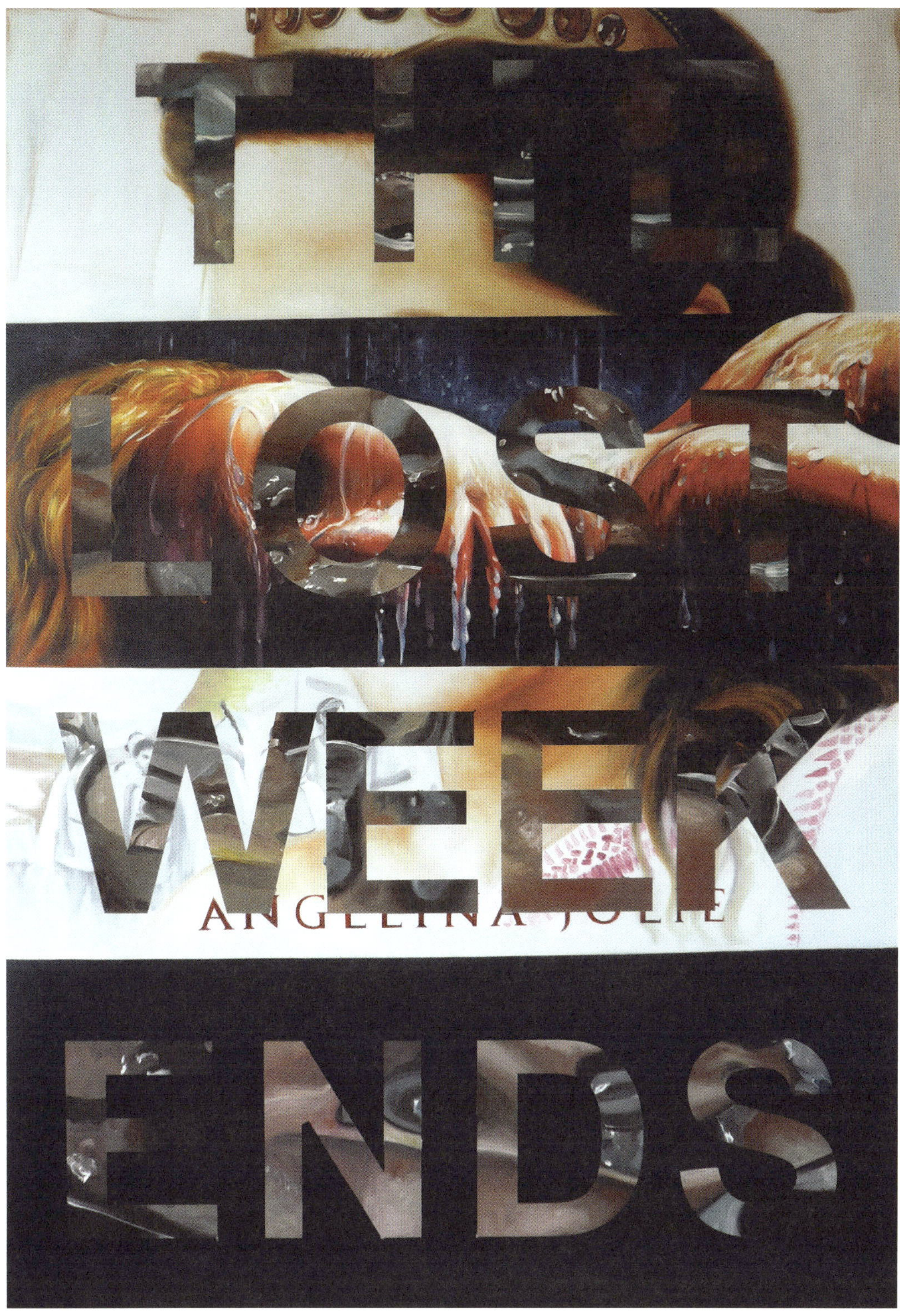

Lost Week Ends 2009

May 2008

Tuesday	Wednesday			
		1 1:00 PM: Livin' Rich 2:30 PM: 2 Furious for Mountains 4:00 PM: A vs. P vs. S	**2** 1:00 PM: All Corn's Children 2:30 PM: Apollo 7 4:00 PM: Beethoven 23	**3** 12:00 PM: Blood Star 1:30 PM: Dark & Silent
6 1:00 PM: Face-On 2:30 PM: Female Euro Travels 4:00 PM: Hard Pie 1	**7** 1:00 PM: Hard Pie 2 2:30 PM: Hard Pie 3 4:00 PM: Hard Pie 4	**8** 1:00 PM: Hill Hogs 2:30 PM: Historyfight 4:00 PM: Hostel & Hutch	**9** 1:00 PM: Inner Seas & Over Seas 2:30 PM: Its All Alive 4:00 PM: Little Men	**10** 12:00 PM: Livin' Rich 1:30 PM: Mile Drive
13 1:00 PM: Mr. 300,000 2:30 PM: Office Job 4:00 PM: Passion of Troy	**14** 1:00 PM: Post Class 2:30 PM: 2nd Chances 4:00 PM: Scotland Yards	**15** 1:00 PM: Sep. Anxiety 2:30 PM: Socio-Psycho Sexy-Politico 4:00 PM: Soldier Minds	**16** 1:00 PM: Swamp Patient 2:30 PM: The Bad 4:00 PM: Broken Chains of Command	**17** 12:00 PM: Tying Knots 1:30 PM: Ultimate G

New New Age Film Festival

Mike Bouchet

Galerie Parisa Kind

Offenbacher Landstrasse 11-13, 60599 Frankfurt am Main T: (+49 69) 60 60 54 38 www.parisakind.com

Free Admission
Screening Schedule

April 2008

Tuesday	Wednesday	Thursday	Friday	Saturday
			11 7:00 PM: Opening Festival Preview	**12** 12:00 PM: 2 Furious for Mountains 1:30 PM: Underestimated, Dangerous, Blue, Wanted
15 1:00 PM: A vs.P vs.S 2:30 PM: Ultimate G 4:00 PM: Tying Knots	**16** 1:00 PM: All Corns Children 2:30 PM: Apollo 7 4:00 PM: Importance of proper raising	**17** 1:00 PM: Broken Chains of command 2:30 PM: Beethovens 23 4:00 PM: The Bad	**18** 1:00 PM: Blood Star 2:30 PM: Dark & Silent 4:00 PM: Swamp Patient	**19** 12:00 PM: Soldier Mindframe 1:30 PM: Face-On
22 1:00 PM: Socio-Psycho Sexy-Politico 2:30 PM: Female Euro Travels 4:00 PM: Its All Alive	**23** 1:00 PM: Sep. Anxiety 2:30 PM: Scotland Yards 4:00 PM: Inner Seas & Over Seas	**24** 1:00 PM: Hostel & Hutch 2:30 PM: 2nd Chances 4:00 PM: Post Class	**25** 1:00 PM: Historyfight 2:30 PM: Passion of Troy 4:00 PM: Hill Hogs	**26** 12:00 PM: Office Job 1:30 PM: Mr. 300,000
29	**30**			

3   *Upsidedown Layer Cake* 2007
Oil on canvas
200 x 140cm
Private collection

5   *Prison Cake* 1996
Linzer Torte with metal file
baked inside
Variable dimensions

6   *RongLevolutions* 1993
Wood, ink, 100m string,
cardboard
14 x 14 x 18cm

8   *Endless Irregular Boxes* 1995
Silk screened cardboard, tape
Variable dimensions

8   *Next Onassis* 1998
Cardboard, packing tape
240 x 260 x 600cm

8   *Testicle Trays* 1994
Vacu-formed plastic, pigment
10 trays
Each tray 5 x 25 x 10cm

8   *Travel Agency Cooking* 2001
2 DVD set "Sounds of the Travel
Agency"(yellow version)
120 min

9   *Translation Booth* 1994
Plywood, paint, corrugated
metal, audiocassette player
and tape
240 x 120 x 120cm

9   *Bong* 1995
Cardboard, adhesive, paint,
pvc tubing
85 x 210 x 70cm

11   *Negative Space* 2002
Inkjet on canvas
120 x 120cm

11   *Where you going kid?* 2003
Inkjet on canvas
180 x 120cm

12   *Small Price* 2008
Oil on canvas
125 x 200cm

12   *Join Her* 2002
Inkjet on canvas
120 x 80cm
Private collection

13   *Lucky Meal* 2008
Oil on canvas
200 x 260cm

13   *Zero Painting* 2007
Diet cola on cotton
120 x 180cm
La Colección Jumex, México

14   *Ask For More Twice* 2007
Diet cola on cotton
180 x 120cm

14   *Ass Rub* 2004
Sandpapered denim
180 x 120cm
Private collection

15   *Tom of Frankfurt* 2004
Bleach on denim
180 x 120cm
Private collection

15   *Tourism* 2008
Oil on canvas
180 x 180cm

15   *Logo Lines 1* 2005
Diet cola on cotton
120 x 180cm
Private collection

16   *Vinyl High* 2007
Oil on canvas
200 x 140cm

16   *Shattered 1* 2007
Oil on canvas
200 x 140cm
Private Collection

16   *Taste New York* 2007
Oil on canvas
200 x 320cm
Private collection

17   *European Gigolo* 2007
Oil on canvas
200 x 140cm

17   *Voodoo* 2008
Oil on canvas
170 x 120cm

17   *XXXXXXXXXXXXXXL* 2008
Oil on canvas
130 x 190cm

19   *Cube model* 1994
cardboard, mylar, packing tape
50 x 120 x 120cm

20   *Cube* 1994
Wood, cardboard, steel, aluminum foil, electric motor
450 x 800 x 750 cm

25   *Please lay down and feel at
home with us* 1995
Acrylic on paper
100 x 150cm

26   *Commune Futon (Bed)* 1995
Fabric, wood, foam,
steel hard ware
30 x 200 x 1750cm

32   *Shitrock Crate* 1999-2007
Plywood, shitrock, foam,
mixed media
120 x 300 x 150cm
Private collection

35   *Eagle Rock Shitrock Sheet* 2000
Inkjet on canvas
Variable dimensions
Private collection

39   *Shuttle explosion* 2003
Bleach on denim
120 x 180 cm
Private collection

66 *My Cola Lite* 2004
2000 liter bottles self produced
diet cola
Dimensions variable

68 *My Cola Lite (Six pack)* 2004
Stamped wood crate, 6 bottles
"My cola Lite"
15 x 60 x 40 cm
ed.10

70 *Cola Container* 2004
Painted steel sea container
240 x 260 x 600cm

71 *Long and Skinny* 2005
Diet cola on cotton
10 panels, 120 x 120 cm each
Private collection

73 *Stadium* 2004
Diet cola on paper
40 x 60cm
Private collection

73 *WC* 2005
Diet cola on paper
40 x 60cm
Private collection

74 *Long and Skinny 2* 2005
Diet cola on cotton
120 x 360cm
Private collection

74 *Freedom Burns* 2004
Diet cola on paper
80 x 60cm
Private collection

74 *Sex has Nothing* 2004
Diet cola on paper
80 x 60cm
Private collection

76 *Heaven and Hell study* 2004
Diet cola on paper
80 x 60cm
Private collection

77 *Positive What Lovin it* 2005
Explosion 1 2005
Thai Sucky-Fucky 2005
Diet cola on cotton,
180 x 120cm
The Astrup Fearnley Collection

77 *Cola Fountain* 2007
Industrial drinking fountain,
CO2 beverage dispenser, self-
produced diet cola syrup
105 x 32 x 32cm

78 *Negative Burst* 2005
Diet cola on cotton,
180 x 120cm
Private Collection

79 *My Arabic Cola Lite* 2005
Diet cola on cotton,
120 x 180cm
Private collection

79 *C Scape* 2005
Diet cola on paper
80 x 60cm
Private collection

88 *Top Cruise* 2005
1000 hand painted
ceramic busts
Dimensions variable
The Astrup Fearnley Collection

91 *Americas Next Top Cruise* 2005
40 gallon glass aquarium, diet
cola, lacquered "Top Cruise"
bust, electric air pump,
rubber hosing
45 x 80 x 25 cm

94 *Almost Every City In The World*
2006
Screenplay: 33,000 A4 paper
sheets, steel, paint
Video: harddrive,
520 hour projection
21 x 31 x 200 cm
Private collection, La Colección
Jumex, México,
LVMH collection

99 *Lyudmilla Putin Jacuzzi*
Cardboard, polyester fiberglass
resin, paint
120 x 240 x 220 cm

100 *Prime Minister Koizumi Jacuzzi*
2006
Cardboard, polyester fiberglass
resin, paint, automotive jack
160 x 220 x 180 cm

102 *Steffi Graf Jacuzzi* 2000
Cardboard, polyester fiberglass
resin, paint, tennis racket
110 x 150 x 160 cm
The Astrup Fearnley Collection

103 *Jude Law Jacuzzi* 2005
Cardboard, polyester fiberglass
resin, paint
120 x 140 x 150 cm
Private collection

103 *Ted Turner* 1999
Oil on canvas
150 x 120 cm

104 *Celine Dion* 1998
Oil on cardbaord
80 x 120 cm

105 *Carmen Elektra Jacuzzi* 2005
Cardboard, polyester fiberglass
resin, paint, water, carrot
140 x 90 x 70 cm
Private collection

107 *Kofi Annan Jacuzzi* 2003
Cardboard, polyester fiberglass
resin, paint, water, salami
110 x 200 x 120 cm

108 *Tatjana Gsell Jacuzzi* 2005
Cardboard, polyester fiberglass
resin, paint, wood, carpet
140 x 340 x 220 cm

110 *Jude Law Jacuzzi* 2005
Cardboard, polyester fiberglass
resin, paint
120 x 140 x 150 cm
Private collection

110 *Jack Welch Jacuzzi* 2005
Cardboard, polyester fiberglass
resin, paint, water
90 x 260 x 105 cm
Private collection

111 *Robert Mugabe Jacuzzi* 2005
Cardboard, polyester fiberglass
resin, paint
140 x 160 x 150 cm
Louis Negre Collection

112 *Banks/Khadaffi Jacuzzi* (left),
Cardboard, polyester fiberglass
resin, paint
120 x 240 x 150 cm
Private collection

112 *Derek Jeter Jacuzzis* (right) 2006
Cardboard, polyester fiberglass
resin, paint
120 x 210 x 160 cm

112 *Lionel Ritchie Jacuzzi* 2007
Cardboard, polyester fiberglass
resin, paint
120 x 220 x 200 cm

113 *Carly Fiorina* 2003
Oil on canvas
200 x 280 cm

113 *S. Penn* 1999
Oil on canvas
50 x 40 cm

114 *K. Lagerfeld Jacuzzi* 2006
Cardboard, polyester fiberglass
resin, paint, vase, flowers, electric air pump
140 x 260 x 180 cm

115 *Schwarzenegger Jacuzzi* 2006
Cardboard, polyester fiberglass
resin, paint
200 x 200 x 800 cm

117 *Are we 3000?* 2007
Oil on canvas
200 x 140cm
Private Collection

118 Tapestry Cartoon Backroom
2007 from L to R

118 *Big Mamma,* 2007
Oil on canvas
200 x 140cm

118 *Cleverxxxsmart* 2007
Oil on canvas
200 x 140cm

118 *Sams Approximation* 2007
Oil on canvas
200 x 140cm

118 *Black Dawn Dreamer* 2007
Oil on canvas
200 x 140cm

118 *Chaoscamper* 2007
Oil on canvas
200 x 140cm

120 *Green Mask* 2006
Oil on canvas
200 x 140cm
Private Collection

121 *Cool Kids* 2006
Oil on canvas
200 x 140cm
Private Collection

121 *Black President* 2006
Oil on canvas
200 x 140cm

121 *Family Foot* 2008
Oil on canvas
90 x 90cm
Private Collection

122 *Elephant Miss Undercover 2*
2006
Oil on canvas
200 x 140cm
Private Collection, Los Angeles

122 *Extended Bad Hours* 2006
Oil on canvas
200 x 140cm
Private Collection

123 *Detention* 2006
Oil on canvas
200 x 140cm
Private Collection

124 *Triple Wolf Ball* 2007
Oil on canvas
200 x 140cm
Private Collection

125 *Spill* 2007
Oil on canvas
200 x 140cm

125 *Peer Pressure* 2008
Oil on canvas
90 x 70cm
Private Collection

125 *Release* 2008
Oil on canvas
90 x 60cm

126 *Red Green Six* 2006
Oil on canvas
200 x 140cm
Private Collection

127 *HeadForestChildSkin* 2005
Oil on canvas
200 x 140cm

128 *Dark Lords* 2006
Oil on canvas
200 x 140cm

128 *Door In The Floor* 2007
Oil on canvas
200 x 140cm

129 *Broke Instinct* 2008
Oil on canvas
200 x 140cm

131 *Diesel fourway* 2007
Oil on canvas
150 x 120cm

133 *Reich Rorsach set 2* 2007
Digital inkjet print on paper
80 x 60cm

134 *I wanna love you* 2007
   Digital inkjet print on paper
   80 x 60cm

135 *Video Bed* 2007
   Custom mattress, foam, cotton,
   video monitor, dvd player, steel
   frame, 43 one hour dvds
   58 x 300 x 300cm

136 *Eddie on Ediie* 2007
   Oil on canvas
   120 x 150cm

137 *Blonde and Brunette Stares* 2007
   Oil on canvas
   150 x 120cm
   Private Collection

138 *Kim on Pink Couch* 2007
   Oil on canvas
   150 x 120cm

139 *CreamMyPussyCats* 2007
   Oil on canvas
   150 x 120cm
   Private collection

139 *Rihanna's Ankle on Blue* 2007
   Oil on canvas
   150 x 120cm
   Private Collection

140 *Half On A Baby* 2007
   Oil on canvas
   180 x 180cm
   Private collection

141 *Enjoy The Backside (Dresser)* 2008
   Oil on canvas
   150 x 120cm

142 *Bang And The Dirt Is Gone* 2007
   180 x 240 cm
   Private collection

143 *Exhibition Poster* 2007
   Offset lithograph
   40cm x 60cm

143 *Lucky Dwarf* 2008
   Oil on canvas
   70 x 90 cm

145 *Reaction time* 2007
   24 hour video on four EP
   VHS tapes
   Variable dimensions

148 *FBI ID Drawings* 2007
   7 drawings and framed mirror
   40 x 30cm each

152 *Peter Jennings Film Festival* 2007
   103 dvds
   Dimensions variable

156 *Guggenheim Toilet* 2006
   Ceramic, fiberglass, paint,
   metal, plastic
   100 x 120 x 60 cm
   ed.3

160 *SpaceBags* 2007
   500 vinyl bags
   bag dimensions are 100 cm
   Dimensions variable

168 *Rest* 2008
   9,940 canned hamburgers
   can dimensions: 5 x 10 cm
   Installation dimensions variable

170 *DecaBurger* 2007
   Bronze, ceramic plate
   38 x 10 x 10cm

171 *Tear* 2007
   D-print
   90 x 120 cm

172 *Rocky Mountain Cheese* 2008
   Oil on canvas
   200 x 200 cm

173 *Teen* 2008
   Oil on canvas
   200 x 200 cm

176 *Triple Chili Cheese* 2007
   Oil on canvas
   130 x 530 cm

176 *DBL DBL BBQ BBQ* 2007
   Oil on canvas
   300 x 300 cm

176 *Italian Summer* 2007
   Oil on canvas
   300 x 420 cm

176 *Everything* 2007
   Oil on canvas
   300 x 300 cm

178 *Angus* 2007
   Oil on canvas
   280 x 420 cm

179 *Happy Pile* 2008
   Offset print collage on wood
   panel, canburger
   120 x 180 cm

180 *Burned* 2007
   Oil on canvas
   280 x 480 cm

190 *16 x 9 Action Film* 2007
   D-5 videotape
   TRT: 144 minute

193 *Good Evening* 2008
   Oil on canvas
   150 x 120 cm

194 *New New Age Film Festival* 2008
   40 feature length videos
   mastered on DV cam,
   DV cam player, Theater seating

198 *First One Wins Illuminated
   Theater Exit Sign* 2008
   Electric exit sign, size 58 sport
   shoe, polished steel chain

199 *Lost Week Ends* 2009
   Oil on canvas
   200 x 140cm

Mike Bouchet

1970	**Born in Castro Valley, California, USA**
1991–1994	**UCLA, California**
2000–2004	**Lives and works in New York City**
2004 –	**Lives and works in Frankfurt, Germany**

Selected Solo Exhibitions

2010   Schirn Kunsthalle, Frankfurt

2009   Autocenter, Berlin, Dec.

2008   "CANBURGER", Galerie Georges-Philipe & Nathalie Vallois, Paris
"New New Age Film Festival", Galerie Parisa Kind, Frankfurt am Main
"16x9 Action Film", Centre Georges Pompidou, Paris

2007   "Shitrock Crate and Tapestry Cartoons", The Box, Los Angeles
"Fat Slices and Conscious Primers", MC Kunst, Los Angeles
"Reaction Time", Circus Gallery, Los Angeles
"16x9 Action Film", MOCA, Los Angeles
"Almost Every City in The World", Galerie Vallois, Paris

2006   "Recent Jacuzzis", Galerie Michael Neff, Frankfurt

2005   "Top, Back and Bottom of Mind Awareness", Maccarone, Inc., New York
"New Jacuzzis", Kunstraum Innsbruck

2004   "Carpe Denim", Galerie Michael Neff, Frankfurt

2003   "Overhead Baggage Treatment", Maccarone, Inc., New York

1999   "Business on Sunset", BOSS Exhibitions, Los Angeles

1993   Untitled solo exhibition, AB Gallery, Los Angeles

Selected Group Exhibitions

2009   "Nothingness and Being", Seventh interpretation of La Jumex Collection,
Curated by Shamim Momin, Mexico City, MEX,
"Quand la première ivresse des succès bruyants …."
CAPC Musée d'art contemporain de Bordeaux, FR
"When the mood strikes… The Collection of Wilfried & Yannicke
Cooreman-De Smedt", MDD Museum Dhondt-Dhaenens, Deurle, BE
"250 Years of Guinness", Sebastian Guinness Gallery, Dublin

2008   "Anthology", Otero Plassart, Los Angeles, USA
"Meet Me Around The Corner",
Astrup Fearnley Museum of Modern Art, Oslo
"No Leftovers", Kunsthalle Bern, Bern, CH
"Walls In the Street" Museum of Contemporary Art, Belgrade
"Working Men", Analix Forever, Geneva
"The Practice of Everyday Life", Feinkost Gallery, Berlin
"Hotel California", Galerie Georges-Philipe & Nathalie Vallois, Paris
"An Unruly History of the Readymade", Jumex Collection, Mexico City

2007   "27 Timer", Hollesgard, Denmark
"Pawnshop", e-Flux, New York
"Mind Hacking II", Muenster, Germany
"Quotidian", BUIA Gallery, New York
"New Economy", Artists Space, New York
Moscow Biennial 2, Moscow, Russia
"Verbale", Innsbruck, Austria
"Uncertain States of America", Warsaw, Poland; Herning Kunstmuseum,
Copenhagen; Beijing, China, Prague

2006   "5 Billion Years", Palais de Tokyo, Paris
        "Uncertain States of America", Reykjavik Art Museum, Iceland
        "E-flux Video Rental", Seoul, Korea, Antwerp
        "Uncertain States of America", Serpentine Gallery, London
        "Mobile: Suro Collection", Triangle Project Space, San Antonio
        "Uncertain States of America" Bard Curatorial Center, New York
        "Sculpture Park", Lahr, Germany
        "Nice Fine Arts", Offenburg, Germany
        Berlin Biennale 4, Berlin
        "Palm D'Or Television Pitch", Frankfurt, Germany
        "Space Boomerang", Swiss Institute, New York
2005   "Strich, Zeichnung, Bild", BAWAG Foundation, Vienna
        "Uncertain States of America",
        Astrup Fearnley Museum of Modern Art, Oslo
        "Off Key", Kunsthalle Bern
        "La Vista Hermosa" Liste, Basel
        "Do You Like Stuff?", Swiss Institute, New York
        "Greater New York 2005", PS1, New York
        "Situational Prosthetics", New Langston Art Center, San Francisco
        "E-flux Video Rental", KunstWerke, Berlin
        "E-flux Video Rental", Portikus, Frankfurt
2004   "Dedicated to a Proposition",
        Extra City, Center for Contemporary Art, Antwerpen
        "Sculpture now", Galerie Michael Neff, Frankfurt
        "Kotzrohr and Popular Ceramics", Video program,
        Wilkinson Gallery, London
        E-flux Video Rental, E-flux New York
        "High Desert Test Sites", Los Angeles, CA
2003   "Hands up, baby, hands up!", Oldenburger Kunstverein
2002   "Out of True", Santa Barbara University Art Museum, CA
2001   "Casino", SMAK, Gent,BE
2000   "Sebastian Clough and Mike Bouchet", Anton Kern Gallery, New York
        "Life After The Squirrel", Location One, New York
1997   "SnowBall", Collaboration with Jason Rhoades and Peter Bonde,
        Venice Biennale
1996   "Size Matters", Special K Projects, Los Angeles
1994   "Common Denomination Language Expo", FAR, Los Angeles
1993   "Slum Loard", Main Street Gallery, Napa, CA
        "In Disposal", Broadway Art Complex, Santa Monica, CA

Public Collections
Astrup Fearnley Museum of Modern Art, Oslo
Centre Georges Pompidou, Paris
DekaBank, Frankfurt
Deutsche Bank, Frankfurt
Jumex Collection, Mexico City
LVMH Collection, Paris
FNAC, Fonds National D'Art Contemporain, Paris
Belvedere Museum, Vienna
François Pinault Collection, Venice
Bernard Arnault Collection, Paris

Articles / Reviews

• "Jeansregen auf der Zeil: Kunstaktion von Mike Bouchet", by: kcd, in: *F. A.Z.*, May 21, 2004, p.52.
• "Mike Bouchet", by Holland Cotter, in: *New York Times*, May 30, 2005
• ",Link Stink' Art", by Howard Stier, in: *New York Post*, 2005, June 2nd, 2005
• "Mike Bouchet", by Martha Schwendener, in: *Artforum*, July 15, 2005
• "Painting the Town", in: *Time Out New York*, August 4-10, 2005
• "An absolute need to haphazard and brutally casual", by Michael Glover, *F.T.* September 11, 2005
• "Mike Bouchet", by Emily Hall, in: *Artforum*, October 2005
• "End Station, Lever Labyrinth, and Mike Bouchet", by John Haber, 2005
• "Mike Bouchet", by JE, in: *Modern Painters*, 2005
• "Mike Bouchet", by Benjamin Carlson, in: *Time Out New York*, 2005
• "Top, Back and Bottom of Mind Awareness", in: *Brooklyn Rail*, 2005
• "Getting Ourselves Back to the Garden", by Betsy Andrews, in: *Gay City*, 2005
• "Space Boomerang", by Elwyn Palmerton, in: *Frieze*, 2006
• "New Economy" by Morgan Falconer, in: *Frieze*, issue 110, October 2007
• "Uncertain States, Prague review" (German) *F.A.Z.*, Nr. 11 / page 31, 14.01.2008
• "Walls in the Street", in: Der Standard 19.6.08
• "Jeans, Filme, Cola und Sex", by Christoph Schütte, in: *F.A.Z.* 8.5.2008
• "Arty Denim" in: *WAD*, issue 230, 2008
• "Le travail, poétique du Quotidien" in: *Crash* n° 45, 2008
• "Codes of Work" in *Espaces Contemporains*, May/June 2008
• "Working Men" in: *Balthazar*, june/july 2008
• "Working Men" in: *artpress*, june 2008
• "16x9 Action Film", by Christian Jankowski, in: *Artforum*, December 2008

Bibliography

• "Jeansregen auf der Zeil: Kunstaktion von Mike Bouchet", by: kcd, in: F. A.Z.,
May 21, 2004, p.52.
• Andjelkovic, Branislava, Lulic, Marko, Trummer, Thomas, "Zidovi na ulici /
Walls in the Street", Siemens Arts Program and Museum of Contemporary Art
Belgrade, 2008
• Aranda, Julieta and Vidokle, Anton, "E-flux video rental catalog, vol. 1",
New York, 2005
• Ardenne, Paul and Poller, Barbara, "Working Men", Geneva, 2008
• Biesenbach, Klaus, "Greater NY 2005", P.S.1 Contemporary Art Center,
NYC, 2005
• Birnbaum, Daniel, Kvaran, Gunnar, Obrist, Hans Ulrich, "American Video Art
at the beginning of the Millenium", Moscow Biennale 2, Moscow 2006
• Birnbaum, Daniel, Kvaran, Gunnar, Obrist, Hans Ulrich,
"Uncertain States of America", Astrup Fearnley Museum of Modern Art, 2005
• Bismuth, Julien, "Mike Bouchet: Celebrity Artist; The Sociographic View",
Kunstraum Innsbruck, Innsbruck 2006
• Cattelan, Maurizio, Gioni, Massimiliano, Subotnik, Ali, "Of Mice and Men":
Berlin Biennale 4, Berlin, 2006
• Fleck, Robert, "L'Art au Corps": Le corps exposé de Man Ray à nos jours",
Musée d'art Contemporain Marseille 1996
• Greenberg Rohatyn, Jeanne, „Casino 2001: First Quadrennial of
Contemporary Art" SMAK, Ghent, 2001
• Huber, Axel and Richter, Babette, "Strich Zeichnung Bild", BAWAG Foundation,
Wien 2005
• Ockenholt, Marianne and Sans, Jerome,"The Snowball", Hatje Kantz,1999
• Pirotte, Philippe, 'Off-key", Kunsthalle Bern, Bern, 2005
• Wahler, Marc Olivier, "From Yodeling to Quantum Physics, vol.1"
Palais de Tokyo, Paris, 2007
• "Visuell Blind Date": Deutsche Bank Collection, Seligenstadt, 2006

Video works

"Dooky Booty", 1995, TRT 4:30

"Dooiiynngg!", 1995, TRT 5:30

"Lila & The Swan (with Norton Utilities)", 1996, TRT 42:00

"5019 York L.A.,CA 90042+Friedrichshof: "Aus mein wurst macht dein wurst!" 1998, TRT 11:00

"InfoLecture", 1999, TRT 21:00

"Comfort Table Lecture Seminar", 1998, in conjunction with Julien Bismuth, TRT 60:00

"BOSS Audition" 2009, in conjunction with Henrik Capetillo, TRT 14:00

"Strongman Commericals", 2003, :90,:60,:30", 2004, TRT 3:00

"Commercia Erotica", 2003, in conjunction with Lucas Ajemian, TRT 3:00

"Programi derene de vojag agentejo" (Green version), 2002, TRT 60:00

"Programi derene de vojag agentejo" (Yellow version), 2002, TRT 60:00

"16x9 Action Film", 2007, 144:00

Overhead Baggage Treatment 2003 video works

Brian Stokes Mitchell Tours 5th Ave, 2003 TRT 60:00

Halle Berry tours the Champs Elysees, 2003 TRT 60:00

In Search of Tuscany with John Guerrasio, 2003 TRT 60:00

Cops in Russia, 2003 TRT 30:00

Blind Date 1 and Cribs with C-Lo, 2003 TRT 60:00

Blind Date and Cribs 2, 2003 TRT 60:00

The New New Age Film Festival, 2008 video works

After Class, 79 min.

Air Friends, 89 min.

Apollo 7, 117 min.

A vs. P vs. S, 84 min.

All Corns Children, 85 min.

Beethovens 23rd, 84 min.

Blood Star, 126 min.

Dark & Silent, 108 min.

Face-On, 104 min.

Fantasy Soldier, 86 min.

Female European Travels, 83 min.

Get Rich or Die Tryin and Stay Alive, 85 min.

Hard Pie 1, 88 min.

Hard Pie 2, 83 min.

Hard Pie 3, 94 min.

Hard Pie 4, 85 min.

Hill Hogs, 81 min.

Historyfight, 89 min.

Hostel and Hutch, 86 min.

Inner Seas Over Seas, 77 min.

It´s All Alive, 86 min.

Little Men, 86 min.

Livin' Rich, 85 min.

Mile Drive, 137 min.

Mr. 300,000, 104 min.

Office Job, 114 min.

Passion of Troy, 86 min.

Scotland Yards, 104 min.

2nd Chances, 97 min.

Separation Anxiety, 96 min.

Socio-Psycho-Sexual-Politico, 106 min.

Soldier min.dframe: Type A and Type B, 88 min.

Swamp Patient, 75 min.

The Bads, 86 min.

The Broken Chains of Command, 92 min.

2 Furious for Mountains, 96 min.

Tying Knots, 89 min.

Ultimate G, 77 min

Underestimated, Dangerous, Blue, Wanted, 110 min.

Wataworld, 86 min.

Colophon

Mike Bouchet
Selected Works 1989-2009

Published by Sternberg Press

© 2009 Mike Bouchet, Sternberg Press, the authors
All rights reserved. No part of this book may be reproduced without the written permission of the publisher.

ISBN 978-1-933128-73-3

Editors: Julien Bismuth, Mike Bouchet
Design: Markus Weisbeck, Surface Frankfurt am Main/Berlin
Printing: Nino Druck GmbH, Germany

Photography: Erik Black, Los Angeles,(pp.6, 8, 20-23, 26, 28, 16), William Taylor, Los Angeles (pp.5, 7, 31, 34, 35)Sebastian Clough, Los Angeles, (pp.8) Wolfgang Guenzel, Frankfurt (pp.14-16, 51, 56-60, 63, 65, 74, 93-96, 99, 105, 117, 127, 148, 149, 194, 198),
Joshua White, Los Angeles (pp.100, 132, 135), Guillaume Grasset, Paris (pp.9, 97, 165-178, 180, 189), Philippe D. Photographie, Brussels (pp.156). All other photographs were provided or taken by Mike Bouchet

Cover image: "Burned", 2007, oil on canvas, 280cm x 480cm

Acknowledgements
The production of this catalogue was accomplished through
the generous support of Gerwin Janke, Galerie Georges-Philippe & Nathalie Vallois, Paris and Galerie Parisa Kind, Frankfurt am Main.

Additional thanks to:
Lucas Ajemian, Daniel Birnbaum, Julien Bismuth, Colin Gardner, Markus Weisbeck

Sternberg Press
Caroline Schneider
Karl-Marx-Allee 78
D-10243 Berlin

1182 Broadway #1602, New York, NY 10001
www.sternberg-press.com